Regional Economics

In this important new book, Roberta Capello presents a modern guide to the theories and models used in regional economics.

Regional Economics provides a comprehensive view of the rich literature developed over the last fifty years on the location of economic activities, urban spatial structure and land use, regional growth and local development.

The explicit identification of the way in which space is conceived in the different theoretical approaches enables the author to provide a coherent framework of the evolution of theories and models in the field of regional economics: from physical space, which characterizes the earliest location theories, to uniform space, typical of neoclassical and Keynesian approaches in the sixties, to diversified-relational space, embedded in local districts and milieu approaches, as well as in learning regions, to diversified-stylized space, which accompanies the cutting-edge theories of the endogenous economic growth and of the new economic geography.

Core topics covered include:

- The identification of market areas for producers, the spatial distribution of alternative production and residential activities in space and the explanation of the existence of an urban system.
- Traditional regional growth theories, both Keynesian and neoclassical.
- Local development theories, such as the concept of the industrial district, regional innovation systems, the learning region and spatial spillovers.
- Recent theories of local growth, embedded in the new economic geography and endogenous growth theories.

Regional Economics contains end of chapter questions and suggestions for core further reading and will be an important tool for any regional economics and policy course – whether applied or theoretical.

Roberta Capello is Full Professor in Regional Economics at the Politecnico of Milan.

ROUTLEDGE ADVANCED TEXTS IN ECONOMICS AND FINANCE

Financial Econometrics
Peijie Wang

Macroeconomics for Developing Countries 2nd edition
Raghbendra Jha

Advanced Mathematical Economics
Rakesh Vohra

Advanced Econometric Theory
John S. Chipman

Understanding Macroeconomic Theory
John M. Barron, Bradley T. Ewing and Gerald J. Lynch

Regional Economics
Roberta Capello

Regional Economics

Roberta Capello

Foreword by Masahisa Fujita
Postscript by Peter Nijkamp

 Routledge
Taylor & Francis Group

LONDON AND NEW YORK

First published 2007 by Routledge
2 Park Square, Milton Park, Abingdon, Oxon OX14 4RN

Simultaneously published in the USA and Canada
by Routledge
270 Madison Ave, New York, NY 10016

Routledge is an imprint of the Taylor & Francis Group, an informa business

© 2007 Roberta Capello

Typeset in Perpetua by
Florence Production Ltd, Stoodleigh, Devon
Printed and bound in Great Britain by
TJ International Ltd, Padstow, Cornwall

British Library Cataloguing in Publication Data
A catalogue record for this book is available from the British Library

Library of Congress Cataloging in Publication Data
A catalog record for this book has been requested

ISBN10: 0–415–39520–8 (hbk)
ISBN10: 0–415–39521–6 (pbk)

ISBN13: 978–0–415–39520–5 (hbk)
ISBN13: 978–0–415–39521–2 (pbk)

To the two Elisas in the family,
my mother and my little niece

Contents

CONTENTS

Figures

Tables

Foreword

Masahisa Fujita

'Yet who can deny the spatial aspect of economic development: that all economic processes exist in space, as well as over time? Realistically, both time and space must be vital considerations in any theory of economy.' Thus spoke Isard, the founding father of regional science, in his master work, *Location and Space-Economy* (1956), which provided the grand synthesis of the economy theory of space from Von Thünen (1826) to the mid-1950s. Exactly half a century later, in this new monograph, Roberta Capello presents a wonderfully informative survey and synthesis of the advancement of spatial economic theory from Von Thünen to the 'new economic geography' today, with special focus on the role of space in economic development.

The history of spatial economics is as rich as it is perplexing. Starting with the monumental work of Von Thünen (1826) on agricultural land use theory, a variety of pioneering ideas had been developed periodically by great location theorists and economists such as Christaller (1933), Hoover (1936), Hotelling (1929), Launhardt (1885), Lösch (1940), Marshall (1920), Ohlin (1933), Palander (1935), and Weber (1909). In the decade of the 1950s, there came into prominence a group of development economists who put a special emphasis on the cumulative nature of development processes in space, presenting their new ideas in exciting terminology such as the *big push* by Rosenstein-Rodan (1943), *growth poles* by Perroux (1955), *circular causation* by Myrdal (1957), *backward and forward linkages* by Hirschman (1958). More recent additions to imaginative terminology include *dynamic scale economies* by Kaldor (1985) and *positive feedbacks* by Arthur (1989). With the advent of the 1970s and 1980s a new perspective emerged, that is, the neo-Marshallian and neo-Schumpeterian literature which interprets development as resulting from the impact of local externalities on the productive and innovative capacity of firms. Then in the decade of the 1990s, a renaissance in spatial economics took place, marking the transition from traditional spatial economics to the new formulations of contemporary spatial economics. Relying on new theoretical tools based on imperfect competition and non-linear dynamical systems, the so-called *new economic geography* has quickly emerged as one of the most exciting areas of contemporary economics. At present, young economists are trying vigorously to push forward the frontiers of research with the intent of elucidating ways to successfully merge the new economic geography with endogenous growth theory.

But despite the long and deep intellectual tradition of spatial economics, its history shows some puzzling aspects. Although the importance of understanding the economic processes in the actual world is no longer at issue, spatial economics for quite some time remained in the periphery of economic science until very recently. This may be due to the traditional view of mainstream economists that international trade theory and its appropriate extensions would be enough to deal with the economic problems in space. Also, as suggested by Krugman (1991a), this may be attributed to the absence in the past of a unified framework that embraces both increasing returns and imperfect competition, the two basic ingredients of the formation of economic landscape.

Whatever may be the reason for these uncommon circumstances of spatial economics in the past, however, the situation has been changing considerably of late. On the one hand, given the recent evident trend towards an increasingly borderless world economy, national boundaries no longer provide the natural unit of economic analysis in space. This has forced economists to rethink fundamentally the economic theory of space by considering seriously the active roles played by a large variety of economic agglomerations, such as cities, regions and industrial districts, in economic processes. On the other hand, the recent development of the new economic geography has demonstrated that increasing returns and imperfect competition are no longer serious barriers in advancing a rigorous microeconomic theory of space economy. Furthermore, the recent neo-Marshallian and neo-Schumpeterian literature has been enriching the economic theory of space by illuminating the impact of local externalities on the productive and innovative capacity of cities and regions.

In this monograph, Roberta Capello has succeeded in presenting a systematic and balanced synthesis of vast literatures in spatial economics or regional economics from Thünen to today's frontiers. The book consists of four parts. Differing conceptions of space account for the division of the book into parts; and differing definitions of growth and development account for its division into chapters. Part 1 examines the traditional *location theory with physical-metric space*. Part 2 deals with *uniform-abstract space theories of regional growth* at constants returns. Part 3 examines *diversified-relational space theories of development* related to location theory. Finally, Part 4 discusses *diversified-stylized space theories of regional growth*, including the new economic geography and the endogenous growth.

The book is written in a quite accessible style, with each subject treated in a balanced manner while clarifying its merits and limitations. Thus, it serves as an ideal textbook on regional economics or geographical economics at the senior undergraduate or junior graduate level. Furthermore, advanced students and scholars in regional and urban economics and economic geography will also gain a lot from reading this fascinating book. Indeed, I enjoyed it and learned a lot, and so will you.

Institute of Economic Research, Kyoto University
Institute of Developing Economies, JETRO
February 2006

Preface

My interest in regional economics started twenty years ago, when I graduated in economics at the Bocconi University in Milan with a thesis on the 'spatial development of innovation'. The chance to pursue research in this field for the rest of my academic life – from a Ph.D. at the Department of Spatial Economics of the Free University, Amsterdam, to research and teaching at the Bocconi University at the beginning of my professional life, and at the Politecnico of Milan as a researcher, at the University of Molise as Associate Professor, and at present back again at the Politecnico of Milan as Full Professor – has inspired my intellectual curiosity in regional economics.

The fascinating aspect of this subject is that, despite its recent birth (compared to other branches of economics), its models and theories have great interpretative capacity with respect to real phenomena in the economic world precisely because they take space into account. Space matters in economic activities. It matters in different ways: as a physical barrier to the movements of goods and people, as a geographical container of specific qualitative and quantitative productive factors, and therefore of specific factor remunerations and development opportunities, and as a productive resource itself by generating (static and dynamic) advantages for firms, and productive activities in general, located on a specific territory. In the fifty years of its existence, regional economics has taken all these interpretations of space into consideration, and produced, since Isard's seminal work *Location and Space-Economy* in 1956, a large variety of theories and models. These incorporate space into logical schemes, laws and models which regulate and interpret the formation of prices, demand, productive capacity, levels of output and development, growth rates, and the distribution of income in conditions of unequal regional endowments of resources. Furthermore, regional economics is today able to include space as an economic resource and as an independent production factor, a generator of static and dynamic advantages for the firms situated within it – or, in other words, an element of fundamental importance in the competitiveness of a local production system.

Faced with the wide variety of models, theories and conceptual approaches that today exist in regional economics, a few years ago I felt that I should reorganize my knowledge by writing a textbook which would oblige me to find a personal way to interpret the development of economic thought in this subject, from the first location theories of the 1940s up until the most recent models of endogenous growth and those of the new economic geography. The basis on which I decided to interpret the development of this subject was the concept of space. The book, in fact, presents the various theories treated by organizing them around the manner in which they conceive space: as physical-metric in the old location theories; uniform-abstract in the growth theories of the 1950s and 1960s; diversified-relational in the theories of the 1970s and 1980s; and diversified-stylized in the modern and updated theories of the new economic geography and those of endogenous growth. The reader will decide whether or not I have succeeded. What I can say from my side is that it has been difficult work but undertaken with inspiration and dedication, and with personal satisfaction when I have felt the different pieces of the puzzle fitting together in my mind.

As is always the case when one reads the original contributions of well-known theoreticians, I have discovered interesting aspects that run counter to general beliefs. I have discovered that divergence, traditionally attributed to Keynesian approaches, instead finds theoretical acceptance in the original neoclassical models; induced by a reality that did not support the results of their original (and most famous) model of interregional factor mobility, the neoclassicals George Borts and Jerome Stein presented a revision of the model in order to demonstrate divergence (and not only convergence) in regional income growth rates.

I have also addressed important issues that seem at present to languish in endless scientific debate. One of these issues is whether regions compete on the basis of comparative or absolute advantages. After reading the various contributions on this matter, I came to the conclusion that those who claim that Ricardo's comparative advantage theorem does not hold for regions are correct. Regions compete on absolute rather than comparative advantages: a conclusion – together with the reasons for it – which I set out in my textbook.

I also came across some general beliefs on important theories conventionally included in regional economics textbooks but which, when analysed, revealed that the original purpose for which they were developed does not permit them to state everything that is generally attributed to them. This is the case of the Heckscher–Ohlin model, which was formulated to interpret specialization patterns in international trade and which is traditionally interpreted as a growth model. But because of its nature and the assumptions on which it is based, this model is unable to interpret growth: rather, it suggests – implicitly and without proof – that there is a tendency towards regional development when this is understood in the sense of greater individual well-being (achieved in the model through 'gains from trade'), and of obtaining and maintaining a role in the division of labour. And this is all that this model can tell us about regional development patterns.

I decided to write the book in my mother tongue, Italian, and it was published two years ago by Il Mulino (Bologna, 2004). However, my concern to reach a wider audience imposed the translation of the book into English. My hope that a translation would be less problematic than writing a new book was not fulfilled, however, for new and different challenges accompany a work of this kind.

First of all, there is the linguistic challenge of preserving the exact meaning of the original text. I benefited greatly in this task from the skilful assistance of my translator, Adrian Belton, who worked hard not only on the first translation but also on all the refinements (several for each chapter) that I imposed upon him.

The second major challenge was to adjust the book to the international arena. This required efforts in various directions. First of all, linking theoretical approaches and models to reality requires the citing of examples from all over the world, not merely from Italy. Secondly, wide-ranging and systematic research on international contributions in all subjects was necessary, for if the bibliographical references were to assist the reader in finding more detailed works on the various topics treated, they had to cover the international arena and be comprehensible to everybody. Especially when the original contributions were in languages other than English (Italian, French, Spanish, German), particular effort was made to find out whether an English translation existed. I managed in most cases, but not in all. Thirdly, and this was the most difficult challenge, I had to cover most of the theories today comprised in the regional economics literature. I tried to be as unbiased as possible, and especially in regard to the most recent theories and approaches developed in the countries of Northern Europe, those stemming from the tradition of the Mediterranean countries, and those produced on the other side of the Atlantic. Success in this endeavour, I believed, would provide the richest and most comprehensive account of the fascinating and intriguing subject of regional economics.

My acknowledgements go first to the people who introduced me to the subject. Roberto Camagni of the Politecnico of Milan opened my mind to Spatial Economics during my first degree earned under his supervision at the Bocconi University; I am especially grateful to him for the twenty years of our inspiring scientific work together, with the hope that many more will follow. His valid scientific and psychological help was once again demonstrated during the writing of this book. Peter Nijkamp of the Free University of Amsterdam has played an important role in my progress by supervising my Ph.D. in regional economics and introducing me to the international scientific arena of Regional Science. Secondly, I am grateful to my students, who over these years have asked for clear explanations and obliged me to delve deeply into each theoretical idea and argument. While writing the textbook, I 'tested' the logic of its four parts and various chapters on my students, first at the University of Molise, and then more recently at the Politecnico of Milan, and their questions and doubts induced me to revise part of the text. My sincere wish is that the future generation of regional economists will benefit from reading this book.

A particular thank you goes to my family and friends who patiently accepted to share my free time with this book.

Roberta Capello
Department of Management,
Economics and Industrial Engineering
Politecnico of Milan
Milan, 3 February 2006

Symbols

An attempt has been made to keep the symbols for variables unchanged throughout all the chapters of this book, and particular effort has been made not to attribute different meanings to the same symbol. However, this has not always been possible when traditional symbols from micro- and macroeconomics are applied: it sometimes happens, in fact, that the same symbol is used with different meanings in the two branches of economics. To avert confusion, there follows a list of the symbols used in the book and their meanings.

τ	=	Unit transport cost
π	=	Unit profit/productivity/productivity growth
Π	=	Total profit
A	=	Technical progress/intermediate purchases and sales/producer
B	=	Producer
C	=	Total costs/consumption/producer
c	=	Average and marginal propensity to consume/average cost
d	=	Distance from the centre
D	=	Demand for a good/cumulated number of adopters
e	=	Net migration balance/export growth rate
E	=	Employment
G	=	Public expenditure
h	=	Growth rate of human capital
H	=	Human capital
I	=	Investments
i	=	Interest rates, sector
j	=	Sector or industry
k	=	Growth rate of physical capital/factor of proportionality between the centre of a certain order and the one immediately below
K	=	Physical capital
l	=	Growth rate of labour
L	=	Labour
m	=	Propensity to import/growth rate of imports/a generic good
M	=	Import/raw materials

n	=	Natural growth rate of population/number of firms/nation or country
p	=	Unit price of a good
P	=	Population/prices
q	=	Size of the house, population density
R	=	Total revenue/public transfers
r	=	Land rent/region
s	=	Average and marginal propensity to save/share of urban land occupied by productive activities/difference between national and regional growth rates
S	=	Supply of a good/savings
t	=	Time/income tax rate
T	=	Land/fiscal revenues
u	=	Utility of a good for a consumer
v	=	Investment accelerator coefficient
w	=	Unit wage/unit wage growth
x	=	Quantity of a good
X	=	Exports
Y	=	Total income/total production
y	=	Income growth rate
z	=	Set of other goods than the house

Introduction

SUMMARY

1   Economics and space

2   Location and physical-metric space

3   Regional growth and uniform-abstract space

4   Local development and diversified-relational space

5   Regional growth and diversified-stylized space: towards convergence?

6   Theories of convergence and divergence: a distinction by now superseded

7   The elements distinctive of theories: the structure of the book

ECONOMICS AND SPACE

Economic activity arises, grows and develops in space. Firms, and economic actors in general, choose their locations in the same way as they choose their production factors and their technology. Productive resources are distributed unevenly in space: they are frequently concentrated in specific places (regions or cities) while they are entirely or partly non-existent in others. Quantitative and qualitative imbalances in the geographical distribution of resources and economic activities generate different factor remunerations, different levels of wealth and well-being, and different degrees of control over local development. The problem of factor allocation – which economists have conventionally treated as being the efficient allocation of the factors among various types of production – is more complex than this, in fact; and it is so because the spatial dimension is of crucial importance.

Space influences the workings of an economic system. It is a source of economic advantages (or disadvantages) such as high (or low) endowments of production factors. It also generates geographical advantages, like the easy (or difficult) accessibility of an area, and a high (or low) endowment of raw materials. Space is also the source of advantages springing from the cumulative nature of productive processes in space: in particular, spatial proximity generates economies that reduce production costs (e.g. the transportation costs of activities operating in closely concentrated *filières*) and, in more modern terms, transaction

1

costs (e.g. the costs of market transactions to negotiate and enforce contracts). These considerations highlight the need to supersede the purely allocative approach typical of a static interpretation of economic phenomena with a dynamic, indeed evolutionary, approach which ties allocative decisions to processes of development. The geographic distribution of resources and potentials for development is only minimally determined by exogenous factors (raw materials, natural advantages). To a much larger extent, it results from past and recent historical factors: human capital, social fixed capital, the fertility of the land (due to the work of man), and accessibility (measured as the weighted distance from the main centres of production and consumption).

Already evident is an aspect that informs the entire treatment of this book: regional economics is *not* the study of the economy at the level of administrative regions, as is often superficially and erroneously believed. Regional economics is the branch of economics which incorporates the dimension 'space' into analysis of the workings of the market. It does so by including space in logical schemes, laws and models which regulate and interpret the formation of prices, demand, productive capacity, levels of output and development, growth rates, and the distribution of income in conditions of unequal regional endowments of resources. Furthermore, regional economics moves from 'space' to 'territory' as the main focus of analysis when local growth models include space as an economic resource and as an independent production factor, a generator of static and dynamic advantages for the firms situated within it – or, in other words, an element of fundamental importance in determining the competitiveness of a local production system.

It may seem somewhat banal to emphasize the importance of space for economic activity. And yet, only recently has it been given due consideration by economic theory. Indeed, in the history of economics, analysts have devoted most of their attention and effort to determining the quantities of resources to be used for various purposes; they have concerned themselves with where those resources and activities are located or where they will be located only in the recent past. Analytical precedence and priority has thus been given to the temporal dimension over the spatial one.

There are several reasons for this belated consideration of space by economists. First, as often pointed out by the founder himself of regional economics, Walter Isard,[1] it has been due to the decisive influence of the neoclassical school, which has conceived the temporal analysis of economic development as crucial and neglected the variable 'space' as a consequence – often in order to simplify the treatment. As Marshall wrote:

> The difficulties of the problem depend chiefly on variations in the area of space, and the period of time over which the market in question extends; the influence of time being more fundamental than that of space.
>
> (Marshall, 1920)

Secondly, the treatment of the variable 'space' in economic analysis – especially if it is included in a dynamic approach – complicates the logical framework. The analytical tools until recently available to economists could not handle temporal and spatial dynamics simultaneously. Nor were they able to cope with the non-linearity of spatial phenomena like agglomeration or proximity economies. Finally, introduction of the variable 'space' required the discarding of the simplifying hypotheses (always dear to economists) of constant returns and perfect competition. According to the logic of a spatial market divided among producers, firms do not compete with all other firms, but only with those closest to them. Spatial distance is thus a barrier to entry which imposes a system of monopolistic competition – which too has only recently been formalized in analytical growth models.[2]

Regional economics therefore seeks to answer the following fundamental questions. What economic logic explains the location choices of firms and households in space? What economic logic explains the configuration of large territorial systems (e.g. city systems)? Why are certain areas – regions, cities, individual territories – more developed than others?

Answers to these questions have been put forward by the two large groups of theories that make up regional economics:

- *location theory*, the oldest branch of regional economics, first developed in the early 1900s, which deals with the economic mechanisms that distribute activities in space;
- *regional growth (and development) theory*, which focuses on spatial aspects of economic growth and the territorial distribution of income.

Location theory gives regional economics its scientific-disciplinary identity and constitutes its theoretical-methodological core. It has typically microeconomic foundations and it adopts a traditionally static approach. It deals with the location choices of firms and households. Linked with it are a variety of metaphors, cross-fertilizations and theoretical inputs (from macroeconomics, interregional trade theory, development theory, mathematical ecology, systems theory) which have refined the tools of regional economics and extended its range of inquiry. In microeconomic terms, location theory involves investigation into the location choices of firms and households; but it also involves analysis of disparities in the spatial distribution of activities – inquiry which enables interpretation of territorial disequilibria and hierarchies. Location theory uses the concepts of externalities and agglomeration economies to shed light on such macro-territorial phenomena as disparities in the spatial distribution of activities, thereby laying the territorial bases for dynamic approaches.

Regional growth theory is instead intrinsically macroeconomic. However, it differs from the purely macroeconomic approaches of political economy in its concern with territorial features. Just as we speak of the micro-foundations of macroeconomics, so we may speak of the locational foundations of regional growth theory.

Numerous cross-fertilizations have taken place between these two branches of regional economics, and they have brought the traditional conceptions of space on each side – *physical-metric* for location theory, *uniform-abstract* for regional growth theory – closer together. I call the more recent conception of space *diversified-relational*: this is the bridge and the point of maximum cross-fertilization between the two traditional branches of regional economics. It yields an authentic theory of regional development based on the intrinsic relationalities present in local areas. These three conceptions of space are today still separate, however, and their integration has only been partly accomplished by the more modern notion of *diversified-stylized* space used by recent theories of local growth.

3

LOCATION AND PHYSICAL-METRIC SPACE

The first and earliest group of theories in regional economics falls under the heading of 'location theory'. This group adopts a purely geographical conception of continuous, *physical-metric* space definable in terms of physical distance and transportation costs. Thus interpreted are the regularities of price and cost variations in space, and their consequences in terms of location choices and the division of the market among firms. This was the conception of space used by the great geographers of the first half of the twentieth century.

Location theory seeks to explain the distribution of activities in space, the aim being to identify the factors that influence the location of individual activities, the allocation of different portions of territory among different types of production, the dividing of a spatial market among producers, and the functional distribution of activities in space. These various phenomena are analysed by removing any geographical (physical) feature that might explain the territorial concentration of activities,[3] so that location choices are interpreted by considering only the great economic forces that drive location processes: transportation costs, which diffuse activities in space, and agglomeration economies, which instead cause activities to concentrate. By balancing these two opposing forces, these models are able to account for the existence of agglomerations of economic activities even on the hypothesis of perfectly uniform space.

Location models differ according to hypotheses on the spatial structure of demand and supply which reflect the aims that the models pursue. There are models whose aim is to interpret the *location choices of firms*, on the assumption of punctiform final and raw materials markets with given locations. Choice of location is determined in this case by an endeavour to minimize transportation costs between alternative locations and under the influence of agglomeration economies (theories of minimum-cost location). Here the obligatory reference is to the models developed by Alfred Weber and Melvin Greenhut. There are then models which seek to identify the *market areas* of firms, that is, the division of a spatial market among producers. In this case, the models hypothesize a demand evenly distributed across the territory which determines the location choices of firms, these being assumed to be punctiform. Locational equilibrium is determined by a logic of profit maximization whereby each producer controls its own market area (theories of profit-maximizing location); the reference here being to the market area models developed by, for example, August Lösch and Harold Hotelling.

There are then models which seek to identify *production areas*. That is, they seek to identify the economic logic whereby a physical territory (land) is allocated among alternative types of production. In this case, the models are based on assumptions about the structure of demand and supply which are the reverse of those made by theories of market areas. The final market is punctiform in space (the town or city centre), while supply extends across the territory. Activities are organized spatially according to access to the final market, and locational equilibrium arises from a balance between transportation costs on the one hand, and the costs of acquiring land for a central location on the other. The models developed by Johann Heinrich von Thünen, William Alonso and the 'new urban economics' school express this logic.

Finally, location theory analyses the economic and spatial mechanisms that regulate the size of territorial agglomerations, their functional specialization, and their territorial distribution. These models put forward a more complex and general theory of location and the structure of the underlying economic relations able to account for the existence of diverse territorial agglomerations within a framework of general spatial equilibrium. The principal contributions to development of this theory have been made by Walter Christaller and August Lösch.

REGIONAL GROWTH AND UNIFORM-ABSTRACT SPACE

The second large group of theories pertaining to regional economics seek to explain why growth and economic development come about at local level. Why are there rich regions and poor ones; regions which grow more than others, and regions which grow less? What factors determine economic growth at local level? In other words, in this case regional economics analyses the capacity of a subnational system – a region, a province, a city, an area with specific economic features – to develop economic activities, to attract them, and to generate the conditions for long-lasting development. Here by 'regional economic development' is meant the ability of a local economic system to find, and constantly to recreate, a specific and appropriate role in the international division of labour through the efficient and creative use of the resources that it possesses. By emphasizing the more economic elements of this definition, regional development can be defined as the ability of a region to produce, with a (comparative or absolute) advantage, the goods and services demanded by the national and international economic system to which it belongs.[4]

The first theories of regional growth were developed midway through the last century. They used a conception of space – as *uniform-abstract*, no longer physical and continuous but abstract and discrete – entirely different from the physical-metric space of location theory. Geographic space was divided into 'regions', areas of limited physical-geographical size (largely matching administrative units) considered to be internally uniform and therefore synthesizable into a vector of aggregate characteristics of a social-economic-demographic nature: 'small countries' in the terminology of international trade but, unlike nations, characterized by marked external openness to the movement of production factors.[5]

The advantage of this conception of space is that it enables the use of macroeconomic models to interpret local growth phenomena. But although these models fit the above-mentioned features, they nevertheless, and it seems inexorably, require the analyst to exclude any mechanism of interregional agglomeration, to discard location theory, to ignore the advantages of local proximity, and instead to assume unequal endowments of resources and production factors, unequal demand conditions, and interregional disparities in productive structures as the determinants of local development. Space is thus no more than the physical container of development and performs a purely passive role in economic growth, while some macroeconomic theories reduce regional development to the simple regional allocation of aggregate national development.

Theories which take this view of space are *growth theories* developed to explain the trend of a synthetic development indicator – income for instance. Although this approach inevitably entails the loss of qualitative information, its undeniable advantage is that it makes modelling of the development path possible. These theories differ sharply in their conceptions of growth: there are those which conceive growth as a short-term increase in output and employment, and others which instead identify the growth path in a long-period increase in output associated with higher levels of individual well-being (high wages and per capita incomes, more favourable prices on the interregional market).

This conception of space has been adopted by the neoclassical regional growth theory, the export-base theory, and the interregional trade theory which developed from various branches of mainstream economics in the 1950s and 1960s: macroeconomics, neoclassical economics, development economics, and economics of international trade.

LOCAL DEVELOPMENT AND DIVERSIFIED-RELATIONAL SPACE

Interpretation of space as *diversified-relational* has restored to theories of regional development one of the key concepts of location theory – namely agglomeration economies – and made them the core of local development processes. According to this conception, which received its fullest development in the 1970s and 1980s, space generates economic advantages through large-scale mechanisms of synergy and cumulative feedback operating at local level.

A number of seminal theories of the early 1960s for the first time conceived space as diversified-relational. Development was defined, in the words of Perroux, as 'a selective, cumulative process which does not appear everywhere at the same time but becomes manifest at certain points in space with variable intensity'.[6] Perroux's definition affirmed the existence of 'poles' at which development concentrates because of synergic and cumulative forces generated by stable and enduring local input/output relations facilitated by physical proximity. Space is thus conceived as diversified and 'relational'.

But it was during the 1970s that studies on 'bottom-up' processes of development, on districts and local *milieux*, gave the notion of diversified-relational space its most thorough formulation. The conceptual leap consisted in interpreting space as 'territory', or in economic terms, as a system of localized technological externalities: a set of tangible and intangible factors which, because of proximity and reduced transaction costs, act upon the productivity and innovativeness of firms. Moreover, the territory is conceived as a system of local governance which unites a community, a set of private actors, and a set of local institutions. Finally, the territory is a system of economic and social relations constituting the relational or social capital of a particular geographical space.[7]

Any connection with abstract or administrative space is thus obviously discounted. Adopted instead is a more intangible account of space which emphasizes – by focusing on the economic and social relations among actors in a territorial area – more complex phenomena which arise in local economic systems.

Precisely because the diversified-relational space theories of the 1970s and 1980s viewed development as depending crucially on territorial externalities in the form of location and spatial proximity economies, they stressed (for the first time in the history of economic thought) the role of endogenous conditions and factors in local development. These theories adopted a micro-territorial and micro-behavioural approach; they can be called *theories of development* because their purpose was not to explain the aggregate growth rate of income

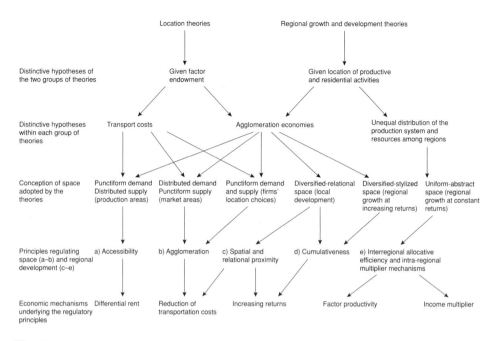

Figure 1 *The principles and hypotheses underlying theories of location and of regional growth and local development*

and employment – as in the case of the above-mentioned uniform-abstract space theories – but instead to identify all the tangible and intangible elements of the growth process.

In the theories which conceived space as diversified-relational, location theory was inextricably and interestingly wedded with local development theory. By pointing out that concentration generates locational advantages, which in their turn create development and attract new firms whose presence further boosts the advantages of agglomeration, these theories elegantly revealed the genuinely 'spatial' nature of the development mechanism.

In this sense, diversified-relational space theories form the core of regional economics, the heart of a discipline where maximum cross-fertilization between location theory and development theory permits analysis of regional development as *generative* development: the national growth rate is the sum of the growth rates achieved by individual regions – as opposed to the *competitive* development envisaged by certain uniform-abstract space theories, where regional development is nothing but the simple regional allocation of aggregate national development.

The intriguing objective of these theories is to explain the competitiveness of territorial systems, the local determinants of development, and the capacity of an area to achieve and maintain a role in the international division of labour. They thus seek to identify the local conditions that enable an economic system to achieve and maintain high rates of development.

Figure 1 summarizes the principles underpinning location theory and regional development theory. The two large theoretical blocks in regional economics – location theory and local growth/development theory – rest on different initial hypotheses: location theory assumes a given factor endowment; local growth/development theory assumes the localization of firms and households. The theories within each group are differentiated by their economic assumptions (transportation costs, agglomeration economies, and the spatial distribution of resources and the productive system) and their conceptions of space (differing spatial structures of demand and supply for location theory; uniform-abstract, diversified-relational and, as we shall see, diversified-stylized space for local growth/development theory). Thus evidenced by Figure 1 are the governing principles of space and regional growth/development that buttressed the approaches: agglomeration and accessibility for location theory; interregional allocative efficiency and intraregional multiplier mechanisms, relational proximity, and cumulative growth processes for theories of local development and regional growth. Figure 1 also highlights the role of agglomeration economies as the hinge between these two broad components of regional economics.

REGIONAL GROWTH AND DIVERSIFIED-STYLIZED SPACE: TOWARDS CONVERGENCE?

Until the end of the 1980s these different conceptions of space developed within regional economics without the slightest convergence between them. In the words of Edvin von Böventer, 'within regional economics one can distinguish between "pure and exact" regional theory without agglomeration economies, on the one hand, and "applied regional theory" which is inexact but takes agglomeration factors into account, on the other hand'.[8] Von Böventer was referring, in the former case, to a rigorously economic and formalized theory of growth, one closer to mainstream economics and envisaging a uniform-abstract space. In the latter case, he had in mind a theory of development without the formal rigour of macroeconomics and predicated on a conception of space where agglomeration economies drive local development.

The 1990s saw the development of more advanced mathematical tools for analysis of the qualitative behaviour of dynamic non-linear systems (bifurcation, catastrophe, and chaos theory) together with the advent of formalized economic models which abandoned the hypotheses of constant returns and perfect competition. These advances made it possible to incorporate agglomeration economies – stylized in the form of increasing returns – into elegant models of a strictly macroeconomic nature.

The reference is in particular to the models of 'new economic geography' and endogenous growth in which space becomes diversified-stylized. These theories anchored their logic on the assumption that productive activities concentrate around particular 'poles' of development, so that the level and growth rate of income is diversified even within the same region. Moreover, these models stylized areas as points or abstract dichotomies in which neither physical-geographical features (e.g. morphology, physical size) nor territorial ones (e.g. the local-level system of economic and social relations) play a role.

These theories achieved considerable success and acclaim in the academic community because they showed that territorial phenomena can be analysed using the traditional tools of economic theory (optimizing choices by individual firms and people), and that the various conceptions of space can – apparently – be synthesized. These models in fact conceived growth as endogenous, generated by the advantages of the spatial concentration of activities, and by the agglomeration economies typical of diversified space theories. They counter-posed dynamic growth mechanisms with increasing returns and transportation costs, thus reprising the economic-locational processes analysed by location theory.

Though diversified (inasmuch as there exist territorial poles of concentrated develop-ment), space in these models is stylized into points devoid of any territorial dimension. Thus inevitably abandoned is the concept of space as territory so favoured by regional economists. This stylized space does not comprise localized technological externalities, nor the set of tangible and intangible factors which, thanks to proximity and reduced transac-tion costs, act upon the productivity and innovative capacity of firms; nor the system of economic and social relations constituting the relational or social capital of a particular geographical area. Yet these are all elements which differentiate among territorial entities on the basis of specifically localized features. As a consequence, these approaches are deprived of the most interesting, and in a certain sense intriguing, interpretation of space as an additional resource for development and as a free-standing production factor. Predominant instead is a straightforward, somewhat banal, view of space as simply the physical/geographical container of development.

To conclude, a certain convergence has come about between the large groups of theor-ies discussed. Diversified-relational space theories, in particular those of (endogenous) local development, merge together ideas put forward by the theories of development and of loca-tion. Diversified-stylized space theories, in particular new economic geography, amalgamate growth and location theories (Figure 2). Nevertheless, a further step forward is still required which would produce an approach combining the economic laws and mechanisms which explain growth, on the one hand, with the territorial features that spring from the intrinsic relationality present at local level on the other. Such an approach would represent the max-imum of cross-fertilization among location theory, development theory, and growth macro-economics; a synthesis which would bring out the territorial micro-foundations of macroeconomic growth models (Figure 2). An undertaking of this kind, though, would require analysis of variables besides the cost of transport, which nullifies the territory's role in the development process. Also necessary would be variables that give the territory prime place – even in purely economic models – among local growth mechanisms. This is the challenge that awaits regional economists in the years to come.

THEORIES OF CONVERGENCE AND DIVERGENCE: A DISTINCTION BY NOW SUPERSEDED

Handbooks on 'regional economics' have often drawn a distinction, indeed a dichotomy, between theories of convergence and divergence: that is, between theories which examine the reasons for diminishing disparities between rich and backward regions, and theories which, on the contrary, explain the persistence of those disparities.[9]

Ranged on the convergence side are theories originating within the neoclassical paradigm and which interpret (in their initial formulation) development as a process tending to equi-librium because of market forces. In equilibrium, not only is there an optimum allocation of resources but also an equal distribution of the production factors in space which guarantees, at least tendentially, the same level of development among regions.

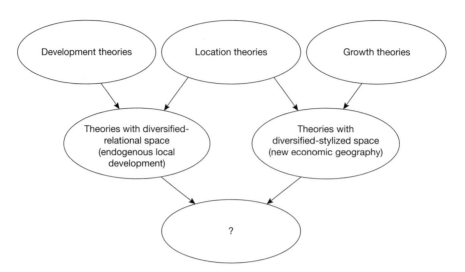

Figure 2 *Convergence among theoretical approaches*

On the divergence side stand theories of Keynesian origin which, by introducing positive and negative feedback mechanisms and the cumulative attraction and repulsion of productive resources respectively in a country's rich and poor areas, envisage not only the persistence but also the worsening of disparities among regions.[10]

In recent years, more refined mathematical and modelling tools have demonstrated that the same theories are able to explain both divergence and convergence. By introducing, for example, scale economies and agglomeration economies into a production function – obviously more complex than that of the 1960s model – the neoclassical model successfully simulates a series of behaviours and tendencies, both continuous and 'catastrophic', very distant from the mechanicism and univocity of the convergence predictions of the original neoclassical model. In the same way, the divergence yielded by Keynesian models (*à la* Myrdal and Kaldor in particular) is called into question if the model's dynamic properties are analysed: according to the parameter values of the dynamic equations describing the model's economic logic, the local system either converges on a constant growth rate or explosively or implosively diverges from it.

It is therefore possible to conclude that there are no longer grounds for any dichotomy to be drawn between theories of convergence and divergence, between optimistic theories and pessimistic ones. However, the problem in and of itself is still very much present, and it is much more complex than was believed in the past. The neoclassical model, elegant in its formulation and consistent in its economic logic, has frequently been criticized as unsuited (in its original formulation) to interpretation of constant and persistent regional disparities. The Keynesian model, in its turn, has been faulted for being unable to foresee territorial limits to the evolution of the cumulative process, although these limits have substantial effects on territorial development paths. But if the 'theories of divergence/convergence' dichotomy is abandoned, the explanatory capacity of each theory can be recovered, to produce a broad array of conceptual tools with which to interpret the complex processes of territorial development. Moreover, I submit, it is much more interesting, as we shall see in the next section, to divide theories according to other and more meaningful features – the definition of space, and the goals implicitly pursued by each theory.

THE ELEMENTS DISTINCTIVE OF THEORIES: THE STRUCTURE OF THE BOOK

This book abandons the distinction between theories of convergence and divergence. Instead it chooses new elements around which to organize theories of growth and development. These elements throw the interpretative capacities and objectives of theories into sharp relief.

The first element is the conception of space, which enables theories to be grouped according to their approach (micro or macro); the roles performed by space in the development process (passive or active); their interpretative focus (growth or development); and the principles determining development and growth (allocative efficiency, cumulativeness, spatial proximity).

A second element differentiating among theories is their interpretation of growth. There are theories which associate growth with employment creation, and models whose policy objective is to reduce unemployment in a context of given but largely under-utilized resources. It is thus easy to disregard the problem of endowment, the allocation of resources and factor productivity, and instead take a short-term perspective which envisages *current* competitiveness of production and structure – a condition which can be extrapolated only for a brief period. There are then models and theories which associate growth with increased individual well-being (unitary wages, per capita income) achievable either through higher levels of productivity (and therefore higher levels of wages and per capita income) or through the productive specialization that permits interregional trade and the purchase of goods on the interregional market at prices lower than they would be if the goods were produced internally. Associated with this view of growth are policy problems concerning poverty, underdevelopment, and inequalities in the spatial distribution of income. The long-period objective of these approaches is to achieve growth of per capita incomes through higher productivity. Finally, there are models and theories whose policy objective is to identify the determinants of an economic system's real competitiveness and its constancy in time.

Emphasizing the different interpretations given to the concept of growth yields more thorough understanding of each theory's objectives, strengths and weaknesses, and real interpretative capacity. A theory developed with a view to short-period employment is unable to demonstrate the determinants of regional competitiveness (which if anything it presupposes), or the elements that give a region a role in the international division of labour, or the mechanisms that enable the region to maintain that role in the long period. Conversely, a theory which seeks to define the key factors in long-period regional competitiveness is unlikely to be interested in quantitative changes in income and their effects on individual well-being (if anything, it implicitly associates better well-being with greater development).

11

Table 1 Elements distinctive of the theories examined and the structure of the book

Definition of space	Elements distinctive of the theories examined	Structure of the book
Physical-metric space	**Location theories**	**PART 1**
	Definition of firms' location choices and of market areas	Chapter 1
	Definition of production areas	Chapter 2
	Definition of the structure of urban systems	Chapter 3
Uniform-abstract space	**Theories of regional growth at constant returns**	**PART 2**
	Preconditions for development	Chapter 4
	Short-term growth of employment and income (with given but largely under-utilized resources)	Chapter 5
	Growth of well-being and per capita income	Chapter 6
Diversified-relational space	**Local development theories**	**PART 3**
	Determinants of competitiveness (exogenous microeconomic factors)	Chapter 7
	Determinants of competitiveness (endogenous microeconomic factors)	Chapter 8
Diversified-stylized space	**Theories of regional growth at increasing returns**	**PART 4**
	Determinants of competitiveness (endogenous macroeconomic factors of demand/supply interaction)	Chapter 9
	Determinants of competitiveness (endogenous macroeconomic supply-side factors)	Chapter 10
	Towards a synthesis	Chapter 11

The book is structured according to these distinctive elements of the theories examined. Differing conceptions of space account for the division of the book into parts; and differing definitions of growth and development account for its division into chapters.

The first part of the book (Part 1) examines location theory. It is organized into chapters which reflect the various hypotheses put forward on space and the objectives pursued by analysing it (Table 1). The first chapter sets out theories which envisage punctiform supply and demand and seek to identify the forces that determine the locational choices of firms. It then deals with theories which assume punctiform supply and spatially distributed demand in order to explain the formation of market areas. The second chapter describes theories which assume spatially distributed supply and punctiform demand to explain the formation of production areas. Finally, the third chapter discusses theories of general spatial equilibrium developed to explain the economic processes which configure large territorial systems, urban systems in particular.

The subsequent parts of the book examine regional growth and development models (Table 1). Part 2 deals with *uniform-abstract space theories of growth* at constant returns. Belonging to this first group are theories of regional growth which derive directly from various branches of mainstream economics: macroeconomics, neoclassical economics, development economics, and international trade economics. For these theories, the engine of development is the unequal distribution among regions of factor endowments and the sectoral structure of supply. This part of the book first examines theories which investigate the preconditions for local development (Chapter 4). It continues with theories concerned with short-period development with given resources (Chapter 5), and it concludes with theories that shift the focus to supply, from the point of view of well-being and full employment (Chapter 6).

Part 3 of the book examines *diversified-relational space theories of development* related to location theory. Microeconomic and micro-territorial in their approach, these theories seek to identify the determinants of local competitiveness. They are sharply distinguished between theories which conceive competitiveness as generated by factors exogenous to the local area (Chapter 7) and ones that, from a more modern perspective, consider endogenous development factors (Chapter 8). The latter are the most 'spatial' theories of economic development; and they are the first to have furnished an economic interpretation of the 'territory' as comprising cooperation and synergy relations among local actors which influence the productive efficiency and innovative capacity of firms, and therefore the local-level rate of development.

Finally, Part 4 of the book discusses *diversified-stylized space theories of growth*. This group comprises the most recent theories, the distinctive feature of which is that they include increasing returns in macroeconomic growth models. Put otherwise: they represent the first attempt to explain local development by combining purely economic and dynamic equilibrium processes with spatial and locational features. The great merit of these theories, in fact, is that they construct elegant economic models comprising agglomeration economies, in the form of increasing returns, which drive virtuous demand/supply processes (Chapter 9), or counteract the decreasing marginal productivity of the individual factors in a virtuous supply-side circle (Chapter 10). Finally, Chapter 11 concludes with a discussion which summarizes the book's analyses, gives a modern interpretation of local development, and outlines the main theoretical challenges that regional scientists will face in the near future.

REVIEW QUESTIONS

1   How do you define regional economics and what are the main topics addressed by this discipline?

2   Would you define regional economics as that part of economics addressing the economic problems of administrative regions?

3   What are the theoretical aspects addressed in regional economics?

4   What are the main topics addressed by location theory? How is space conceived within location theory?

5   What are the main topics addressed by regional growth theory? How is space conceived within regional growth theory?

6   What is the difference between regional growth and local development theories?

7   What is the difference in the way space is conceived in the theories of regional growth and local development?

FURTHER READING

Alonso, W. (1964) 'Location theory', in Friedmann, J. and Alonso, W. (eds), *Regional development and planning: a reader*, Cambridge, Mass.: MIT Press, pp. 78–106.

Hoover, E. M. (1948) *The location of economic activity*, New York: McGraw-Hill.

Isard, W. (1949) 'The general theory of location and space', *Quarterly Journal of Economics*, vol. 63, no. 4, pp. 476–506.

Isard, W. (1956) *Location and space-economy*, Cambridge, Mass.: MIT Press.

Meyer, J. R. (1963) 'Regional economics: a survey', *American Economic Review*, vol. 53, pp. 19–54.

Richardson, H. W. (1973) *Regional growth theory*, London: Macmillan.

Von Böventer, E. (1975) 'Regional growth theory', *Urban Studies*, vol. 12, pp. 1–29.

Part 1

Location theory: physical-metric space

Chapter 1

Agglomeration and location

SUMMARY

1 Agglomeration economies and transportation costs
2 Localization economies and transportation costs
3 Market size and transportation costs
4 Economies of scale and transportation costs
5 Spatial demand, market equilibrium and firm location
6 Interdependency in location choices: the Hotelling model

AGGLOMERATION ECONOMIES AND TRANSPORTATION COSTS

Space is inextricably bound up with economic activity. This statement is prompted by the rather banal observation that all forms of production require space. But it also derives from the fact that not all geographical areas afford the same opportunities for production and development. The uneven distribution of raw materials, production factors (capital and labour) and demand (final goods markets) requires firms, and productive activities in general, to select their locations just as they select their production factors and technology. And just as the choice of the factors and technology decisively influences the productive capacity of firms and their position on the market, so location crucially determines the productive capacities of firms and, in aggregate terms, of the geographical areas in which they are located. To ignore this dimension – as traditional economic theory does – is to disregard a factor which sheds significant light on the mechanisms underlying firms' behaviour and economic activities in general, and which drive economic development.[1]

The notion of space was first introduced into economic analysis by theories on industrial location. The aim of these theories was to explain location choices by considering the two great economic forces that organize activities in space: transportation costs and agglomeration economies. These forces push the location process in opposite directions since they simultaneously induce both the dispersion and the spatial concentration of production.[2]

It is because of agglomeration economies that spatial concentration comes about. Widely used in regional economics, the term 'agglomeration economies' denotes all economic advantages accruing to firms from concentrated location close to other firms: reduced production costs due to large plant size; the presence of advanced and specialized services; the availability of fixed social capital (e.g. infrastructures); the presence of skilled labour and of managerial expertise, and of a broad and specialized intermediate goods market. All of these are resources whose availability, or production, require a high level of demand.

The advantages that induce firms to opt for concentrated location can be grouped into three broad categories:[3]

1   *Economies internal to the firm, also called economies of scale.* These arise from large-scale production processes yielding lower costs per unit of output.[4] In order to reap the advantages of large-scale production, the firm concentrates all its plants in a single location. The advantages in this category derive, not from proximity to other firms, but from the pure concentration of activity in space.

2   *Economies external to the firm but internal to the sector, or localization economies.* These spring from location in an area densely populated by firms operating in the same sector. Whereas scale economies depend on the size of the firm (of its plants), localization economies are determined by the size of the sector in a particular area with a wide range of specialized suppliers and in which skilled labour and specific managerial and technical expertise are available.

3   *Economies external to the firm and external to the sector, or urbanization economies.* These derive from the high density and variety of productive and residential activities in an area; features which typify urban environments. The advantages in this category accrue from the presence of large-scale fixed social capital (urban and long-distance transport infrastructures, advanced telecommunication systems) and a broad and diversified intermediate and final goods market. These advantages increase with the physical size of the city.

All the above advantages result from the concentration of economic activities in space. However, there are two forces which work in the reverse direction and give rise to dispersed location. The first is the formation in the agglomeration area of increasing costs or diseconomies, these being (a) the prices of less mobile and scarcer factors (land and labour), and (b) the congestion costs (noise and air pollution, crime, social malaise) distinctive of large agglomerations. These diseconomies are generated above a certain critical threshold.[5] However, the second factor – transportation costs – is of greater interest, because these costs countervail the spatial concentration of activities whatever level of agglomeration has been reached. For in conditions of perfect competition, perfectly mobile production factors, fixed raw materials and demand perfectly distributed across the territory, the existence of transportation costs may erode the advantages of agglomeration until activities are geographically dispersed and the market becomes divided among firms, each of which caters to a local market.

The theory of localization defines 'transportation costs' as all the forms of spatial friction that give greater attractiveness to a location which reduces the distance between two points in space (e.g. production site and the final market; place of residence and the work-place; the raw materials market and the production site). Transportation costs are accordingly the economic cost of shipping goods (the pure cost of transporting and distributing them); the opportunity cost represented by the time taken to cover the distance which could instead be put to other uses; the psychological cost of the journey; the cost and difficulty of communication over distances; the risk of failing to acquire vital information.

Transportation costs are therefore essential to location theory in its entirety, for they differentiate space and enable its treatment in economic terms. They are, moreover, comprised in the concept of agglomeration economies as the costs of interaction and distance: if transportation costs were nil, there would be no reason to concentrate activities, because doing so would not produce 'economies'. In this sense, agglomeration economies are 'proximity economies': that is to say, they are advantages which arise from the interaction (often involuntary) among economic agents made possible by the lower amount of spatial friction in concentrated locations.

As a later chapter will show, agglomeration and proximity form the linkage between location theory and the theory of regional development. Indeed, development theory in the 1970s and 1980s took agglomeration, in the sense of proximity, to be the decisive endogenous factor in cumulative and territorialized processes of economic development.[6]

Two distinct groups of theories on the location of industrial activities can be identified on the basis of objectives that they set themselves, and according to the hypotheses that they assume about the spatial structure of the market:

- *Cost minimization theories*. These hypothesize a punctiform outlet market and a punctiform source of raw materials supply located at different points of space, in order to investigate the location choices of firms at minimum transportation costs. In that they analyse the location choices of individual firms, these theories are based on a partial equilibrium framework.[7]
- *Profit maximization theories*. On the hypothesis that demand is geographically dispersed and supply is concentrated in some points of the market, these theories account for the division of the market among several firms in terms of profit maximization. They assume that the extent of each firm's market and its location depend on consumer behaviour and on the location choices of other firms. These theories are conceived largely within a partial equilibrium framework; an exception is Lösch's model, which envisages a general spatial equilibrium (several firms simultaneously in economic-location equilibrium).

Cost-minimization theories offer answers to questions such as the following: Given the price and location of raw materials and the outlet market, where does the firm locate? How do location choices change when one hypothesizes a place in which agglomeration economies (e.g. the greater availability and higher quality of labour, broader outlet markets) exist? Profit-maximization theories seek to answer questions such as these: Given a certain spatial distribution of demand, how do firms divide up the market? Once the firm's location has been defined, how does it change with variations in the initial production conditions (e.g. variations in production or transportation costs) or in the location choices of other firms?

19

This chapter sets out the main theories that endeavour to answer these questions. It will begin by showing that when demand and supply are punctiform in space, agglomeration economies (in the form of localization economies) influence firms' location choices even when these are intended to minimize costs (of production and transport); and in their nature as urbanization economies they may give rise to location choices which appear illogical if considered solely in terms of costs minimization. The chapter then shows that, when supply is punctiform and demand is distributed uniformly in space, transportation costs influence the division of the market among firms; and moreover that, in the presence of scale economies or variations in their magnitude, market areas change in their extent. Finally, the chapter will explain how location choices depend closely on the choices of other firms, and also on consumer behaviour.

LOCALIZATION ECONOMIES AND TRANSPORTATION COSTS

Weber's model

One of the first and best-known studies on the spatial concentration of industry dates back to 1909. In that year, the economist Alfred Weber constructed an elegant location model where the costs of transportation among production site, raw materials markets, and the final goods market (which together define a minimum transportation cost) are directly compared against localization economies. The prevalence of one element over another determines the geography of industry location.[8]

Weber's model is based on the following simplifying assumptions:

■ there is a punctiform market for the good (*C* in Figure 1.1a);
■ two raw materials markets, also punctiform, are located at a certain distance from each other (M_1 and M_2 in Figure 1.1a);
■ there is perfect competition in the market, i.e. firms are unable to gain monopolistic advantages from their choice of location;
■ demand for the final good is price-inelastic;[9]
■ the same production technique is used in every possible location; production costs are therefore given and constant.

The location choice results from a complex calculation performed in two stages.

In the first, the firm looks for the location that assures the minimum transportation costs between the production site, the raw materials market and the final market for the good produced. In the second stage, the firm compares the advantages of agglomeration (localization economies) against the higher transportation costs that it would incur by choosing the new location instead of the one with minimum transportation costs.

The first stage of calculation identifies the location that assures minimum transportation costs. Let *x* and *y* be the tonnes of raw materials present respectively in markets M_1 and M_2 and required to produce one unit of output, and let *z* be the tonnes of the finished good to be transported to the final market *C*. Total transportation costs (*CT*) are expressed as a function of the weight of the good to be transported and the distance to cover:[10]

(a) The locational triangle: choosing the location with the minimum transportation costs

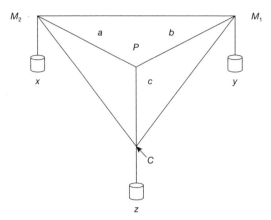

(b) The agglomeration areas

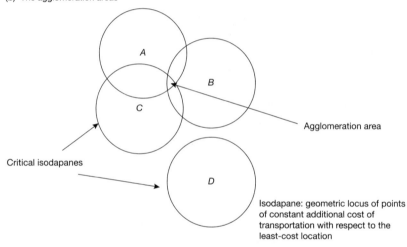

Figure 1.1 *Weber's location equilibrium*

$$CT = xa + yb + zc \tag{1.1}$$

where a, b and c are respectively the distances in kilometres between the raw materials markets and the production site, and between the latter and the final market; xa, yb and zc represent the 'forces of attraction' that push the firm respectively towards points M_1, M_2 and C (Figure 1.1a).

The minimum cost location solution can be identified:[11]

1 at a point inside the triangle formed by joining M_1, M_2 and C if none of the 'forces of attraction' exceeds the sum of the other two. In economic terms, this situation occurs when the cost of transporting the z tonnes of the good one kilometre further away from the outlet market is less than the costs of transporting the x and y tonnes of raw materials one kilometre further away from their source market;

2   at corner C of the triangle, i.e. the final market, if the sum of the costs of transporting the x and y tonnes of raw materials one kilometre further away from their market is less than the cost of transporting the z tonnes of final good produced one extra kilometre. This situation comes about because of the greater relative weight, in the composition of the finished product, of ubiquitous raw materials with respect to those that must be transported. Weber calls this condition 'market-oriented';

3   at a point closer to the raw materials markets if the sum of the costs of transporting the x and y tonnes of raw materials one kilometre more is greater than the extra cost of transporting the z tonnes of the finished good. This situation can be explained by the lesser relative weight, in the composition of the final good, of ubiquitous raw materials with respect to localized raw materials, and/or the product's loss of weight during the manufacturing process. Weber calls this location 'raw material-oriented'.

Weber provides a practical solution to the problem of identifying the minimum point. He hypothesizes a triangular board (the location triangle) in which three holes are drilled at the vertexes M_1, M_2 and C. Threads are passed through these holes (Figure 1.1a) and their ends are knotted together on the upper surface of the board. Weights respectively proportional to x, y and z are attached to the other ends of the threads below the board. The point at which the knot of the three threads lies on the upper surface of the board corresponds to the point of minimum transportation costs.

In the second stage of the location choice process, the firm compares the least-cost location with an alternative one where it can enjoy localization economies – for instance the availability of labour at lower cost and/or better quality.

Assuming that P in Figure 1.1a is the location point with the lowest transportation costs, Weber describes the 'isodapanes': curves along which the additional transportation cost that the firm must pay in order to cover a certain distance from the least-cost location remains constant.[12] On the assumption that other firms operate in the same sector, and that these firms obtain advantages from concentrated location such that they have a pecuniary advantage equal to v, the decision to relocate will be taken if and only if each firm's isodapane measuring an extra transportation cost equal to the agglomerative advantage (v) intersects with the isodapanes of the other firms. In this case, in fact, within the area of intersection the additional transportation costs are less than the advantages generated by concentrated location. In Figure 1.1b, firms A, B and C find themselves in this situation and they relocate. But not so firm D, for which the agglomerative advantage is no greater than the additional transportation cost.[13]

Criticisms of the model

Weber's model has made a permanent and major contribution to industrial location theory. Its principal merit is that it uses entirely rational modes of reasoning: for instance, comparison between the advantages of an alternative location and the additional transportation costs that it would generate. Nevertheless, the model has a number of shortcomings:

- its static nature. The model identifies the least-cost location on the basis of productive efficiency, but it ignores dynamic aspects such as innovation at the microeconomic level, while, at the macroeconomic one, it neglects changes in income distribution and in the relationships among agglomeration advantages, rents and wages;[14]
- its transport-oriented nature. The cost of transportation defines first and foremost the most efficient location; only subsequently does it identify alternative locations. Some critics have claimed that this approach is less efficient than one based on the direct search for a point of minimum total production cost;[15]
- its abstractness, which makes the least-cost location difficult to calculate in real settings. It is rather unlikely, in fact, that the weight of raw materials in the final weight of the good can be calculated, distinguishing *inter alia* the weight of the raw materials to be transported from those present at the production site;[16]
- its nature as a partial equilibrium model which entirely neglects possible interactions among firms;
- its supply-side bias. The criticism most frequently made of the model is that it is excessively oriented to the supply side: it makes no mention of demand factors, assuming that demand is unlimited and inelastic to price variations.

MARKET SIZE AND TRANSPORTATION COSTS

Weber's model assumes that demand is punctiform and therefore has no physical or economic dimensions. But this is to gainsay the existence of population agglomerations where outlet markets for goods and production factors are larger and of better quality than elsewhere. In other words, Weber's model ignores large urban agglomerations whose exist-ence is due to the advantages ('urbanization economies') that residential and productive activities obtain from habitative density. For people, these advantages are the availability of a wide range of services, from recreational amenities (cinemas, theatres) to transport facil-ities (international communication hubs, airports and stations). For firms, they are broad and diversified markets for production factors and final goods, a concentration of social fixed capital, and the efficient production of public services.

If the existence of final markets of different sizes (and densities) is hypothesized, it can easily be shown that the location choices of industries change with respect to those made both when final markets are punctiform and when their distribution is geographically uniform.

Melvin Greenhut has conducted interesting analyses of how the market's physical size determines the location of industrial firms. On the hypothesis that the distribution of demand is geographically homogeneous, Greenhut finds that firms do not always decide to locate in the region with the least distance between the final market and the raw materials market – as they would do if minimum cost were their only consideration.[17]

In proof of this statement, Greenhut assumes that:

1 there exist two areas, regions *A* and *B*, each of which has a final market and a source of raw materials;
2 region *A* has a larger final market than region *B*;

23

3   there exist punctiform raw materials markets;

4   firms can operate in one or other of the areas, but they cannot purchase raw materials in one region to sell on the other region's final market; the markets of the two regions are entirely separate;

5   the unit costs of production are the same in the two regions;

6   unit costs of transportation are constant, so that total transportation costs are proportional to distance;

7   the unit costs of transportation are the same in the two regions.

If the distance between the outlet market and the raw materials market is less in region *A* than it is in region *B*, the location choice of a firm in region *A* – which has greater density of productive and residential activity – is conditioned by two factors: (a) the lower transportation costs in region *A*; (b) the greater earnings available in that region from higher local demand for the good. Both these factors generate higher profits in region *A*.

If, conversely, the distance between the outlet market and the raw materials market is greater in region *A* than it is in region *B*, the existence of a larger market in *A* explains why firms choose to locate in that region even though the distance between the final market and the raw materials market is greater than it is in region *B*. The presence of a large market, in fact, may amply offset the higher transportation cost that the firm must pay in *A*, thus yielding profits greater than those obtainable in the alternative location.

ECONOMIES OF SCALE AND TRANSPORTATION COSTS

Market areas

The models discussed thus far account for the existence of industrial agglomerations by weighing localization or urbanization economies against transportation costs. Now we examine a second group of industrial location models which are instead intended to show that the co-existence of economies of scale (these being the first form taken by agglomeration economies and arising solely from the concentration of industry in a point of space) with transportation costs gives rise to a spatial division of the market among firms.[18] It is now necessary to abandon the hypothesis of a punctiform market structure and to assume that demand is uniformly distributed geographically.

How market areas are formed for each firm is demonstrated on the basis of the following assumptions:

■   demand is distributed uniformly along a linear market and is entirely price-inelastic;[19]

■   two firms offer the same product with identical cost functions (an assumption that, as we shall see, the model makes only initially);

■   the locations of the two firms are given;

■   the cost of transportation per unit of distance (e.g. the cost of transportation per km) is constant, so that the total cost of transportation is proportional only to the distance covered;

■   the cost of transportation is paid by the consumer.

Defining the market areas of the two firms is straightforward. Let A and B be the two firms located at two points on a linear market (for example a beach or a straight road) (Figure 1.2a). The price at which the firm sells the good on the market is the sum of the good's production price (p^*), and the cost of transportation:

$$p = p^* + \tau d \tag{1.2}$$

where τ denotes the unit cost of transportation per unit of distance, and d the distance covered by the consumer to purchase the good.

The greater the distance from the production site, the more the purchase price of the product increases because of the transportation cost incurred by the consumer in travelling to purchase the product. The distance from the production site obliges consumers located in a to purchase the good at a higher price, equal to p_1 in Figure 1.2a. Attracted by a lower price, the consumers choose to buy the good from the firm located closer to them. In Figure 1.2a, for example, the difference in price between p_1 and p_2 induces consumers located in c to purchase the product from firm A rather than from firm B. It is obvious that this condition applies to all consumers located between points a and b: throughout this area, firm A offers the good at a cheaper price than does firm B. The same reasoning holds for consumers located from b onwards: they find it more economical to patronize firm B, which offers the same good as A at a lower price. Point b represents the threshold between the two market areas: the point, that is, where the consumer is indifferent between purchasing from firm A or firm B because both charge the same price for the good.

The model just described rests on the hypothesis that the cost functions of the two firms are the same, and that transportation costs are paid by the consumers. But what happens if we assume that the firms benefit from economies of scale and that they pay the transportation costs?

If one of the two firms (in this case firm B) enjoys economies of scale (i.e. its production cost is lower than that of firm A), the threshold separating the two firms' markets, represented by point b, shifts in position so that it marks out a larger market area for firm B (Figure 1.2b). Firm A is able to stay in the market because of the distance that separates it from B.

In Figure 1.2c, firm B enjoys both economies of scale ($p_B^* < p_A^*$) and lower transportation costs ($\tau_B < \tau_A$) (more efficient transport and packaging technologies), and it takes over a large part of A's market. A's control is further reduced and now covers a small area ($a - b$) adjoining its production site. Interestingly, owing to reduced spatial friction (expressed by low transportation costs), B even deprives A of market areas which were previously its undisputed monopoly. The extreme case is that in which B's advantage in terms of economies of scale is so overwhelming that firm A is forced out of the market (Figure 1.2d).

Although simple, this model yields results of considerable interest:

1   Consumers located closer to the production site obtain an economic advantage in terms of lower transportation costs (when these are assumed to be borne by consumers) and therefore pay a lower overall price for the good, provided the firm does not engage in price discrimination.

25

(a) Supply and transportation costs equal for the two producers

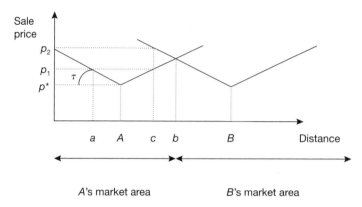

A's market area   B's market area

(b) Transportation costs equal for the two producers and economies of scale for producer B

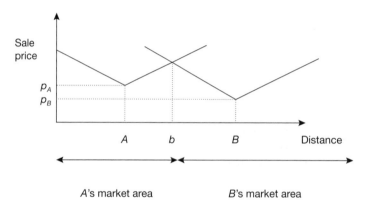

A's market area   B's market area

Figure 1.2 The division of the market between producers

2   The firm may discriminate on price within its market area, where it operates a monopoly, without losing market shares. Numerous methods of price discrimination can be used if the cost of transportation is paid by the firm and not directly by the consumer. The firm may impose the same sale price – equal to the price at which the good is sold to the remotest consumer in its area – on all consumers, and thus appropriate all the surplus earned from those located closest to it; or it may discriminate among groups of consumers by charging higher prices to consumers located in one area ($a - A$ in Figure 1.3) than to those in another area ($A - b$), thus extending its market area from b to b'.[20]

3   It follows from points (1) and (2) that physical distance is a barrier to entry into local markets: a firm does not compete with all the others, but with those located closest to it. Consequently, the model of competition among firms in a spatial market is the model of monopolistic competition à la Chamberlin and Lancaster[21] where price discrimination is based, not on product differentiation as in traditional microeconomic models, but on the distance that separates purchaser from producer.

(c) Reduced transport costs and economies of scale for producer B

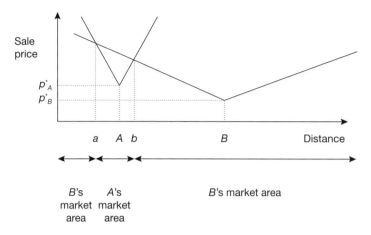

(d) Economies of scale for producer B such to force producer A out of the market

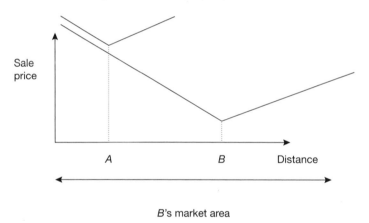

Figure 1.2 The division of the market between producers (continued)

A subsequent refinement: Hoover's theory

The model just described was subsequently refined by Edgar Hoover, who found a simple way to endogenize economies of scale in the model and have them depend indirectly on distance. He did so as follows.

Hoover's assumptions are similar to those of the previous model. Demand for a good is uniformly distributed along a linear market. Two firms, *A* and *B*, are located at two extremes of the market and they produce a homogeneous good. Unlike in the previous model, however, transportation costs are paid by the firm, and production by both firms is characterized by economies of scale until a certain level of output has been reached. Beyond this level, the economies of scale turn into diseconomies which – as is usual in neoclassical microeconomic models[22] – push up average production costs if the quantity of output increases.

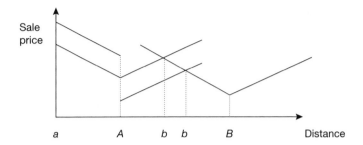

Figure 1.3 *Effects of price discrimination on the market areas*

In order to sell their goods at a distance from the production site, firms must pay a transportation cost proportional to the distance over which the goods must be shipped. A decision by firm *A* to increase its market changes its production costs with respect to the initial level *a*: on the one hand, in fact, by extending its market, the firm obtains economies of scale and produces at a lower cost per unit of output, equal to *b*; on the other, the distance between the new market areas and the production site requires the firm to pay the transportation costs represented by the line *bb'* (Figure 1.4a). At distance *D*, the cost of distribution (or sale price) – which comprises both the new production cost and the transportation cost – is equal to *E*.

If this reasoning is applied to a variety of distances from the production site, lower levels of production cost are obtained as combinations of the different sizes of the markets being served at different distances. The distance/cost relation is negative as long as economies of scale operate; but once the point of most efficient production (the lowest least average cost point) has been reached, the economies of scale change – according to the model's hypothesis – into diseconomies, and the distance/cost relation becomes positive. In fact, an increase in production comes about at production costs higher than previously because of diseconomies of scale and transportation costs. For distance *F* in Figure 1.4a, the sale price is now *E"*. By combining the various distribution costs thus obtained, a curve, U-shaped with respect to distance, can be constructed. This curve Hoover calls the 'margin line', and it represents an average production cost given by the sum of production and transportation costs.

The same procedure can be used to construct a 'margin line' for firm *B*. The intersection between the two 'margin lines' obviously represents the demarcation line between the two firms' markets: *A* serves the market extending from its production site to *L*; *B* controls the market extending from *L* to its production site.

It is possible to determine in the case of Hoover's model, too, what happens to the division of the market between the two firms if one of them (firm *A*) manages to achieve economies of scale – for instance by introducing a technological innovation: distance remaining equal, *A*'s production costs will be lower, and the entire margin line will shift downwards. The final outcome will be that the boundary between the two firms' market areas moves to *L'*, and therefore in favour of firm *A* (Figure 1.4b).[23]

28

(a) Construction of the 'margin line'

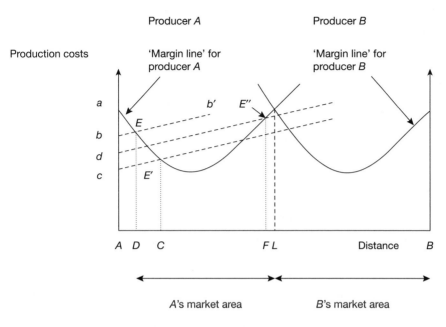

(b) Increase in economies of scale for producer A: effect on the division of the market

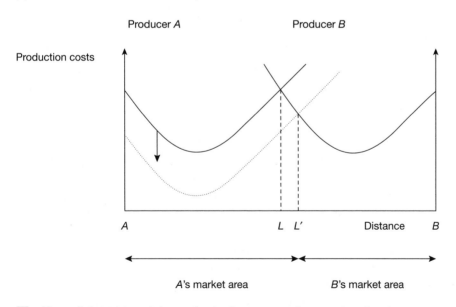

Figure 1.4 Division of the market in the presence of economies of scale

SPATIAL DEMAND, MARKET EQUILIBRIUM AND FIRM LOCATION

The next step is to define the quantities of the good offered by the firm that consumers are willing to purchase when they have to cover different distances to do so – given a certain cost of producing the good and a certain transportation cost (again assumed proportional to the distance). Necessary for this purpose is construction of an *individual spatial demand curve* which shows the different quantities of the good x that individuals are willing to purchase from firm i according to their distance from the firm and according to the production price (or factory price) set by the firm on the basis of production conditions (costs profile, economies of scale). Once the individual spatial demand curve has been plotted, the market's spatial demand curve can be calculated as the simple sum of the individual quantities demanded at the various distances from the firm by the n consumers existing in the market. When analysed together with the usual firm's supply curve of microeconomic theory, the market's spatial demand curve defines the market equilibrium.[24]

The spatial demand curve constructed by August Lösch is shown in Figure 1.5, which consists of four graphs. Graph (a) represents the price/distance relation; a straight line, the slope of which depends on the value of the unit cost of transportation (τ), as in Figure 1.2. Graph (b) shows the individual demand curve of traditional microeconomics, which evinces a negative relation between price and quantity: as the price of the good increases, the quantity that the consumer is willing to buy diminishes. Graph (c) has the simple function of mapping the variable on the axes. Finally, graph (d) plots the individual spatial demand curve.

At a distance of d_1, the firm offers good x to the consumer at price p_1. At this price, the consumer is interested in purchasing quantity x_1 of the good, as shown by the individual demand curve. Thanks to the transposition of the axes in the third graph, the quantity can be easily transferred to the fourth one. The same reasoning applies to other distances: moving clockwise, identified at d_2 is the quantity x_2 demanded by the consumer. Uniting the various quantity/distance combinations in the fourth graph produces the individual spatial demand curve.[25]

On the assumption that all consumers have identical individual spatial demand curves, total demand for the firm's good at every distance will be the sum of the individual quantities demanded at the various distances by the n consumers existing in the market. Assuming a uniform density of consumers for each unit of distance, q, the total demanded quantity of the good will be equal to the area below the individual demand curve multiplied by the density q (area ODX in Figure 1.6a).

Assuming a homogeneous plane, and no longer a simple linear market, Lösch uses the same procedure to identify the firm's market areas. Rotating the triangle formed by the individual demand curve 360 degrees around the vertical axis plots a circular market. Multiplying the volume of the cone thus obtained by the density q yields the total quantity of the good demanded in a circular market (Figure 1.6b).[26]

Interestingly, the size of the market area delineated by Lösch's 'demand cone' depends – given a certain structure of demand – on transportation costs and on the conditions under which the good is offered. An increase in the transportation costs inclines the individual spatial demand curve and restricts the firm's market area (Figure 1.7a). A higher sale price

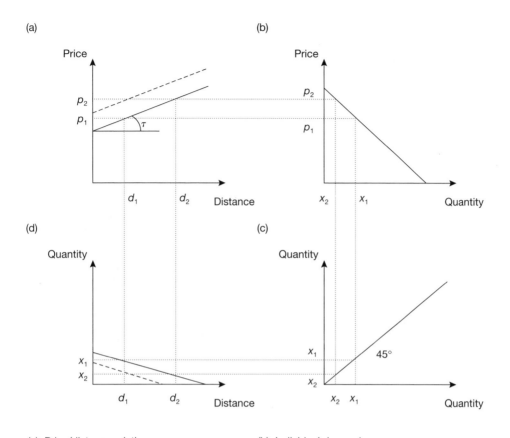

(a) Price/distance relation
(b) Individual demand curve
(d) Individual spatial demand curve
(c) Transposition

Figure 1.5 *Construction of the individual spatial demand curve*

(a) In the case of the linear market, spatial market demand is represented by the area below the individual demand curve multiplied by population density q.

(b) In the case of the circular market, spatial market demand is represented by the volume of the Lösch demand cone multiplied by population density q.

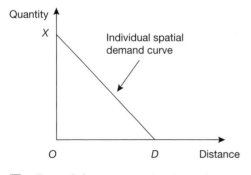

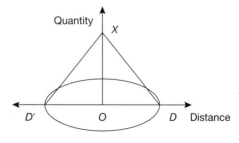

Figure 1.6 *Spatial market demand*

reduces the quantity of the good demanded by the consumer, distance remaining equal, and the individual spatial curve consequently undergoes a parallel shift downwards which reduces the firm's market area (Figure 1.7b).[27]

Having defined the demand curve, Lösch now describes the firm's economic-spatial equilibrium[28] and the firm's location. The firm acts as a monopolist in its market area, which is protected by distance (externally to it demand for the good falls to zero owing to the excessive transportation cost) and produces in conditions of profit maximization and surplus profits.[29] The market, at the spatial level, is made up of numerous non-overlapping market areas with broad spaces in which there is unsatisfied demand (Figure 1.8a).

However, this is a short-term equilibrium. The existence of surplus profits from production of the good and of still unexploited market areas induces new firms to enter the market and to locate in the areas not yet covered by supply. The market entry by new firms has two joint effects: (a) the spatial market is occupied until areas come to overlap; (b) the profit margins of individual firms are eroded by a decrease in demand, which is now divided among several firms, and by an increase in costs due to greater demand for production

(a) Increase in transportation costs

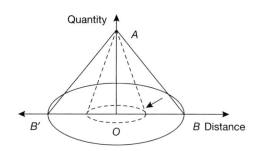

(b) Increase in the price of the good

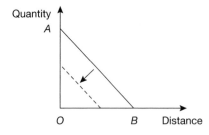
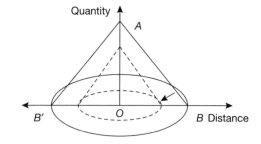

Figure 1.7 Variations in market areas

(a) Conditions of maximum profit:
short-term equilibrium

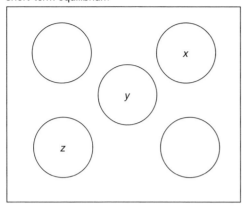

(b) Entry of new firms in the market

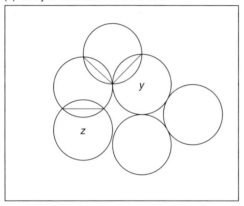

(c) Long-term equilibrium

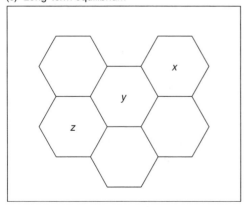

Figure 1.8 Evolution towards a long-term spatial market equilibrium

factors and intermediate goods with which to produce additional quantities of the good. The situation soon arises in which firms are no longer interested in entering the market because the surplus profits have been absorbed by the increasing production costs. The long-term equilibrium of the market has thus been reached.

Faced with overlapping market areas, and if the good is homogeneous, consumers choose to purchase the good offered at the lower price, which is the price determined by the shortest distance between buyer and producer (Figure 1.8b). The result of the process is a long-term market equilibrium in which a spatial market assumes a pattern of regular hexagons with no overlapping areas (Figure 1.8c).

INTERDEPENDENCY IN LOCATION CHOICES: THE HOTELLING MODEL

The models described thus far assume that – given the locations of producers, and given demand uniformly distributed geographically (in linear or circular form) – the market is divided into areas within each of which there operates a single firm. None of these models hypothesizes that, once the market has been divided up, the firms will consider the possibility of relocating. Nor do they consider the existence of interdependency mechanisms operating in the location choices of firms, and which, as we shall see, give greater density to the spatial distribution of activities.

The earliest theory of interdependence among location choices was set out in the well-known duopoly model developed by Harold Hotelling – although various other authors have contributed to the theory.[30]

The model's assumptions are very similar to those of the market areas model:

- the existence of only two firms (duopoly);
- a linear market (a beach, for example) homogeneously distributed along which is demand for the good produced, which is also homogeneous (the same brand of ice cream, for example);
- nil costs of relocation;
- demand entirely inelastic to price: that is, a quantity of the good demanded by the consumer which does not change with variations in price (tourists on the beach purchase the same quantity of ice cream regardless of the price at which it is sold).[31]

Assuming that the firms are initially located at A and B (Figure 1.9a), if one of them – for example A – relocates to A', the division of the market will obviously change in favour of A, which acquires a new market share by appropriating it from firm B. It is likewise in the interest of firm B to relocate, for example to B', because by so doing it can take over a portion of A's market. The process continues until the firms are located at the centre of the spatial market, each sharing one half of it (Figure 1.9b). Only this arrangement gives stability to a situation which otherwise, according to Hotelling, would be indeterminate under these hypotheses.[32]

(a) The mechanism towards equilibrium

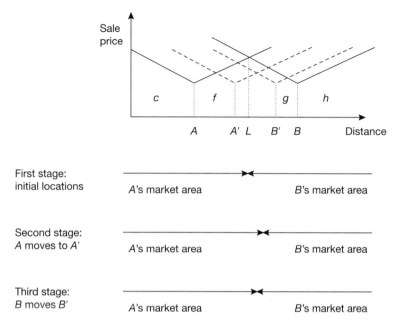

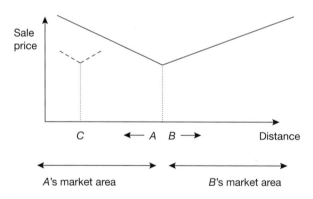

Figure 1.9 *The Hotelling duopoly*

Hotelling's model highlights the following two important considerations:

1 Even in the presence of transportation costs, there is a natural tendency for firms to cluster in space; a tendency which may help explain the existence of large agglomerations, most notably cities.

2 The competitive solution obtained by market forces does not coincide with the public interest: the average distance that consumers must cover to purchase the good once

the firms have achieved location equilibrium (Figure 1.9b) is – assuming an initial location pattern like that in Figure 1.9a – greater than the distance that they previously had to travel. This has long provided theoretical justification for planning actions intended to influence location choices. However, this is not to imply that private initiatives never coincide with the public interest; rather that the coincidence between private and public interest should be proved and not taken for granted.

Criticisms of the Hotelling model have centred on the close dependence of its results on its initial hypotheses.[33] First, if a cooperative solution is admitted, the two firms may agree not to change their initial locations (which generate market shares exactly equal to the final ones) and thus avoid the costs of relocating. Second, if the possibility of new market entrants is admitted, the spatial concentration disappears; for it is in the new firms' interest to avoid a central location and instead exploit more peripheral ones (for example at C in Figure 1.9b). From these locations they are able to take over portions of A's market, upsetting the location equilibrium as a consequence. Third, if the hypothesis of demand curve rigidity is discarded, the result of a central location is once again doubtful. In fact, if the price influenced sales (i.e. on the assumption that demand is elastic to price), the firms would select locations closer to the final consumer in order to minimize the transportation cost borne by the latter (which is reflected in the good's final price) and thus maximize their revenues. A shift by both firms from a central location to a more peripheral one would yield greater revenues. In fact, at the new locations A' and B' in Figure 1.10, consumers would obtain a greater saving in terms of transportation costs (depicted by the area cross-hatched with vertical lines in Figure 1.10) than they would obtain from a central location (depicted by the area cross-hatched with horizontal lines). Their demand for the good would consequently increase.

CRITICAL REMARKS

As is frequently the case, models developed to define the market areas are characterized both by substantial interpretative capacity and by weaknesses due to abstraction and to the hypotheses necessary to reduce the complexity of the real world.

The great merit of these models is that they interpret the location choices of firms solely in the light of the large-scale forces that drive location processes: transportation costs on the one hand, agglomeration economies on the other. By balancing these two opposing forces, these models are able to explain the existence of agglomerations of firms on the hypothesis of a perfectly homogeneous space. In other words, they do not resort to geographic factors, which furnish an excessively banal explanation of the concentration of economic activities in space.

A second salient feature of these models is their ability to incorporate spatially-extended demand into the location choices of firms. The existence of this spatial market obliges firms to take location choices which extend well beyond the logic of minimizing transportation costs between production sites and distant points of sale, and which as a consequence are more realistically oriented to controlling the market.

These models have the further merit of conceiving – within a framework of location choices – interdependency among the behaviours of different firms. A location choice does

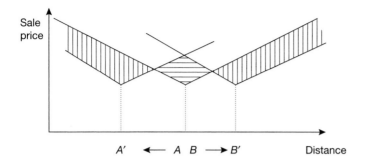

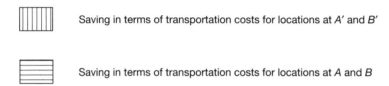

Figure 1.10 Advantages in terms of transportation costs for alternative locations

indeed depend on the size of the market to which it gives access; but it is not taken regardless of the choices of other firms. This feature turns analysis of location equilibrium into an iterative game whose solution depends on the game's hypotheses themselves.[34]

Another strength of these models is their demonstration of the real role of distance in economic analysis: distance is a barrier to market entry which enables each individual firm to exercise a monopoly within its market area.

However, although these positive features give significant interest to these models, a number of weaknesses intrinsic to them should not be overlooked. Mention has already been made, in regard to Hotelling's duopoly, of the strong influence exerted by the initial hypotheses on the final result. The most influential of these hypotheses is the price-rigidity of demand. Once it has been discarded, a series of alternative location equilibria arise. More peripheral with respect to the centre of the market, from the point of view of sales maximization these equilibria yield competitiveness gains in market areas more distant from the centre and where prices are higher.

To repeat a point made earlier, if the hypothesis of a homogeneous spatial market is discarded, it may be possible to explain location choices which are counter-intuitive if viewed solely in terms of transportation costs. Because of these weaknesses, it has been pointed out that although these models assume the existence of demand distributed in space – and although they thus have sales depend on transportation costs – they still inadequately account for the effects of demand on the final equilibrium.[35]

A final consideration concerns the low incidence of transportation costs in the final value of the goods typically produced by present-day industry. This incidence has been estimated at only 3–8 per cent, which suggests that these models have a rather limited capacity to interpret reality: it is difficult to argue, in fact, that geographical agglomerations exist owing to the centre of gravity of certain industries. These models seem more realistically applicable to tertiary activities. Because of the low unit value of many services, for example commercial ones – which increases the incidence of transportation costs (we always choose the nearest baker's shop to buy our bread) – and the importance of face-to-face relations in many advanced services (law, accountancy, health care), in the case of services the costs of transportation and closeness to the firm of the service significantly influence consumer choices.[36]

CONCLUSIONS

This chapter has surveyed the earliest theories of location developed to explain the determinants of location choices by industrial firms. The oldest of the models discussed – Weber's model – assumes demand and supply structures which are punctiform in space. On this hypothesis, the model elegantly and convincingly explains the existence of territorial agglomerations on the basis of two great economic forces which induce either the concentration or the dispersion of activities in space: agglomeration economies on the one hand, transportation costs on the other. Still today, these forces are components of more modern, and in certain respects more complex, models which seek to conjugate location choices with local growth dynamics (see Chapter 9), and it is on the balancing of them that the geographical organization itself of activities depends.

The chapter has also described models which envisage a punctiform source of demand and a supply uniformly distributed in space. Starting from these assumptions on the spatial structure of demand and supply, these models simply but convincingly demonstrate the importance of distance in determining the behaviour of consumers and firms in the market. Distance is a spatial friction – a cost associated with movement in space – which in economic terms raises a barrier to entry in the local market, for it protects the firm against competition and permits monopolistic behaviour, such as price discrimination, within the local area.

Still to be examined are location models based on the hypothesis of a punctiform source of demand and a supply distributed in space. This is the topic of the next chapter.

REVIEW QUESTIONS

1 What are the economic forces explaining the location of activities in space?

2 What are the different categories of agglomeration economies?

3 What is the definition of transportation costs in regional economics?

4 Why do transportation costs play an important role in location theory?

5 In Weber's model, what are the elements on which location choice is based? How is the location point achieved by the firm in Weber's model?

6 If final markets of different size are conceived, how and why does the location choice of a firm change?

7 How are the market areas of different producers identified? What is the role played by distance in the identification of the market areas?

8   What is the definition of a spatial demand curve? How is it obtained?

9   How does the location choice of firms change when interdependence in location choices is assumed?

10   Which spatial structure of demand and supply is behind the 'market areas' theory? Is it the same structure as in Weber's model?

SELECTED READING ON EMPIRICAL FINDINGS

About industrial location choices

Li, S. and Ho Park, S. (2006) 'Determinants of locations of foreign direct investment in China', *Management and Organization Review*, vol. 2, no. 1, pp. 95–119.

Urata, S. and Kawai, H. (2000) 'The determinants of the location of foreign direct investment by Japanese small and medium-sized enterprises', *Small Business Economics*, vol. 15, no. 2, pp. 79–103.

Woodward, D. P. (1992) 'Locational determinants of Japanese manufacturing start-ups in the United States', *Southern Economic Journal*, vol. 58, no. 3, pp. 690–708.

FURTHER READING

Beckmann, M. J. (1968) *Location theory*, New York: Random House.

Chamberlin, E. H. (1936) *The theory of monopolistic competition*, Cambridge, Mass.: Harvard University Press.

Greenhut, M. (1959) 'Size of markets versus transport costs in industrial location surveys and theory', *Journal of Industrial Economics*, vol. 8, pp. 172–84.

Hoover, E. M. (1948) *The location of economic activity*, New York: McGraw-Hill.

Hotelling, H. (1929) 'Stability in competition', *The Economic Journal*, vol. 39, no. 153, pp. 41–57.

Isard, W. (1956) *Location and space-economy*, Cambridge, Mass.: MIT Press.

Smith, D. M. (1971) *Industrial location: an economic geographical analysis*, London: Wiley & Sons.

Weber, A. (1929) *Alfred Weber's theory of the location of industries*, Chicago: University of Chicago Press.

Chapter 2

Accessibility and location

SUMMARY

1   Accessibility and transportation costs: land value and use
2   The location of agricultural activities: the Von Thünen model
3   The urban location of firms: the Alonso model
4   The urban location of households
5   Recent developments: general equilibrium models
6   Generalized accessibility and the gravity model

ACCESSIBILITY AND TRANSPORTATION COSTS: LAND VALUE AND USE

The previous chapter showed how some location models interpret the location choices of firms solely in terms of the two strategic economic forces that characterize location processes: transportation costs, which induce the dispersion of activities, and agglomeration economies, which instead give rise to concentration. By balancing these opposing forces, the models examined were able to account for the existence of agglomerations of economic activities. They did so, moreover, by hypothesizing a perfectly uniform space without the geographic features that can straightforwardly explain the spatial concentration of economic activities.

The previous chapter also showed that the underlying logic of models which define market areas entails specific assumptions concerning the spatial structure of supply and demand: production develops at specific points in space, and it supplies geographically dispersed markets.

The theories examined in this chapter reverse these hypotheses on the spatial structure of demand and supply. For the models now discussed, in fact, the production site assumes a spatial dimension and extends across a territory, while the consumption site (the market) is punctiform. This reversal of assumptions about the territorial structure of production and the market is not a purely academic exercise. Rather, it is entailed by the problem that these models set out to solve, for they abandon the endeavour to identify the market areas of each producer and address an issue which has not yet been mentioned: how to define a 'production area', meaning by this the physical space (the land) occupied by an individual economic activity.

In these theories, location choices are dictated by a specific principle of spatial organization of activity: namely 'accessibility', and in particular accessibility to a market or a 'centre'. For firms, high accessibility means that they have easy access to broad and diversified markets for final goods and production factors, to information, and to the hubs of international infrastructures. For people, accessibility to a 'central business district', and therefore to jobs, means that their commuting costs are minimal, while at the same time they enjoy easy access to a wide range of recreational services restricted to specific locations (e.g. theatres, museums, libraries) and proximity to specific services (e.g. universities), without having to pay the cost of long-distance travel.

High demand for accessibility to central areas triggers competition between industrial and residential activities for locations closer to the market, or, more generally, closer to the hypothetical central business district (the city centre).

All the location choice models described in this chapter have an important feature in common: the cost of land, or land rent. Assuming the existence of a single central business district, owing to high demand for central locations with their minimum transportation costs, land closer to the centre costs more; a condition accentuated by the total rigidity, at least in the short-to-medium period, of the urban land supply. The models described in this chapter resolve the competition among activities on the basis of a strict economic principle: firms able to locate in more central areas are those able to pay higher rents for those areas.

Unlike the industry location theories (in particular Weber's model) which identify a different location equilibrium according to the spatial principle that patterns activities in space (agglomeration economies rather than minimum transport costs), these models envisage just one factor organizing activity in space: land rent, this being the sole principle which explains location choices by all activities, whether agricultural, productive or residential.

The strength of these models is the elegant and irrefutable logic with which they account for the distribution of productive, agricultural and residential activities in a geographic space from which they eliminate every differentiating effect except for physical distance from the centre. Given their assumptions on the structure of demand and supply in space, these models are particularly well suited to analysis of the location of industrial and residential activities in urban space. In an urban environment, in fact, it is easy to hypothesize the existence of a single business district (a city centre) which, for firms, performs the function of collecting, distributing and exporting the city's products, and for households is the place where jobs are available. These models are able to establish where an individual firm or household will locate.

The first model analysing the spatial distribution of alternative production activities was developed in the early nineteenth century by Johann von Thünen. Only in the 1960s did pioneering studies by Walter Isard, Martin Beckmann and Lowdon Wingo prepare the ground for Alonso's formulation of Von Thünen's historical model applied to an urban context.[1] The model of the monocentric city soon became a free-standing school of thought within location theory, where it was labelled 'new urban economics'. This corpus of theories endeavoured to develop general equilibrium location models in which the main interest is no longer decisions by individual firms or households. Instead, the main areas of inquiry become definition of the size and density of cities, and identification of the particular pattern of land costs at differing distances from the city that guarantees achievement of a location equilibrium for all individuals and firms in the city.[2]

As we shall see, these theories are set forth as elegant models demonstrating the economic nature of spatial phenomena and showing that they can be analysed with the conventional tools of economic theory. They are in fact an application of microeconomic theory to the study of the intra-urban structure.

The chapter first describes Von Thünen's basic model, which, in simple terms and with strict economic logic, explains the spatial distribution of agricultural production around a medieval town. It then presents the models subsequently developed on the same theoretical bases to examine the location of firms and households in urban areas.[3] Moreover, brief discussion will be made of the general equilibrium models developed in this regard, since they have constituted one of the most important fields of urban economics since the 1980s. The chapter concludes by outlining a method which can be used to measure the attractiveness of an urban centre for firms and households located in its surroundings.

THE LOCATION OF AGRICULTURAL ACTIVITIES: THE VON THÜNEN MODEL

Johann Heinrich von Thünen developed the first location model based on the hypothesis of a continuous production space and a single punctiform final market.[4] His model has generated the entire corpus of theories on the urban location of economic activities.

Von Thünen's model is based on a set of assumptions which all subsequent theories would adopt:

1   there exists a uniform space where all land is equally fertile and transport infrastructures are identical in all directions (isotropic space);
2   there is a single centre, the medieval town, where all goods are traded (i.e. there is a specific market place);
3   demand is unlimited, an assumption which reflects the supply-oriented nature of the model: the location equilibrium depends solely on the conditions of supply;
4   the production factors are perfectly distributed in space: the allocation of land among alternative production activities does not derive from an uneven spatial distribution of the production factors;
5   there is a specific production function, with fixed coefficients and constant returns to scale, for each agricultural good; this assumption entails that the quantity of output obtainable from each unit of land and the unit cost of production are fixed in space;
6   perfect competition exists in the agricultural goods market: farmers therefore take the prices of the goods they produce to be given;
7   unit transport costs are constant in space: the total cost of transportation depends on the distance between the production site and the town, and on the volume of production. Transportation costs may vary according to the crop.

Assuming the existence of a certain number of farmers, Von Thünen addresses the problem of how to determine the allocation of land among farmers working in the area surrounding the market place.[5]

He bases his model on a concept of rent as a residual which would also characterize subsequent models: the price that farmers are willing to pay for land is the remainder left when transportation and production costs, including a certain remuneration (profit) for the farmer, have been subtracted from revenues.

In formal terms, if x is the quantity of a good produced by a farmer, c the unit cost of production, p the price of the agricultural good, τ the unit cost of transportation, and d the distance to the market, rent r is defined as:

$$r(d) = (p - c - \tau d)x \qquad (2.1)$$

This equation states the levels of rent that farmers are willing to pay for land at different distances from the market place where goods are traded. It is represented graphically by a straight line, with slope $-\tau d$ and intercepts equal to $(p - c)x$ and $(p - c)/\tau$, respectively denoting the maximum value of rent in the town and the maximum distance from the town, where land value is nil.

From equation (2.1) one can straightforwardly obtain the impact on rent due to a shift in space (e.g. of one kilometre) by calculating the first derivative of rent with respect to distance:

$$\frac{dr(d)}{dd} = -\tau x \qquad (2.2)$$

As (2.2) shows, the variation in rent is exactly equal to $-\tau x$: a shorter distance from the centre generates a saving in total transport costs equal to the increase in the rent required to occupy more central locations.[6]

On the assumption that there are three farmers (A, B and C), each of them producing a specific agricultural product with a differing degree of perishability, a rent supply curve can be constructed for each farmer. Because goods are perishable to differing extents, the rent supply curves assume different positions and slopes (Figure 2.1). The farmer who produces the most perishable good will have a productive process that uses the land in the most intensive and economically efficient way (geometrically, the highest intercept on the Y-axis, equal to $(p - c)x$), and he will be more willing to pay the rent charged for land one kilometre closer to the town (geometrically, the steeper slope of the straight line, equal to $-\tau x$). As the farmers compete for the more accessible land, each unit of surface area will be allocated to the farmer willing to pay the highest rent for that land. As far as a', the land will be allocated to farmer A, who offers the highest rent for the most central locations, from a' to b' to farmer B, and from b' to c' to farmer C: the actual rent realized by the landowner from cultivation of his land is the envelope of the three rent supply curves.

One of the main strengths of this model is its ability to demonstrate that it is simple distance from, or accessibility to, the town (expressed by transportation costs) which accounts for differences in land rent. It thus departs from the classical Ricardian view that

43

differences in land profitability are due to different degrees of fertility.[7] By so doing, it is able indirectly to explain the location of economic activities in space – a result which is a significant achievement.[8]

THE URBAN LOCATION OF FIRMS: THE ALONSO MODEL

In the early 1960s, first William Alonso and then Richard Muth reconsidered Von Thünen's model and adapted it to an urban context,[9] thus paving the way for numerous subsequent studies. Alonso and Muth extended the bases of Von Thünen's pioneering model, making it more specific to the urban case; but they also made it more general by abandoning the hypothesis that only transportation costs express spatial friction and the preference for more central locations.

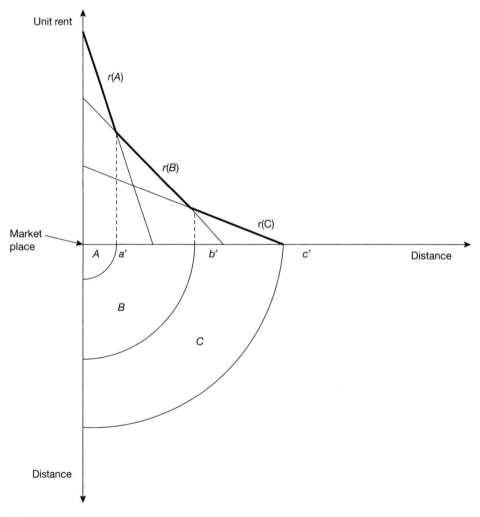

Figure 2.1 Land allocation among three farmers: the Von Thünen model

The assumptions of Alonso's model are the same as those of Von Thünen's model of agricultural activity described above. It envisages a city (no longer a plain) characterized by uniform space (homogeneous spatial distribution of the production factors) and endowed with infrastructures which cover the entire city in all directions (isotropic space). The city has a single centre – the city centre or business district – which is generically defined as the most attractive location for all firms and households. Given these assumptions, the city is analysed along only one dimension: a radius comprising different distances from the city centre to the periphery.

The base model addresses a problem similar to the one which preoccupied Von Thünen. As firms compete for central locations, the model shows how the urban space is allocated among alternative types of production once the market cost of land at different distances from the centre is known.

Also Alonso's model defines rent as the remainder left when the entrepreneur has subtracted production costs (including transportation costs) and a desired level of profit from the revenue obtained by selling the good. Formally, rent is expressed as:

$$r(d) = (p_x - \pi - c_x(d))x(d) \tag{2.3}$$

where r denotes the unit rent, p_x the unit price of the good produced by the entrepreneur, c_x unit production costs (including transportation costs), π the profit, d the distance from the centre, and x the quantity of the good produced.

Because production costs include transport costs, in the Alonso model they depend on distance, as they do in the Von Thünen model. However, unlike in the latter, revenues too depend on distance: a less suburban location gives greater proximity to broader markets, and consequently access to higher earnings (consider the sales of a shop located in the city centre compared to one in the periphery, especially if they sell luxury items).

Equation (2.3) expresses the 'bid rent', or the rent (by square metre) that the entrepreneur is willing to pay at differing distances from the centre, once costs and the entrepreneur's intended profit have been subtracted from revenues. Profits remaining equal, a more central location implies a willingness to pay higher rent because the entrepreneur incurs lower transport costs and obtains higher revenues. Likewise, a suburban location can yield the same profit if and only if less rent is paid for the land: the saving on land cost must offset the higher transport costs and the lower revenues that less central locations entail (Figure 2.2a).

The slope of the bid-rent curve, which expresses the variation in the cost of land due to a one unit of variation in the distance from the centre, is given by:

$$\frac{\partial r(d)}{\partial d} = (p_x - \pi - c_x(d)) \quad \frac{\partial x(d)}{\partial d} - \frac{\partial c_x(d)}{\partial d} x(d) \tag{2.4}$$

This shows that, at one unit of distance further away from the centre, the unit rent offered to maintain the same profit level π diminishes because of increased transport costs and decreased revenues.

45

(a) Bid-rent curve

(b) Location equilibrium for the firm

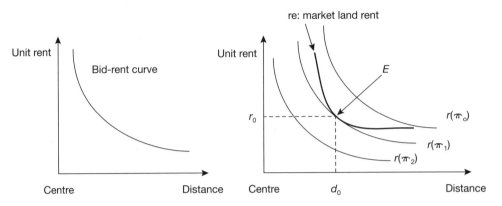

(c) Location equilibrium for firms with different propensities for central locations

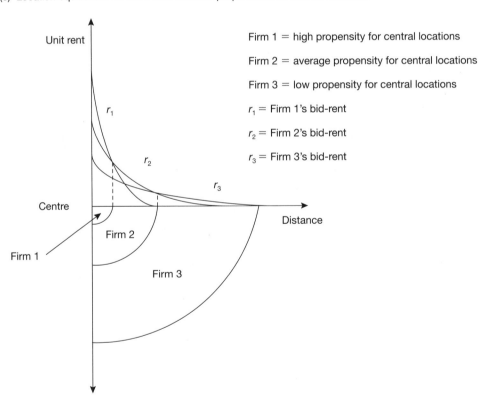

Figure 2.2 *The bid-rent curve and the location equilibrium for firms*

At every distance from the centre (for example d_0 in Figure 2.2b), if the firm wants to increase its profits, it must offer a lower rent. Conversely, at the same distance, it can offer a higher rent if it is willing to accept lower profits. It is therefore possible to plot different bid-rent curves for an individual firm, all of them with the same slope, and each of them defined on the basis of a different profit level which increases towards the origin (Figure 2.2b).

In a partial equilibrium framework, which assumes as known the 'market land rent curve' (i.e. the real market cost of land: curve *re* in Figure 2.2b), it is possible to define the optimal location for the firm. Along the market land rent curve (*re*), the firm will choose the location yielding the highest profit, which is expressed by the tangency of the market rent curve with the lowest bid-rent curve. In Figure 2.2b the location equilibrium is reached at point *E*, and thus at a distance d_0 from the centre and with a rent equal to r_0.

Finally, on the hypothesis of three firms operating in sectors for which central locations are of differing importance (for instance, a fashion boutique, a computer retailer, and a baker's shop), it is possible to identify for each of them a bid-rent curve whose position and slope differ because the firm's sales have greater or lesser sensitivity to a central location. Following a pattern exactly like that described by Von Thünen, the three firms arrange themselves on the urban land according to their willingness to pay: at each distance from the centre, the firm willing to pay the highest rent will be accorded use of the land (Figure 2.2c).

A final aspect is of interest. The differing 'fertility' of various types of land has traditionally been viewed as determining differences among agricultural rents.[10] In this model it can be interpreted in the modern sense as the differing 'productivity' of more central urban land due to its greater accessibility to information. If revenues and costs vary with distance, rent is the value that reduces all net revenues to those obtained from marginal lands.[11]

THE URBAN LOCATION OF HOUSEHOLDS

The model for households, this too formulated by William Alonso, is entirely similar in its theoretical basis and analytical structure to the model just discussed for firms. In this model, location choices are no longer made by firms, but by households. The main difference from Alonso's model for firms is the influence exerted on location choices by a new variable: the size of the house. A household may in fact decide to forfeit housing space in order to move closer to the city centre. The saving obtained by purchasing a smaller house, and from the lower transportation costs associated with more central locations, enables the household to pay the higher unit cost of land typical of less peripheral urban areas.

The households model therefore comprises three variables: the cost of land (or of the house), the size of the house, and transport costs.

Assume the following utility function[12] for the household:

$$u = u(d, z, q) \tag{2.5}$$

where d is the distance from the centre, q is the size of the house, and z is the set of all the other goods that the household needs.

Given a certain distance from the centre and any combination of house size q and other goods z, a reduction (even slight) in the size of the house causes a loss of satisfaction for the household which must be offset – in order to maintain its utility constant – by an increase in the quantity of other goods in the household's possession. This condition is depicted by Figure 2.3a, which shows the so-called indifference curves for the various 'house size/quantity of other goods' combinations that leave the household's utility unchanged.[13]

Each indifference curve represents a certain level of utility, which rises as the distance from the origin increases (Figure 2.3a).[14] The household will seek to position itself on the highest indifference curve, subject to its budget constraint: that is, provided its income equals the expenditure that it must undertake. The budget constraint is written as:

$$y = p_z z + r(d_0)q + \tau d_0 \qquad (2.6)$$

where y is the household's income, $r(d_0)q$ and τd_0 are respectively expenditure on the house and transportation costs at distance d_0, and $p_z z$ represents the cost of purchasing other goods. On solving (2.6) for z, we obtain:

$$z = \frac{y - r(d_0)q - \tau d_0}{p_z} \qquad (2.7)$$

Graphically, the budget constraint is represented by a straight line with intercept $(y - \tau d_0)/r(d_0)$ if the household decides to spend all its income on the house, not on purchasing units of other goods, and $(y - \tau d_0)/p_z$ when, conversely, the household decides to use its entire income to purchase other goods.

The condition which maximizes the household's utility, under the budget constraint, is represented by the point of tangency between the budget line and the indifference curve. The household cannot go beyond that level of utility because it lacks the income to do so; at the same time, it is irrational for the household to position itself below that level of utility, given the income available to it (Figure 2.3a).

In mathematical terms, the same condition holds if the slopes of the two curves are equal:[15]

$$\frac{u'_q}{u'_z} = -\frac{r(d_0)}{p_z} \qquad (2.8)$$

Assuming that good z is expressed in numeraire – i.e. its price is equal to one – the slope of the budget line is exactly equivalent to the rent $r(d_0)$. Equation (2.8) shows that, in equilibrium, the household is indifferent to substituting the other goods with size of the house when the relative utility deriving therefrom (u'_q/u'_z) is equal to the rent.[16] Each household thus expresses that maximum amount that it can pay for each distance from the centre compatibly with a certain utility level that it wishes to attain (u^* in Figure 2.3b).[17] In order for the household to express less demand for the good 'house' (i.e. it settles for a smaller house) and spend income on other goods, maintaining utility constant, the price of the house must increase. The other goods thus become relatively less costly and therefore relatively more attractive to the consumer. In Figure 2.3b, this means that for the household to remain on the same indifference curve, the budget constraint must slope like line *bb*.

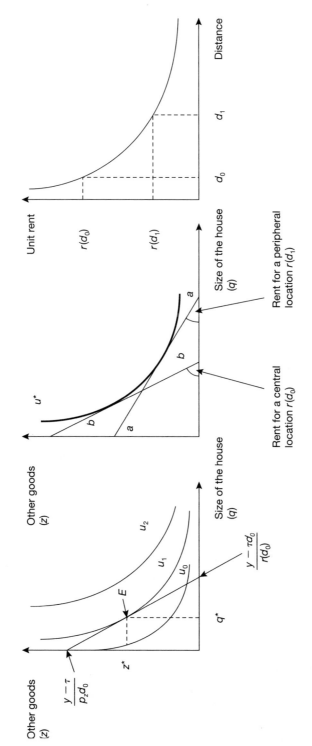

Figure 2.3 *The household's optimal choice and the bid-rent curve*

We now move an important step forward. We are able to obtain the bid rent: given a certain level of utility, this is expressed by the different slopes of the budget line for different distances from the centre. As the distance from the centre decreases, the budget line grows more rigid, owing to an increase in the maximum rent offered for a location at that distance, as shown by Figure 2.3c.

The analysis thus far yields the following important result: bid-rent curves are nothing but a transformation that maps indifference curves in consumption space (the trade-off between goods z and house size q in Figure 2.3b) into corresponding indifference curves in urban space (the trade-off between rent and distance in Figure 2.3c).[18]

The slope of the rent curve with respect to distance, or the bid-rent gradient, expresses the increase in the unit cost of land (of the house) that the household is willing to sustain in order to move one unit of distance closer to the centre, maintaining its utility constant. In formal terms it corresponds to:[19]

$$\frac{q\,\partial r(d)}{\partial d} = -\tau \qquad \text{or} \qquad \frac{\partial r(d)}{\partial d} = -\frac{\tau}{q} \tag{2.9}$$

Equation (2.9), known as the 'Muth condition', defines indifference to alternative locations by expressing a condition whereby alternative locations maintain the household's utility constant. In fact, (2.9) is nothing other than (2.2) in Von Thünen's model, from which it differs only by including an additional variable: the size of the house (q), which decreases on moving closer to the centre because physical space becomes more expensive. In this case, the household is indifferent to less peripheral locations when the saving made possible by lower transport costs *and the purchase of a smaller house* equals the higher unit costs of land typical of central locations. The shape of the bid-rent curve is therefore not linear but exponential (as in Von Thünen), while still exhibiting a negative slope.

As in the case of firms (Figure 2.2b), location equilibrium is obtained by superimposing the market land rent curve (which expresses the real market prices of land, defined exogenously) on the bid-rent curves. The point of tangency between the actual rent curve and the lowest bid-rent curve (relative to the highest utility) represents the household's optimal location choice (Figure 2.4).

An interesting final element for analysis is the effects of an increase in household income on the location equilibrium. Let us take a certain house size as given. The household will choose to locate at a distance from the centre where a further shift towards the periphery (the cost of transportation c in Figure 2.5a) would equal the marginal advantage represented by the saving on the cost of land (v in Figure 2.5a). An increase in income may give rise to reverse relocation choices: if the household is more interested in a larger-sized house, the advantage in terms of saving on the price of the house increases (curve v shifts to v' in Figure 2.5b) and the household will locate in a more peripheral area. When the household is instead more concerned about the greater opportunity cost of transportation (curve c rises to c' in Figure 2.5b), it will choose a more central location.[20] In the presence of both effects, it is generally believed in the American literature that the former (the size of the house) prevails, with the consequence that the location equilibrium shifts towards the periphery.

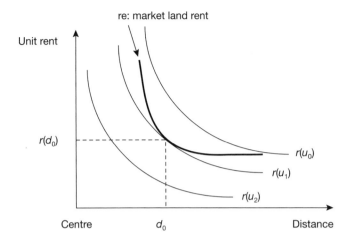

Figure 2.4 *The location equilibrium for households*

(a) Costs and benefits of accessibility   (b) Effects of a change in income

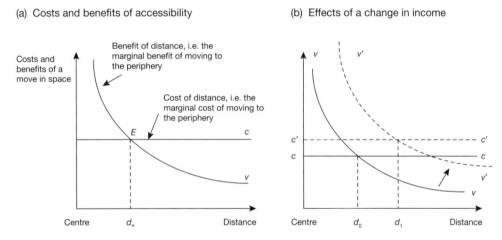

Figure 2.5 *Costs and benefits of accessibility and the effects of a change in income on the location choice*

RECENT DEVELOPMENTS: GENERAL EQUILIBRIUM MODELS

Characteristics of general equilibrium models

The models just described have guided us through the location choices of an individual firm and an individual household, but they have done so within a partial equilibrium framework. Moreover, given their inability to derive actual land prices, in order to define the location equilibrium, they have assumed as known the market land rent curve expressing the real market cost of land.

The general equilibrium approach developed since the mid-1980s in 'new urban economics' – or less emphatically 'economics of the monocentric city' – enables us to remedy both shortcomings of the previous models. General equilibrium models, in fact, seek to endogenize the market land rent value, i.e. to obtain it from the location equilibrium conditions themselves. They are conceived with the aim of identifying the urban density, city size, and land prices which produce a location equilibrium where all households are equally satisfied (or all firms earn equal profits), keeping the logical-conceptual framework identical to that of the partial equilibrium models.[21] Numerous studies have been produced on these matters, their intention being no longer to identify the location of an individual household or firm, as in the partial equilibrium models, but rather to identify the land price conditions that produce a location equilibrium characterized by equal utility for all households or equal profit for all firms, and to determine the residential density of each city under these conditions.

In the case of firms, on the hypothesis that: (a) the value of land at the edge of the city is equal to the value of agricultural rent and known, (b) the equilibrium quantity of the good (i.e. the quantity that simultaneously satisfies the demand and supply conditions for the good), (c) the prices of the other production factors (besides land), and (d) the level of profit desired by firms, the models identify the maximum size of the city, the density of firms, and the trend of land prices in space (the actual rent curve). The same characteristics (maximum size, density, and land price in space) are identified by the models in the case of households, once the population wanting to locate in the city, the price of other goods, and household's desired utility have been given exogenously.[22] This endeavour has been carried forward on various hypotheses: the existence of a 'closed city', i.e. a city whose demographic size is given in the case of households (or market equilibrium in the case of firms), and an 'open city', i.e. the case in which also the size of a city is endogenously defined.

Although the models now discussed are striking in their elegance and economic logic, they are often extremely complex. Consequently, the descriptions that follow have been simplified as far as possible, and they are accompanied by illustrations.

The general equilibrium model for firms

The purpose of the general equilibrium model is to identify – given a percentage (s) of urban land used for productive activities – the equilibrium density of the n firms located on the urban land, all of them specialized in production of the same good (and therefore characterized by the same production function).[23]

The model hypothesizes a Cobb–Douglas production function[24] comprising only two production factors (land and capital), which can be substituted for each other, and with constant returns to scale:[25]

$$Y_d = aT_d^\alpha K_d^{1-\alpha} \tag{2.10}$$

in which Y is the quantity of the good produced by the firm, a is a constant representing technical progress, T and K are respectively the quantities of land and capital used in the production process, while α and $(1 - \alpha)$ respectively denote the efficiency of the production factors 'land' and 'capital' in the production process.

The various combinations of production factors required to achieve a certain level of production (Y) are represented in Figure 2.6a by the isoquant curves. These represent higher levels of production at increasing distances from the origin. When they are compared against the isocost line, which represents the factor combinations that keep total production costs constant, they identify the land/capital combination which maximizes the firm's profit (or, revenues remaining equal, minimize its costs) given a certain distance (d_0) from the centre (point E in Figure 2.6a).[26]

If the firm wants to increase the amount of urban land that it uses, but producing the same quantity at the same costs, it will have to reduce the amount of capital invested in the production process. The firm will have an incentive to choose this option when the land is more attractive, i.e. when its cost is lower (Figure 2.6b). Thus, as previously obtained with the households model, the different slopes of the isocost line for different distances from the centre, assuming p_K as numeraire, identify the bid-rent curve (Figure 2.6c) – given a certain profit level (i.e. along a given isoquant curve). As the distance from the centre decreases, the budget line grows more rigid because the maximum bid-rent for that distance increases, as shown in Figure 2.6.

The rent curve is defined as:[27]

$$\frac{T_d}{Y_d} \frac{\partial r(d)}{\partial d} = -\tau(\lambda) \tag{2.11}$$

(2.11) is the Muth condition in the case of firms. It states that a firm is indifferent to location when the new location's advantage in terms of saving on transport costs is equal to the increase in the cost of urban land. In order to cover the increase in land cost, the firm will be tempted to use a lesser amount of land, which has become relatively more costly, and to replace it with additional quantities of the other good, capital, for example by constructing taller buildings. It will thus use less land per unit of output (T_d/Y_d will be lower).[28]

We may thus once again state that each firm is indifferent to alternative locations along the bid-rent curve. In other words, the cost of moving in space is nil, so that any alternative location along the bid-rent curve leaves the firm's profit unchanged.

Moving to the general equilibrium case, on the assumption that the n firms all have the same production function, and that the equilibrium quantity of the good in the city ($Y*$) is known, it is possible to use the 'boundary rent curve' to identify the intensity of land use, the maximum profit level achievable by each firm, and the total size of the city.[29] The boundary rent curve defines, for each maximum profit level of firms (and therefore for each bid-rent curve), at which size of the city the quantity produced at equilibrium in the urban market exactly equals the quantity given exogenously.[30]

Assuming land value at the edge of the city as known and equal to the value of agricultural land, the equilibrium bid-rent curve can be identified. It will be the bid-rent curve that intersects the boundary rent curve for the value of land at the city's edge (*brc* in Figure 2.7a).

The reasons for this statement are the following. Higher bid-rent curves are logically excluded from the definition of an equilibrium condition, since they define levels of

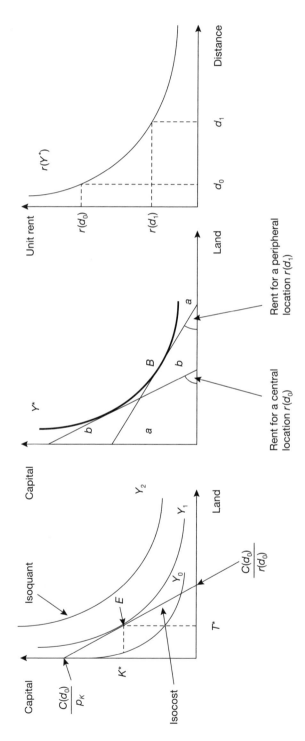

■ *Figure 2.6* *The firm's optimal choice and the bid-rent curve*

individual profits lower than the one that firms can actually achieve (in Figure 2.7a, in fact, point E is determined for higher profit levels than point A). Lower bid-rent curves are also logically unacceptable for defining an equilibrium condition since they determine a land value at the urban edge which is lower than the agricultural rent. The only acceptable bid-rent guaranteeing an equilibrium is therefore the one which crosses the boundary rent curve at the level of agricultural rent.

Point E in Figure 2.7a therefore defines:

- the market land rent curve, previously defined exogenously and coincident with the bid-rent curve, for city sizes smaller than d_{max}, and with r_a for larger sizes;
- the individual profit level (π_1) achieved by firms in the city;
- the maximum size reached by the city (d_{max}).

This model also shows that firms locate in the urban area according to a specific equilibrium density distribution which is obtained once the maximum size has been identified. Indifference to alternative locations obtains for every distance from the centre, because the lower rent charged for suburban locations exactly offsets higher transportation costs and allows savings on capital costs (reducing the amount of land used per unit of output).

An interesting case is the one in which an open city – where firms can relocate to other urban areas – is hypothesized. There are several boundary rent curves in this case, each of them expressing an equilibrium production level in the goods market (Figure 2.7b). The location equilibrium is obtained by exogenously defining a profit level externally and internally to the city equal to π^*. The point at which the bid-rent curve guaranteeing the profit level π^* intersects with the agricultural rent defines the size of the city (and its density). The intersection of the bid-rent curve with one of the boundary rent curves shows the equilibrium quantity actually produced ($brc(Y_1)$ in Figure 2.7b).

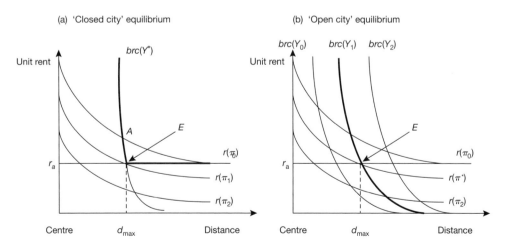

Figure 2.7 *General equilibrium for firms*

The general equilibrium model for households

Reasoning which is very similar (in its logical structure if not in all its hypotheses) to that used by the general equilibrium model for firms defines the location equilibrium of n households in a city. The general equilibrium for households first requires that the indifference to alternative locations, as expressed by Muth's condition, must hold for all the n households. On the hypothesis that households have the same incomes and the same preference structures, they exhibit location indifference along the same bid-rent curve. Figure 2.8a shows various bid-rent curves, with higher levels of utility for curves closer to the origin.

However, the market land rent curve is no longer known, as it was in the partial equilibrium model. It must be determined by comparing the bid-rent curves of the various households, just as the market land rent curve was defined in Von Thünen's model by the envelope of the bid-rent curves of the three farmers.

As in the above case of firms, it is possible to use the boundary rent curve to define the market land rent curve (and therefore the utility of households). For every level of household utility (and therefore for every bid-rent curve and for every maximum urban size at every distance from the centre), this curve defines what size of the city ensures that the total population is equal to that given exogenously (Figure 2.8).

This curve delimits the urban area for different levels of utility and different maximum sizes of the city, subject to the condition that the total population is equal to the population given exogenously: if the utility increases, so does the amount of space required by each household, with the consequence that residential density diminishes.[31]

As in the case of firms, assuming the value of land on the urban edge as known and equal to the value of agricultural land, it is possible to identify the equilibrium bid-rent curve. This will be the bid-rent curve that cuts the boundary rent curve for land value at the city's edge (*brc* in Figure 2.8a). If the boundary rent curve intersects with the highest bid-rent curve (point A in Figure 2.8a), households will be forced to shift down to lower rent curves, which express greater utilities. Instead, if it intersects with lower bid-rent curves, there

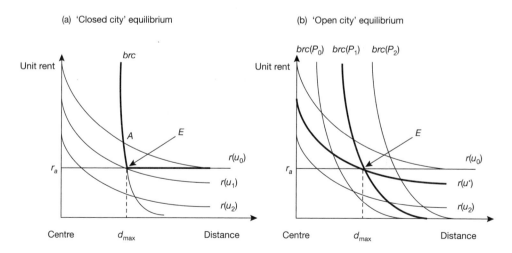

Figure 2.8 General equilibrium for households

will be no equilibrium because the land value offered by households at the outermost edge of the city will be less than the agricultural value.

As in the case of firms, point E in Figure 2.8a defines:

- the market land rent curve, previously defined exogenously and coincident with the bid-rent curve, for city of sizes smaller than d_{max}, and with r_a for larger sizes;
- the utility level (u_1) achieved by households in the city;
- the maximum size, and the density, reached by the city (d_{max}).

In the case of an open city – where households can relocate to other urban areas – there exist (as previously in the case of the model of firms) several boundary rent curves, each of them defining a different level of population (Figure 2.8b). Equilibrium is obtained by exogenously defining a level of utility externally and internally to the city which equals u^*. The point at which the bid-rent curve guaranteeing utility level u^* intersects with agricultural rent defines the size of the city (and its density). The intersection of the bid-rent curve with one of the boundary rent curves shows the population in equilibrium ($brc(P_1)$ in Figure 2.8b).

Finally, we may discard the hypothesis that all households have the same income and assume that there exist three classes with different incomes and different preference structures. The slopes of the bid-rent curves will differ according to level of income. As income increases, the different classes of households will be willing to pay more for houses in order to locate (one unit of distance) closer to the centre (Figure 2.9).[32] The three classes of households are distributed across the urban area as in Von Thünen's model: each area will be occupied by the class of households that makes the highest rent bid. Market land rent will be the envelope of the bid-rent curves at each distance from the centre, so that the city can be depicted as a set of concentric rings each containing the class of households willing to pay the highest rent for that distance (Figure 2.9).

Firms and households

Finally, a brief description of some models of monocentric cities which, with minor adjustments, enable simultaneous analysis of the location of firms and households. On the hypothesis that the rent gradient of firms is higher than that of households (i.e. firms are willing to pay higher unit rents in order to move one unit of distance closer to the centre), the bid-rent curves for firms and households will be those shown in Figure 2.10.

These models lead to two important results. The first is that they identify the bid-rent curves of firms and households endogenously. Let us assume that at time t_0 households choose a level of rent r_0 characterized by a certain level of utility. For equilibrium to come about, the level of utility must be such that it determines an amount of population and a labour supply equal to the labour demand of firms. If households have chosen too a high level of utility, and therefore make rent bids which are too low, the population located in the city (in the range $d_1 – d'_{max}$) may be insufficient to satisfy the labour demand by firms. The availability of work will attract new households into the city, with a consequent increase in demand for urban land which pushes the bid-rent curve up to r_1 in Figure 2.10. The city will expand (d''_{max}) until labour-market equilibrium has been re-established at a lower level of utility.

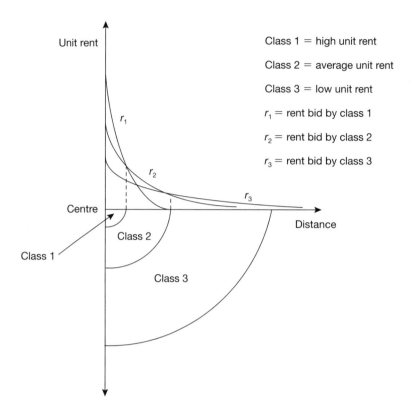

Figure 2.9 Location equilibrium for different classes of households

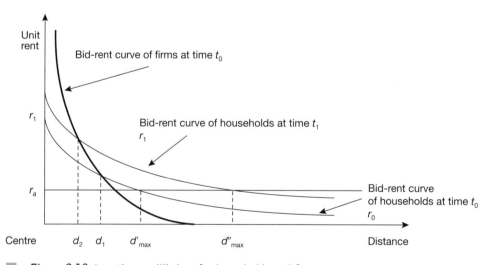

Figure 2.10 Location equilibrium for households and firms

The second important result of these models is that they divide the urban area between productive and residential activities. Urban land will be allocated to the activities able to pay a higher rent for each distance from the centre – as in Von Thünen's model. In this case, the central areas will be occupied by firms, while households will be pushed towards suburban areas: a theoretical result which closely reflects what actually happens in reality.

CRITICAL REMARKS

Starting from hypotheses similar to those of Von Thünen's classic model, with considerable formal elegance and economic rigour, the models described in this chapter adopt a neoclassical framework of profit maximization for firms, and utility maximization for households, to identify the location equilibrium conditions for productive and residential activities, the spatial pattern of urban land prices, and the density and size of the city.

The models draw on microeconomic concepts to explain purely spatial phenomena, such as the distribution of activities in space and the location choices of households and firms. They are thus able to break down the disciplinary barrier between mainstream and urban economics which for long hampered development of a general theory of space. Traditional economics has consequently been enriched with theories that interpret space in purely microeconomic terms; while urban economics has acquired a traditional economic logic with which to interpret location choices.

Moreover, although these models are highly abstract, owing to their unrealistic hypotheses (isotropic space, a city with a single centre), they are able to describe conditions which closely match actual reality: an urban land rent gradient negative with respect to distance from the centre (Figure 2.11), the central location of activities with high value added (business and management), broad suburban spaces for residential activities.

However, despite their logic, elegance and economic rigour, these models have a number of theoretical elements which weaken their overall logical structure. One of them is the decisive role played by commuting in determining location equilibrium. If real behaviour does not comply with the perfect rationality envisaged by the models, so that commuting is of less importance for a person's utility, the entire theoretical-conceptual edifice collapses. However, this shortcoming can be partly remedied, if we acknowledge that the costs of transportation to the centre and the desire to reduce them may reflect other important aspects of an individual's utility function when s/he makes location choices, like accessibility to information, recreational services, and opportunities for social interaction.

A second shortcoming is more serious. These models concern themselves neither with how a city centre is organized nor with what happens outside the city itself. They restrict themselves to interpreting locational behaviour within the area extending between an hypothetical aspatial centre and the physical boundary of the city. Moreover, when these models are used to interpret location equilibrium, not internally to a city but among cities, and therefore on the hypothesis that the city is part of an urban system and that firms and households may decide to relocate to other cities with attractively higher levels of utility or profit, they display a clear interpretative weakness. On the hypothesis that households have equal preference structures and firms have equal production functions, there can only be indifference to alternative locations in other cities if all these exhibit – in the logic applied here to describe

59

(a) Retail

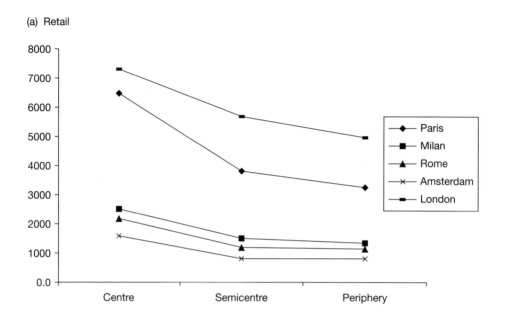

(b) Offices

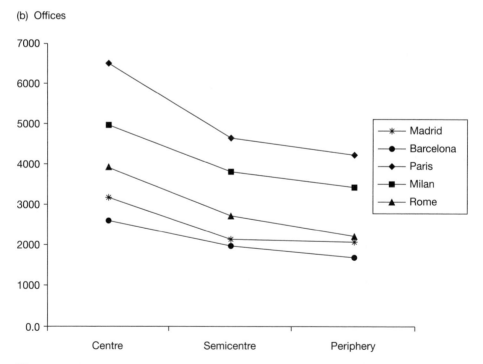

Figure 2.11 Urban rent gradients in some major European cities (rental values per sq m. per annum in euros – 2003)

Source: Our elaborations on ONCOR European Property Bulletin data, 2004

them – the same bid-rent curve and the same boundary rent curve, and are therefore all of the same size. If this is the case, there will be an urban system made up of cities which are all of equal size;[33] but this circumstance is amply contradicted in the real world. In order to deal with this defect, the conceptual framework should be able to accommodate the hypothesis that locational advantages differ according to the size of the city, and that rents – the monetary counterpart of the advantages that households and firms obtain from central urban locations – vary (distance from the centre remaining equal) from city to city.

Only thus is it possible to conceive a location equilibrium with cities of different sizes. Yet this also requires acceptance of the idea that large, medium-sized and small cities are structurally different and perform different functions in the overall economy, and consequently have specific production specializations: a hypothesis at odds with the basic features of these models, and which instead opens the way for the general equilibrium models discussed in the next chapter.

GENERALIZED ACCESSIBILITY AND THE GRAVITY MODEL

Throughout this chapter, the location of activities in urban space has been explained in terms of accessibility to a generic central business district – the locus of trade, information, and social and economic interaction. The centre attracts firms and households which, in their turn, influence the centre in diverse ways: commuter movements, diffusion of knowledge and information, cooperation networks and personal relationships. These forces of attraction (and repulsion) affect not only the centre but every pair of points in space (two different zones of the same city, but also two different cities) and they are generated by the intensity of the flows of people, information and goods between those points. In fact, these flows measure the relations that may arise between the activities located at the two points in space and, at aggregate level, the greater attractiveness of one zone with respect to the other (one city with respect to the other).

Surprisingly, flows of people, goods and information across a territory seem to organize themselves on the basis of gravitational fields sensitive to the amount of activities located on the territory, and to their relative distance.[34]

Since the work of George Kingsley Zipf in the years after the Second World War,[35] territorial flows of information, goods and people have been estimated using the gravity model, so called because it is based on Newton's law of universal gravitation. The model states that every point in space undergoes (or exerts) an influence proportional to its mass and inversely proportional to the distance that separates it from the other point in space.[36]

In general, the *model of flow* (so called because of its ability to estimate flows between two territorial entities) is expressed as:

$$T_{ab} = K(P_a^{\alpha} P_b^{\beta})/d_{ab}^{\gamma} \tag{2.12}$$

where T is the intensity of interaction between a generic pair a and b of points in space, K is a constant of proportionality, P is the mass of points a and b respectively, d is the distance between a and b. α and β are assumed equal to 1. The distance exponent, γ, represents the impedance or friction exerted by physical space on movement (of goods or people). Its value therefore differs according to the phenomenon studied (consider, for example, the greater weight of the distance covered between home and shop to purchase staple goods like bread or milk, compared to luxury goods like jewellery). The mass P of the territorial entities is often expressed in terms of population.

When the gravity model is generalized so that it can be applied to estimation of flows between a generic point and n points in space (between one zone of a city and all the other zones of the city), the analogy still holds between gravitational physics and interpretation of territorial phenomena, as well as depicted by the following gravity model (labelled *model of potential* for its capacity to measure the attractiveness potential of a place):

$$E_a = K \sum_j P_j / d_{aj}^{\gamma} \qquad\qquad (2.13)$$

where E represents the potential energy produced on a by a set of masses Pj each at a distance d from a.[37] Once again, parameter γ denotes spatial friction, which may differ from the value of 1 assumed in the original gravitational physics model, thereby enabling application of the model to territorial phenomena with an extra degree of freedom.

In economic terms, (2.13) represents 'generalized accessibility or interaction'. It measures the accessibility (or attractiveness) of every point with respect to the space that surrounds it.[38] A great deal of information is comprised in the generalized accessibility of a hypothetical zone i. It expresses 'demographic potential' when it estimates the commuter flows from all the other zones of the city to zone i; 'market potential' when it interprets the flow of people (potential customers) from all the other zones to zone i if it is an area of commercial activity; 'income potential' when a per-capita income is associated with individuals (potential customers); and 'location potential' when it is used to explain location choices (made according to the place with the greatest location potential) and the set of flows away from that location (demand for mobility and transport). Finally, location potential also explains the value attributable to a particular location (the rent of the previous models) in view of its attractiveness and generalized accessibility.

(2.12) and (2.13) can be easily estimated with simple econometric models, following their conversion into logarithmic form and the consequent linearization of the equations. Knowing the physical distance between two cities (or between two places in a city), the populations of the two places and interaction flows between two places, T – or of one place with j other places, E – it is statistically possible to obtain the values of K, α, β and γ.

In operational terms, these models have obvious predictive capacity if they are used to estimate the potential impact of the location of a new productive activity in a particular area. In the case of a project to build a shopping centre in a generic zone i, for example, once the values of K, α, β and γ have been estimated, and once the distance between two points in space and the increase in population expected in the area (e.g. new jobs) are known, equation (2.12) is able to predict the number of people who will move from a zone of the city to zone i. Furthermore, the model of potential (equation 2.13) is able to predict the demand for transport, the market potential (potential number of shoppers at the shopping centre), and the income potential associated with construction of the shopping centre.

CONCLUSIONS

The chapter has described models, of a strictly neoclassical nature, which seek to account for the allocation of land between alternative activities within a spatial structure of uniform supply in space and a punctiform source of demand. High demand for access to central areas triggers competition between firms and households to obtain locations closer to the market, or more generally to a hypothetical central business district.

Land rent is the main factor that organizes activities in urban space. According to strict economic logic, competition for land closer to the centre is resolved by its allocation to activities able to pay higher rents.

The virtues of these models are their rigour and their stringent economic logic. Their main weakness emerges when they set out to explain the location choices made by households and firms between cities with different levels of utility or profit.

Indifference to alternative locations, which is the long-period equilibrium condition, is guaranteed if and only if cities offer the same utility and the same profit; and therefore, according to the model's logic, if and only if cities are of the same size. Yet this implies the existence of an urban system consisting of cities which are all of the same size – a circumstance widely belied by reality. In order to understand the economic reasons for the existence of urban systems with cities of different sizes, consideration must be made of the functional characteristics of cities. This is an aspect which the models described thus far are unable to handle, and which is instead addressed by the models discussed in the next chapter.

REVIEW QUESTIONS

1 Which principle is behind the organization of activities in space in a monocentric city?

2 How is competition for central locations among alternative activities solved?

3 How is rent defined in the Von Thünen model?

4 How is location equilibrium of productive activities in Alonso's model achieved?

5 How does Alonso's model change when residential activities are taken into consideration?

6 How would you define the 'Muth condition'?

7 Why is the bid-rent rent also defined as 'indifference curve in urban space'?

8 What are the main purposes of general location equilibrium models?

9 What is the 'boundary rent curve' and how is the location choice achieved in a general equilibrium model?

10 Which of the main critics moved to the 'new urban economics'?

SELECTED READING ON EMPIRICAL FINDINGS

About land use and land prices

Brueckner, J., Thisse, J.-F. and Zenou, Y. (1999) 'Why is Central Paris rich and downtown Detroit poor?: an amenity-based theory', *European Economic Review*, vol. 43, pp. 91–107.

Fanning Madden, J. (1981) 'Why women work closer to home', *Urban Studies*, vol. 18, no. 2, pp. 181–94.

Gin, A. and Sonstelie, J. (1992) 'The streetcar and residential location in nineteenth century Philadelphia', *Journal of Urban Economics*, vol. 32, no. 1, pp. 92–107.

Wheaton, W. (1977) 'Income and urban residence: an analysis of consumer demand for location', *American Economic Review*, vol. 67, no. 4, pp. 620–31.

FURTHER READING

Alonso, W. (1964) *Location and land use: towards a general theory of land rent*, Cambridge, Mass.: Harvard University Press.

Beckmann, M. J. (1969) 'On the distribution of urban rent and residential density', *Journal of Economic Theory*, no. 1, pp. 60–8.

Fujita, M. (1989) *Urban economic theory: land use and city size*, Cambridge: Cambridge University Press.

Huriot, J.-M. (1988) *Von Thünen: économie et espace*, Paris: Economica.

Richardson, H. W. (1977) *The new urban economics: and alternatives*, London: Pion.

Chapter 3

Hierarchy and location

SUMMARY

1   Hierarchy and urban systems

2   The geographical approach: Christaller's model

3   The economic approach: Lösch's model

4   Some recent developments

5   Towards a new theory of urban systems: city networks

HIERARCHY AND URBAN SYSTEMS

The location theories discussed in the previous chapters analysed the location choices of individual firms or people. They disregarded, however, the existence of other activities or individuals and of dichotomous location alternatives: urban or non-urban areas, central or peripheral ones, areas with high or low concentrations of activities. When they considered the existence of several activities, they ruled out the possibility that these might locate in alternative urban centres. And when they dealt with several cities, they reached the somewhat paradoxical conclusion that the existence of urban systems apparently in equilibrium entailed that those cities must all be of the same size. Only thus could indifference to alternative locations be guaranteed because the levels of profit and utility were the same in all the cities.[1]

Thus far, therefore, we have not met theories able to explain the location choices of several firms and households among alternative urban centres. Nor, consequently, have we found a theory of location able to explain why in reality there exist numerous cities, of different sizes and performing different functions, which depend partly or wholly on larger cities for higher-quality services and activities. In other words, we have so far been unable to explain why an urban hierarchy exists.

The theories presented in this chapter seek to account for the existence of urban systems made up of cities of different sizes. The aim of these theories is to formulate rules able to interpret the *urban hierarchy* by explaining:

- the size and frequency of urban centres at every level in the hierarchy, and therefore the market area of each of them;
- the distance between a particular city and those at the levels immediately below or above it, and therefore the geographical distribution of all the urban centres.

The founders of this school of thought, known as 'central place theory', were the geographer Walter Christaller and the economist August Lösch.[2] These were the first to formulate models able to explain the urban hierarchy, and they prepared the ground for subsequent analyses.

THE GEOGRAPHICAL APPROACH: CHRISTALLER'S MODEL

The original model

Christaller's model is based on the assumption that an urban centre exists where there are goods and services to be traded. This central 'place' (hence the name 'central place theory' given to the literature that Christaller's model inspired[3]) must produce or supply goods or services to a population spatially dispersed across a uniform and isotropic surrounding territory.[4] The aim of the model is to show how products and services (especially tertiary functions) come to be territorially organized into an urban hierarchy.

For this purpose Christaller introduces the concepts of *threshold* and *range*. These express in geographical terms the economic forces that organize activities in space: transportation costs and agglomeration economies, or economies of scale. The range of a service is the maximum distance that consumers are willing to travel to purchase it (which includes the maximum transportation costs that they are willing to pay in doing so). The threshold of a service is the distance that, when rotated around the supply centre, marks out a circular area with sufficient population to generate a level of demand such that the service can be produced profitably. A service is produced only if the range exceeds the threshold. In other words, a service is produced only if there is sufficient demand for it to be supplied at a profit.[5]

The central place is located at the centre of a circular market area, which is the optimal location because consumers located in the area are able to minimize their total transport costs.[6]

In equilibrium, the circular market areas defined by the range of the service assume the shape of a hexagon. This geometric shape enables Christaller to maintain three fundamental assumptions: (i) minimization of transport costs for consumers (the hexagon, in fact, is the geometric shape closest to a circle); (ii) even distribution of the service supply, so that the territory is covered without areas being left unserved; and (iii) competition among producers, which requires that market areas must not overlap.[7] In equilibrium, a 'honeycomb' lattice consisting of *n* centres producing for *n* hexagonal market areas, all of the same size, arises in space (Figure 3.1).

According to Christaller, moreover, each service has a range which determines the size of its market area: high-quality services, produced and supplied in large urban centres, have more extensive ranges which delineate market areas broader than those in which lower-quality services are supplied.

66

(a) The market principle

(b) The transportation principle

(c) The administrative principle

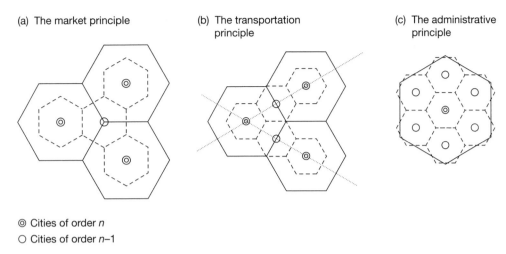

◎ Cities of order *n*
○ Cities of order *n*–1

Figure 3.1 *Organization of market areas according to Christaller's three principles*

Having defined the regular hexagon-shaped market areas – where an *n*-order service is supplied – Christaller identifies the market areas of the immediately lower-order service. He hypothesizes for this purpose that the first relative production units of the lower-order service choose to locate in the central place where higher-order services are already being produced – that is, the centres of the hexagons – so that they can benefit from agglomeration economies.

Because the range of the lower-order service is by definition less than that of the higher-order service, the market area served by production units located at the centre of the hexagon is smaller than the hexagon itself. Consequently, a part of the territory is left uncovered. This unsatisfied demand attracts new service production units into the area. These choose their locations according to three different principles that Christaller envisages as shaping market areas in space:

1   the *market principle*, which postulates location equidistant from a triad of higher-order centres represented by the vertex of the larger-sized hexagon (Figure 3.1a). Optimization of this location fulfils the criterion of minimizing the number of centres able to cover all the territory of the higher-order market. According to this location pattern, there are $1 + 6/3 = 3$ lower-order centres in a higher-order market area;

2   the *transportation principle*, which applies to a location equidistant from a pair of higher-order centres (Figure 3.1b). This choice optimizes the location of lower-order centres on the basis of minimization of transport costs to the higher-order centres. In each higher-order market area there are $1 + 6/2 = 4$ lower-order centres;

3   the *administrative principle*, identified by location in the centre of the triangles making up the hexagon (Figure 3.1c), so that the purpose of optimization is to prevent higher-order centres from competing to administer lower-order ones. This aim is achieved if the lower-order centres pertain to a single higher-order centre. In this pattern, there are $1 + 6 = 7$ lower-order centres for each market area of a certain order.

The model thus generates a hierarchy of urban centres: for each centre (or market area) of order n there are k centres (market areas) of order $n - 1$; k is the factor of proportionality between the centre of a certain order and the one immediately below it, and it assumes value 3, 4 or 7 according to the predominant location principle (market, transportation or administrative).[8] In Christaller's model, this proportionality factor is constant throughout the urban hierarchy. For each k, simple rules can be applied to obtain the number of centres of each order, the distance between the centres of each order, and the size of the market area.[9]

The model reaches an important conclusion: each large centre produces the goods/services relative to its hierarchical level and all lower-order goods/services. The large centre's advantages therefore derive from the functional level typical of its hierarchical order. Hence, the size of the city becomes a proxy for the urban function, and each higher-order centre has a descending array of lower-order centres until the lowest-level agglomeration is reached.[10]

Christaller's model therefore generates a system of hierarchical spatial relations which gravitate on the surrounding market area. Although the model is mainly geographical in nature, it gains robust internal consistency from the economic postulates on which it is based:[11]

- *optimal behaviour by consumers*, who minimize transportation costs so that they can purchase the service offered. The market areas are separate from each other and do not overlap;
- *homogeneous geographical space* in which the agglomeration of activities comes about for economic, not physical-geographic, reasons;
- *a transportation cost proportional to the distance covered*;
- *existence of economies of scale*, these being implicit in the concept of threshold;
- *equity in supply of the service*, which is implicit in the statement that the territory must be covered so that all consumers have access to all services/goods.

When Christaller applied his model to reality, he obtained surprising results. He first analysed the urban structure of Southern Germany, exogenously defining six levels of centres with a centrality indicator consisting of the number of telephones connected to the inter-urban network. When he then applied the market principle, he found a striking correspondence between the number of centres identified by his model and the number that actually existed in reality:

Hierarchical level	1	2	3	4	5	6	7
Theoretical number of centres	1	2	6	18	54	162	486
Observed number of centres	1	2	10	23	60	105	462

It needs to be stressed that Christaller's model is able to answer the questions put at the beginning of the chapter: it demonstrates the existence of an urban hierarchy in which each city of a certain size performs a specific function. Moreover, the model is able to furnish rules with which to identify the number of centres of a certain order, the size of each market area of each centre, the distances among centres of the same order, and therefore their geographical distribution.

Mathematical formalization

The Christaller model was purely qualitative in its original formulation. However, a very simple quantitative version of it has recently been proposed.[12] Let p_1 denote the population of the lower-order settlement, and r the population of the rural area depending on p_1. The population of the area served by p_1, called P_1, is easily identified:

$$P_1 = p_1 + r \qquad (3.1)$$

On the hypothesis that each city has a population in its area which is a constant fraction c of the area, i.e.

$$p_j = cP_j \qquad \text{with } 0 < c < 1 \qquad (3.2)$$

(3.1) can be rewritten as:

$$p_1 = c(p_1 + r) \qquad (3.3)$$

so that:

$$P_1 = \frac{cr}{1 - c} \qquad (3.4)$$

(3.4) states that the population of the city of order 1 is equal to $c/(1-c)$ times the population of the rural area. In the central place literature $c/(1-c)$ is termed the 'urban multiplier'.

Let us assume that there are n levels of urban centres and that each centre serves itself and s 'satellite' centres around it.[13] The population of a region served by a higher-order city, called P_n, is obtained from the population of the lower-order area which it controls $(1+s)$, considering that centre n maintains a population of order n, not $n-1$, within its area:

$$P_n = P_{n-1}(1 + s) - p_{n-1} + p_n \qquad (3.5)$$

Bearing (3.2) in mind, (3.5) can be rewritten as:

$$P_n = P_{n-1}(1 + s) - cP_{n-1} + cP_n \qquad (3.6)$$

so that:

$$P_n = \left(\frac{1 + s - c}{1 - c}\right) P_{n-1} \qquad (3.7)$$

Because in Christaller's model s and c are constant throughout the urban hierarchy, (3.7) identifies a constant relation between the size of the region's population and that of the lower-order region.

(3.7) can be written in generic form:

$$P_n = \left(\frac{1 + s - c}{1 - c}\right)^{n-1} P_1 \tag{3.8}$$

Substituting P_1 with (3.4), when we multiply the right-hand member by $(1 + s - c)/(1 + s - c)$, we obtain:

$$P_n = \left(\frac{1 + s - c}{1 - c}\right)^{n} \frac{rc}{1 + s - c} \tag{3.9}$$

(3.9) states that, knowing the population of rural settlements r, we are able to find the size of the market area and the population of centres of any order whatever.

THE ECONOMIC APPROACH: LÖSCH'S MODEL

The original model

In 1940, Lösch developed a general equilibrium model in order to remedy a major short-coming of Christaller's model: its assumption of a proportionality factor constant throughout the urban hierarchy.

Lösch's model also generates a hexagonal structure of market areas, but it does so on the basis of purely economic principles:

- competition among firms: this does not permit the existence of uncovered market areas, since the potential profits available in non-controlled spatial markets attract new firms into those areas;
- consumer rationality: when consumers have to choose between two possible suppliers, their rationality induces them to select the one which offers the good at the lowest price; and therefore, according to the logic of the model, they select the producer located closest to them (see Chapter 1).

Lösch's model defines market areas by explicit (though exogenous) cost and demand curves of goods, and thus achieves spatial equilibrium of an individual sector. The model identifies a stable spatial economic equilibrium in the hexagonal market areas which arise when firms no longer have incentives to enter the market.

Unlike Christaller, Lösch identifies several factors of proportionality – also called nesting coefficients – which operate up the urban hierarchy: Christaller's $k = 3$, 4 and 7 is still valid, but other values of the coefficient of proportionality are considered, in particular 9, 12, 13, 16, 19, 21 (Figure 3.2). Lösch assumes, in fact, that there is a specific value of the nesting coefficient, and therefore a specific size of the hexagonal market areas, corresponding to each type of good or service. Lösch's coefficients are simple geographic multiples of Christaller's coefficients (3, 4 and 7), and they therefore comply with Christaller's three principles:[14]

- 9 and 21 with the market principle: $9 = 1 + 6 + 6/3$, and $21 = 1 + 6 + 6 + 6 + 6/3$;
- 16 with the transportation principle: $16 = 1 + 6 + 6 + 6/2$;
- 13 and 19 with the administrative principle: $13 = 1 + 6 + 6$ and $19 = 1 + 6 + 6 + 6$;
- 12 with the market principle and then the transportation principle: $12 = 1 + 6 + 6/3 + 6/2$.

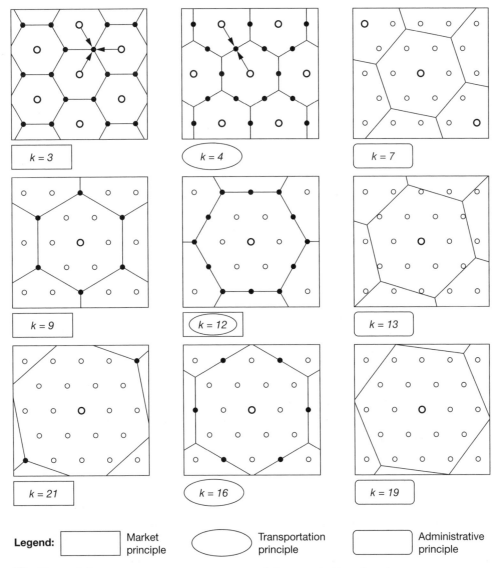

Figure 3.2 The nine most compact patterns of the organization of centres

Relaxing the assumption of a proportionality factor constant throughout the urban hierarchy has significant consequences. It eliminates the two-way relation between size of the centre and specialization, and it enables consideration to be made of such important empirical situations as the different functional specializations of centres of the same size and the possibility that centres have functional specializations: hence a centre may perform only the function of its order and not of all the others, as the Christaller model imposes.

The way in which Lösch arrives at the overall structuring of the territory on the basis of his hypotheses is interesting but analytically unsatisfactory. For Lösch, the organization of economic space results from the superimposition of several hexagons, of different sizes and structures (corresponding to different types of goods and services). All hexagons have a common centre, which produces all the goods (Figure 3.3a). The final structure of the territory is obtained by rotating the superimposed hexagons to obtain the maximum density of centres in some areas, and the maximum coincidence of different production locations (Figure 3.3b). The result is a series of circular alternate sectors of high and low settlement densities. These sectors radiate out from a large city to form a structure which complies with an efficiency principle for the transportation system (Figure 3.3c).[15]

Lösch's model yields more realistic and less paradoxical patterns than those produced by Christaller's model. However, they are obtained at the expense of blurring the concept of urban hierarchy: there are no elements in the high density spaces of urban centres that can be used to identify a hierarchical structure of centres – due to a lack, amongst other things, of a clear division of labour among them.[16]

Also Lösch demonstrates the validity of his model empirically, in his case by applying it to the territory of Iowa in the United States. Hypothesizing an urban structure comprising six hierarchical levels and a nesting factor of 4, he obtains the following results:[17]

hierarchical level	0	1	2	3	4	5
theoretical no. of centres	0–1	2–3	9–10	39	154	615*
actual no. of centres	0	3	9	39	153	615
theoretical distance among centres (miles)	179	90	45	22	11	5.6*
observed distance among centres (miles)		94	50	24	10	5.6

(*) = observed value

As said, for empirical verification of his model Lösch preferred to use a nesting coefficient of 4, which corresponds to Christaller's proportionality coefficient for his transportation principle. This principle is compatible with the territory selected by Lösch for his empirical analysis, which was a plain traversed by rectilinear transport infrastructures.[18]

Mathematical formalization

Like Christaller's model, Lösch's has also attracted the interest of numerous economists, some of whom have proposed a mathematical formalization of it.[19]

The formal approach uses five equations to state the economic conditions that the model regards as crucial for achievement of general spatial economic equilibrium. The latter arises from two specific factors: each producer seeks to maximize his/her profit; and each

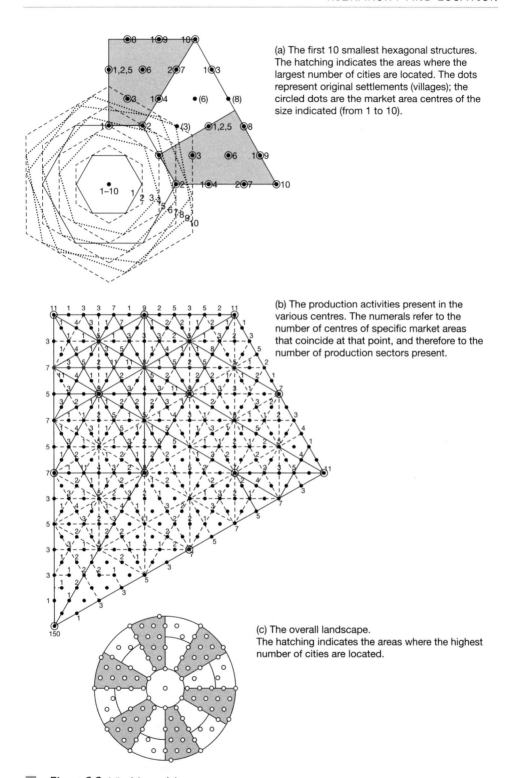

(a) The first 10 smallest hexagonal structures. The hatching indicates the areas where the largest number of cities are located. The dots represent original settlements (villages); the circled dots are the market area centres of the size indicated (from 1 to 10).

(b) The production activities present in the various centres. The numerals refer to the number of centres of specific market areas that coincide at that point, and therefore to the number of production sectors present.

(c) The overall landscape.
The hatching indicates the areas where the highest number of cities are located.

Figure 3.3 Lösch's model

consumer seeks to maximize his/her utility by accessing the least costly market. Moreover, the existence of several firms in the same sector gives rise to competition among them which nullifies extra-profits.

The conditions are the following:

1   The locations of producers must be the most advantageous possible, so that no movement in space improves profitability.
2   The number of possible locations must be such that coverage of the entire territory is guaranteed.
3   Extra-profit must be nullified, so that stability is ensured in the market and the entry of new firms is prevented.
4   The firm's volume of production and the size of its market area must be as small as is compatible with its average production costs. If change in the size of the market is associated with a price increase greater than the increase in average production costs, this will generate extra-profit and therefore create room for new firms to enter the market.
5   The good's sale prices on the border between market areas must be equal in order that consumer indifference between alternative locations is guaranteed at the border.

These economic conditions can be straightforwardly translated into equations.
    Defining:

m	=	generic good, in which $m = 1, 2, \ldots M$;
n	=	generic centre of goods production, in which $n = 1, 2, \ldots N$;
x_{mn} e y_{mn}	=	the spatial coordinates indicating each production centre's position in space. There are two of them for each place n;
X_{mn}	=	quantity produced of good m in the production centre n;
Π_{mn}	=	total profit obtained from sale of the good m in the production centre n;
c_m	=	average production cost of good m;
P_m	=	sale price of good m;
A	=	total size of the territory, while $A_{m1}, A_{m2}, \ldots, A_{mn}$ represent the sizes of the market areas in which the generic good m is sold;
C_{mn}	=	boundary of the market area of the production centre n for good m;
d_{mn}	=	the distance between the production centre n and the boundary of its market area;
τ	=	the unit cost of transportation for the good m;

we can rewrite the five conditions as the following equations:

1. First-order conditions ensuring profit maximization in each location:

$$\frac{\partial \Pi_{mn}}{\partial x_{mn}} = 0 \quad \text{and} \quad \frac{\partial \Pi_{mn}}{\partial y_{mn}} = 0 \qquad 2N \text{ in number (2 for each market area } n)$$

2. Condition for the territory to be entirely covered by the supply of each individual good:

$$\sum_{m=1}^{M} A_m = A \qquad \qquad M \text{ in number}$$

3. Condition for the absence of extra-profit in each production centre:

$$p_{mn} = c_{mn} \qquad \qquad N \text{ in number}$$

4. Condition of minimum market area size so that marginal changes in average costs equal marginal changes in the good's price in each production place:

$$\frac{\partial p_{mn}}{\partial X_{mn}} = \frac{\partial c_{mn}}{\partial X_{mn}} \qquad \qquad N \text{ in number}$$

5. Condition of equality in prices at each market-area boundary:

$$p_{mn} + \tau d_{mn} = p_{mn'} + \tau d_{mn'} \qquad C \text{ in number}$$

The number of equations to be estimated in the model is therefore $4N + M + C$, which is equal to the number of unknowns, these being:

- the size of the market areas A_{mn}, which are equal in number to the centres N;
- the prices p_{mn} for each centre, N in number;
- the number of production centres N_m, for each good m, M in number;
- the coordinates of each centre x_{mn} and y_{mn}, $2N$ in number;
- the boundaries of the market areas, C.

Equality between the number of unknowns and the number of equations is the necessary condition for a solution to exist. However, because the system is non-linear, there may be multiple solutions or no solution at all. There are various ways to simplify the system of equations. The number of unknowns can be reduced by imposing a regular shape on the market areas, as in Lösch's original model. In this case, each area's number of boundaries becomes known. Moreover, with $N_m - 1$ market areas of the good m being known, the n-th market area is the difference from the total size of market A.

The formalized version of Lösch's model has a number of shortcomings, however.

- Because the number of centres in which production takes place is not known, solution of the model is highly complex, in that the number of equations to estimate in order to satisfy the first condition is a priori unknown.
- Even more than in the original non-formalized model, no account is taken of the possible existence of agglomeration economies in the form of both the urbanization economies typical of a higher-order centre and the localization economies of more specialized centres.

75

- The non-linearity of the system is such that it guarantees neither the existence nor the uniqueness, nor the stability of the equilibrium solution.

CRITICAL APPRAISAL OF THE TWO MODELS

Christaller's and Lösch's models are widely recognized as being the first models of general spatial equilibrium. Assuming uniform space, they were able to explain (a) the existence of sets of different-sized cities, (b) the role of each of them, and (c) the distance among them. In short, these models were the first to make interpretation of city systems possible; and only very recently have new models of general location equilibrium been proposed. However, their logical structure appears unable to account for the existence, in equilibrium conditions, of urban centres of different sizes.[20]

Still today, therefore, Christaller's and Lösch's models are unique tools with which to interpret the structure of city systems. On the basis of the simple existence of the two well-known economic forces determining location choices (agglomeration economies and transportation costs), location equilibrium arises from a logic of profit optimization for firms and utility optimization for customers.

However, the two models have a number of weaknesses widely emphasized in the literature.[21] Some of them stem from the abstract nature of certain assumptions – for example the spatial homogeneity of resources and constant unit transportation costs – but they do not undermine the interpretative capacity of the models, and they can be easily justified by the need to simplify the complexity of the real world. But other shortcomings are more critical because they affect the models' inner consistency, namely:

- The lack of analysis of demand, this being assumed to be evenly distributed in space and immobile.[22] Likewise, these models exogenously define the quantity of each good demanded by each individual. In other words, they are approaches which largely pertain to production theory.
- The lack of interdependence between the production and location choices of firms. Given the models' hypothesis of geographically homogeneous production resources and demand, on the supply side proximity to other firms does not influence cost functions; on the demand side there is no interdependence – of complementarity or substitutability – between goods.[23] Demand for a good is independent of the price of other goods and independent of the locations of the producers of other goods.
- The static nature of the models. This restricts their use in analysis of the evolution and dynamics of the urban hierarchy.

The first two of these shortcomings are serious, for they reflect contradictions between the results and the initial hypotheses which undermine the interpretative logic of the models. Indeed the assumption that demand is uniformly distributed across the territory conflicts with the models' pivotal result that population concentrates in urban centres.[24] The concentration of producers at certain points in space, in fact, rules out any possibility of homogeneous demand, because it induces consumers to resort to a central place offering optimal conditions (goods which are cheap because of low transportation costs).

The models ignore any location interdependence on both the supply and the demand sides. On the supply side, they fail to consider any input/output relation that might favour location choices dictated by proximity to other suppliers. As a consequence, they have no production function which ties the production of one good to another. On the demand side, they have no utility function which associates one good with another. The models admit no substitutability or complementarity and consequently take the form of superimposed partial equilibria.

Paradoxically, Christaller, and more specifically Lösch, invoke a concept of agglomeration economies in order to explain firms' choices; yet they subsequently ignore the advantages of such economies, thereby undermining their models' inner consistency. Despite these defects, however, given their uniqueness, and in many respects their unsurpassed economic and geographic conceptualization of the urban hierarchy, Christaller's and Lösch's models still occupy a central place in spatial economics.

SOME RECENT DEVELOPMENTS

Christaller and Lösch were the pioneers of what has been called the 'central place theory'. Since their ground-breaking studies, considerable efforts have been made to improve the original models and to remedy their shortcomings and internal contradictions. This section outlines some of these theories, providing references in the footnotes to texts which deal with formal aspects.

The first important achievement of these more recent theories has been to develop models of a more strictly economic nature, and of increasing analytical complexity, which enable demand aspects to be included in the general equilibrium. Among them, the model of Martin Beckmann and John McPherson has been widely successful.[25] This model is able to overcome the restriction imposed by a constant nesting coefficient (the k in Christaller's model, which Lösch also sought to eliminate), and the constant ratio between the population of the centre and the population of the surrounding area up the urban hierarchy (or within the same hierarchical level of services, when these are supplied by centres of different sizes). Beckmann and McPherson's model hypothesizes that the proportionality factor differs according to the hierarchical level of centres and the service supplied at level n. The significance of the proportionality factor is no longer geographic but economic (although it is measured in terms of population), and it states the total number of individuals resident in the centre of order n necessary to supply the corresponding service to each inhabitant of its market area (including the centre itself). In other words, it expresses the number of people necessary to produce the good for the entire market area.

More recently, Hubert Beguin has extended the Beckmann and McPherson model to include two economic aspects which the original model identified as determinants of the ratio between the centre's population and the population of the surrounding area:[26] labour productivity (i.e. the number of people necessary to produce one unit of the good m), and the structure of individual consumption (i.e. the quantity of good m demanded by each inhabitant of the market area of centre n). Beguin is able to show that, in reality, the structure of the urban hierarchy – in terms of the ratio between the central area's population and that of the rural area surrounding it – depends upon:

77

- variation of labour productivity across the various levels of the centre's hierarchy (increasing, decreasing and constant returns to labour);
- the distribution of the various types of goods/services in overall demand;
- the income elasticity of demand for various goods.

'Central place' theory has accomplished a second step forward by introducing the advantages of localization economies into Christaller's and Lösch's models. A noteworthy contribution in this regard has been made by W. Long,[27] who incorporates interdependence among goods into a model *à la* Christaller. He hypothesizes that the quantity purchased of a good *m* does not necessarily diminish with distance from the centre. Although the price of good *m* increases as one moves further away from the centre, it may subsequently decrease as one approaches other centres, owing to the localization economies deriving from proximity to these new centres. Long also states that the range of a good may change according to whether it is produced in a smaller centre or a larger one. To the latter he attributes a shorter range due to the presence of a larger number of substitute goods on the broader urban market. It is evident that the introduction of these hypotheses disrupts the regularity of Christaller's and Lösch's patterns, and that interdependence mechanisms, on both the demand and supply sides, may distort the results obtained by the original models. However, Long's model is no more than a preliminary exercise, whose mathematical complexity does not yet allow analytical solutions to be obtained.

Finally, central place theory has taken a third step forward in response to the need to understand not only the urban structure but also its evolution and its dynamics. Here the main contribution has been made by John Parr with his comparative statics model,[28] which analyses the evolution of the spatial organization of the urban hierarchy on the following hypotheses:

- the formation of successive levels of the hierarchy from the lowest to the highest;
- change in the allocation of economic functions at the hierarchy's various levels;
- alterations in the hierarchical structure, i.e. in the number of levels associated with the various sizes of centres: formation of a new level in the hierarchy, change in the extension in the market area of a hierarchical level, disappearance of a hierarchical level.

Parr modifies the structure of the hexagonal market areas envisaged by Christaller's original model: in the cases described above, they are transformed into rectangular or triangular or again hexagonal areas of varying sizes up the urban hierarchy.

TOWARDS A NEW THEORY OF URBAN SYSTEMS: CITY NETWORKS

In recent years, the urban systems of the advanced countries have evolved in a manner evidently at odds with Christaller's hierarchy model. Medium-sized cities (40,000 to 200,000 inhabitants) have undergone marked development and are now characterized by close interdependencies among centres of the same order, pronounced productive specializations, and the absence of hierarchical relationships within individual urban systems. Developments over the past twenty years therefore show that urban systems have little in common with Christaller's hierarchical structure. They instead display the following features:[29]

- urban specialization, especially in industry but also in services, which contradicts the Christaller model's prediction of the hierarchical despecialization of each centre;
- incomplete presence of the entire mix of functions in each city;
- high-rank functions in lower-order centres;
- horizontal linkages among cities performing similar functions: for example, the network of cities specialized in international financial services;
- synergies among similar centres performing advanced production functions and services, as exemplified by sub-regional industrial districts.

These empirical findings demonstrate the inadequacy of Christaller's traditional model, which fails to explain phenomena widely apparent in the evolution of the urban systems of the advanced countries. They have led to the development of a new conceptual paradigm – that of *city networks* – which furnishes a more convincing and coherent interpretation of emergent territorial patterns.

This new paradigm envisages the possibility that close relationships may arise among urban centres which cooperate and interact on the basis of specific economic relations. These relations may be vertical among cities of different orders, or (and this is the much more innovative aspect) they may be horizontal among cities of the same order which interact on the basis of complementarity or synergy. In the light of these two processes, it is possible to identify two types of city network:[30] *complementarity networks* consisting of specialized and complementary centres linked by a set of input–output relations. Sectoral specialization guarantees economies of scale and agglomeration economies even in centres of small size. Examples of this type of urban network are the specialized cities of Randstad (Holland), or the polycentric structure of the cities of the Veneto region in Italy; and *synergy networks* consisting of similar and mutually cooperating centres; economies of scale are guaranteed by the cooperation network itself, which links the markets of the individual centres together. Examples of this type of network are financial centres operating worldwide, whose markets are virtually linked by advanced telecommunications networks, or networks of cities connected by the religious tourism itineraries created during the Vatican Jubilee celebrations.

A third category, which can also be conceived as a sub-category of the second one, can be identified in *innovation networks* consisting of centres which cooperate on specific infrastructural or productive projects in order to achieve a critical mass in terms of both demand and supply. Examples of this type of network are agreements among French cities for the construction of infrastructures.

The new paradigm for interpretation of city systems has numerous novel features. First, the concept of 'city network' abandons the territorial logic of hierarchical relations among cities controlling non-overlapping market areas and closely embedded in each other. It instead focuses on long-distance relationships among cities of the same size performing very similar functions, which by definition cannot exist in Christaller's model.

79

Furthermore, the model based on 'network' relationships among cities discards the principles of economic efficiency (minimization of transportation costs and maximization of the market area controlled from the centre) which underpin the organization of urban centres in hierarchy models. Now of prime importance are new principles of economic efficiency which govern the organization of urban systems and originate from the positive effects of cooperative or complementary activities. In the case of synergy networks, the advantages are termed 'network externalities',[31] which accrue to all and only the members of the network. An example is provided by the advantages obtained by international financial centres from the creation of the telematic networks and the 'virtual' market that enable them to operate across great distances and enjoy relative economies of scale. In the case of complementarity networks, the advantages are those of the territorial division of labour and specialization that can be achieved through economies of horizontal integration among production units, and vertical integration in specific specialization chains.

According to the city network paradigm, therefore, relations among urban centres are no longer governed by a clear hierarchy among centres, or by competition among them in which localization economies and input–output relations strengthen the growth of one centre necessarily to the detriment of another. Economic relations among centres are now based on cooperative links which enable urban economies of scale to be achieved, without cities necessarily having to grow in terms of physical size.

We are now able to give a definition of the network paradigm. City networks consist of sets of horizontal, not hierarchical, relationships among complementary or similar centres. These relationships generate economies or externalities of, respectively, specialization/division of labour and of synergy/cooperation/innovation.

Empirical studies have amply demonstrated the tendency of urban systems to organize themselves into networks, but they have not investigated the magnitude of the advantages created by this type of organization.[32] Only recently have the first attempts been made to verify the positive effects arising from cooperative or complementary activities. An econometric study applied to the 'Healthy Cities Network' of the World Health Organization – an institutional network of urban centres set up in order to promote and coordinate urban policies for the protection of the quality of life in cities – has demonstrated that a network organization has positive effects. The cities most closely involved in the network were most successful in terms of the implementation of their urban policies.[33]

It is still too early for the city network paradigm to be called a theory, given that it still lacks adequate theorization. However, it seems certain to flank (and in certain respects supersede) Christaller's traditional territorial approach to the study of urban systems and their evolution. It is beyond doubt, in fact, that the paradigm represents a major theoretical advance on the urban hierarchy model. A good example of its interpretative force is its ability to sever the mechanistic relation between specialization and city size imposed by Christaller's model. It explains, for example, why Zurich, a city of only 300,000 inhabitants, fulfils a function of prime importance in international finance together with megalopolises like New York and Tokyo: a circumstance impossible to conceive or explain on the logic of Christaller's hierarchical model.

CONCLUSIONS

The chapter has analysed theories capable of interpreting the economic reasons for the existence of urban systems made up of cities of different sizes, and in doing so to remedy the evident limitations of other approaches, in particular those described in Chapter 2. Central place theories and the seminal works of Christaller and Lösch explain how urban systems organize themselves on the territory according to strict economic principles. Their merits and shortcomings have been analysed, and the latest advances in central place theory rectifying the weaknesses of the original models have been outlined.

The chapter has concluded with discussion of 'city networks theory', which is the most recent conceptualization of the organization of urban systems. This approach no longer interprets urban systems in terms of purely hierarchical relations among cities (which allow for control over non-overlapping market areas embedded in each other). It instead envisages horizontal relations among urban areas of the same size and performing similar functions. These relations exist in the real world but do not find theoretical explanation in Christaller's model. Although this approach yields a conceptual interpretation of evident real phenomena, it is still a paradigm which lacks an adequate theory that would give it wider scientific recognition.

REVIEW QUESTIONS

1   What is the main aim of the 'central place theory'?

2   What is the meaning of threshold and range in Christaller's model?

3   How does Christaller identify hexagonal market areas?

4   What are (in Christaller's model) the principles governing activities in space, and how do they differentiate among one another?

5   What are the economic postulates of Christaller's model?

6   What are the main differences between Lösch's and Christaller's models?

7   How does Lösch identify hexagonal market areas?

8   What are the main limits envisaged in Lösch's and Christaller's models? Have they been overcome? If yes, how?

9   What are the reasons behind the development of the city network theory?

10 What are the main conceptual elements contained in the city network theory? Which empirical results have been achieved to support this conceptual framework?

SELECTED READING ON EMPIRICAL FINDINGS

About city networks and urban systems

Boix, R. (2004) 'Redes de ciudades y externalidades', *Investigaciones Regionales*, no. 4, pp. 5–27.

Capello, R. (2000) 'The city-network paradigm: measuring urban network externalities', *Urban Studies*, vol. 37, no. 11, October, pp. 1925–45.

Dematteis, G. (1994) 'Global networks, local cities', *Flux*, no. 15, pp. 13–17.

Gottman, J. (1991) 'The dynamics of city networks in an expanding world', *Ekisticks*, no. 350–1, pp. 227–81.

Pumain, D. and Saint-Julien, T. (eds) (1996) *Urban networks in Europe*, Paris: John Libbey Eurotext.

Taylor, P. S. (2001) 'Specification of the world city network', *Geographical Analysis*, vol. 33, no. 2, pp. 181–94.

FURTHER READING

Beckmann, M. J. and McPherson, J. (1970) 'City size distribution in a central place hierarchy: an alternative approach', *Journal of Regional Science*, vol. 10, pp. 25–33.

Camagni, R. (1994) 'From city hierarchy to city network: reflections about an emerging paradigm', in Lakshmanan, T. R. and Nijkamp, P. (eds), *Structure and change in the space economy: Festschrift in honor of Martin Beckmann*, Berlin: Springer Verlag, pp. 66–87.

Camagni, R. and Capello, R. (2004) 'The city network paradigm: theory and empirical evidence', in Capello, R. and Nijkamp, P. (eds), *Urban dynamics and growth: advances in urban economics*, Amsterdam: Elsevier, pp. 495–529.

Christaller, W. (1933) *Die zentralen Orte in Süddeutschland*, Darmstadt: Wissenschaftlische Buchgesellschaft, English edn (1966), *The central places in Southern Germany*, Englewood Cliffs, NJ: Prentice-Hall.

Lösch, A. (1954) *The economics of location*, New Haven, Conn.: Yale University Press.

Part 2

Theories of regional growth: uniform-abstract space

Chapter 4

Productive structure and development

SUMMARY

1   The different interpretations of regional growth and development
2   The different conceptions of space
3   The theory of the stages of development
4   Stages of development and disparities
5   Industrial structure and regional growth: shift-share analysis
6   The centrality/peripherality approach

THE DIFFERENT INTERPRETATIONS OF REGIONAL GROWTH AND DEVELOPMENT

This chapter and those that follow examine the second broad area of regional economics: *regional development theory*. Although there are numerous and markedly different approaches to regional development, all of them endeavour to identify the factors responsible for the development path assumed by a local system. They analyse local development in terms of (a) absolute growth (from the viewpoint of the *efficient allocation of local resources*) and (b) relative growth (among regions) in order to interpret regional disparities and possible paths of convergence and divergence in levels and rates of income growth, doing so from the viewpoint of *even income distribution*.

Regional economics shifts the focus of analysis from location choices – so far examined in location theories – to the processes involved in the economic development of subnational areas. It seeks to explain, given a certain quantitative and qualitative distribution in space of resources and activities, the capacity of a local system – whether a region, a city, a province, or a geographical area with specific economic features – to develop economic activities or to attract new ones from outside, and to generate local well-being, wealth and enduring growth.

Consequently, the theories and models discussed in this and the following chapters deal with regional development, by which expression is meant the capacity of a region to find (and constantly to recreate) a specific and appropriate role within the international division of labour through the efficient and creative use of the resources possessed by the local economic system. Regional underdevelopment and regional imbalances arise from differing capacities to exploit and to organize local resources (environmental, economic, physical and human) and to attract new resources and activities into an area. Regional development theory seeks to identify the factors that generate this capacity, and the external processes and the relations that either strengthen or weaken it. The level and evolution of these tangible and intangible factors determine the *development* path of a region and its well-being. However, for the sake of brevity, the theories and models often sum up the various elements determining the development patterns of an economic system in a single indicator – the *growth* of a region's per capita output or income. Although this approach to development has the obvious drawback that qualitative information is lost, it has the indubitable advantage that analytical modelling of the development path becomes possible. In this case, we shall be dealing in what follows with *regional growth theories*. When the analysis instead concerns the tangible and intangible elements (often difficult to formalize) which define and conserve the well-being of a society, we shall be dealing with *local development theories*.

As we shall see, no single definition has been given to the concept of regional growth. Rather, the various theories on the subject pertain to three 'philosophies' which have interpreted economic dynamics. The first, that of the classical (and neoclassical) economists of the eighteenth and nineteenth centuries, interprets the growth process in terms of productive efficiency, of the division of labour in a Smithian sense, and of production factor productivity, and hence examines the dynamics of wages, incomes, and individual well-being. The second philosophy adopts a short-term view of growth and concentrates on the exploitation of given and unused capital resources and of large labour reserves. The third philosophy – the most modern of them – interprets the growth path as a problem concerning competitiveness and long-term dynamics and therefore takes the constant innovation of an economic system to be essential for development patterns.

We can use these three philosophies and their three views of the economic dynamic to classify the theories analysed later into three groups and highlight their normative aims.

The theories belonging to the first group aim to identify the *factors that generate employment and income* in a local system over the short period. They hypothesize the existence of unused production capacity (capital stock) and large labour reserves. In these conditions, local economic growth does not depend on the structure and dynamic of supply (which by definition is able to expand and respond rapidly to market requirements); rather, it is driven by growing demand for locally produced goods which exerts an income multiplier effect through increases in consumption and employment.[1] This was the definition given to growth by the first theories of the 1950s (see Chapter 5), which presupposed a problem of unemployment.

A second group of theories seeks to identify the economic mechanisms which enable a region to move out of poverty, start along a growth path, and ensure a certain level of *well-being and per capita income for its inhabitants*. Growth is a problem of individual well-being to be addressed in two ways: by acting upon factor productivity, thereby obtaining increases in real per capita wages and incomes, and by fostering processes of production specialization which yield advantages deriving from the purchase of goods on interregional markets at prices lower than they would be if the goods were produced internally to the region. These theories also comprise the notion of relative growth – of divergence/convergence in levels and rates of growth among regions – in that they measure the magnitude and trend of disparities among per capita incomes.[2] Growth was viewed in this way by most of the theories developed in the 1960s (see Chapter 6). Problems of poverty, underdevelopment, and inequalities in the spatial distribution of income are the normative aspects of concern to these models.

The theories in the third group embrace a more modern conception of growth. They investigate the local conditions that enable the economic system to achieve high levels *of competitiveness and innovativeness* and, more crucially, to maintain those levels over time. Growth is defined as an increase in a region's real production capacity and its ability to maintain that increase. This conception is adopted by present-day theories and models of regional growth (see Chapters 7 to 10).

This classification is useful for two reasons. First, it prevents the attribution to theories and models of aims that they do not in fact set for themselves. For example, it is wrong and misleading to think that theories which seek to identify processes of employment growth on the assumption of given but unused resources are able to suggest policies for long-term development. Indeed, it is hazardous to base normative action intended to foster a long-term dynamic on theories which concern themselves with the short period.

Second, the distinction drawn by the above classification of conceptions of growth dispels some apparent contradictions in theories and models of regional development. According to the conception of short-period income growth, an increase in exports is a development mechanism because it creates income. Yet from the viewpoint of individual well-being, it removes goods from final consumption and consequently hampers growth. Likewise, when development is viewed in terms of a short-period increase in income, emigration from a region is a cost because it deprives the area of effective demand (although it does so only at the level of subsistence consumption). But if the concern is with individual well-being, emigration is viewed as a positive factor in a region's development because it redresses imbalances (and consequently inefficiencies and income differentials) in the local labour market. On this view, surplus labour has nil marginal productivity and tends to spend any increase in income on consumption, rather than on savings and production investments.[3] Far from being a resource for production development, it is an obstacle to growth, and its reduction statistically increases per capita income.[4] Finally, if the focus is on an area's potential for long-period development, the population is once again viewed as a resource which should not be wasted on emigration.

The element that triggers the growth process can be deduced from these various interpretations of development. A short-period increase in income can be straightforwardly achieved through growth in demand for locally produced goods and services. The latter takes the form of effective sectoral demand, also external to the local economy and possibly dynamic, which sets off a virtuous 'demand/supply' mechanism through Keynesian multiplier effects on income. In this case, the engine of development is *demand*. From this point of view, therefore, no consideration is made of the ability of supply to keep up with growing demand, given the assumption that there are no limits on local production capacity. But although this assumption may well be realistic in the short period, it is unsustainable in the long one. By contrast, if the focus is on individual well-being and long-period competitiveness, the engine of development must necessarily lie on the *supply* side, and specifically in the availability of production factors (labour, capital, entrepreneurship), and in the absolute and comparative advantages of the local firms which determine an area's production capacity and its position on the world market.

Finally, it is evident that those who set out to analyse development and growth must necessarily assume a dynamic perspective, whatever conception of development they may have – short- or long-period, posited on employment, on per capita income and individual well-being, or on competitiveness.

In order to simplify their formal treatment, less recent models often assume that the effects of development only last for the period in which they arise. The use of a single-period framework makes it possible to employ *static or comparative static models* in which changes in the levels of the variables, in a single period, come about independently of the time variable. More recently, however, much use has been made of *dynamic, initially linear, models* which enable analysis of how equilibrium conditions change over time. In this case, reference is no longer made to static equilibrium conditions defined by the *level* of a certain variable. Rather, the intention is to identify stationary equilibrium conditions in which it is the *rate of growth of the variable* that remains constant over time. *Stable or unstable dynamic equilibria* can be identified according to whether the system is able to return to equilibrium when it has deviated from the equilibrium growth rate, or whether it has departed from it permanently. Most recently, regional development has been studied using non-linear dynamic models which yield, as we shall see,[5] multiple, stable or unstable, oscillating or even 'chaotic' equilibria. It would be of great interest if proof were forthcoming that the results on equilibrium stability obtained with a static or dynamic linear model change when non-linearities are introduced into the structural relations that characterize the model. This outcome would demonstrate that the traditional dichotomy between 'divergence theories' and 'convergence theories', so often stressed in the literature and economics handbooks, has been superseded.

THE DIFFERENT CONCEPTIONS OF SPACE

A further important element in understanding the theories and models set out in the literature is the rather different *conception of space* that they use, for it plays a crucial role in identification of growth determinants.

The earliest theories of regional development were growth theories which sought to explain trends in income and employment over the short and medium-to-long period. To do so they abandoned the concept of physical-metric space employed by location theory and replaced it with a notion of *uniform-abstract* space – a space in which supply conditions (factor endowment, sectoral and productive structure) and demand conditions (consumer tastes and preferences) are identical everywhere in the region. This is the case of the neoclassical theories of regional growth, the export-base theory, and the theory of factor endowments, all of which, with this definition of space, deliberately disregard any economic diversity within a region. They instead hypothesize a uniform territory in which production processes have no cumulative and synergic effects, and in which there are none of the agglomeration economies that instead play such a major role in the location theories examined in previous chapters.

A space of this kind allows local growth phenomena to be interpreted using macroeconomic models adapted to the specificities of the local area. In fact, on the assumption of a uniform-abstract space in which the economic variables assume the same values throughout the region (conceived as a point in space), it is possible to stylize the region's economic behaviour in aggregate macroeconomic models and theories. The analyst is thus able to predict the economy's development on the basis of interactions among certain variables (for example, the propensity to import or to consume, or the capital/output ratio). These theories are *theories of regional growth* which seek to interpret the trend of a synthetic development indicator like income, with an inevitable loss of qualitative information but the undoubted advantage that they make it possible to model the development path analytically.

This conception of space was adopted by the first theories of regional growth. These theories were facilitated in their task of interpreting local development paths by already well-established economic approaches, although these had to be adapted to specific interpretative needs. The neoclassical theory of regional development, the Harrod–Domar model, and the theory of factor endowments discussed in this part of the book derive in fact from macroeconomics, neoclassical economics, development economics, and the economics of international trade. These theories view economic growth as driven by economic differences among regions and by the interregional relations generated by those differences: weak regions with poor factor endowments, low resources productivity and limited production capacity are matched by regions with high endowments of capital, technologies, and know-how.

A second interpretation of space is comprised in the notion of *diversified-relational* space. Unlike the previous interpretation, this one hypothesizes the existence of marked polarities in geographical space, and of specificities in the relationships among people, society, and the territory on which development is based. This conception of space both allows and requires analysis to shift from a macroeconomic and macro-territorial approach to a micro-territorial and micro-behavioural one. These theories can therefore be defined as theories of development which seek not so much to explain a rate of aggregate growth of income or output as to identify all the elements – tangible and intangible, exogenous or endogenous – that characterize the development process. This conception of space is adopted by the theories examined in the next part of the book (Part 3). The growth pole theory, analysis of the role of multinational companies in local development, and studies on the diffusion of innovation in space, endeavour to identify the (exogenous) causes of territorial polarities on which development depends. The heavy emphasis placed upon the role of local relations in development explains why these theories conceive space as 'relational' as well as diversified. Such relations are local input–output relationships between a leader firm and other local firms, between a large multinational company and the local industrial system, between innovators (external to the region) and local imitators.

This interpretation of space is expressed most forcefully by theories on industrial districts, *milieux*, or 'learning regions' which look for the endogenous determinants of development. These theories maintain that cumulative development processes stem from the concentration itself of activities in space. This is the source of economic and social relations

89

which – facilitated and strengthened by proximity – act upon the productivity and innovativeness of local firms. Once again, the emphasis on local economic and social relations leads to definition of space as a relational space. For these theories, it is territorial concentration itself that generates development and the increasing returns which (in the form of agglomeration economies) make the growth process self-fuelling and give rise to a virtuous circle of development. However, development is selective: it only comes about in areas where the spatial concentration of production exerts its positive effects on the efficiency parameters of production processes. Space thus becomes an independent economic resource and production factor. It generates static and dynamic advantages for the firms situated within it; and it crucially determines the competitiveness of a local production system.

Because theories of endogenous development are mainly concerned with externalities, and localization and 'district' economies, we may say that they represent the 'core' of regional economics – the hub of the discipline where location theories and development most closely interweave and merge. These theories permit definitive abandonment of the notion of *competitive* development (embraced by some neoclassical theories of the 1960s), which derived from the simple regional distribution of an aggregate growth rate, and the adoption instead of a notion of *generative* development where the national growth rate is the sum of the growth rates of individual regions.

Finally, the most recent theories (described in the last part of the book) conceive space as *diversified-stylized* in that it comprises development-generating polarities. These polarities have no territorial dimension, however, because they are stylized into simple points in space. This conception has been adopted by the theories of new geographical economics and endogenous growth theories, and it enables them to construct elegant economic models which include the synergies and cumulative feedback processes that arise in space. Because polarities are punctiform, they can be handled by traditional macroeconomic models (in fact, they once again become regional growth models), while economic growth is selective and cumulative because of the presence of increasing returns which stylize the advantages of concentrated location.

This new conception of space has partly resolved the problem from which regional development theories have always suffered: their inability to construct formal models which combine specifically territorial features, like externalities and agglomeration economies, with macroeconomic laws and processes of growth. However, it should be pointed out that the assumption of a stylized rather than relational space deprives the polarities envisaged by such models of a territorial dimension able to give space – through synergy, cooperation, relationality and collective learning – an active role in the growth process. The introduction of agglomeration advantages in stylized form, through increasing returns, cancels out the territorial dimension. In so doing it divests these theories of the aspect of greatest importance to regional economists: namely space as territory defined as a system of localized technological externalities, or as a set of material and non-material factors which by virtue of proximity and reduced transaction costs act upon firms' productivity and innovativeness.[6] Finding a way to incorporate the territorial dimension into theories already able to merge physical-metric, uniform-abstract and diversified space is the challenge that now faces regional economists.

Before early theories of regional growth are described, this chapter reviews the theories that have identified the *industrial structure* and *geographical location* as the *preconditions for local development*. These are theories which seek to determine the tangible and intangible elements necessary for the growth process to begin.

They conceive space as uniform but not abstract (here the reference is to the theory of the stages of development, and to the theory which associates phases of development with levels of regional disparity). By identifying the economic and social characteristics of the development path, in fact, they deal with a real rather than abstract space, although they still treat the territory as being internally uniform.

These theories are of interest for their simplicity, and also for their long-sightedness. They contain in embryonic form the development-generating factors – local production specialization, transport infrastructures, capital, advanced services, location close to large outlet markets – which later theories would amplify and elaborate.

As we shall see, these theories link closely with those on underdevelopment (for example the theory of the stages of development), and in so far as they take their theoretical framework from these theories, they share their strengths and weaknesses.

THE THEORY OF THE STAGES OF DEVELOPMENT

One of the earliest theories of development applicable to territories of all sizes – from nations to regions to local economies – is the theory of stages of development. This was the earliest attempt by location theorists to combine analysis of the location patterns of firms with interpretation of the effects of location choices on development.[7]

The simplicity of the theory is both its strength and its weakness. It depicts regional development as a natural sequence of phases, each characterized by growing factor productivity and an increasing capital/labour ratio which yield ever higher levels of well-being and per capita wealth.[8]

The theory identifies the following sequence of development stages:

1 *autarky*, when the local economic system is self-sufficient within a subsistence economy: everything produced locally is used (and produced in sufficient quantities) for local consumption;
2 *specialization*, when the creation of transport infrastructures makes trade in agricultural goods possible and the local economy begins to specialize in certain primary goods;
3 *transformation* of the local economy from agriculture to industry as a result of the take-off of industrial activities closely connected with the processing of primary goods (agricultural and mining products), and with the needs of a growing population (building construction). These industrial activities often develop on the basis of knowledge and expertise external to the area;
4 *diversification* of manufacturing activity due to increasing demand for intermediate goods, the growth of income, and the consequent appearance of new sectors catering to the consumption needs of a growing and increasingly diversified population;
5 *tertiarization*, the expansion of tertiary activities in response to what has by now grown into an advanced industrial system.

91

This simple theory captures a number of important features of a development process. First, it highlights the productive specialization which – according to the standard Smithian conception of the division of labour – is the source of greater labour productivity. Productivity increases derive from what have been termed 'roundabout methods': increasingly indirect production processes divided into vertically specialized phases, cycles and processes which enable the simplification and mechanization of every production phase.[9] As a result of debate within development theory on the underdeveloped countries, this theory has also emphasized the importance for development of the simultaneous growth of diverse sectors and infrastructures in a process of 'balanced development'. The latter has a number of advantages and externalities[10] deemed to be the main sources of increasing returns at territorial level, and the engine of local growth. The most significant of them are the following:

- externalities deriving from *interdependencies among sectors* which, via input–output linkages, ensure development of the local economy as a whole if there is an initial growth impulse in a single sector;[11]
- externalities arising from *interdependencies between demand and supply* which generate cumulative development processes based on a growth of supply in line with the preferences structure of local consumers;[12]
- externalities arising from *investments in different infrastructures* for integrated projects selected on the basis of the infrastructural needs of local demand, whether this is planned or even only potential. Investments in transport infrastructures are of particular importance because expansion of the market controlled by local firms depends on them.[13]

According to this theory, underdevelopment is an area's forced persistence in a particular phase.[14] The causes of this situation are conditions internal and external to the area. The internal ones relate to a lack of the sources of territorial-level increasing returns just mentioned. If a local economy does not have sufficient savings to invest in capital or infrastructures, or if its market is too small, its productivity level will remain extremely low and will fuel a vicious circle of underdevelopment – limited market expansion, low savings and low consumption, reduced stock of capital in the economy, and low income (Figure 4.1). Besides an insufficient critical mass of demand, savings and infrastructures, there are various external constraints that operate as well. If the region belongs to a system of more developed regions, it is likely that demand/supply interactions or sectoral interdependencies, stimulated by internal demand for relatively advanced products, will be set in motion externally to the region. The leakages to more advanced regions may be so strong that they restrict the local effects of expansion in demand – a risk, as we shall see, that other theories of regional development have considered carefully.[15]

The proponents of 'balanced development' accordingly suggest that, in early phases, development policies should channel public investments into a few large and diversified sectors with significant weights at local level (strong sectors). The purpose is twofold: (a) to minimize leakages to advanced areas and (b) to remedy the insufficient saving formation typical of backward economies. Later, when the take-off of the strong sectors has expanded private resources, a share of public investments may be directed to other sectors.

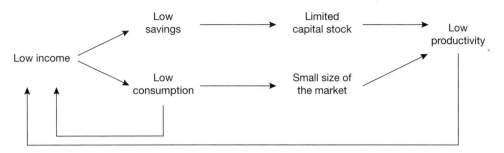

Figure 4.1 *The vicious circle of underdevelopment*

This simple theory highlights a number of important features of the development process: the role of infrastructures and their development, with particular regard to demand; the role of the production specialization at the basis of increasing returns in factor productivity; and the importance of transport in increasing the size of the market and production. However, it is rather difficult to accept the idea that development moves through necessarily identical stages in all regions, when these are characterized by different economic, social and historical conditions; and, moreover, when they are embedded in very different economic contexts. In light of these considerations, we shall see how the economist Douglass North rejected the idea of a natural development process and developed his export-base theory, furnishing a more convincing explanation of the development of the western American regions in the 1950s.[16]

STAGES OF DEVELOPMENT AND DISPARITIES

In the mid-1960s, J. G. Williamson reprised the idea that development proceeds through stages and analysed how regional disparities evolve within a country.[17]

Williamson's thesis, with which other regional economists agree,[18] is that development in its early stages is concentrated and polarized in a country's central area. Only subsequently does it spread to more peripheral areas and to weaker sectors. The consequence of this 'two-speed' development is that the regional gap widens in the early phases of a country's economic development, and then narrows when the national income reaches a certain level. It therefore follows an inverted U-shaped trajectory (Figure 4.2).

The reasons for the widening gap between strong and weak regions in the early phases of development relate to to the following well-known 'crowding-out' effects which favour the strong economy over the weak one:

- emigration of skilled labour from weak areas to strong ones;
- capital flows to the wealthier regions, to which they are attracted by higher demand, by the availability of infrastructures, services and a potential market, and by better environmental conditions for firms;
- allocation of a larger share of public investments to strong areas, in response to explicit actual or potential demand;
- limited interregional trade in resources, so that, in early stages, the rich area does not exert pull effects on the poor one.

93

Over time, these processes exacerbate regional disparities within a country until mechanisms working in the opposite direction begin to operate, for example:

- the creation of new jobs in less developed areas, as well, with the consequence that emigration diminishes or even ceases;
- reduced attractiveness of the more advanced areas due to the saturation of markets and physical congestion, with the consequent prohibitive costs of land and an inevitable fall in the average profit rate;
- growth of public investments in the weak areas, which has a twofold effect: the birth of a local production system which requires major investments in social capital, and the growth of private investments in the strong areas;
- the onset of pull effects exerted by the strong area on the weak one.

Although the empirical evidence confirms that regional disparities increase during the early phases of a country's development, it does not bear out the hypothesis that the growth differentials subsequently diminish. The theory therefore seems excessively optimistic in its interpretation of disparities as following a natural, deterministic and universal law. Technological progress, social changes, and the evolution of knowledge are all factors which may give advanced regions a greater capacity to attract capital and labour from the weaker regions, and to obtain public investments in modern social capital and advanced infrastructures (e.g. hub airports, high-speed trains). Consequently, in the advanced regions, the frontier of decreasing returns on investments is reached at higher levels of income. In graphic terms, this means that the U-curve of regional disparities moves rightwards and upwards, as in Figure 4.2, so that, given a level of income Y', the country may find itself with a higher level of regional disparities: E' rather than E''.

It is also likely that development in the weak regions will come about on the basis of 'traditional' industries which require non-innovative production processes and standard technologies – as implied by Vernon's life-cycle theory.[19] Accordingly, the gap between the leader and follower regions may persist in qualitative rather than quantitative terms.

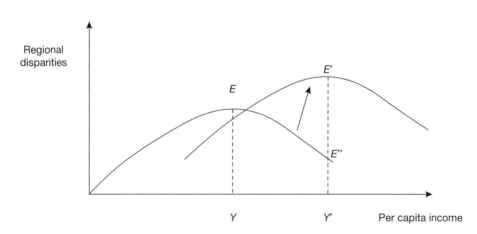

Figure 4.2 Williamson's curve of regional disparities

INDUSTRIAL STRUCTURE AND REGIONAL GROWTH: SHIFT-SHARE ANALYSIS

Its simplicity notwithstanding, the theory of development stages yielded an important finding, which analysts reprised and amplified at the end of the 1950s: the sectoral composition of a region explains its rate of growth. Given their low levels of factor productivity and small capital/labour ratios, mainly agricultural regions experience low growth rates, whilst industrialized regions, by contrast, record high factor productivities and therefore high rates of development.

However, when the sectoral structure of a region is taken to be the main determinant of economic growth, some of the simplifications in the above line of reasoning must be removed. Interpretation of a region's growth rate solely in terms of sectoral composition aggregated into only three sectoral macro-categories (agriculture, industry and services) – as in the theory of the stages of development – entails the hypotheses that each sector within a macro-category has the same productivity, and that the latter does not vary according to the region in which the sector produces.

It is obvious that both these hypotheses are somewhat unrealistic. Sectors in a particular macro-category have very different productivities. Consider, within the category 'industry', the differing capital intensities (capital/labour ratios) that distinguish heavy industries (chemicals, pharmaceuticals) from light industries such as textiles, clothing and food. It is likewise evident that a sector located in two regions which differ in their infrastructure endowments, quality of production factors, and technological knowledge will achieve different levels of productivity in the two regions.

At the end of the 1950s these considerations prompted a group of economists to develop more composite analysis of the relation between production structure and regional growth. This gave rise to the well-known statistical method for determining a region's relative growth rate known as 'shift-share analysis'.[20]

The theory's basic idea is that the regional growth rate is influenced by three factors: the industrial structure, sector productivity, and the dynamics of demand and consumer preferences.

On the assumptions that the same sectors have the same productivities regardless of their location, and that the region has the same sectoral composition as the country as a whole, the region's rate of growth should be equal to that of the country. However, the regional growth rate often differs from the value that it should assume were it to grow at the same rate as that of the country. In formal terms, it is equal to:

$$y_r = y^* + s \qquad (4.1)$$

where y denotes the income growth rate, r the region, and s the difference between the national and regional growth rates, while the asterisk on the variable y indicates the growth rate that the region should achieve if it is to be the same as that of the country as a whole. The difference between the national and regional growth rates – called 'shift' (s) – may depend on two effects: first, the *composition effect* (proportion effect) exerted by the region's sectoral structure – also termed the 'MIX effect' – and deriving from the presence in the region of sectors with more marked dynamics at national level due to increasing demand in those sectors. The composition effect can be measured as:

$$\text{MIX} = \sum_{i=1}^{n} \frac{E_{ir}^0}{E_r^0} \left(\frac{E_{in}^1}{E_{in}^0} - \frac{E_n^1}{E_n^0} \right) \tag{4.2}$$

where E represents the sectoral variable analysed (employment or value added), i denotes the sector, while n and r respectively stand for the country and the region. The term in brackets measures the difference, in the period of time from 0 to 1, between national-level employment in sector i and the average national increase in employment. This is multiplied by the relative weight of the sector in the local economy. The record effect is the *competition effect* (differential shift) of the region's sectoral structure – or the 'DIF effect' – which derives from the regional economy's capacity to develop each of its sectors at greater average rates than those achieved by the corresponding national sectors. The DIF effect can be calculated as follows:

$$\text{DIF} = \sum_{i=1}^{n} \frac{E_{ir}^0}{E_r^0} \left(\frac{E_{ir}^1}{E_{ir}^0} - \frac{E_{in}^1}{E_{in}^0} \right) \tag{4.3}$$

In this case the term in brackets measures the increase in sector i at regional level compared to the increase in the same sector at national level. As in the case of the MIX effect, the increase is multiplied by the sector's relative weight in the local economy.

When applied at a disaggregated sectoral level to a region, the shift-share analysis highlights the aspects that the theory of the stages of development simplistically ignored: on the one hand, the differing productivity of the same sector in different areas (measured by the DIF effect); on the other, each sector's contribution to regional growth differentials. The strength of this approach is its ability to distinguish between structural factors (MIX effect) and short-term ones (DIF effect) in regional growth differentials, and to isolate those that drive regional development: demand-side elements measured by the MIX effect on the one hand, and supply-side elements of local competitiveness measured by the DIF effect on the other.

It is possible to illustrate the foregoing analysis by means of a graph where the national rate of employment growth (although other sectoral variables, like value added, can be used) is plotted on the X-axis, and the regional one on the Y-axis. Each sector is represented by a point indicating its growth at the national and regional level respectively. Moreover, by showing the average national and regional growth rates on the graph, and by drawing a 45-degree line from the origin (along which the sectors record a rate of regional growth equal to the national rate), it is possible to mark out different areas representing different development conditions (Figure 4.3).

Development conditions favourable to the region are represented by a large number of sectors lying above the 45-degree line (areas *A*, *D* and *E*): these represent a capacity for local growth superior to the national capacity, and therefore a favourable DIF effect. In this case, development is driven by the competitiveness of the local sectors. Positive growth conditions are represented by a large number of sectors to the right of the line representing the national sectoral average (areas *A*, *B* and *C*): these are sectors which achieve growth rates above the national average. Specialization by the region in these sectors denotes local

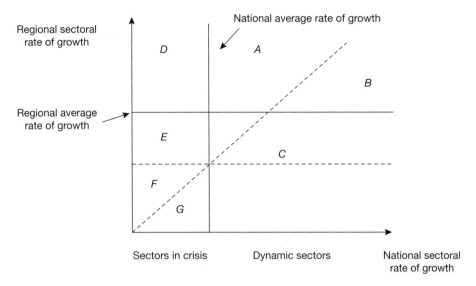

Figure 4.3 *Relative sectoral development: composition and competition effects (shift-share analysis)*

Source: Camagni 1992a, p. 165

growth driven by increasing demand at national level: that is, by a favourable MIX effect. Conditions favourable to a region's growth are represented by a large number of sections occupying area *A* of the graph, which indicates that both the MIX and DIF effects are favourable; or area *B*, where the regional dynamic is weaker but nevertheless sufficient to maintain a generally high level of development: these, in fact, are sectors above the regional average. Conditions equally positive for a region are represented by a large number of sectors located in areas *D* and *E*, where the competitiveness of local sectors is sufficiently high to offset the 'crisis' in which the sectors find themselves at national level. Limited national demand for these goods is more than offset by the competitiveness of local firms, which are able to conserve and increase their market shares. This was the case of the Italian industrial districts in the 1970s, when they maintained positive growth rates despite the general crisis which hit the economies of the industrialized countries after the oil shocks.[21] Crisis conditions for a local economy are instead represented by a large number of sectors in areas *F* and *G* of Figure 4.3: these are sectors in crisis at the national level and which have even lower growth rates at the local one. Also indicative of a crisis is the presence of a large number of sectors in area *C*, where the growth of national demand is not enough to off-set the limited competitiveness of local sectors.

The usefulness of graphics in depicting the results of shift-share analysis is demonstrated by Figure 4.4, which shows such analysis applied to three different geographical areas.[22] One can see at a glance the differences in competitive capacities recorded between 1995 and 2001 for the European areas of Vienna (Austria), Provence (France) and South Yorkshire (UK). Vienna and South Yorkshire show a clearly unfavourable DIF in numerous sectors; Provence instead has a large number of sectors with local growth rates superior to national ones (Figure 4.4 a, b and c).

(a)

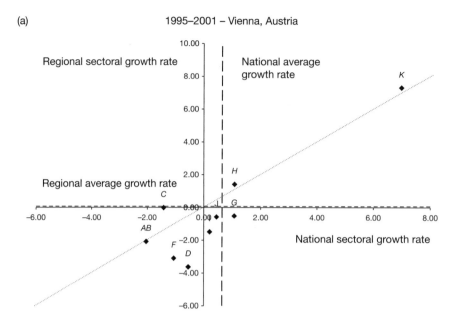

(b)

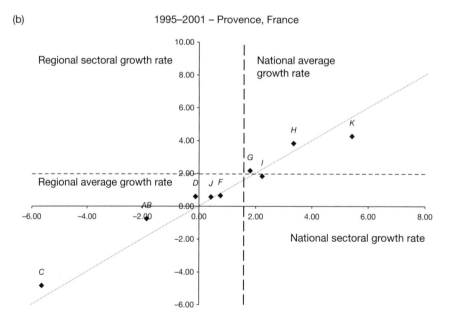

Figure 4.4 Relative sectoral development: composition and competition effects (shift-share analysis) in three different geographical areas

Source: Our elaborations on Eurostat REGIO data

(c)

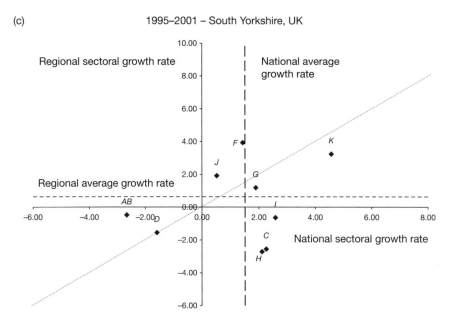

NACE classification of sectors:

A, B Agriculture, hunting, forestry and fishing
C   Mining and quarrying
D   Manufacturing
F   Construction
G   Wholesale and retail trade; repair of motor vehicles, motorcycles and personal and household goods
H   Hotels and restaurants
I   Transport, storage and communication
J   Financial intermediation
K   Real estate, renting and business activities

Source: our elaborations on Eurostat REGIO data

Figure 4.4 *Relative sectoral development: composition and competition effects (shift-share analysis) in three different geographical areas (continued)*

The limitations of this method are well known. The results are highly sensitive to the degree of sectoral disaggregation used in the analysis, and also to the method employed to calculate the region's weight relative to the country.[23] Moreover, the method is purely descriptive: it is entirely unable to explain the relative performances of regions. Its application, in fact, only allows analysis of the growth conditions of regions; it cannot be used to show the causes of their development paths. Identification of the determinants of growth is still the primary goal of all theories of regional development, and it is to these that the following chapters are devoted.

THE CENTRALITY/PERIPHERALITY APPROACH

Strictly geographical in nature,[24] the centrality/peripherality approach regards distance from the centre of economic activities as the cause of delayed development. The approach originated in Walter Isard's 1950s theory of development potential, and in H. Giersch's analysis

99

of the barycentric location of core European regions, which was subsequently reprised by J. Friedmann in his theories of underdevelopment.[25]

The simplicity of this approach is also its strength. It simply points out that geographic centrality is in itself a factor fostering development, while peripherality hampers it. Access to information, technological knowledge, outlet markets of goods, and markets for production factors are a necessary condition for the growth of a local market, while peripherality – defined as the distance from a hypothetical economic centre (or 'core') – entails higher transport costs for finished goods, raw materials, semi-finished goods, greater costs of information acquisition, delays in the adoption of innovations: all of which features hamper income growth and competitiveness.

This model works very well for Europe, where a strong, developed and highly industrialized centre has formed over time, contrasting with more peripheral, less dynamic and more backward areas. Mediterranean regions, but also Nordic ones, or regions in Western Europe, have always recorded lower levels of development than have central regions. The European Union's 'Objective 1' covers the least advanced regions in the Union, and all of them are geographically peripheral. However, it is not always the case that the geographical centre of a country is also its economic centre. Consider the United States: a country with a less developed 'centre', and where geographically peripheral regions located on the coasts comprise the country's main economic activities, areas of development and wealth.

CONCLUSIONS

This chapter has reviewed the second broad area of analysis conducted by regional economics: regional growth and development. It has shown the difference between growth theories and development theories, the former being concerned to explain trends in a single indicator, a region's per capita income; the latter to analyse trends in the tangible and intangible aspects of development. It has also examined the different definitions given to the concept of growth or development: this can be conceived as short-term growth of employment and income, growth of well-being and per capita income, or long-period growth of competitiveness. Identifying how theories conceive growth aids the comprehension of theories, and the removal of apparent contradictions among them. Also important for understanding the theories and models of regional economics is the concept of space. This differs considerably, ranging from uniform-abstract space (which represents a geographical-administrative conception of space) to diversified-relational space (where territorial factors account for local development) to diversified-stylized space. This last conception hypothesizes development-generating polarities, and therefore the existence of agglomeration economies and increasing returns in growth processes, but it removes the spatial dimension from those polarities. By so doing, it enables space to be incorporated into macroeconomic models of growth; yet at the same time it deprives space of an active role in explanation of development. The chapter has concluded by outlining the early theories that sought to explain the conditions necessary for growth to come about.

REVIEW QUESTIONS

1   What is the difference between regional growth and local development?

2   Which are the different interpretations of growth given in the different theories of local development and regional growth?

3   Why is it sensible to divide theories on the basis of their conception of growth?

4   Which are the different conceptions of space in the different theories?

5   Which are the strengths and weaknesses of the stages of development?

6   What do the MIX and DIF effects measure? How are they calculated?

7   Would you define shift-share analysis as an interpretative or a descriptive methodology?

SELECTED READING ON EMPIRICAL FINDINGS

About accessibility and regional development

Bruinsma, F. R. and Rietveld, P. (1993) 'Urban agglomerations in European infrastructure networks', *Urban Studies*, vol. 30, pp. 919–34.

Bruinsma, F. R. and Rietveld, P. (1998) 'The accessibility of European cities: theoretical framework and comparison of approaches', *Environment and Planning A*, vol. 30, pp. 499–521.

Capello, R. (2006) 'Knowledge and accessibility for regional cohesion in the enlarged Europe', special issue of *Scienze Regionali – Italian Journal of Regional Science*, vol. 5, no. 2

Handy, S. L. (1997) 'Measuring accessibility: an exploration of issues and alternatives', *Environment and Planning A*, vol. 29, pp. 1175–94.

Hansen, W. G. (1959) 'How accessibility shapes land use', *Journal of the American Institute of Planners*, vol. 25, pp. 73–6.

Linneker, B. J. and Spence, N. A. (1992) 'Accessibility measures compared in an analysis of the impact of the M25 London Orbital Motorway on Britain', *Environment and Planning A*, vol. 24, pp. 1137–54.

Shen, Q. (1998) 'Location characteristics of inner-city neighbourhoods and employment accessibility of low-wage workers', *Environment and Planning B*, vol. 25, pp. 345–65.

Spiekermann, K. and Wegener, M. (2006) 'Accessibility and spatial development in Europe', *Scienze Regionali – Italian Journal of Regional Science*, vol. 5, no. 2, pp. 15–46.

Vickerman, R., Spiekermann, K. and Wegener, M. (1999) 'Accessibility and economic development in Europe', *Regional Studies*, vol. 33, pp. 1–15.

Vickerman, R. W. (1996) 'Location, accessibility and regional development: the appraisal of trans-European networks', *Transport Policy*, no. 2, pp. 225–34.

About the shift-share analysis

Andrikopoulos, A., Brox, A. J. and Carvalho, E. (1990) 'Shift-share analysis and the potential for predicting regional growth patterns: some evidence for the region of Quebec, Canada', available on line.

Barf, R. A. and Knight III, P. (1988) 'Dynamic shift-share analysis', *Growth and Change*, vol. 19, no. 2, pp. 1–9.

Fritz, O. and Streicher, G. (2005) 'Measuring changes in regional competitiveness over time. A shift-share regression exercise', Working Papers 243, WIFO Publications.

Lasuen, J. R. (1971) 'Venezuela: an industrial shift-share analysis 1941–1961', *Regional and Urban Economics*, vol. 1, no. 2, pp. 153–220.

Ray, M. A. and Harvey, J. T. (1995) 'Employment changes in the European Economic Community: a shift-share analysis', *Review of Regional Studies*, vol. 25, no. 1, pp. 97–110.

FURTHER READING

Capello, R. (2006) 'Knowledge and accessibility for regional cohesion in the enlarged Europe', special issue of *Scienze Regionali – Italian Journal of Regional Science*, vol. 5, no. 2.

Friedmann, J. (1966) *Regional development policy: a case study of Venezuela*, Cambridge, Mass.: MIT Press.

Isard, W. (1954) 'Location theory and trade theory: short run analysis', *Quarterly Journal of Economics*, vol. 68, no. 2, pp. 305–20.

Keeble, D., Owens, P. L. and Thompson, C. (1982) 'Regional accessibility and economic potential in the European Community', *Regional Studies*, vol. 16, pp. 419–32.

Perloff, H., Dunn, E., Lampard, E. and Muth, R. (1960) *Regions, resources and economic growth*, Boltimore: John Hopkins.

Spiekermann, K. and Wegener, M. (2006) 'Accessibility and spatial development in Europe', *Scienze Regionali – Italian Journal of Regional Science*, vol. 5, no. 2, pp. 15–66.

Chapter 5

Demand

SUMMARY

1 Demand and regional growth

2 Interregional relations: accounting aspects and macroeconomic elements

3 The exporter region: the export-base model

4 Estimation of the 'economic base' and of the regional multiplier

5 Input–output analysis

6 The importer region: the Harrod–Domar model

7 Balance of payments and local growth: Thirlwall's Law

DEMAND AND REGIONAL GROWTH

The previous chapter described the conditions necessary for a growth process to begin. The existence of infrastructures and production services, a shift of the productive structure to sectors with greater value added and higher factor productivity, and the access to central markets which breaks down the barriers due to peripheral location: all these factors determine whether a region will be able to move to a growth path.

This chapter begins with an examination of the theories which in the 1950s and 1960s (when regional economics was still in its infancy) investigated the economic determinants of development and the mechanisms that enable a system to grow and achieve higher rates of output, greater levels of per capita income, lower unemployment rates, and higher levels of wealth. We shall see that these models interpret development by using a synthetic indicator: the *growth* of a region's output or per capita income. Although this approach has the indubitable advantage of making analytical modelling of the growth path possible, it requires the assumption of a uniform-abstract space wherein supply conditions (factor endowment, sectoral and productive structure) and demand conditions (consumer tastes and preferences) are everywhere identical and can be expressed with a vector of aggregate socio-economic-demographic characteristics. We may accordingly call the theories examined in this and the next chapter *theories of regional growth*.

There are numerous factors which may trigger a growth process: among them increased demand for locally produced goods; greater local production capacity; a more abundant endowment (quantitative and qualitative) of local resources and production factors; and a larger amount of savings available for investments in infrastructures and technologies intended to increase the efficiency of production processes.

This chapter will examine theories and models which conceive growth as resulting from greater *demand* for locally-produced goods and which adopt the typically Keynesian notion that development consists in the growth of output, income and employment. Acccording to this approach, greater demand for a locally-produced good does not confine its positive effects to employment and the incomes of those employed in the sector producing that good. Because of interdependencies in production and consumption, greater demand also generates increases in employment and income in activities upstream from the expanding sector, and in service activities supplied to the local population as a whole. In the end, therefore, increased demand for a local good gives rise to higher income and employment in the entire area.

These models therefore envisage demand as the engine of growth; a hypothesis quite acceptable to regional economies. Regions are in fact small geographical entities where it is rarely the case that all necessary goods are produced locally; and, conversely, where those goods that are produced frequently exceed local demand for them and are sold on domestic or even international markets (consider the number of cars manufactured in Turin or Detroit: a number certainly excessive to the needs of the city's residents!).

Demand is often external in these models, in fact, and stems from interest in a local good expressed on the world market. Hence, the growth of a region depends on the extent to which its productive structure specializes in goods demanded by consumers world-wide. There are numerous local economic systems in the world whose products are sold inter-nationally: the textiles of Prato (near Florence, in Italy), the glassware of Murano (near Venice, in Italy), the cars of Turin, Detroit or Munich, the olive oil of Greek and Italian regions, the wines of areas in France and Italy, to mention only some. Expansion in demand for the goods produced in these areas determines whether or not the entire territory will grow. As shown by the export-base model (the best-known in this family of theories), increased exports of a good generate greater local production, with positive effects on income and local employment and – via interdependencies in production and consumption – on employment and income in activities upstream and downstream from the production of that good. Considering that consumption usually grows with income, any additional expenditure will be transformed into income, the growth of which will in its turn augment expenditure, in a circular process characterized by increasingly smaller income increments.[1]

Reasoning in terms of demand-driven development has a number of consequences. First, an approach of this kind can only interpret a *short-term* process of growth, because it implic-itly assumes the competitiveness of *current* production and the economic system; an assumption which can only be sustained in the short period.

Second, development is associated with the pursuit of higher levels of employment and income: no consideration is made of either individual well-being or the competitiveness of the local production system. The latter aspect is perhaps the most problematic, in that analysis centred on the demand components assumes the existence of unused capacity (capital stock) and large reserves of labour on which the system can draw to meet increasing demand: in other words, the competitiveness of the local system is taken for granted. Yet this is an assumption that can only hold for the short period. To return to the example of the Detroit (or Turin) car industry, it is true that local income and employment depend on world demand for cars. In the short period, therefore, it is possible to hypothesize that Turin's or Detroit's productive capacity will be able to satisfy increasing demand. But in the long period, the area's development will depend on the car industry's ability to maintain its position on the world market, and to compete on the basis of the quality and innovativeness of its products. These elements, however, are entirely absent from the Keynesian models of demand which will be examined in this chapter.

Given the assumption of surplus in production resources, Keynesian theories should be used with caution when they are employed in interpretation of a long-period growth path – and especially when they are used to devise measures to support a local long-period dynamic. By contrast, when these theories are applied to the specific problem of high unemployment in the presence of given productive capacity, they have two evident merits: the simplicity and rigour of their economic logic, and the ease with which they can be applied to concrete situations. We shall see below that when Keynesian theories shed their short-period perspective and assume a long-term, multi-period one – as exemplified by the Harrod–Domar model – they are able to abandon strictly demand-related aspects and give due importance to supply elements (the availability of savings and capital formation) in the interpretation of growth processes. For all these reasons, Keynesian theories deserve specific treatment in a handbook on regional economics.

INTERREGIONAL RELATIONS: ACCOUNTING ASPECTS AND MACROECONOMIC ELEMENTS

The regional balance of payments

The growth models described in this and the next chapter argue that, whilst countries can rely on their internal capabilities to develop, regions are economic systems of small size and therefore have only limited markets for both goods and production factors. Moreover, because their productive structures are often highly specialized, their economic systems produce a surplus of specialized goods but are unable to furnish the local market with a wide range of resources and physical capital, which must therefore be wholly or partly purchased on external markets.

The relations that a regional economic system establishes with the rest of the world influence its development, and the economic mechanisms underlying these exchanges determine the macroeconomic conditions which accompany the region's growth path. All these intertwined aspects can be easily understood by looking at the social accounting systems used to record the relations of an economic system (at national or regional level) with the rest of the world, and the effects of these relations on the levels of production, income and capital formation.

The *balance of payments* is the accounting instrument which records, at aggregate level, all the economic and financial transactions undertaken by a regional system with the rest of the world in a particular period of time, for example one year. It is compiled for national systems, but it can also be drawn up in simplified form for regional systems. In the latter case, too, it is an important logical device, and it will prove useful for understanding the models which follow.

A balance of payments consists of three distinct parts, in each of which receipts and payments are recorded (Table 5.1). The first is the *current account*, which is divided into the trade balance, services balance, and unilateral transfers. The trade balance records the values of exports (credits) and imports (debits).[2] Entered among receipts in the services balance is expenditure within the region by non-residents (e.g. tourists from outside the region), and among payments, expenditure by residents external to the region. Also recorded as receipts are all revenues generated by local production factors outside the region (residents working in neighbouring regions, the profits of resident-owned businesses operating externally), and as payments, the earnings of production factors which produce in the region. Finally, the current account also includes, under the heading 'unilateral transfers', the region's gratuitous receipts or payments: the former include transfers by the central government to the region in the form of pensions, unemployment benefits, development aid, and remittances by emigrants (funds sent regularly by emigrants to their families in the region); the latter consist of remittances sent by immigrants to other regions: in the case of wealthy regions with a large number of immigrant workers, this item may be conspicuous. The sum of the trade balance, the services balance and unilateral transfers is the current account balance: that is, the balance of all the *real* transactions undertaken by the region with the rest of the world.

The second component of the balance of payments, the *capital account*, records financial transactions in regard to the opening of debits or credits for payment of the goods recorded in the trade balance, and direct investments by or to the region. These investments take a variety of forms: as receipts, investments by state-owned enterprises, investments by privately-owned firms in the region, investments in property assets; and, conversely, public and private investments outside the region as payments.

The third component of the balance of payments, termed the *balancing account*, records the monetary counterparts (inflows and outflows of money) of the transactions in goods or capital performed by the region.

Individual transactions are recorded by means of the double-entry system. This is a method which records a credit and a debit for every transaction undertaken. For example, a purchase of goods from another region to the amount of 100,000 euros is recorded as a credit under the heading 'imports' in the trade account, and at the same time as a debit of 100,000 euros in the balancing account. If the same goods were bought with a business loan, the purchase would still be recorded as imports in the trade balance, but the loan would enter among the receipts of the capital account. Because of the double-entry principle, therefore, the balance (the difference between the totals of the credit and debit columns of an account) of the entire balance of payments is always zero: the overall balance is always 'in balance'.

Table 5.1 The regional balance of payments

(a) CURRENT ACCOUNT

Receipts

Payments

(1) Trade balance

1. Value of Goods Exported
- Value of goods exports

1. Value of Goods Imported
- Value of goods imports

(2) Services balance

2. Value of Services Exported
- Expenditures by non-residents for services (e.g. expenditures by tourists in the region)
- Remuneration of employees and property income owned by residents outside the region (e.g. incomes of workers commuting to the region; profits of resident-owned firms located in other regions)

2. Value of Services Imported
- Expenditures by residents for external services (e.g. expenditures by residents on tourism outside the region)
- Remuneration of employees and property income owned by non-residents in the region (e.g. incomes of workers commuting from other regions; profits of non resident-owned local firms)

(3) Unilateral transfers

3. Positive Unilateral Transfers
- Remittances by emigrants
- Public transfers to the region
  - pensions
  - unemployment benefits

3. Negative Unilateral Transfers
- Remittances by immigrants

Current Account Balance: *Receipts – Payments*

(b) CAPITAL ACCOUNT

Credits

Debits

1. Commercial Credits Received by Local Importers
2. Direct Investments from Other Regions and Abroad
- investments by state-controlled enterprises in the region
- investments by private firms located outside the region
- investments in property assets by non-local private firms and public bodies (purchases of buildings and land)

1. Commercial Credits Granted by Local Exporters to External Importers
2. Direct Investments in Other Regions and Abroad
- investments in external property assets (purchases of buildings and land outside the region)
- investments by local firms outside the region

Capital Account Balance: *Receipts – Payments*

(c) BALANCING ACCOUNT

Outflows

Inflows

- Money outflows

- Money inflows

Account Balance: *Receipts – Payments*

The balance of payments and the value of regional output

The individual balances – of trade, services, the current account and the capital account – are used to calculate regional macroeconomic values by means of a series of closely inter-connected social accounting schedules.[3]

The first is the gross domestic product account (or simply 'production account') which summarizes supply and demand items (Table 5.2a).[4] Recorded on the credit side are the region's resources (the value of domestic output and imports), and on the debit side, the uses made of those resources, which may be consumed, invested or exported.[5] A positive balance of payments (due to positive trade and service balances) signifies that a proportion of domestic production has been undertaken for an external market, and it is entered as a component of gross domestic product (the value of local production in a certain period of time), as in Table 5.2a.

A second schedule sets out regional gross disposable income account. For accounting purposes this is defined as the sum of aggregate production, net compensation of employees from outside the region, and unilateral transfers. The gross disposable income is either consumed or saved (Table 5.2b).[6] Public transfers to backward regions increase the gross disposable income via the item 'net current transfers from outside' without influencing gross domestic product.

A third schedule is the capital formation and financial account. Here, receipts consist of internal and external savings and capital transfers, while payments are real (not financial) investments made internally to the region (by local and external firms) and capital account taxes or transfers paid (Table 5.2c). The balance records the internal financial resources in surplus (if the balance is positive) or in deficit (if it is negative). At the level of the aggregate economic system, deficit internal resources must equal the resources obtained from outside the region. Conversely, if internal resources are in surplus, they must equal the resources employed externally to the region. This means that, in accounting terms, the current account balance always equals the balance of the capital formation account.[7]

Macroeconomic conditions in interregional relations

The mechanisms by which interregional relations determine the levels of output (gross domestic product), income (gross disposable income) and capital formation subsume very different macroeconomic conditions. A positive balance of the current and capital accounts – a balance which favours local growth – may in fact result from the following very different circumstances:

(a) a large volume of exports, due to a highly competitive productive system able to finance the imports which the region requires. This situation suggests that positive macroeconomic conditions characterize the region; a competitive productive system, in fact, signals the existence of high levels of real production, employment and income;

(b) large public transfers (which are included among current account items as net current transfers) generating an increase in income but not in local production (gross

Table 5.2 The main social accounts at regional level

(a) Gross Domestic Product Account

Resources	Uses
Gross domestic product at market prices	Final internal consumption
Imports of goods and services	• public
	• private
	Final consumption by other regions
	• public
	• private
	Gross fixed capital formation
	• net fixed capital formation
	• depreciation
	Changes in inventories
	Exports of goods and services

(b) Gross Disposable Income Account

Sources	Uses
Gross domestic product at market prices	Final internal consumption
+ *Net compensation of employees*	• private
and property income	• public
from outside the region	
Total (Gross income at market prices)	Final consumption *from the rest of*
	the world
	• private
Gross income at market prices	• public
+ *Net current transfers from outside*	Gross saving
+ Net indirect taxes	• internal to the region
− Subsidies	• *from the rest of the world*
Total (Gross disposable income)	

(c) Capital Formation and Financial Account

Receipts	Payments
Gross domestic savings	Gross fixed capital formation
• internal to the region	• internal capital formation
• *from the rest of the world*	• capital formation *from the rest*
	of the world
Capital transfers (inward – credits)	*Capital transfer (outwards – debits)*

Items from the balance of payments are in italics.

domestic product). In this case, growth is financed by other regions, income does not reflect any real local productive capacity, and the region is 'living beyond its means'. If the flows of external financing cease, as a result of a political decision or because of a national economic crisis, local growth may halt and have no chance of spontaneous recovery. The macroeconomic conditions that accompany this development path are likely to be a limited local degree of competitiveness associated with unemployment and stagnation;[8]

(c) inward interregional capital movements for the purchase of property assets such as land and buildings, which increase regional wealth held in liquid form and may engender greater spending on consumption. However, in this case too, the macroeconomic accounting equilibrium may conceal a situation of unemployment and stagnation;

(d) inward interregional capital movements for direct investments in the region, with a positive impact on gross domestic product due to greater real investments stimulating employment and the region's real productive capacity. It is very unlikely that a positive balance of payments obtained by this means will conceal unemployment, especially in the long run;

(e) inward capital movements of a short-term financial nature (business loans) which give rise to greater import volumes. The macroeconomic conditions concealed behind this accounting relation are less clear-cut.

In the theories that follow we shall see how these conditions alternate among models of local growth. The first theory examined – the export-base theory – argues that growth depends substantially on the competitiveness of the local production system (case (a) above): an (exogenous) increase in exports raises income and employment levels. The next model discussed, the one developed by Harrod and Domar, stresses the importance of inflows of savings and capital for the growth of income and employment: the logic of this model corresponds to cases (c), (d) and (e) above. Finally Thirlwall's Law warns that development may be hampered by a negative trade balance if exports are conceived as the sole means to finance imports: that is, if only case (a) above holds.

THE EXPORTER REGION: THE EXPORT-BASE MODEL

Hoyt's model

The export-base model is the best-known of those developed to determine the role of demand in growth and development. The main idea behind this model, in all its versions, is that while large economic systems, such as those of large countries, are able to rely on their own internal forces for their development, smaller economic systems – regions or cities, many of them specialized – cannot rely solely on endogenous capacities to achieve development: their economic growth is closely conditioned by factors external to the local system.[9]

The origin of the export-base model is interesting. In the 1930s, the Federal Housing Administration asked a planner, Homer Hoyt, to provide a simple instrument to forecast the physical growth of cities. For this purpose, Hoyt developed the first export-base model at the urban level. He distinguished employment in the base sector (L_b) (the sector in which the area specializes) from employment in the services (or non-base) sector (L_s) and formulated the following relations:[10]

$$
\begin{aligned}
L_T &= L_b + L_s \\
L_s &= aL_T \qquad \text{with } 0 < a < 1 \\
L_b &= \bar{L}_b
\end{aligned}
\qquad (5.1)
$$

Total employment (L_T) is by definition the sum of employment in the two sectors. Employment in the base sector is exogenous to the economic system, while employment in the services sector is a share a of total employment. With appropriate substitutions and after some simple steps, we obtain:

$$
L_T = \frac{1}{1-a} L_b \qquad (5.2)
$$

and in growth rate terms, within a single period:

$$
\Delta L_T = \frac{1}{1-a} \Delta L_b \qquad (5.3)
$$

Equation (5.3) states that when employment increases in the base sector, total employment undergoes a more than proportional increase, whose amount is defined by the urban multiplier $(1/(1-a))$ – which by definition assumes values greater than one.

Assuming a simple proportion, equal to f, between total employment and the population resident in the area, we can write:

$$
P = fL_T \qquad \text{with } f > 1 \qquad (5.4)
$$

By unifying equations (5.4) and (5.3), the growth of the resident population (and therefore the physical growth of the area) can be straightforwardly calculated as:

$$
\Delta P = f \Delta L_T = \frac{f}{1-a} \Delta L_b \qquad (5.5)
$$

The export-led Keynesian model

During the 1950s – it seems entirely independently of each other – the economist Douglass North, and subsequently Charles Tiebout and Richard Andrews, developed an economic version of the Hoyt model. They replaced the physical variables of Hoyt's model with aggregate macroeconomic variables – income, demand internal and external to the region – in order to determine the economic growth of areas rather than their physical development.[11]

The economic version of the model was based on a traditional Keynesian aggregate demand model where aggregate income or production, Y, equals the components of aggregate demand, consumption C, exports X and imports M (assuming for simplicity, for the time being, that there is no public sector, G and $T = 0$):

$$Y = C + X - M$$

where:

$$X = \bar{X} \qquad \text{with } 0 < c < 1 \text{ and } 0 < m < 1$$
$$C = cY$$
$$M = mY \qquad\qquad\qquad\qquad\qquad\qquad\qquad\qquad (5.6)$$

While exports are hypothesized as exogenous to the model, consumption and imports depend on the level of income and on the respective propensities to consume, c, and to import, m.

With simple substitutions and the consequent logical steps, equation (5.6) can be rewritten as:

$$Y = \frac{1}{1 - (c - m)} X \qquad\qquad\qquad\qquad\qquad (5.7)$$

In growth rate terms, equation (5.7) becomes:

$$\Delta Y = \frac{1}{1 - (c - m)} \Delta X \qquad\qquad\qquad\qquad\qquad (5.8)$$

This states quite simply that when an area's exports increase, production and income increase more than proportionally, as long as the marginal propensity to spend $(c - m)$ is less than unity – a condition guaranteed by the values that c and m assume by definition.[12]

Equation (5.8) is analogous to (5.5) in the previous model. Both state that external demand – measured in terms of exports (expressed in values or in units of employment in the sector producing for sales outside the region) – generates and determines the amount of local growth, doing so through its multiplier effects on local income (in the economic model), and on employment in the base sector (in the model with physical variables).

Equation (5.8) states that more rapidly developing regions are those able to maintain a surplus of exports over time – unless the expansion of initial exports is cancelled out by an even greater volume of induced imports. In fact, a greater propensity to import signals that most of the multiplier effects fall outside the region.

The export-led model can be expanded in two directions. In the first, consideration is made of all the components making up aggregate demand: with respect to the model just described, private investments, public spending and tax rates are also considered.[13] In this version of the model, the possible determinants of growth are not only an increase in exports but also a growth of investments or public spending. The second direction – the one taken by interregional income theory – consists of a model which is similar to the previous one but constructed on interregional bases. Exports of a region depend on the income produced in other regions – with the advantage that the link between the growth of local income and the growth of income in other regions can be taken into consideration.[14]

It is now possible to examine certain key aspects of this theory, aspects which also high-light its limitations. First, the theory does not imply, nor does it elaborate, an equilibrium growth rate. If a region has resources and productive capacity, an expansion of activity in the base sector (of exports in the economic version) generates a regional rate of growth without economic or physical constraints on development. Entirely lacking, in fact, is any treatment of the supply structure. Second, the theory does not concern itself with processes of convergence or divergence among regions, and therefore with relative growth. Convergence is only possible in so far as low-income regions are more likely to increase their exports. Yet there is nothing in the model able to interpret that likelihood. Finally, the theory is unable to define the determinants of growth because it takes the growth of exports (or increased employment in the base sector) to be a matter of fact, not as a result of the model.

An early dynamic version of the model

An early dynamic version of the model was formulated towards the end of the 1970s in order to deal with one of the main criticisms brought against the original model: the constancy of the ratio between employment in services and total employment.[15] Employment in services, in fact, may easily increase independently of the trend in the base sector, for example as the result of autonomous investments in the region, or of a growth in per capita income. This possibility is included in a model very similar to Hoyt's, where the variable 'income' replaces the variable 'employment', the aim being to study the time trends of the growth rates of the variables. Equation (5.1) therefore becomes:

$$Y_T = Y_b + Y_s$$

where:

$$Y_b = \overline{Y}_b$$
$$Y_s = a_0 + a_1 Y_T \qquad (5.9)$$

where Y_b and Y_s denote the incomes generated respectively by the base sector and the services sector. The latter is made to depend on total income, as in Hoyt's model, and on a constant a_0 which measures exogenous variations in the income of the services sector. Simple substitutions produce the static equilibrium equation:

$$Y_T = \frac{a_0}{1 - a_1} + \frac{Y_b}{1 - a_1} \qquad (5.10)$$

In development rate terms, equation (5.10) becomes:[16]

$$\frac{\Delta Y_T}{Y_T} = \frac{\Delta Y_b}{1 - a_1} \frac{1}{\dfrac{a_0 + Y_b}{1 - a_1}} = \frac{\Delta Y_b}{a_0 + Y_b} = \frac{\Delta Y_b}{Y_b} \frac{Y_b}{a_0 + Y_b} \qquad (5.11)$$

113

Equation (5.11) demonstrates the important role of constant a_0 in a dynamic process. If it assumes zero value, total income increases at the same rate as the base sector's income, which bears out the hypothesis of the constant ratio between employment (or income) in the services sector and total employment (or income). If, instead, constant a_0 assumes values greater or less than zero, the growth rate of income differs from that of income in the base sector, assuming respectively higher values (in the case of negative values of a_0) or lower ones (in the case of positive values of a_0). A study of the American regions has shown that a_0 often assumes negative values, and therefore that the growth rate of a regional income is higher than that of the base sector, because of a higher income growth rate in the services sector. In the United States, the higher income growth rate in the services sector is mainly determined by public investments (in the construction industry, for example), by an income elasticity to demand for local public services greater than unity, and by import substitution mechanisms which develop as local activity grows.

A recent dynamic version of the model

More recent years have seen formulation of a dynamic version of the export-base model, the purpose of which is to verify the stability conditions of the equilibrium solution.[17]
Starting from the well-known aggregate demand relation:

$$Y(t) = C(t) + X(t) - M(t) \tag{5.12}$$

and introducing time lags in the relations between consumption and income, and between imports and income, it is possible to state that consumption and imports at time t are defined by income at $t-1$:

$$C(t) = cY(t-1) \tag{5.13}$$

$$M(t) = mY(t-1) \tag{5.14}$$

Equation (5.12) thus becomes:

$$Y(t) - (c-m)Y(t-1) = X(t) \tag{5.15}$$

Assuming that external demand for locally-produced goods increases exponentially over time at a constant rate $g > 0$, the dynamic of regional income assumes the time trend shown by Figure 5.1.[18] With an initial income level equal to Y', the growth of exports induces income to grow towards $Y*$. The same tendency is apparent if the region has an initial income level of Y''.

Interestingly, according to the same logic, if $g < 0$, income converges on a negative level $Y**$, declining at a constant rate g provided that $0 < c - m < 1 + g$. The condition for convergence to come about is that the propensity to consume locally $(c - m)$ must be less than 1, a condition already contained in the static model and respected by definition. The dynamic characteristics of this model are quite simple, given the linear structure of its

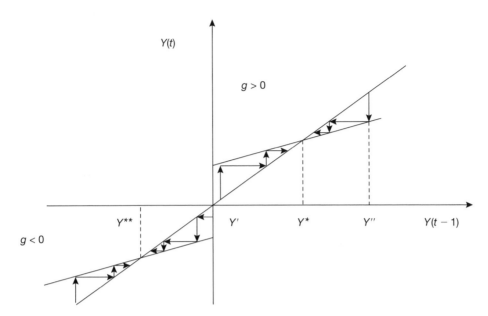

Figure 5.1 *The dynamic equilibrium of the export-base model. Convergence towards development (g > 0) or decline (g < 0) at a constant rate g*

underlying relations. However, if non-linearity is introduced into these relations, it is possible to obtain explosive trends or sudden crises, depending on the structural changes which occur in the system.[19]

A CRITICAL ASSESSMENT OF THE MODEL

General remarks

The great merit attributed to the export-base model, in all its versions, is that it has analysed regional development from the point of view of a small economic system. Using the purely economic logic of Keynesian macroeconomics, the model is able to demonstrate the decisive role performed by interregional trade relations in the growth of a small economic system. Given the difficulty of characterizing a local economic system as a self-sufficient economy, exports are treated in these models as a major component of aggregate demand, and autonomous investments only as a minor one.

The export-base model also reminds us that *productive specialization* is a key determinant of economic growth. The role assumed by a region in the international division of labour depends on its ability to identify the specific productive assets with which it can offer goods on a much broader market and acquire demand extending well beyond local barriers. This thesis is still largely valid today, and in the 1970s it was strongly supported by bottom-up development theories. Moreover, for the period in which this thesis was conceived, it represented a significant advance in regional development analysis. Given the way in which it is conceived, the export-base model also warns of the risks to specialized local economic

115

systems when international demand for their products exhibits marked long-period fluctuations. On the logic of the model, in fact, just as an increase in demand for locally produced goods is a source of development, so a decrease in such demand may presage a recession.

This approach to local growth, with its conceptual simplicity, economic logic, and simple application to real situations (given that it needed a relatively small dataset), enjoyed considerable success for a number of years in both regional and urban economics. This success, however, induced analysts to ignore the intrinsic limitations of the model, which were mainly due to its a-spatial nature adapted from macroeconomics to a local context. A region is interpreted by this model as an internally uniform space which differs from an external space (like a nation does from the rest of the world) in terms of its different productive structure and specialization. But the model provides no explanation for this distinction. Its interregional version counterposes a region to others assumed to differ from it in their propensities to import and consume, and in their export capacities. All of these differences are hypothesized, but none of them are explained. The model is therefore able to identify, but not to interpret, the determinants of local development. For this reason, it is a model well suited to describing the development of areas historically specialized in certain industrial sectors, or in so-called 'Ricardian goods', or those goods connected with the availability of natural resources (e.g. minerals, specific agricultural products). Specialization in Ricardian goods does not need to be explained, therefore, but is taken for granted. In all other cases, however, the way in which the export-base is determined and converted into greater competitiveness has to be interpreted by analysing the structure and the dynamic of local supply, which are unfortunately entirely neglected by the model.

A second criticism concerns the high level of aggregation at which the analysis is conducted. No distinctions are drawn among different productive activities or different industrial specializations. The model implies that the multiplier effects of exports on income are of the same magnitude whatever sector produces the goods exported. But this implication is refuted when one considers that every sector of specialization generates a multiplier effect of greater or lesser proportions according to whether the demand for intermediate goods created by the production of export goods is addressed to internal producers, or whether, instead, it gives rise to greater imports from other regions.[20] Pioneering studies by Chenery in the early 1950s used a North/South Italy input–output table to show that the large-scale investments made in the Italian Mezzogiorno at the time benefited the industrialized North more than the developing South because of the marked leakage effects in the Mezzogiorno's income multiplier.[21]

Moreover, the model assumes that there is no obstacle against an expansion of supply. If external demand increases, the system has the resources with which to augment productive capacity: unemployed production factors and productive capacity – either unused or expandable at nil cost – are assumed to be available. If this is not the case, an increase in demand engenders a short-term rise in prices, rather than a real physical expansion of production activity.

Use of the model for long-period predictions is restricted by its intrinsic assumption that multipliers are stable over time.[22] In the long period, in fact, it is easy to foresee – along a development path – that the productive diversification of the local economy will generate import substitution effects at odds with the multiplier's constancy. In the long period it is likely (and desirable) that an area's specialization will shift to more advanced sectors with higher value added, given the probability that, along its development path, the region will be able to transfer resources from declining sectors to emerging ones. If study of regional development confines itself to the logic of constancy in specialization, it may overlook one of the most interesting aspects of dynamic analysis: the structural change that accompanies long-period development.

For the same reason, a further shortcoming of the model is that it deliberately ignores the role of the residential (or services) sector in an area's growth, in that growth is solely dependent on the dynamic of the base sector. The level and quality of local, financial, managerial, marketing and technological services instead largely determine the long-period productivity and competitiveness of base sectors, especially in modern economies.

Estimation of the 'economic base'

Interest in application of the export-base model has led to the development of various methods with which to distinguish a region's base sector from its services sector, a distinction easy to draw in theory but difficult to apply in practice. The method most commonly suggested for this purpose is the location quotient technique, which distinguishes the two sectors according to the sector's employment share at regional level compared to the same sector's share at national level:[23]

$$QL_{ir} = \frac{E_{ir}}{E_r} \Bigg/ \frac{E_{in}}{E_n} \tag{5.16}$$

where i, r and n respectively denote the sector, the region, and the nation, and E is total employment (although it can represent any sectorally disaggregated variable available at regional level – income for example). If the ratio between the shares is greater than unity, then the surplus is interpreted as a measure of production exceeding local demand, and therefore as consisting of net exports. With the exporting sectors thus established, summing employment (or income) yields an estimate of employment (or income) in the base sector.

However, the use of the location quotient to define the base sector has a number of shortcomings.[24] First, it assumes that consumers have the same tastes and preferences over space. If they did not, the surplus might not signify that production is more than enough to meet local demand, but rather that the structure of local demand is different from that of the country as a whole. Second, the method assumes that the economy concerned is a closed system: it presumes, in fact, that the nation does not export, so that the share of employment (or income) at the denominator represents only demand internal to the country. Because this is an unrealistic assumption, the location quotient underestimates the base sector. Finally, if the location quotient is instead calculated on the basis of units of production, the method assumes equal levels of productivity across space, which is a further unrealistic assumption.

Another method proposed for estimation of the base sector is the minimum requirements technique.[25] This starts from the assumption that the lowest share of employment in a sector in all regions is the minimum share necessary to satisfy the needs of a region, and that if the employment share in that sector is larger than in other regions, it signals that productive capacity is in excess of the region's requirements. The sum of employment in sectors with employment shares above the minimum determines employment in the base sector. This method too has its limitations. First of all, a region may have a very small proportion of employment in a sector, not because it produces only to satisfy its own needs, but because it is a net importer in that sector – an aspect which makes selection of the benchmark region highly arbitrary. Second, this method requires the same assumptions about the constancy of demand and productivity across space that have already been mentioned in regard to the location quotient technique.

Estimation of the regional multiplier

Assuming that the above-mentioned shortcomings are acceptable, application of the export-base model in prediction of a region's development requires estimation of the income multiplier. Early attempts in this direction began by identifying the base sector with the methods (with their shortcomings) just described.[26]

But there are at least two other methods commonly used to estimate the regional multiplier. The first of them consists in empirical estimation of the multiplier (i.e. the various marginal propensities). Originally proposed by Archibald, this method estimates the multiplier via direct estimation of the propensity to purchase goods locally.[27] It examines official figures on household consumption – detailed by spending category at national level – in order to identify goods and services with a high probability of being purchased locally (retail services, public services, cinemas, educational services, and so on). It then calculates the local shares compared to national ones and aggregates total spending for each. Repetition of the exercise for a certain number of years yields a time series of local spending which, when regressed on disposable income, produces an estimation of the marginal propensity to consume income at local level, $(c - m)$.[28] Once this value is known, the value of the regional multiplier can be easily obtained.

The second method was first proposed by Allen. It abandons the idea of directly estimating local spending, or the various marginal propensities (to consume and to import from other regions or abroad). Instead, it takes as a proxy for the regional multiplier the inverse of the 'leakages' on a region's gross domestic product. Allen identifies four channels of leakages from the multiplier effect on income: savings, interregional imports, imports from abroad, and direct and indirect taxes. Once the values of these are known, and their shares of income calculated, the inverse is nothing other than the value of the multiplier.[29]

INPUT–OUTPUT ANALYSIS

While export-base methods are able to measure the extent to which local product changes with variations in external demand, there is a technique – called input–output analysis – which enables estimation to be made of the impact of growth in demand in a particular sector on output by each individual sector of the local economy, and on total output. Accordingly, export-base models can be classified as input–output models with only two sectors.

118

Using Wassily Leontief's model of sectoral interdependencies as its basis, input–output analysis can be used to predict the effects exerted by a growth of demand in a particular sector on the rest of the local economy. We shall see how.

Input–output analysis involves construction of a square $n \times n$ matrix. Recorded in this matrix are all the flows of sales (in the rows) and purchases (in the columns) that take place in a year among the n local production sectors: or in other words, the intermediate flows of goods (expressed in values) among the various sectors.[30] Completing the matrix are series of columns and rows. Recorded in the former are sales by each sector to final demand (public and private consumption, investments and exports); recorded in the latter are purchases of the original production factors, labour and capital (and therefore wages and profits) and purchases from abroad – and from outside, in the case of a sub-national input–output matrix (imports).[31]

By construction, the sum of each row represents each sector's revenue from sales of goods to other sectors and to final demand. The sum of each column represents the costs incurred by each sector in order to purchase intermediate goods, and goods produced externally, and to remunerate the production factors, wages and profits. The row values equal the column values. Moreover, the sum of final demand equals the sum of the income components or of value added, this being the regional output Y (Table 5.3).

With A_{ij} denoting the value of goods that sector i sells to sector j, and C, G, I, X and R respectively denoting private consumption, public spending, investments, exports and the value of output, the row sum (the revenue of a generic sector i) is given by:

$$\sum_j A_{ij} + (C_i + G_i + I_i + X_i) = R_i \qquad \forall i \tag{5.17}$$

Table 5.3 Simplified structure of an input–output table

Selling sectors	Intermediate demand Purchasing sectors 1...n			Final demand C	G	I	X	Total output
1	A_{11} ·	A_{1j} ·	A_{1n}	C_1	G_1	I_1	X_1	R_1
.	.	. . .	.	.	.	.	.	.
.	.	. . .	.	.	.	.	.	.
.	.	. . .	.	.	.	.	.	.
.	.	. . .	.	.	.	.	.	.
n	A_{n1} ·	A_{nj} ·	A_{nn}	C_n	G_n	I_n	X_n	R_n
Labour (wages)	W_1 ·	W_j ·	W_n					W
Other components of value added (profits)	Π_1 ·	Π_j ·	Π_n		Y			Π
Imports	M_1 ·	M_j ·	M_n	M_c	M_g	M_i		M
Total output	R_1 ·	R_j ·	R_n	C	G	I	X	

and the column sum (the costs of a generic sector j) by:

$$\sum_i A_{ij} + W_j + \Pi_j + M_j = R_j \qquad \forall j \tag{5.18}$$

where W and Π are respectively wages and the other components of value added (profits). The regional gross domestic product Y is given by:

$$W + \Pi = Y = C + G + I + X - M = R - \sum_j \sum_i A_{ij} - M \tag{5.19}$$

The flows of goods between sector i and sector j can be expressed by the so-called 'technical coefficients' a_{ij}, which state the (technical/structural) relation between production by sector i and by sector j. In other words, the technical coefficients state how many euros of output by sector i are necessary for the production of one euro by sector j:[32]

$$A_{ij} = a_{ij}R_j \qquad \text{and} \qquad a_{ij} = A_{ij}/R_j \tag{5.20}$$

Substituting equation (5.20) in equation (5.17) and writing final demand as a single item D, we obtain, for every sector i:

$$\sum_j a_{ij}R_j + D_j = R_i \qquad \forall i \tag{5.21}$$

Equation (5.21) expresses the value of production (revenue) obtained by sector i selling output in part to final demand D and in part to other sectors.

After linear algebra operations on the matrix of the technical coefficients, equation (5.21) can be rewritten as:[33]

$$R_i = \sum_j b_{ij}D_j \qquad \forall i \tag{5.22}$$

where b_{ij} is the 'inverse Leontief matrix' or the 'multiplier matrix'. This matrix enables calculation of the value of output by each sector i generated directly or indirectly by one euro of final demand addressed to each sector j. In fact, it allows calculation not only of the direct effects of a certain amount of demand but also the indirect effects operating via final demand itself. For example, equation (5.22) is able to determine not only the production of wood generated by demand in the construction industry but also the production of wood generated by demand in the furniture industry, this demand being in its turn generated by increased demand in the construction industry. Whereas in export-base theory the Keynesian multiplier is synthesized into a single value, in input–output analysis it is disaggregated into a $n \times n$ set of multipliers relative to every sector or good demanded.

Input–output analysis is therefore a useful tool for forecasting the effects of a hypothetical increase in demand in a particular sector. If the technical coefficients matrix a_{ij} is known, it is possible to calculate the effect of an increase in external demand for a good (sector) ΔD_j on:

- the value of production by individual local sectors i: $\Delta R_i = b_{ij}D_j$;
- local wages: $\Delta W = \sum_i \Delta R_i a_{wi} = \sum_i b_{ij}D_j a_{wi}$, where $a_{wi} = W_i/R_i$;

- local employment, assuming a constant sectoral average wage w_i^*: $\Delta L = \Sigma_i \Delta W_i / w_i^*$;
- local income: $\Delta Y = \Delta W + \Delta \Pi = \Sigma_i R_i (a_{wi} + a_{vi})$, where v denotes the other components of income besides wages.

The limitations of this methodology are well known. First, the constancy of the technical coefficients to increased production, as well as their constancy over time, requires all production to be at constant returns, and technical progress to be non-existent. The difficulties increase when input–output analysis is used at sub-national, regional or urban level. In this case, if the instrument is used to forecast the trend of the local economy, the technical coefficients matrix must be divided into an intraregional trade flow matrix and a interregional trade flow matrix. This enables measurement of the impact of increased demand in a particular sector on the local economy, and it excludes the 'leakages effects' on other areas of the country. But dividing the coefficients matrix in this way is a complex undertaking. It is usually performed with one of the following two methods: (a) the compilation of empirical survey-based tables, which is an accurate but extremely costly method; (b) desk research on the sector's specialization, on the assumption that the sector is able to meet increased demand only if it pertains to the specialization of the area.[34]

The use of input/output analysis to forecast and simulate the effects of economic policy measures at the local level entails the assumption that technical coefficients are constant over time. Consequently, the results of such analysis should be interpreted with caution.

THE IMPORTER REGION: THE HARROD–DOMAR MODEL

The original model

In 1939 the economist Roy Harrod, and then entirely independently in 1957, Evsey Domar, investigated the rate of growth required for an economic system to maintain its initial macroeconomic equilibrium.[35] The model formulated by Harrod and Domar concludes that equilibrium of an economic system is more the exception than the rule, given that the growth path is highly unstable and very likely to diverge from the equilibrium growth rate.

The Harrod–Domar model was subsequently used to interpret the dynamics of regional economic systems.[36] The assumption behind this regional version is that imports – when analysed as the channel through which capital goods and savings are acquired from other regions – determine the local economy's growth rate; moreover, they allow for equilibrium growth conditions less restrictive – and therefore more easily sustainable over time – than those which applied to a national economy closed to foreign trade. Hence, while the export-base theory highlights the importance of external demand as the engine of development, the Harrod–Domar model emphasizes that the regional dynamic may also be driven by investments originating from other regions which stimulate local output and income: cases (c), (d) and (e) discussed on p. 110.

As we shall see, the Harrod–Domar model also differs from the export-base theory in that it is a multi-period model. It abandons the strictly short-period logic that we have seen thus far and assumes a longer-term perspective. Moreover, far from conceiving saving as a deduction from effective demand, this approach stresses the importance of saving as a means with which to acquire resources for productive investments.

The model is based on the following assumptions:

1 production of a single good, which can be used either as a final good (in which case it is consumed and exits the economic system) or as a capital good (in which case it remains in the system and engenders the production of other goods);

2 the non-perishable nature of the capital good, which means that there is no need to differentiate between investments in new capital and investments to amortize capital assets;

3 a constant propensity to save;

4 fixed production coefficients, i.e. constancy in the quantities of the production factors 'capital' and 'labour' necessary for one unit of output – which is equivalent to assuming the absence of technical progress;

5 growth of labour at a constant rate n equal to growth of the population;

6 investments proportional to the increase in demand as defined by the accelerator theory:

$$I_t = v_t (Y_{t+1}^* - Y_t) \qquad \text{with } 0 < v_t < 1 \qquad (5.23)$$

where v_t – the 'acceleration coefficient', assumed constant by the model – measures the increase in capital (I_t) with a unit increase in demand $Y_{t+1}^* - Y_t$. It therefore expresses the capital/output ratio;

7 income proportional to the increase in investments, as suggested by the Keynesian multiplier theory:

$$Y_{t+1} - Y_t = \frac{1}{s} (I_{t+1} - I_t) \qquad \text{with } 0 < s < 1 \qquad (5.24)$$

where s is the propensity to save and $1/s$ is the factor of proportionality (or the Keynesian multiplier) between investments and income: unit increases in investment have a more than proportional effect (equal to $1/s$) on income.

An increment in aggregate demand entails an increase in the capital and labour production factors necessary to adjust production to the new level of consumption. Assuming full employment in order to maintain this equilibrium condition, on the hypothesis of constancy in the technical coefficient of production (L/Y), the labour growth rate must be equal to the population growth rate, n.

On the capital side, as suggested by equation (5.23), an increase in demand generates an increase in investments, the financing of which requires an amount of savings (S) equal to the necessary investment (I). If this is the case, the economy grows at a rate – called the 'warranted growth rate' (y_t) – equal to:

$$y_t = \frac{\Delta K}{K} = \frac{I}{K} = \frac{sY}{K} = \frac{sY}{Y} \frac{Y}{K} = \frac{s}{v} = n \qquad (5.25)$$

Equation (5.25) states that the growth rate must be equal to the ratio between the propensity to save s and the acceleration coefficient v, which in turn must be equal to the rate of growth of the labour force. If this is the case, the initial equilibrium between aggregate demand and production will be maintained over time.[37]

However, if the system grows at the warranted growth rate y_t, it moves, in Harrod's words, along a 'knife edge' between the risk of explosion on the one hand, and of recession on the other. Any disequilibria generated by conditions external to the system, in the absence of exogenous interventions, tend to be aggravated by signals emitted by the market which induce firms to operate in the direction opposite to the one required for equilibrium to be re-established. In an economic system, in fact, planned investments in excess of actual savings ($I > S$) signal that effective consumption is greater than expected saving, and therefore that effective demand is greater than expected demand.[38] Firms react to the short supply of goods in the system by increasing their investments – a reaction which, paradoxically, worsens the disequilibrium. The increase in investments generates, via the multiplier effect on income, a more than proportional increase in income and aggregate demand. The latter increasingly diverges from expected demand, with severe inflationary effects in the long run. In the same way, if planned investments are less than effective saving ($I < S$), this signals that expected demand is greater than effective demand. Firms react to a surplus of supply in the system by reducing their investments, thereby slowing the growth of effective demand even further, and in the long period causing recession.

In short, the model shows that there are forces within an economic system in initial disequilibrium which push it further and further away from stationary equilibrium and, according to the initial conditions, towards either inflationary conditions or deep recession.

The regional version of the model

When the Harrod–Domar model is adapted to the regional context, it yields interesting results in addition to the ones furnished by the national version. The distinctive feature of the model's regional version is its macroeconomic equilibrium condition, which for a regional economy is:

$$S + M = I + X \tag{5.26}$$

where M and X respectively denote the imports and exports of capital from/to one region and the other. Regions are not closed economic systems (if they were, the regional model would not be different from the national one): they have close relations with other regions, with which they exchange goods and production factors.

For a generic region i, equation (5.26) can be rewritten as:

$$(s_i + m_i)Y_i = I_i + X_i \tag{5.27}$$

that is:

$$\frac{I_i}{Y_i} = s_i + m_i - \frac{X_i}{Y_i} \tag{5.28}$$

123

where m is the propensity to import capital proportional to income. Equation (5.25) thus becomes:

$$y_i = \frac{s_i + m_i - \dfrac{X_i}{Y_i}}{v_i} = n_i \qquad (5.29)$$

Equation (5.29) states that – unlike in a closed economy – capital may grow at the same rate as output (thus guaranteeing the steady state) even if investments tend to outstrip savings, provided that the gap between savings and investments is covered by a surplus of net imports.[39] A regional economic system can finance investments not only with internal savings but by importing capital goods from other regions.[40] Net exports may likewise help maintain the steady-state equilibrium, when there is a surplus of internal saving, because they make up the shortfall between low internal consumption and the level of production corresponding to full use of productive capacity.

Similarly, full employment in a region with an internal shortage of labour may be maintained by an inflow of workers from other regions, while outflows of migrants to other regions may off-set unemployment in the region. The labour-market equilibrium condition is therefore:

$$y_i = n_i - e_i \qquad (5.30)$$

where e_i is the net migratory balance (emigrants minus immigrants) in each period of time as a percentage of the regional population P_i.

A first important result obtained by the regional version of the Harrod–Domar model is that the conditions for constant-rate growth are less restrictive – and therefore more easily sustainable over time – than those governing a national economy closed to foreign trade. However, once again the steady-state equilibrium can be interpreted as the exception rather than the rule, given that there are no conditions in the model ensuring interregional flows of labour and capital sufficient to guarantee growth at a constant rate. That is to say, there are no conditions within the model which guarantee that the interregional flows of production factors will equilibrate the system.

A second important result of the model in its 'regional' version is the following: regions characterized by net surpluses of imports, that is, those for which

$$m_i - \frac{\sum\limits_{j} X_j}{Y_i} > 0 \qquad (5.31)$$

are regions which grow more rapidly than others – propensity to save and capital/output ratio remaining equal. In fact, according to the logic of the model, a net surplus of imports gives rise to a higher growth rate because this surplus represents extra savings injected into the economic system from outside, as shown by equation (5.29).

Finally, the third important result of the Harrod–Domar model concerns the time trends of differences among regional growth rates. If, as is the case in the real world, there are initial differences among the growth rates of regions, the model shows that these differences not only persist but increase with the passage of time. In fact, when the initial growth rate of region i is higher than that of region j ($y_i > y_j$), it follows from equation (5.29) that

$$\frac{\sum_j m_j Y_j}{Y_i} \quad \text{where by definition} \quad \sum_j m_j Y_i = \sum_j X_j \tag{5.32}$$

diminishes, giving further impetus to y_i.

The two latter findings remind us, on the realistic assumption that a poor region is a net importer of capital from rich regions, that the model hypothesizes convergence by regional growth rates on steady-state equilibrium. In fact, equations (5.31) and (5.32) state that the growth rate of a poor region is constantly higher than the rates of the advanced ones: a situation brought about by convergent development and which demonstrates that, in contexts characterized by a scant propensity to save and a low capital/output ratio, the propensity to import performs a crucial role in intra- and international regional re-equilibrum processes.

Finally, more detailed analysis of the s/v ratio is required, given its importance in equation (5.29) for explanation of the regional growth rate. This equation states that greater growth is achieved by regions with high propensities to save and with low capital/output ratios (v); regions, therefore, which make efficient use of capital or have low capital-intensive sectoral structures (service sectors, for example). This latter feature has enabled the Italian region of Lombardy to attain high levels of development despite a long-standing low accumulation rate (1970s and 1980s). By contrast, the Italian Mezzogiorno, where investments were made in capital-intensive sectors for at least thirty years (1955–85), has achieved limited growth despite large injections of (public) investments and external savings.

This observation enables us to state that, whereas in the single-period Keynesian model saving is detrimental to growth because it subtracts from effective demand and limits multiplier effects – as indicated by the term $1-c$, equal to s, at the denominator – even in Keynesian models (if they adopt a genuinely dynamic, multi-period and long-term perspective) the availability of saving and capital formation, i.e. supply rather than demand elements, explain regional growth.

Critical assessment of the model

The Harrod–Domar model is well suited to describing and interpreting the growth of regional economic systems apparently characterized by critical macroeconomic conditions. Limited internal savings, a low capital/output ratio, and a negative trade balance are expected to hamper macroeconomic growth. But this situation is contradicted in the real world by numerous regional systems, and it can only be explained if a decisive role is given to the external capital which makes up the internal saving shortfall.[41] When the same logic is used to identify the relative growth path, it is able to account for converging growth rates of regions which differ markedly in their levels of internal investment and saving – levels that would otherwise signal divergence.

Although the regional Harrod–Domar model furnishes useful insights, it can be criticized on various grounds, all of them concerning the fact that it was originally developed to interpret the macroeconomic conditions of a country's growth and was only subsequently adapted to a regional setting.

The first weakness of the model is its inability to predict whether interregional flows of production factors will restore equilibrium. This inability is due to the absence of mechanisms which regulate and interpret those flows. However, since the model was not originally formulated to explain flows of production factors, it is obvious that a theory of resource mobility is entirely lacking.

A second and evident limitation of the model is that it is unable to demonstrate clear tendencies towards divergence or convergence among regions. It is true that in the real world backward regions are generally net importers of capital, and therefore that, on the logic of the model, they are faster growing regions; as a consequence, they are able to converge on the growth rates of advanced regions. Yet it is equally true that in the real world backward regions are generally also net exporters of labour: a situation which, according to the logic of the model, is accompanied by lower rates of income growth, and divergence rather than convergence.

Finally, although we may accept the model's finding that backward regions are net importers of capital (as happens in the real world), the model provides no explanation as to the determinants of this greater capacity to attract capital. While in the national version of the model, the reasons can be conceived as favourable macroeconomic conditions attracting capital (a higher interest rate), in its regional version they should be identified in location factors typical of any geographical area, which can only be identified using a microeconomic approach. Not surprisingly, therefore, they are entirely absent from a macroeconomic model with uniform-abstract space like the one developed by Harrod and Domar.

BALANCE OF PAYMENTS AND LOCAL GROWTH: THIRLWALL'S LAW

At the beginning of the 1980s, the importance of exports for a region's growth was once again affirmed. Whilst the export-base model interprets exports as signalling the competitive advantage of a region, and therefore its potential development, the theory now discussed – known as Thirlwall's Law – gives exports a decisive role in the development process: they sustain the trade balance, and in the absence of other mechanisms, they enable the financing of the imports necessary to satisfy internal demand.[42] In fact, if exports were scant and failed to meet the area's import needs, a disequilibrium would arise in the regional trade balance; and this, over the long period, would restrict imports, the satisfaction of local demand, the needs of local industry, and development. On this view, an area's failure to develop is due to disequilibrium in the regional trade balance.[43]

A region can therefore maintain a certain level of growth if there is equilibrium in its trade balance. Assuming that the growth rate of exports depends on the growth rate of world income (y_w), weighted by the elasticity of export demand to world income (α), and the growth rate of imports (m), in its turn dependent on the growth rate of regional income (y_r), weighted by the elasticity of import demand to local income (β),[44] equilibrium in the regional trade balance is ensured if the following equality holds:

$$\alpha y_w = \beta y_r \qquad\qquad\qquad (5.33)$$

that is:

$$y_r = \frac{\alpha}{\beta} y_w \qquad\qquad\qquad (5.34)$$

This last relation states that a regional growth rate depends on the growth rate of world income and on the ratio between the two elasticities of demand to income. In order to stimulate local development a region must foster an industrial structure with sectors whose exports have high elasticity of demand to world income (α) and, at the same time, whose imports have low elasticity of demand to local income (β). On this approach, therefore, local development is nothing other than a problem of industrial conversion to sectors whose exports and imports have respectively greater or lesser elasticities of demand to income.

The interest of this theory resides in its twofold contention that (a) imports are a *sine qua non* for internal production, which requires raw materials and non-locally-produced intermediate goods; and (b) that exports are crucial for growth because they are the most immediate source of import financing.

However, there are other import-financing methods that enable the limits imposed on growth by a negative trade balance to be bypassed, as shown above ('Interregional relations'). Numerous examples can be cited in the real world of rich exporting regions which co-exist with backward regions; in the latter, public transfers and private investments from advanced regions finance a negative trade balance and local income growth in the long run.

It therefore seems that, like any demand-driven theory, Thirlwall's Law has a certain validity if it is used to explain short-period development, given that its concern is not to interpret the specialization and competitiveness of the productive system.

CONCLUSIONS

This chapter has analysed Keynesian models of regional growth in which demand components are the engine of development. They are theories which interpret regional development as growth in employment and income driven by increased demand. The chapter has frequently pointed out that these theories restrict themselves to describing short-period growth: they entirely ignore the structure and dynamic of the production system, taking it for granted that a region can increase supply in response to expanding – also external – demand.

For these reasons, it is risky and misleading to use Keynesian theories in interpretation of a long-term growth path, or as the basis for policy measures to support a long-run dynamic. If they are instead used to overcome the specific normative problem that they address – reducing unemployment in the presence of a given productive capacity – they have obvious merits: they are simple and at the same time rigorous in their economic reasoning, and they are easy to apply to a real context.

Finally, the chapter has shown that when Keynesian theories discard the short-time perspective and adopt a long-term, multi-period one, as in the case of the Harrod–Domar model, they are able to abandon demand aspects and highlight the importance of supply components – such as the availability of saving and capital formation – for interpretation of the regional growth process.

MATHEMATICAL APPENDIX

The differences equation (5.15) is solved, as usual, by separating the solutions of the homogeneous and particular equations.

The homogeneous equation, which we define as $Q(t)$, is:

$$Q(t) - (c - m)Q(t - 1) = 0 \qquad (5.1a)$$

Setting

$$Q(t) = K\varphi^t \qquad (5.2a)$$

we obtain

$$K\varphi^t - (c - m)K\varphi^{t-1} = 0 \qquad \text{i.e. } \varphi = c - m \qquad (5.3a)$$

(5.2a) thus becomes:

$$Q(t) = K(c - m)^t \qquad (5.4a)$$

with constant K, whose value is not yet known.

The particular equation is defined as:

$$R(t) - (c - m)R(t - 1) = X(0)(1 + g)^t \qquad (5.5a)$$

Defining:

$$R(t) = h\psi^t \qquad (5.6a)$$

(5.5a) becomes:

$$h\psi^t - (c - m)h\psi^{t-1} = X(0)(1 + g)^t \qquad (5.7a)$$

and therefore:

$$h\psi^t(1 - \frac{(c - m)}{\psi}) = X(0)(1 + g)^t \qquad (5.8a)$$

This holds if and only if:

$$\psi = (1 + g) \tag{5.9a}$$

and

$$X(0) = h - \frac{(c - m)h}{\psi}$$

$$h = \frac{X(0)\psi}{1 - \dfrac{c - m}{\psi}} \tag{5.10a}$$

Recalling that $\psi = (1 + g)$, (5.10a) becomes:

$$h = \frac{X(0)(1 + g)}{(1 + g) - (c - m)} \tag{5.11a}$$

Substituting the values of h and ψ in (5.6a), the particular solution of (5.5a) becomes:

$$R(t) = \frac{X(0)(1 + g)^{t+1}}{(1 + g) - (c - m)} \tag{5.12a}$$

The solution of (5.15) is given by the sum of the homogeneous solution $Q(t)$ and the particular solution $R(t)$, i.e.

$$Y(t) = K(c - m)^t + \frac{X(0)(1 + g)^{t+1}}{(1 + g) - (c - m)} \tag{5.13a}$$

which is nothing other than (5.13n). Using the initial condition to define K, which is still unknown, we obtain:

$$Y(0) = K(c - m)^0 + (1 + g)^0 \frac{X(0)(1 + g)}{(1 + g) - (c - m)} \tag{5.14a}$$

or:

$$K = Y(0) - \frac{X(0)(1 + g)}{(1 + g) - (c - m)} \tag{5.15a}$$

which is nothing other than (5.14n).

If $c - m < 1$, the $\lim_{t \to \infty} K(c - m)^t = 0$. It follows that the regional income converges on a development path with constant equilibrium rate g, as shown graphically by Figure 5.1.

REVIEW QUESTIONS

1   Which conception of space is used in the regional growth theories of the 1950s and 1960s and why?

2   How can one define a theory of regional growth driven by demand dynamics?

3   How is the balance of trade structured? How do the trade balance, the service balance and the capital transfer balance enter the regional social account?

4   Which macroeconomic conditions can be hidden behind a regional income balance in the presence of openness of the region to external trade?

5   What is argued by the export-base theory (in all its formulations) and what are the strengths and weaknesses of this theory?

6   Which are the methodologies to measure the regional consumption multiplier?

7   How can an input–output table be built and for what purposes? What do the technical production coefficients and the coefficient matrix represent?

8   Which additional element is contained in the Harrod–Domar model in its formulation at the regional level? What are the main weaknesses and strengths of this model?

9   Is it true that regional growth can be hampered by a negative trade balance? Explain why.

SELECTED READING ON EMPIRICAL FINDINGS

About regional multipliers

Allen, K. J. (1969) 'The regional multiplier: some problems in estimation', in Cullingworth, J. B. and Orr, S. C. (eds), *Regional and urban studies: a social science approach*, London: Allen & Unwin, pp. 80–96.

Archibald, G. (1967) 'Regional multiplier effects in the United Kingdom', *Oxford Economic Papers*, vol. 19, pp. 22–45.

Daley, W. M. (1997) *Regional multipliers. A user handbook for the regional input–output model-ling system (RIMS II)*, U.S. Department of Commerce, Economics and Statistics Administration, U.S. Government Printing Office, Washington, DC 20402, third edn, avail-able on line.

Faggian, A. and Biagi, B. (2003) 'Measuring regional multipliers: a comparison between different methodologies in the case of the Italian regions', *Scienze Regionali – Italian Journal of Regional Science*, no. 1, pp. 33–58.

Steele, D. B. (1969) 'Regional multipliers in Great Britain', *Oxford Economic Papers*, New Series, vol. 21, no. 2, pp. 268–92.

About input–output analysis

Camagni, R. (1982) 'L'Impatto sull'economia Sarda della spesa e dell'investimento turistico in Costa Smeralda', *Quaderni Sardi di Economia*, no. 4, pp. 371–413.

Carter, H. O. and Brody, A. (eds) (1970) *Applications of input–output analysis*, Amsterdam: North-Holland.

Chenery, H. (1962) 'Development policies for Southern Italy', *Quarterly Journal of Economics*, vol. 76, pp. 515–47.

Cuihong, Y. (2002) 'The impacts of water conservancy investment by using input–output technique: a case of China', paper presented at the 14th International Conference on input–output technique, held in Montreal, Canada, 10–15 October.

Harringan, J. (1982) 'The relationship between industry and geographical linkages: a case study of the United Kingdom', *Journal of Regional Science*, vol. 22, no. 1.

Hewings, G. J. D., Israilevich, P. R., Sonis, M. and Schindler, G. R. (1997) 'Structural change in a metropolitan economy: the Chicago Region 1975–2011', in Bertuglia, C. S., Lombardo, S. and Nijkamp, P. (eds), *Innovative behaviour in space and time*, Berlin: Springer Verlag, pp. 183–212.

Israilevich, P. R., Hewings, G. J. D., Schindler, G. and Mahidhara, R. (1996) 'The choice of an input–output table embedded in regional input–output models', *Papers in Regional Science*, vol. 75, pp. 103–19.

Ning, A. and Polenske, K. P. (2005) 'Application and extension of input–output analysis in economic-impact analysis of dust storms: a case study in Beijing, China', Paper for presentation at the 15th International Input–Output conference held in Beijing, China, June 27 to July 1.

Nyhus, D. (1983) 'Observing structural change in the Japanese economy: an input-output approach', in Smyshlyaev, A. (ed.), *Proceedings of the fourth IIASA task force meeting on input–output modeling*, International Institute for Applied System Analysis, Laxenburg, Austria.

Polenske, K. (1970) 'An empirical test of interregional input–output models: estimation of 1963 Japanese production', *American Economic Review*, vol. 60, pp. 76–82.

FURTHER READING

Chenery, H. (1962) 'Development policies for Southern Italy', *Quarterly Journal of Economics*, vol. 76, pp. 515–47.

Domar, E. D. (1957) *Essays in the theory of economic growth*, London: Oxford University Press.

Harrod, R. F. (1939) 'An essay in dynamic theory', *The Economic Journal*, vol. 49, no. 193, pp. 14–33.

Hoyt, H. (1954) 'Homer Hoyt on the development of economic base concept', *Land Economics*, pp. 182–7.

North, D. (1955) 'Location theory and regional economic growth', *Journal of Political Economy*, vol. 63, pp. 243–58.

Richardson, H. W. (1978) *Regional and urban economics*, Harmondsworth: Penguin Books.

Thirlwall, A. P. (1980) 'Regional problems are balance of payments problems', *Regional Studies*, vol. 14, pp. 419–25.

Chapter 6

Factor endowment

SUMMARY

1 Factor endowment and regional growth
2 Regional growth and factor mobility
3 Factor immobility, specialization and well-being
4 Absolute vs. comparative advantage in regional growth
5 The theory of customs unions

FACTOR ENDOWMENT AND REGIONAL GROWTH

The remaining chapters of the book examine theories which focus exclusively on supply components to explain long-period regional dynamics. In the light of the theories described in the previous chapter (in particular the export-base model), therefore, they not only view exports as the engine of development but take a step further by identifying the factors responsible for the greater export capacity, and therefore the competitiveness, of a local economic system. If an economic system is able to export – or in other words, if it is able to gain a role in the international division of labour – it must enjoy some form of advantage: it must be able to produce goods at lower prices, supply higher-quality products, and place new goods on the market. An economic system can fulfil these various requirements if it has more efficient productive processes, a complex and advanced local industrial system, modern production services and infrastructures, good quality resources, and advanced production technologies – and also if its area comprises broad, diversified and advanced knowledge developed by complex cultural, social and economic processes.

There are therefore numerous sources of territorial competitiveness; and not surprisingly very different approaches have been taken to their analysis. This chapter presents theories which have concentrated on *factor endowment* as the source of territorial competitiveness. Although they differ in certain of their basic assumptions, these theories comprise a broad corpus of strictly neoclassical models which adopt diverse hypotheses on the mobility of goods and production factors in their treatment of growth from a *resource-based* perspective.

133

Imbalances in interregional factor endowments, and differences in levels of factor productivity, account for the advantage enjoyed by a local system in its relations with the rest of the world. These are the elements which underlie the growth path and which condition its timing and the form that it takes.

According to these theories, it is trade in goods or factors that explains the adjustment of the relative prices of goods and factors, increased productive capacity, and the achievement of full employment. For theories which assume the perfect mobility of production factors among regions (neoclassical growth models), differing remunerations of the production factors reallocate resources in space, and thus generate a higher rate of growth – according to typically neoclassical reasoning.[1] For theories which instead conceive goods as mobile (theories of interregional trade), differing levels of factor productivity give the region a comparative advantage in the production of a particular good, which it is able to export owing to price differential. Moreover, it is in the region's interest to resort to the external market for the purchase of those goods that it produces at a lower level of productivity than other goods. These imported goods are sold on the external market at prices that are more competitive than they would be if the goods were produced internally to the region.

It should be noted that the concept of 'growth' is used here with a meaning other than that given to it by the theories discussed in the previous chapter. The reason for this difference in the meaning of growth is the fact that these models have different policy concerns: not high unemployment – to be reduced by increased demand for local goods – but problems of poverty, underdevelopment, and inequalities in the distribution of income. Growth is consequently no longer interpreted as an increase in employment and short-term income; rather it is conceived as individual well-being (and its interregional convergence), which is achieved either through increases in factor productivity, and consequently in wage levels and per capita income (neoclassical macroeconomic models), or through specialization processes which generate interregional trade, and consequently advantages deriving from the purchases of goods offered on the external market at prices lower than they would be if the goods were produced internally.

These theories have a number of distinctive features which should be borne in mind. The first group of them – classical and neoclassical with factor mobility – are distinctive in that they make reference to a concept of 'relative growth', the purpose being to identify and explain paths of convergence or divergence in the levels and rates of output growth. In this respect, neoclassical models of factor mobility are still today erroneously viewed as only able to explain a tendency of local economies towards convergence. But the modern versions of these theories show that, if increasing returns are introduced into the neoclassical production function, behaviours and tendencies are produced which differ greatly from the original model's mechanistic and univocal result of re-equilibrium in income levels among regions.[2] Moreover, after modification of the original model by its authors to comprise two sectors, it is able to explain divergent trends in income levels if an initial equilibrium condition is assumed (see 'The two-sector model' below).

The distinctive feature of the second group of theories – classical and neoclassical, on interregional trade – is that they employ the concept of *relative advantage*, or *comparative advantage*, first formulated by Ricardo in his classical model of international trade and on the basis of which it was possible to identify a region's specialization. Among all the goods that can be offered on the external market, the region exports those that it produces at relatively lower production costs. This difference in production costs is due to the differing relative productivities of the factors used to manufacture the goods. This statement essentially means the following: even if a region produces all goods at higher prices, so that it is generally more inefficient in its production processes than any other region in the country, it may nevertheless be *relatively less inefficient in producing one particular good*. The region will thus be able to obtain a role for itself in the international division of labour by specializing in production of the good in which it is relatively more efficient. As we shall see, this argument has major normative implications, for it asserts that there is always an automatic mechanism guaranteeing the existence of some specialization, regardless of productive efficiency, and therefore that economic policy measures to foster development are unnecessary. The significance of this assertion is so far-reaching that it requires total guarantee of its truthfulness, although, as we shall see, this truthfulness is undermined by the ease with which economic mechanisms operating at national level are automatically expected to apply at regional and local level as well. The models described in this chapter draw their theoretical framework from the classical and neoclassical theories of growth and international trade. Once again, therefore, they are approaches to regional *growth* which envisage a uniform-abstract space in order to treat economic conditions, everywhere identical, in terms of aggregate economic indicators.

The next section discusses models constructed on the assumption of perfect mobility of the production factors, at nil transportation costs, and immobility of the goods produced.[3] It reverses the terms of this hypothesis and considers the idea that it is the production factors which are immobile, while the goods produced are perfectly mobile. In the case of production factors with nil transport costs, it will be shown that the neoclassical theory, besides being a theory of local growth, is also a theory of the mobility of the production factors. If goods are perfectly mobile, the theory of local growth is also a theory of interregional trade.[4] The latter derives from neoclassical theories of international trade which comprise models notable for their elegant economic logic but criticizable for the facility with which they are applied to a local setting.

REGIONAL GROWTH AND FACTOR MOBILITY

The one-sector model

The pioneering neoclassical model of regional growth was formulated by the economists George Borts and Jerome Stein at the beginning of the 1960s. It makes the usual assumptions of a neoclassical growth model:

- perfect competition in the goods market;
- perfect competition in the production factors market, which means that production factors are remunerated at their marginal productivity, guaranteeing profit maximization for the entrepreneur;
- full employment achieved by means of flexibility in the remuneration of the production factors;

135

- perfect mobility of the production factors among regions, at nil cost;
- total immobility of the goods produced;
- adjustment of the capital/labour ratio according to the dynamics of the production factors; there is therefore perfect substitutability between the two factors in the production of two goods.

In neoclassical theory, economic development depends on technical progress on the one hand, and on growth of the production factors on the other. These components are synthesized into the regional aggregate production function, which is expressed by a Cobb–Douglas function with constant returns:[5]

$$Y = AK^{\alpha}L^{1-\alpha} \tag{6.1}$$

where $0 < \alpha < 1$ and Y denotes income, A technical progress, K capital, L labour, and α and $1-\alpha$ respectively the efficiency of capital and labour.

In logarithms, the change in income Y over time is[6]

$$y = a + \alpha k + (1 - \alpha)l \tag{6.2}$$

where the lower-case symbols y, a, k, l respectively represent the growth rates over time of income, technical progress, capital and labour. Equation (6.2) states that whether income will grow over time depends on the growth of technical progress, and on the growth of capital and labour. Equation (6.2) can also be rewritten as:

$$y - l = a + \alpha \, (k - l) \tag{6.3}$$

which highlights a further important aspect: growth in the productivity of labour and/or per capita income (indicated by the left-hand member of the equation) is equal to growth in technical progress and the capital/labour ratio. In the absence of technical progress, per capita output can only increase if the growth of capital exceeds that of labour. For the same reason, the steady state – i.e. the dynamic equilibrium in which the capital/output ratio or per capita output remain unchanged as income increases – is guaranteed when the growth rate of capital equals that of labour.

According to the neoclassicals, growth is a matter of the optimal allocation of inter- and intra-regional resources. In an open economy with perfect factor mobility, a more efficient interregional allocation of resources requires the production factors to shift to where their productivity is highest, and where they receive the greatest remuneration. In a region, therefore, the growth rate of capital (k) depends on the amount of internal savings (sY) available to finance investment (ΔK), and on the differential between capital remuneration in the area (i_r) and capital remuneration in the rest of the world (i_w). In symbols, this means that:

$$k = \frac{sY}{K} + \mu \, (i_r - i_m) \tag{6.4}$$

In the same way, labour grows with the growth of the population (n) and the increase in the differential between wage remuneration in the region and the rest of the world ($w_r - w_m$):

$$l = n + \lambda(w_r - w_m) \tag{6.5}$$

μ and λ represent the extent to which capital and labour move according to remuneration differentials.

Assuming the existence of two regions – a poor South with more labour than capital, and a North with conversely more capital than labour – capital migrates from the rich area to the poor one; and, conversely, labour migrates from the South to the North. As a consequence, owing to different levels of factor productivity, remunerations are higher in the region where the factor is less abundant (Figure 6.1). The outflow of labour from the South enables it to increase productivity and therefore to increase remuneration of the labour factor. The same positive effect ensues from the outflow of capital from the North. The reallocation process halts when the regions attain the same factor productivities, the same remunerations, the same factor endowments, and therefore the same levels of income, in full employment. In Figure 6.2, where the complete availability of labour in the two regions is implicit in the x-axis, the area below the marginal productivity curve is the region's volume of output. The reallocation of resources generated by the differentials in factor remuneration therefore gives the North net advantages in terms of the increased production depicted by the dashed area in Figure 6.2a, while that of the South is equal to the dashed area in Figure 6.2b.

Put in dynamic terms, the model reaches steady-state equilibrium when capital and labour grow in exactly the same proportions. Figure 6.3 shows the shapes of the curves for which the growth rates of capital and labour are nil.[7] Straightforwardly obtained from these is the curve that represents constant growth of the capital/labour ratio used to analyse the dynamic properties of equation (6.3):[8] the steady-state equilibrium is reached at a certain positive value of the K/L ratio. Mathematical proof can be provided of the existence, uniqueness

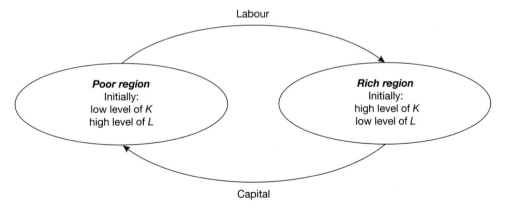

Figure 6.1 *Interregional flows of production factors in the one-sector and two-regions model*

(a)

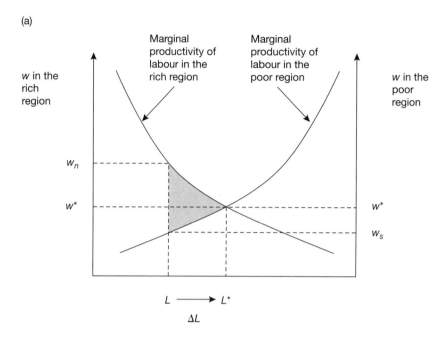

(b)

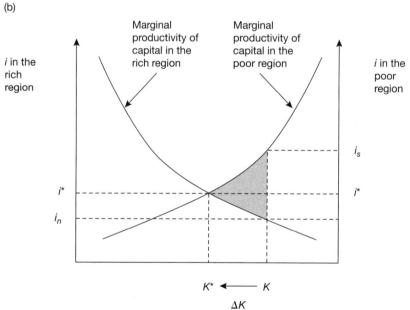

Figure 6.2 Production advantages from resource reallocation

Source: McCombie, 1988

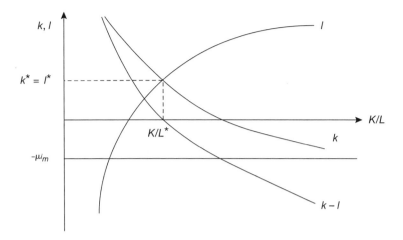

Figure 6.3 *Steady-state equilibrium in a neoclassical model*

and stability of the equilibrium solution: the latter coincides with the point at which the growth rate of the capital/labour ratio is nil. If the capital growth rate curve meets the labour curve for negative values, the region does not grow but instead constantly declines. We shall see later how dynamic equilibrium may fail to come about if increasing or decreasing returns are incorporated into the model.

The two-sector model

When the neoclassical theorists were confronted by empirical evidence which apparently refuted their conclusion that capital flows to regions with low income levels, they were obliged to develop a different approach which would furnish a better interpretation of the real movement of the factors, and which would in particular confirm the tendency of capital to shift to areas with higher wage remunerations.[9]

The model which the authors of the original one developed for this purpose – known as the two-sector model – incorporates more realistic assumptions and emphasizes the role of the inefficient allocation of resources within the same region as the determinant of intra- and interregional flows of production factors. The result is surprisingly different from that produced by the one-sector model: again according to neoclassical logic, the production factors migrate because they are attracted by higher remunerations. However, the subsequent reallocation of resources, due to an external shock that moves the regions far from the initial steady-state equilibrium, pushes local economies towards permanently different growth rates.[10]

The model is based on the following assumptions, some of which were already made by the one-sector model:

- the existence of two regions, each of which has two sectors producing two goods, one for export and one for domestic use, the former characterized by high labour productivity, the latter by low productivity. These sectors are often identified as industry (with high productivity) and agriculture (low productivity);

■ disequilibria in the trade balance, which by hypothesis are off-set by private capital movements;

■ perfect competition in the goods market: the quantities sold by the individual regions do not influence the good's price on the world market, whilst the price of the domestic good is determined by local demand and supply;

■ use of the capital factor only in the industrial sector: an assumption which does not affect the final result, as subsequently demonstrated by the authors;

■ constant returns in the production of the goods;

■ remuneration of the production factors at their marginal productivity;

■ equality between the cost of the production factors and the value of the marginal product of the factors, which guarantees profit maximization for firms.[11]

Starting from a situation of initial equilibrium, in which the growth rate is stable and *uniform* between the regions, and in which capital and labour grow in each of them at a constant rate equal to that of income, the model shows how the growth rates of the two regions vary if an exogenous shock is introduced.[12] Suppose that demand for the good exported by one of the two regions increases: the price of the good rises as a direct consequence; this effect has a positive impact on the value of the marginal product of the factors in the region. The outcome is an intra- and interregional reallocation of production resources, as follows:

■ capital stock in the sector producing for export increases as a result of the inflow of external capital attracted by greater remuneration;

■ labour demand by local firms increases because of the increase in the value of the marginal product of labour (generated by the rise in the exported good's price);

■ the greater demand for labour attracts workers both from the local agricultural sector and from other regions, given the higher remunerations available;

■ finally, the expansion of production and employment in the sector producing for export has a backwash effect on the agricultural sector, which records an increase in demand for the good, and, consequently, in production and employment.

In this model, therefore, production growth results from a more efficient allocation of resources to the manufacturing sector, with its higher productivity. After an initial stimulus triggered by increased demand for the exported good, the endowment of productive resources in the manufacturing sector is augmented by investments from outside, and by migrations of workers from other regions and from the agricultural sector.[13]

Two main conclusions ensue from this model. They differ from – indeed they conflict with – those of the single-sector model examined in the previous section. First, the production factors now move to the same high-wages region (Figure 6.4): the model is therefore supported by its authors' empirical results on the American regions.

The second conclusion is even more interesting: the model demonstrates that there is a tendency for regional growth rates to *diverge*. The reason for this is as follows: the income

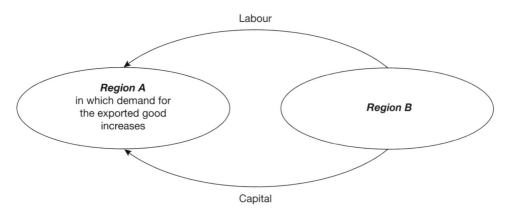

Figure 6.4 Interregional flows of production factors in the two-sectors and two-regions model

generated in the region exporting the manufacturing good differs from disposable income in an amount that equals the remuneration of the capital borrowed externally.[14] Internal saving, calculated as a share of disposable income, will therefore never be enough to finance local production. The shortage of capital guarantees high remuneration of this production factor, and this stimulates a constant inflow of capital from outside. As a result, the region's growth rate is persistently higher than that of other regions. The flow of workers into the exporter region alters the capital/labour ratio and thus attenuates the divergence in growth rates.[15] The agricultural sector acts upon growth rate disparities in two ways in the model: it supplies labour to the exporter sector, so reducing the divergence between growth rates; and in the growth process, its augmented goods demand stimulates production and attracts new workers from outside, once again mitigating growth rates disparities.

Interestingly, although the two-sector model starts from completely different assumptions and although it develops within a necessarily different conceptual framework, it reaches the same conclusion as the Harrod–Domar model. Both models argue, in fact, that if a region is a net importer of capital, it will have higher growth rates. Moreover, in line with Keynesian models of cumulative development *à la* Myrdal/Kaldor, the two-sector model demonstrates that this advantage persists over time, and thus aggravates regional disparities.

Contrary to the widely-held belief, the neoclassical model also envisages divergence among growth rates, not just their convergence. It does so by assuming an initial steady-state, thus eschewing the one-sector model's hypothesis of initial disequilibrium between regions. More recently, when the model has been given dynamic formulation with increasing returns, it has been able to account for divergence in growth rates even on the basis of initial disequilibrium conditions.[16]

Critical assessment of the neoclassical approach

The elegant and rigorous economic logic of the neoclassical models just described still gives them wide currency among analysts of regional growth. Generally acknowledged as their main merit is their attribution of a prime role to production factor mobility in the regional growth process. This mobility has greater impact at the regional rather than national level because there are fewer spatial and social frictions impeding resource mobility between regions than between countries.

Wealthy regions are highly attractive to labour. But the decreasing returns consequent on the intensive use of labour may diminish their competitiveness. In the same way, backward regions offer locational advantages due to their relatively lower wages and unit labour costs, and therefore attract capital (or at least they do so in the one-sector model) which increases the competitiveness of local industry. Traditional labour-intensive manufactures may therefore be advantageous to backward or newly-industrialized areas.[17]

However, the persistence of marked regional disequilibria suggests that these locational advantages are not enough to close the gap between advanced and backward regions. Strong areas are able to absorb the decreasing returns that accompany industrialization and high capital intensity, while the weak regions of the advanced countries have to compete with the low unit labour costs characteristic of the underdeveloped countries, and are therefore squeezed between the rich North and the poor South.[18]

The persistence of regional disequilibria also suggests that migratory flows, as the neoclassical theories interpret them, encounter a number of obstacles in reality, the first and perhaps most obvious of them being the economic and psychological costs of resources mobility. Assumed to be nil in the models examined above, these costs may instead explain why the factors do not move in the direction indicated by the model, or may not move at all.

Capital tends to remain in rich regions because of cumulative processes and synergies attendant on the process of development. Technical progress in the form of product and process innovations, new knowledge, processes of collective learning, and agglomeration economies in general, induce firms to invest only in rich regions already endowed with capital. Often supplementing these economic advantages are social and environmental conditions unfavourable to productive activities in regions with low per capita incomes.

Labour mobility, too, may encounter obstacles. First, the flow of labour to rich regions may well depend on the state of the strong region's economy: migratory flows may not take place to a rich but stagnant region with limited prospects of economic growth.[19] Moreover, migration from weak areas to strong ones is often selective, involving higher-skilled workers, who are able to find employment matching their expertise in the strong region. This type of migration inevitably deprives the weak area of more efficient and skilled resources, and thus works against possible convergence rather than for it. Finally, there may well exist 'imperfections' in the labour market which distort the perfect competition mechanism at the basis of the neoclassical logic, so that wages may increase even in the presence of unemployment in other regions; indeed, they may exacerbate that unemployment.

According to the theory of the 'Italian dual economy' propounded by Lutz,[20] wage increases imposed by the trade unions in strong areas (though the argument applies to strong sectors or firms as well) create wage dualism and segmentation in the national labour market. According to Lutz, the strong area reacts to the increased labour cost by laying off workers and introducing more advanced technologies. The unemployed workers move to the weak area, where they are willing to accept lower-paid jobs with very low levels of

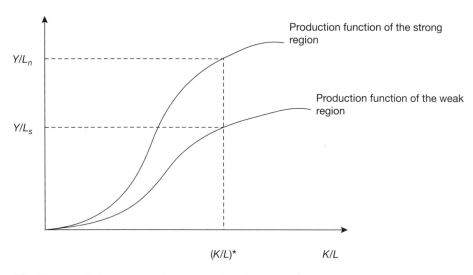

Figure 6.5 *Different production functions in two regions*

productivity. Moreover, the homogenized wage levels among regions – brought about by national-level bargaining despite the presence of wide factor productivity differentials – are dangerous labour-market imperfections, in that they eliminate the economic incentives which induce interregional mobility, of capital in particular. On this neoclassical view, persistent underdevelopment may well be due to the presence of institutional and social factors which restrict the mobility of resources to more efficient allocations, besides the low specialization and scant competitiveness which, according to the two-sector model, determine the initial growth of regions.

Finally, the uniqueness of the production function for all regions is somewhat unrealistic. If it is removed, the results of the model change: in the presence of different technologies, an equal capital/output ratio among regions no longer guarantees an equal level of production (Figure 6.5). In the real world, regions are very likely to produce different goods, while the spatially uneven distribution of specific technological knowledge and factors necessary for firms also partly explains the limited mobility of capital among regions.

FACTOR IMMOBILITY, SPECIALIZATION AND WELL-BEING

Specialization and comparative advantage: Ricardo's classical model

It was stressed in the previous chapter that one limitation of the demand-driven theories of regional growth is their inability to explain regional specialization. One of the first attempts to find an endogenous explanation for a region's specialization consists in the application of international trade models to interregional trade. These models are applied at regional level in the belief that, since interregional trade flows are larger and freer than international ones (owing to shorter distances and the absence of economic barriers to trade), theories developed at international level can be applied at the regional one as well.[21]

However, this contention may be erroneous. Although a region tends to specialize as much as and perhaps more than a nation, and although trade with the rest of the world may therefore be extremely important for its growth and well-being, the economic factors which influence international trade cannot be transposed indiscriminately to the regional level. Either they do not work exactly as they do at national level (flexibility of prices and wages, equilibrium in the balance of payments) or they do not exist (exchange rate fluctuations).

There is a further aspect that should be emphasized. These models were not developed to explain growth. They were instead conceived to interpret the specialization patterns of areas in the production of goods and the advantages deriving from trade – assuming the factoral endowment as given. They therefore determine the conditions that generate the greater sectoral specialization of regions, local production remaining equal. The advantage of specialization is the higher level of individual well-being that results from the lower relative prices of goods, which suggests a tendency to local development.

According to the models inspired by the theory of international trade, regions (and countries) exchange their goods on the basis of a *comparative advantage*, not an absolute one. This amounts to saying that even if a region produces all goods at higher costs and prices, and is thus generally more inefficient than the rest of the country in the production of all goods, it may be *relatively less inefficient in the production of one particular good*. It thus acquires a role in the international division of labour by specializing in the good that it produces at relatively less inefficient conditions. This result, known as the 'Torrens–Ricardo paradox', becomes clear on examining the logic of the model which produced it: David Ricardo's theory of comparative costs.[22]

The assumptions of the model are the following:

- there are two regions, the North and the South, which produce two goods, *A* and *B*;
- there is only one production factor, labour, whose productivity differs between the two regions;
- goods are produced without increasing or decreasing returns: marginal costs are constant;
- there is perfect mobility of production factors within the region, and perfect immobility of them between regions;
- there is no money, so trade takes place in 'units of goods' according to a barter system.

Table 6.1a reports the production costs of the goods in terms of the hours of labour required to produce them. The North produces one unit of both *A* and *B* with one labour-hour, while the South requires 2 labour-hours to produce good *A* and fully 4 hours to produce good *B*. The South is therefore more inefficient than the North in the production of both goods. If we stop at this point, according to the logic of absolute advantage, the North has no reason whatsoever to trade with the South and to purchase goods 'more expensive' than those which it produces internally.

Table 6.1 *Absolute and comparative advantages in the production of two goods in two regions*

Goods	A	B
Regions		
(a) Absolute advantage (labour-hour per unit of good)		
North	1	1
South	2	4
(b) Comparative advantage (opportunity cost in terms of units of the good forfeited in order to obtain an additional unit of the other good)		
North	1	1
South	1/2	2

According to the logic of the model, differences in absolute production costs are not enough to explain the advantages of trade between North and South: the analysis, according to Ricardo, should instead be made on the basis of *comparative costs*, or *opportunity costs*, defined as the quantity of another good that must be forfeited in order to be able to produce one unit more of a particular good. In our numerical example, in order to produce one extra unit of good *A* in the North, it is necessary to forfeit one unit of good *B* (and in the same way, to produce one extra unit of good *B* it is necessary to forfeit one unit of good *A*). In the South, to produce one extra unit *A* it is necessary to forfeit 2 units of good *B* (and to produce one extra unit of good *B* it is necessary to forfeit half a unit of good *A*).

Table 6.1b shows the comparative costs in production of the two goods in the two regions. The North is more efficient than the South in the production of good *B*; vice versa, the South is more efficient than the North in the production of good *A*. As a result, the North specializes in the production of only good *B*, and the South in good *A*, and the two regions exchange the amounts of those goods that are surplus to local demand.

How much do the regions gain from the trade? Let us suppose that the price of good *B* in the international market is fixed at 1.5 units of *A*, this being the intermediate price between the price of one unit of *A* in the North and 2 units of *A* in the South. Hence, if the North shifts one labour-hour from production of *A* to production of one unit of *B*, and exports the extra unit thus produced, it receives in exchange 1.5 units of *A*; whereas if it produces only one unit of *A* in that hour it will receive only 1 unit of *A*. The North thus saves half an hour of labour (0.5). Likewise, if the South specializes in the production of *A*, in one hour of extra labour (allocated to the production of *A*) it produces half a unit of *A*, forfeiting a quarter of a unit of *B*. By trading the half unit of *A* on the market at the ratio 1:1.5, the South obtains one-third (0.33) of a unit of *B* (0.5*1:1.5), instead of the one-quarter that it could produce internally: the South saves one-third (0.33) of a labour-hour.[23]

Both regions benefit from the exchange: their 'gains from trade' induce them to produce the good with which they enjoy a comparative advantage. Each region sees trade as an opportunity to obtain the imported good by resorting to a production technique superior

145

to the one available within the region, and which allows the imported good to be produced at a lower 'labour value'. This increases the population's well-being.[24] Hence the reallocation of labour to more efficient uses yields greater individual well-being and a higher level of production.

The assumptions of constant costs and the unlimited availability of the production factor imply that regions achieve complete specialization: each region is induced to produce one single good, the good with which it enjoys a comparative advantage.

The main result of the model is that, according to the theorem of comparative advantage, there is an automatic mechanism – generated by the market – which ensures that a region will always have some specialization regardless of its real capacity to produce competitively. This obviously leads to the radical claim that regions are *always* able to attain a role in the national and international market whatever their real productive capacities may be. When this does not happen – as evinced by the wide regional disparities that still exist in the advanced countries – it is only because there are elements which distort the normal workings of the factors market. However, before dispensing with policies to support local competitiveness and the convergence of regional growth paths, as the theory of comparative advantage suggests, it is necessary to determine whether the validity of the theory of comparative advantage holds at regional level. It will be shown below that it is highly unlikely that the theory of comparative advantage does so, with the consequence that regions compete solely on the basis of absolute advantage.

The Ricardo model has a number of weaknesses. Principal among them is that the difference in labour productivity between the two regions, which generates the comparative advantage, is not explained. Nevertheless, the concept of comparative advantage has intrigued economists because of the rigorous, and highly counter-intuitive, logic on which it is constructed, with the result that it has been too hastily incorporated into regional economics.[25] Only recently has its applicability to the regional context been explicitly disputed.[26]

The theory of factor endowments: the neoclassical Heckscher–Ohlin model

Within a neoclassical framework, in 1933 a Swedish economist, Bertil Ohlin, reprised a study already begun by Eli Heckscher in 1919 to formulate a model of international trade which remedied some of the unrealistic assumptions of previous theories and is known as the 'Heckscher–Ohlin model'.[27]

The Heckscher–Ohlin model (also known as the model of factor-endowment) is structured on the assumption that production factors are immobile: an assumption typical of international trade models and the opposite of the assumption made by the neoclassical growth model. It accounts for the tendency of regions to assume sectoral specialization by evidencing the reasons for the differing factoral productivities of regions (or countries), which are assumed to be exogenous in Ricardo's model. Given immobile production factors and freely tradable goods, the factor-endowments model shows that it is more convenient for a region to specialize in manufactures which make the most intense use of the most abundant production factor in the area because it is relatively less costly. Of all the goods that the region can sell on the external market, it should specialize in the one which it can manufacture at relatively lower production costs and then export thanks to the price differential. In the same way, it is more convenient for the region to resort to the external market to purchase goods offered at prices lower than those which, because of the lower level of productivity, the region would be able to achieve by producing those goods internally.

To reach these important conclusions, the model starts from the following assumptions:

- there are two regions, North and South, each producing only two goods with only two factors, capital and labour;
- each good is produced with a different factor intensity: good A, steel, requires more capital than labour; good B, corn, requires more labour than capital;
- the production factors are qualitatively identical but differ in quantity between the two regions; the North has more capital than the South; the South has a greater quantity of labour;
- the production functions are identical in the two regions. This assumption precludes the possibility that the comparative advantage derives from interregional differences in production technology, contrary to the Ricardo model;
- there is perfect competition in the market for production factors. Consequently, the equilibrium price of each good is equal to the marginal cost required to produce it, and the price of each factor equals the value of marginal productivity;
- demand conditions are identical in the two regions: hence they do not alter the direct relation between the relative prices of the goods before and after trade. In other words, the different price of a good in the two regions does not reflect differences in consumer preferences, but is due only to differences in the relative prices of the factors;
- production factors are immobile; the regions have the same factor endowments before and after trade;
- the goods produced are traded on the national and international markets; trade is free of any obstacles, such as tariffs or transport costs.

One of the simplest versions of the model takes the following form. In the North, which is the high capital-intensity region, labour costs more than capital because it is available in limited quantities. Consequently, the North employs less labour and more capital to produce steel than does the South, where capital costs more than labour $((K/L)_A^N > (K/L)_A^S$ in Figure 6.6).

The same applies to the production of corn: the North will tend to produce one unit of corn at a higher capital/labour ratio than that at which the unit is produced in the South. Note that in both regions, for any relative factor price, given that corn is a labour-intensive good, a unit of corn is produced at a capital/labour ratio lower than that of a unit of steel.

The argument thus far produces the following important result: in the South, where labour costs less than capital, it is obvious that the price of a unit of corn in relation to a unit of steel will be lower than in the North. Conversely, in the North, where capital is more abundant, and therefore less costly, the price of the labour-intensive good, corn, will be higher in relation to steel than it is in the South.

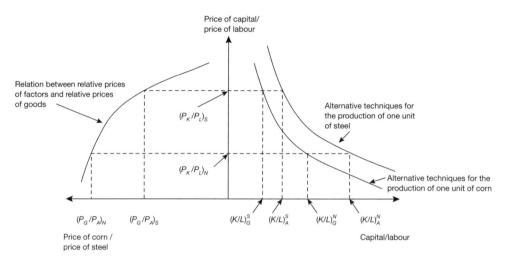

Figure 6.6 *Relative prices of factors and goods for different capital/labour ratios*
Source: Armstrong and Taylor, 2000, p. 125

These differences in relative prices generate comparative advantages for the two regions. It is economically convenient for the South to specialize in the production of corn and to trade the surplus for steel, which is less costly if purchased on the external market. Conversely, it is economically convenient for the North to specialize in the production of steel, and to obtain corn on the international market at prices lower than domestic ones.

The adjustment process does not stop here, however. Specialization, even if only partial, in production of one of the two goods requires the regions to reallocate capital and labour between the two types of production, and this alters the relative prices of the factors. The North, which must shift resources from the production of corn to the production of steel – the high capital-intensive good – will now experience relatively greater demand for capital than for labour, with a consequent reduction in the availability of capital and an increase in its relative price. In the South, as a consequence of its specialization in corn, demand for labour will be relatively greater than demand for capital, producing a relatively greater increase in wages with respect to the cost of capital. The result, as illustrated by Figure 6.7, is the equality of the relative prices of the goods on the international and domestic trade markets ('law of one price').

Empirical verification of the Heckscher–Ohlin model has often produced results at odds with the theoretical conclusions. The best known of these contradictory findings is the Leontief paradox.[28] When testing the model in the case of the United States during the 1950s, Leontief found that the exporting sectors of the USA – a capital-abundant country – were in fact high labour-intensity sectors. Using a different methodology, Moroney and Walker obtained the same result as Leontief: the labour-abundant southern regions of the United States were in fact exporters of capital-intensive goods.[29] Furthermore, the industrialization of the northern Italian regions in the period 1960–1990 led to their predominant

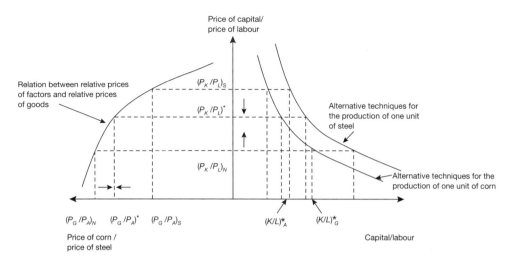

Figure 6.7 *Equality in the relative prices of factors and goods as a result of interregional trade*

Source: Armstrong and Taylor, 2000, p. 130

specialization in light industry – textiles, clothing, electronics – whilst the labour-abundant Italian South specialized in heavy industries like steel and petrochemicals.[30]

The first explanation for the empirical paradoxes of the Heckscher–Ohlin model is that production factors differ among regions not only quantitatively but also qualitatively. Leontief himself pointed out that it is impossible to treat labour as a homogeneous factor when testing the model. Different occupations and differing endowments of skilled labour may largely explain the specializations of regions – as demonstrated by the 'new factor-proportion theory' of international trade.[31] A second interpretation of the empirical paradoxes centres on the fact that the theoretical model does not allow for technical progress: product and process innovations may, in fact, generate substantial advantages even in traditional sectors, making them competitive in advanced regions endowed with modern and advanced capital – as pointed out by the proponents of the 'neo-technological' approach to international trade.[32] Finally, in regions where high public capital investments are made – like Southern Italy in the period 1960–1980 – or where large public incentives are offered in order to attract large firms – like the North of Great Britain and Ireland – industrial specialization is the result of these intervention policies rather than of market forces.

The results obtained by the model are interesting and they constitute its acknowledged merits. The model reminds us that interregional trade functions as a perfect substitute for factor mobility, because it equalizes the prices of the factors even in the absence of the geographical mobility of resources. Moreover, as said, the model is able to explain productive specialization (exogenous in the export-base model and in the classical Ricardian model), and to show increases in well-being.

It should be borne in mind, however, that under the model's intrinsic logic – with its assumptions of a given factor endowment, constant returns to scale and constant factor intensity per unit of output – it is not possible to associate greater specialization with greater

149

output. We may therefore conclude that the model, as it is formulated, is unable to define a process of regional growth. If anything, it suggests – implicitly and without proof – that there is a tendency towards regional development when this is understood in the sense of greater individual well-being (achieved in the model through 'gains from trade') and the obtaining and maintaining of a role in the division of labour.

ABSOLUTE VS. COMPARATIVE ADVANTAGE IN REGIONAL GROWTH

As we have seen, the model of interregional trade yields the important finding that regions, whatever their level of efficiency, always obtain a role in the international division of labour by specializing in production of the good which gives them a comparative advantage. There is therefore an automatic mechanism which guarantees that a region will have some sort of specialization regardless of its productive efficiency.

Given the importance of this assertion, one may legitimately enquire whether it applies to nations as it does to regions; or whether, instead, if a region is inefficient in the production of all goods, it may end up by producing nothing, leaving it to the region most efficient in absolute terms to produce all goods. In theoretical terms, this is to enquire whether regions compete on the basis of an absolute advantage, and not a comparative one.

It has been recently argued that regions differ from countries in that they compete on the basis of an absolute advantage.[33] To understand this assertion it is necessary to look at the adjustment processes which restore equilibrium in international trade, and at the operation of the principle of comparative advantages in the presence of exogenous shocks. The starting-point is the observation that, although the Ricardo model yields the result that trade is always in the interest of a country, it actually occurs only if there are absolute advantages in commerce between economic actors which compare the (absolute) prices of a good in the two countries, given a certain exchange rate.[34] In the higher-productivity country, wages are necessarily higher than in the less efficient country, where factor remunerations are defined on the basis of lower levels of productivity and overall output. It is logically likely that productivity gaps will be on average perfectly off-set by wage gaps (calculated in the same currency) – which demonstrates that comparative advantages are also absolute advantages.

However, let us assume the hypothesis that the monetary wage is kept artificially high in the less productive country so that it equals the wage in the efficient country, which is, say, 1 euro an hour (we are speaking here in terms of national, not regional economies). In this case, assuming that the exchange rate is 1:1, if labour productivity is equal to that shown in Table 6.1a, the monetary conditions of trade are those in Table 6.2: the North has absolute advantages in the production of both goods because of its labour force's greater productivity. The North produces everything; it achieves more than full employment; and it has a positive trade balance because it exports the surplus goods produced to the South – which instead produces nothing; suffers high unemployment; and has a constant deficit in its balance of payments. At national level, three automatic re-equilibrating mechanisms reinstate a regime of comparative advantages:

Table 6.2 *Monetary conditions of trade*

Goods	A	B
Regions		
North	1 euro	1 euro
South	2 euro	4 euro

1   in a fixed exchange rate regime, the North's persistently positive trade balance accumulates gold (or, in more modern terms, money) in the country, activating Hume's well-known 'price-specie-flow' mechanism:[35] an acceleration in the circulation of money generates inflation; this in its turn gives rise to an increase in prices and wages which erodes the country's absolute advantage in the production of all goods;

2   in a flexible exchange rate regime, the North's persistently positive trade balance induces revaluation of the exchange rate, and therefore induces an increase in the prices of exports and a decrease in the prices of imports. The result is again a loss of competitiveness by goods produced by the North which favours the South, which regains competitiveness in the goods for which it enjoys a comparative advantage;

3   the imbalance between demand and supply in the North's labour market pushes up wages, once again generating a loss of competitiveness by the North which favours the South.

These mechanisms restore a comparative advantage regime which enables the less competitive country to produce and thereby regain a role in the international division of labour.

However, although this holds for a country, it may not do so for a region. First, monetary wages may not reflect marginal productivities at regional level. On the one hand, wages are fixed at regional level on the basis of national-level agreements reflecting the country's average productivity; on the other, if low productivity is due to conditions external to firms (difficult accessibility, low quality of services), workers will not accept lower pay levels in a context where factor mobility is free. For this reason, the idea that wage gaps off-set productivity gaps, protecting the comparative advantage, is unrealistic.

We may therefore argue that the automatic re-equilibrating mechanisms which operate between countries are less efficient if the territories analysed are regions, because:

(a)   at regional level, a positive trade balance may be maintained by outgoing interregional capital movements, and it does not necessarily generate increases in local prices and wages.[36] More evidently, this mechanism operates in backward regions with negative trade balances: a situation which may persist if it is financed by public transfers in the form of pensions and unemployment benefits, or by inflows of external capital. If this is the case, the trade balance is not a macroeconomic constraint; and as a consequence, the re-equilibrating mechanism is not activated;

(b) there are no re-equilibrating mechanisms based on exchange rate flexibility at regional level because a single money regime operates;

(c) at regional level, there are only re-equilibrating mechanisms generated by disequilibria in the labour market. But neither in this case does the labour market mechanism operate as efficiently as it does at national level. When there are labour-market disequilibria, in an intra-national context of high factor mobility it is more likely that workers will migrate to high-wage regions, and less likely that wages will fall in weak regions and rise in strong ones. The real-wage readjusting mechanisms do not have sufficient time to exert their positive effects.

The upshot, therefore, is that when some regions are more efficient in absolute terms than others, they tend to produce all goods, while the others are at risk of mass unemployment and 'desertification'. These conditions will persist because the pure macroeconomic re-equilibrating mechanisms that seemingly ensure the relative competitiveness of territories at national level do not exist, or do not work, at the regional level. Hence derives the need to 'safeguard' the real competitive capacities of regions, because it is on these that long-term development opportunities depend.

THE THEORY OF CUSTOMS UNIONS

There is an important area of analysis in the theory of international trade which concerns itself with the effects of the creation of customs unions, like the European Common Market of 1958 or the Single European Market of 1993.[37] Some studies have examined regional aspects, given curiosity about the effects of the creation of the Single Market on regional growth and disparities. In recent years, the decision to institute a 'Europe of 25' has sparked animated debate on how entry into the European Union of the former members of the Communist bloc has affected both regional disparities within each country of the East and the growth paths of the regions of the fifteen original member-states of the Union.[38]

Creation of a customs union entails the abolition of economic and institutional barriers to international trade through the elimination of customs tariffs/duties, harmonization of technical standards in production and of rules on the quality certification of products, on their safety and transport, abolition of disparities in the indirect taxation of consumption goods, and common regulation of the capital market. The main consequences are an expansion of outlet markets and the creation of a large integrated market in which geographic-institutional distance among local markets affords them increasingly less 'protection' – as testified by the large-scale globalization processes of today's economy.

According to the theory of customs unions, the expansion of markets produces a number of important macroeconomic effects:

1   a marked increase in competition on markets;

2   greater economies of scale in goods production because of the larger size of outlet markets;

3   the creation of trade in final and intermediate goods because local markets are no
    longer the only ones available. Each region purchases from the most efficient supplier
    in the European market;
4   increased investments prompted by forecasts of greater competition: an effect which
    comes about even before the creation of a single market, in that it is the result of
    market expectations to which firms adjust;
5   demand for a greater variety of goods because of increased per capita income
    (income effect);
6   a shift of demand to goods produced with more efficient techniques guaranteeing
    lower prices for the same quality;
7   technology and knowledge transfers from strong to weak regions.

With the possible exception of the last of these effects, it is likely that all of them
will favour the richer and more advanced regions – given that these possess the financial,
productive and knowledge resources necessary to withstand increased competition on
markets, to respond to a diversification of demand, to exploit increasing economies of scale,
and to make decisive, targeted and timely investments as creation of the single market
proceeds. An interesting example is provided by the widening of regional disparities in the
former Communist countries consequent upon their entry into the European Union –
between central and peripheral regions, and between ones lying more to the east or to the
west (especially those bordering on the European Union). In these countries, in fact, the
empirical evidence suggests that, although there is an evident diffusion of economic activity
previously concentrated in metropolitan regions, the process works selectively in favour of
the regions situated closest to the European Union.[39]

This is also apparent at the more micro-territorial level between the strong and weak
areas of a particular region. For instance, the creation of the Single European Market in
1993 had positive effects on the large Italian cities of Milan, Rome and Naples, which in
the years immediately prior to 1993 had undergone a marked process of economic recovery
and development after years of recession.[40]

The last of the effects listed above – technology transfer from the 'centre' to the
'periphery' – can be interpreted as favourable to backward areas. Nevertheless, it requires
a local capacity to exploit technologies in pursuit of specific local competitiveness targets
which is often lacking in weak areas.

We may therefore conclude that customs unions theory warns that the creation of a large
single market may have repercussions on regional growth: it offers major opportunities for
development to local systems, but these opportunities may not be equal for all of them and
they may work instead in favour of advanced and dynamic regions, thus widening regional
disparities.

Customs unions theory states that, in broad integrated economic areas, the production
factors, technical knowledge and consumption patterns circulate freely, generating substantial homogeneity in productive capacity and demand. But perfect homogeneity in incomes
and factor endowments heightens the tendency towards productive despecialization.

153

The distinction between international and domestic trade disappears, and all output by the integrated area is traded according to criteria pertaining to the internal market and inter-regional trade. Thus explained is the growth of intra-industry trade: that is, the exchange of similar goods 'in two directions' – or 'horizontal trade' – which for some time has developed greatly in the advanced countries. This process, too, has interesting effects on the development of local systems.

Explanations of the apparently paradoxical phenomenon of trade in the same goods among countries and regions have been based on two groups of components:

- *demand components*: following the pioneering studies of Linder, the well-known Lancaster model has explained horizontal trade as stemming from the existence of 'horizontally' differentiated products. Goods have specifications which depend on different mixes of the same characteristics – the overall quantity of these characteristics remaining equal – which consumers can obtain by changing brand, supplier or producer. Free choice by consumers among these differentiated products, which they purchase according to specific individual utility functions, is the basis of horizontal trade;[41]
- *supply components*: in this case, horizontal trade in identical goods is explained by analysing how a good is produced and, especially, distributed in modern economies. It is through its sales and distribution network that a firm establishes and defines its advantage on a particular market. On this view, product differentiation stems only from the ways in which firms sell their products and control their market shares.

The implications for regional development are obvious. If we accept the idea that supply components – different modes of production and distribution – explain horizontal trade, regions must compete on the basis of more efficient and less costly production achieved by exploiting economies of scale, technical progress, and process and product innovations: all of which are elements very distant from the macroeconomic advantage envisaged by the theory of comparative advantage, and which obviously bear out the idea the competitiveness is based on an absolute advantage for regions. This is the thesis argued by the theories treated in the next part of the book.

CONCLUSIONS

This chapter has examined neoclassical theories of regional growth, where 'growth' is understood as an increase in individual well-being (and its interregional convergence). For the first group of theories – the neoclassical macroeconomic models – greater individual well-being is achieved through increases in factor productivity, and consequently in wage levels and per capita income (neoclassical macroeconomic models). For the second group of theories – which comprises the classical and neoclassical models of trade – higher levels of individual well-being are achieved through processes of regional specialization. Greater specialization pushes towards interregional trade and consequently yields advantages from the purchase of goods offered on the external market at prices lower than if the goods were produced internally.

The chapter has examined a number of commonplace assumptions about these theories. As regards the neoclassical macroeconomic models, it has shown that their interpretation as 'theories of convergence' is too restrictive: the modern versions of these theories demonstrate that inclusion of increasing returns in the neoclassical production function produces a set of behaviours and tendencies at odds with the mechanistic and univocal result of re-equilibrium between regional income levels obtained by the initial model. Moreover, the original model, which was modified by its authors to envisage the existence of two sectors, is able to explain divergences in income levels if initial equilibrium is hypothesized.

As regards the second group of theories – classical and neoclassical – on interregional trade, the chapter has shown that it is not possible to make immediate use of Ricardo's concept of comparative advantage when explaining the competitiveness of regions. Indeed, the chapter has demonstrated that the economic mechanisms on which the concept of relative advantage rests at national level do not apply at the regional one. This means that regions compete not on the basis of a comparative advantage, but an absolute one; an advantage that must constantly be recreated over the long period. The theories examined in the next chapters are specifically concerned with identifying the factors responsible for this advantage.

REVIEW QUESTIONS

1 Which conception of growth is at the basis of the neoclassical regional growth models?

2 What are the results achieved in the one-sector model and how do they differ from the results achieved by the two-sectors model?

3 Which aspects of the two-sectors model are reminiscent of the results obtained in other models?

4 What are the weaknesses and strengths of neoclassical regional growth models?

5 Is the statement that regional growth models always interpret convergence processes valid?

6 What is meant by the statement that regions compete on the basis of a 'comparative advantage'?

7 What is the result achieved by Ricardo's model?

8 What is the main theory in the Heckscher–Ohlin model and which conception of growth is the model able to interpret?

9 What are the reasons behind the idea that regions compete on the basis of an absolute advantage?

10 What is the theory of customs unions theorizing?

SELECTED READING ON EMPIRICAL FINDINGS

About regional competitiveness

Department of Trade and Industry (DTI) (2005) *Regional competitiveness and the state of the regions*, on-line edition, UK.

Edmonds, T. (2000) *Regional competitiveness and the role of the knowledge economy*, Research Paper 00/73, House of Commons.

Eskelinen, H., Maskell, P., Vatne, E., Malmberg, A. and Hannibalsson, I. (1998) *Competitiveness, localised learning and regional development*, London: Routledge.

Huovari, J., Kangasharju, A. and Alanen, A. (2003) 'Regional competitiveness in Finland', paper presented at the ERSA conference, held in Finland. Available on line.

Leontief, W. (1953) 'Domestic production and foreign trade: the American capital position re-examined', *Proceedings of the American Philosophical Society*, vol. 97, pp. 332–49.

About advantages and disadvantages of customs unions

Emerson, M. (1992) *One market one money: an evaluation of the potential benefits and costs of forming an economic and monetary union*, Oxford: Oxford University Press.

Resmini, L. (2007) 'Regional patterns of industry location in transition countries: does the economic integration with the EU matter?', *Regional Studies*, forthcoming.

FURTHER READING

Borts, G. H. and Stein, J. L. (1964) *Economic growth in a free market*, New York: Columbia University Press.

Camagni, R. (2002) 'On the concept of territorial competitiveness: sound or misleading?', *Urban Studies*, vol. 39, no. 13, pp. 2395–411.

Cecchini, P. (1988) *The European challenge: 1992*, Aldershot: Wildwood House.

Leontief, W. (1953) 'Domestic production and foreign trade: the American capital position re-examined', *Proceedings of the American Philosophical Society*, vol. 97, pp. 332–49.

Lutz, V. (1962) *Italy – a study in economic development*, London: Oxford University Press.

McCombie, J. S. L. (1988) 'A synoptic view of regional growth and unemployment: I – the neoclassical theory', *Urban Studies*, vol. 25, no. 4, pp. 267–81.

Ohlin, B. (1933) *Interregional and international trade*, Cambridge, Mass.: Harvard University Press.

Ricardo, D. (1971) *Principles of political taxonomy and taxation*, Harmondsworth: Penguin Books.

Part 3

Theories of local development: diversified-relational space

Chapter 7

Territorial competitiveness and exogenous development

SUMMARY

1   Diversified space: the components of territorial competitiveness
2   The growth-pole theory
3   The role of multinational companies in local development
4   The spatial diffusion of innovation
5   Infrastructures and regional development
6   New communication technologies and regional development

DIVERSIFIED SPACE: THE COMPONENTS OF TERRITORIAL COMPETITIVENESS

This part of the book examines an approach to the study of regional development which runs counter to those treated thus far. It differs from them in its conception of space. Whilst the theories discussed in previous chapters use the term 'space' to denote territorial areas assumed to be internally homogeneous and uniform, the theories now considered conceive 'space' as *diversified*. This change of perspective allows economic activities and production factors, demand and sectoral structure, to be treated as spatially dishomogeneous within a region, so that territorial relations are cast in new light.

This new conception of space enables identification of highly distinct polarities in a territory. Activities, resources, economic and market relations structure themselves around these polarities to generate a cumulative process of territorial agglomeration and a virtuous circle of development. This conception of space restores one of the inspiring principles of location theories – that of agglomeration economies as the source of local development – to theories of regional development. It is evident that any connection with geographical space, abstract or administrative, is thus severed. A more complex conception of space takes over, one based on the economic and social relations that arise in a territorial area. Whence derives the expression *diversified-relational space*.

When space is conceived of as 'diversified-relational', theories radically change in their nature. A macroeconomic and macro-territorial approach gives way to a micro-territorial and micro-behavioural one. The notion of a region as a portion of a national system acting and reacting economically as a single, internally homogeneous unit is abandoned. Its place is taken by individual economic actors (large or small, public or private, multinational or local) whose behaviour is studied in terms of location choices, productive and innovative capacity, competitiveness, and relations with the local system and the rest of the world.

The qualitative nature of theories – only in recent years superseded thanks to the more advanced and sophisticated modelling techniques examined in the next part of the book[1] – led in the mid-1970s to the distinction in the literature between '"pure and exact" regional theory without agglomeration economies, on the one hand, and "applied regional theory" which is inexact but takes agglomeration factors into account, on the other hand' drawn by Edwin Von Böventer.[2]

The theories analysed in this part of the book resemble those discussed in the previous chapter in that they conceive of development as a process generated and sustained by supply-side elements. But we shall see that they embrace a conception of development which has little to do with that of the theories previously examined. They abandon the short-run view of development as a simple increase in income and employment, and also that of individual well-being, and assume a longer-term perspective. They identify all the tangible and intangible elements in a local area which determine its *long-term competitiveness* and enable it to maintain that competitiveness over time. To reprise the distinction between development and growth, this part of the book deals with theories of local development, while the endeavour to identify the (short- or long-period) growth path pursued thus far is abandoned.

The theories analysed here therefore seek to identify the factors which render the costs and prices of production processes lower than they are elsewhere. These factors are (a) elements *exogenous* to the local context, which originate externally to the area and are transferred into it either fortuitously or deliberately, and (b) *endogenous* elements which arise and develop within the area and enable it to initiate a process of self-propelling development.

Exogenous elements comprise the following: the fortuitous local presence of a dominant firm or a multinational company; the diffusion in the area of an innovation produced elsewhere; or the installation of new infrastructures decided by external authorities. Although these elements have nothing to do with local features and productive capacities, once they are present in an area they may catalyse new economic activities and development. Endogenous elements are entrepreneurial ability and local resources for production (labour and capital); and in particular the decision-making capacity of local economic and social actors able to control the development process, support it during phases of transformation and innovation, and enrich it with external knowledge and information. All these are factors strengthened and enhanced by a concentrated territorial organization which generates local processes of knowledge-acquisition and learning; networks of economic and social relations which support more efficient and less costly transactions;[3] and advantages of economic and physical proximity among economic actors.

The assumption of diversified space entails definitive abandonment of the notion that regional development consists solely in the allocation of resources among regions. Instead, regional development must be conceived of as stemming from local productive capacity, competitiveness, and innovativeness. The neoclassical model of interregional growth (Borts and Stein's one-sector model) presumed that the national growth rate is exogenously determined, and that the problem for regional development theory is explaining how the national growth rate is distributed among regions. According to this logic of *competitive development*, the growth of one region can only be to the detriment of the growth of another region, in a zero sum game.[4] The theories examined here adopt a notion of *generative development* whereby the national growth rate is the sum of the growth rates achieved by individual regions. National economic development may well increase because of growth achieved by a particular territorial area, and this growth may also come about – in the presence of increasing returns (as for the theories discussed in the next chapter) – with the same resources.

This chapter examines theories which identify the elements exogenous to the system which determine long-term competitiveness: the presence of a dominant firm, or of a multinational company; the diffusion of an innovation originating in another area; the construction of transport and social infrastructures, and finally the adoption of advanced communication technologies. Left for treatment in the next chapter are theories which, with intriguing and impressive insight, seek to identify the endogenous elements that determine local competitiveness. These theories hypothesize the existence of increasing returns generated by territorial agglomerations; they in fact conceive the development path as dependent on the efficiency of a territorially concentrated organization of production, not on extra economic resources or on their more efficient spatial allocation.

THE GROWTH-POLE THEORY

The economic approach: Perroux's contribution

The first theory which abandons the notion of uniform-abstract space to conceive of a diversified-relational space is the 'growth-pole theory' first formulated in 1955 by the French economist François Perroux. The basis of Perroux's theory is encapsulated in his celebrated statement – which despite its simplicity has been important in its consequences: 'Development does not appear everywhere at the same time: it becomes manifest at points or poles of development, with variable intensity; it spreads through different channels, with various final effects on the whole of the economy'.[5]

Thus, in the same period when the principal models of interregional growth were being produced, Perroux formulated a theory of local development which envisaged selective growth at certain points in space where a 'propulsive unit' triggered the development process. Perroux identified this element as the fortuitous presence in the area of a dominant firm, which he called '*l'industrie motrice*' owing to its capacity to influence through its investment decisions the levels of investment undertaken by the firms connected with it.[6] Because of its vigour and technological dynamism, the dominant firm responds to the needs of an external market (and here the influence of the export-base model is evident). And thanks to its dominant position in the sector and in the economy, it generates a series of positive effects on the sector to which it belongs, and on the economy as a whole.

161

A technological innovation by the dominant firm which reduces the price of a good, or enhances its quality, increases external demand for that good. This stimulates greater production of the good which in its turn generates a growth-pole through a series of positive effects:

- *a Keynesian multiplying effect on income* which horizontally pervades the entire economy. Increased production by the dominant firm augments employment in both the firm itself and in those connected with it, with a consequent increase in incomes and consumption;
- *a multiplying effect à la Leontief*, connected with intersectoral input–output effects, which vertically pervades the dominant firm's filière. Firms and sectors upstream from the dominant firm see their production and outlet markets expand. Relations among firms act as channels transmitting the development without which the growth-pole could not exist (the theory thus closely reflects a conception of diversified-*relational* space);
- *an acceleration effect* on firms' investments. Growth of demand for the dominant firm's goods and those of the firms connected with it stimulates investments (there is an evident reference here to the Harrod–Domar model). These investments are facilitated by higher profits which generate higher levels of reinvestment of those same profits. Like the input–output effect, this acceleration effect operates vertically along the dominant firm's filière. This gives rise to selective development because, especially in its direct effects, development may be confined only to the sector to which the dominant firm belongs, and to the sectors connected with it;[7]
- *a polarization effect* which produces what Perroux calls a 'growth-pole'. Increased demand for intermediate goods and services generated by the dominant firm induces other firms to locate close to it in order to (a) minimize their transportation costs in serving the propulsive firm, (b) exploit the infrastructures and fixed social capital activated by the pole, (c) improve the local managerial or entrepreneurial skills produced by the economic activities generated by the dominant firm, and (d) exploit the greater demand produced by higher employment.

This theory comprises a number of key features for the interpretation of development already put forward by previous theories: the importance for the development process of infrastructures, services and input/output relations among firms and sectors that balanced development models had already emphasized; the positive effects of growth in demand (real and expected) on the level of investments already highlighted by the Harrod–Domar model; and the Keynesian income multiplying mechanisms already present in the export-base model.

The difference resides in the way in which these factors are conceived – no longer in macroeconomic and macro-territorial terms, but rather in microeconomic and micro-behavioural ones.[8] Development is generated by the dynamism of a firm and by its links with other firms, and the cumulative growth process is the result of rational behavioural reactions by the various actors involved in the dominant firm's activities.

Perroux thus for the first time incorporated into a theory of local development the possibility of selective development: that is, development confined to particular sectors or particular areas of a region by cumulative processes which work to the advantage of specific sectors and areas. In Perroux's approach, therefore, growth does not necessarily and automatically spread through all the economy's sectors and through the national and regional territory.

The territorial approach: Boudeville's contribution

Although the growth-pole theory aimed to interpret local development, it lacked a clear local dimension. According to Perroux's theory, the channels through which development spreads are input/output relations, but it gives these relations no concrete spatial location. Not surprisingly, therefore, it has been argued in the literature that economic space and geographic space do not coincide in Perroux.[9]

In 1964, Jacques Boudeville endeavoured to emphasize precisely this spatial/territorial component of the growth-pole theory, by imposing clear geographic boundaries on the positive development effects generated by the propulsive industry. By constructing a simple extension of Perroux's theory, Boudeville identified three ways to define the geographic boundaries of polarization effects. For this purpose, he used the following three hypotheses on the geographic location of the actors involved in the development process, or on the geography of positive spillover effects:

1   the propulsive industry and the firms connected with it are geographically clustered;[10]
2   the propulsive firm is located in a city. Hence – in keeping with the classical tradition of urban economics – the input/output relations which generate development can be hypothesized as operating within that same urban area;
3   the positive effects generated by the dominant firm impact only upon the local area. This amounts to hypothesizing the absence of leakages in the income-multiplying effects evidenced by the export-base theory, and to arguing that a growth-pole comes into being when the positive effects of a dominant firm are confined to the local area.

These three interpretations have an important feature in common: for all three of them the key factor in development is no longer, as in Perroux, sectoral interdependence alone. For local economic development to come about, there must be a *spatial concentration* of production activities which determines the positive final effect exerted by the dominant firm on local development.

This last point has an important implication, which represents a watershed with respect to the logic used by previous interregional growth models to interpret regional development: the spatial concentration of economic activity is a territorial organization of production which generates development more efficiently than does spatial dispersion. The growth-pole theory was therefore the first step towards conceiving space as an active factor in development. It opened the way for the analyses of endogenous development presented in the next chapter. For these analyses, the spatial concentration of activities is the source of increasing returns in the form of agglomeration economies, localization economies, technological externalities, and localized learning processes – all of which are elements that enhance the competitiveness of local firms and foster local development.

Critical assessment of the theory

The merits of the growth-pole theory have already been pointed out. It suggested, for the first time, the existence of selective local development which works in favour of some sectors and some specific local areas but does not necessarily benefit the region as a whole. The real world is constellated by strong areas (with greater densities of manufacturing activity, and a greater capacity for economic growth) and weak areas, even within the same region: for the first time, the growth-pole theory is able to explain phenomena of concentrated settlement.

Moreover, the theory has the outstanding merit of recognizing input/output relations among sectors on the one hand, and the spatial concentration of productive activities on the other, as the crucial factors in development. As regards sectoral relations, it is the first theory of regional development to have emphasized the competitiveness of certain sectors and industrial dynamics in explanation of local development.[11] As for agglomeration economies, this is the first time that these become an essential component of theories of local development as well.

Finally, it is a theory which brings together notions developed by other, and apparently entirely distinct, theories. The ideas of the central place theory[12] reappear in Perroux's argument that the pole furnishes higher-level services (services to businesses, infrastructural and health services, educational, recreational and cultural ones) for a broader area, and that the availability of these services attracts new businesses into the area around the pole. Once again, firms take their location decisions in the light of the two crucial features emphasized by location theory: transportation costs (in this case of intermediate goods delivered to the dominant firm) on the one hand, and agglomeration economies on the other, generate a polarization effect and give rise to a theory of local development.

The experiences of the European countries where public intervention has been inspired by this theory – intervention either through the creation of state-controlled enterprises (as in Italy) or through policies to attract foreign companies (as in the United Kingdom and Ireland) – have revealed many of the flaws in growth-pole theory.

A first defect of the theory is its failure to explain the reasons for the initial presence of a propulsive industry in an area: the theory assumes this presence to be exogenous. Because the growth-pole theory does not explain why the propulsive firm has located in that particular area, it is unable to distinguish the effects of a natural pole from those of a planned pole.

Incentivizing the location of large firms in weak areas through government growth policies is an excessively banal normative interpretation of Perroux's and Boudeville's theory. For a pole to come into being, the large firm, or the industrial complex, must be embedded in a broad production filière which subcontracts and outsources numerous activities; investment by the dominant firm thus generates very strong multiplying effects, and it is in these that the definition of a pole resides. In order to generate the effects of a natural pole, a planned pole must necessarily be able to create a local network of inter-sectoral relations if the positive effects of the large firm's dynamism are to remain *in situ*. And this is an aspect which the majority of public intervention schemes guided by this theory have greatly undervalued.[13] There are, in fact, numerous examples of the creation of large local industrial complexes (e.g. steel and petrochemicals) in the Italian Mezzogiorno which have established intersectoral relations outside the region and transmitted the beneficial effects of development beyond the confines of the local economy.

A second shortcoming of the growth-pole theory is that it has deliberately ignored the negative effects (Albert Hirschman's 'backwash effects'[14]) accompanying the formation of a pole, emphasizing only its positive ones (Hirschman's 'spread effects'), and stressing expectations of success in creation of a pole. But it may easily happen that the location of a large firm in an area has an initial crowding-out effect on local firms – especially crafts businesses – resulting from the shock on prices and wages generated by the advent of the large firm, with a markedly negative impact on local employment.[15]

Figure 7.1 illustrates the evolution over time of the negative and positive effects exerted on an area's economy by the formation of a pole. The positive effects tend to appear in the long period, after initial resistance has been overcome and relations have been established between the dominant firm and local businesses. The negative effects, which are very pronounced in the first period, subsequently attenuate, when the local economy has re-organized itself around the large firm. The result is a pattern of net effects (so-called 'net spillover effects') which is initially markedly negative but then becomes positive when the development-generating effects absorb the negative ones. It has been estimated that the period of net negative impacts may last even for decades.

Moreover, close inspection of the growth-pole theory reveals a contradiction in its logic when applied for normative ends. If the aim is to develop a weak area, the domin-ant firm must have need of only few local inputs; but for this reason it is unable to generate large-scale spillover effects on the local economy. In order to obviate this difficulty, Italy switched in past decades from sectors like steel and petrochemicals (1960s) to mechanical engineering and car production (1970s and 1980s) – sectors requiring greater inputs and therefore presumed to generate spillovers. In this case, however, the growth-pole policy did not produce the expected results, which demonstrates that the process is a highly complex one, and requires interventions of another kind: not only incentives to industry but also support for the development of intangible elements such as human capital, know-ledge, and learning.

The growth-pole theory has indubitably played an important part in the history of economic analysis of local development. It was the first theory to be able to interpret development using a microeconomic approach. It showed that factors like sectoral com-petitiveness and territorial concentration are crucial for development, and it introduced the notion of selective development in some areas and some sectors. On the theoretical front, however, it was unable to explain why an engine of development (a dominant firm) should be present in some areas and not in others. Because of this shortcoming, normative application of the theory has resulted in sometimes severe policy failures.

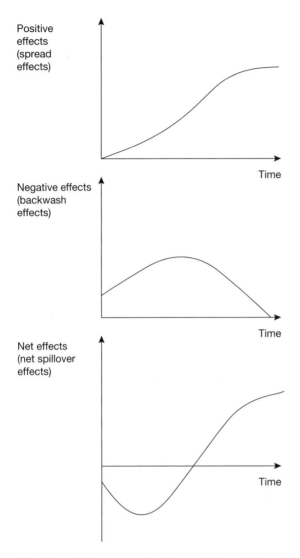

Figure 7.1 *Temporal evolution of the positive and negative effects of a pole*

THE ROLE OF MULTINATIONAL COMPANIES IN LOCAL DEVELOPMENT

On the basis of criticisms of the neoclassical model for its optimistic view of capital mobility, and of Perroux's equally optimistic view of the role in local development of large-sized firms, in the 1970s a theory was put forward which interpreted regional development in terms of the impact of large multinational firms on local growth. The micro-behavioural nature of this model's reasoning justifies its inclusion in this chapter.

Adopting a 'radical' approach, this theory focuses on the impact of the location choices of multinational firms on regional development. Its overall thesis is that the location decisions of multinational firms are driven by the profit motive. This, the theory argues, is evident in their choice of areas with low labour costs for the location of labour-intensive unskilled production activities.[16] On this logic, weak regions are the preferred sites for these kinds of low-value-added functions, and the development (crisis) of these areas is strictly linked to their success (failure). Breaking the production cycle down into its various functions and finding an appropriate location for them is, according to the theory, the winning strategy for multinational firms. However, this strategy tends to consolidate the division of labour between rich regions as the centres of advanced managerial high-value-added functions, and poor ones destined to receive lower-level activities. There is therefore the risk that what Lipietz calls an 'integration/domination' relationship with the advanced regions may become permanent.[17]

On this radical view, it is capitalist accumulation which causes spatially uneven development. The workings of the capitalist system reproduce and exacerbate regional disparities over time, widening the gap between rich and poor areas within the country. Accentuating this tendency are further risks for weak areas inherent in a capitalist economy: principally the hyper-mobility of capital, which entails constant changes in the physical location of multinationals. This exposes weak regions to expansion followed by decline of their economies, with rapidly alternating waves of growth and recession. The very rapidity with which growth comes about generates crises: the scarcity of infrastructures, labour and productive capacity in periods of expansion induces a rise in local wages and prices which impoverishes the entire regional economy.[18]

The persistence of regional imbalances despite public interventions in favour of large firms in the North of the United Kingdom, the South of Italy, and Ireland has empirically belied the claims of this 'radical' current of thought.

The 1980s saw the advent of a more balanced school of thought which emphasized also the positive processes engendered in local economies by the presence of multinationals.[19] The elements cited are the following:

- a strengthening of the productive system in areas with scant entrepreneurship;
- enhancement of industrial agglomeration effects;
- job creation at the local level;
- stimulus for new industrial investments upstream and downstream from the multinational firm;
- the creation of new firms upstream and downstream from the multinational;
- increased managerial and technological expertise in the area;
- localized technological spillovers;
- cross-fertilization between firms and local institutions in the provision of vocational training.

The intensity with which these processes arise in the local economy depends on the characteristics of the multinational firms which locate in the area and on the characteristics of the area itself. The degree of the group's vertical integration, the technological intensity of its production process, the size of its filière, its position in that filière, the type of investment (greenfield or the purchase of already-existing firms), and the extent to which

167

production is outsourced, are all aspects of the *modi operandi* of multinationals which affect the benefits that they generate for the local economy.

As for an area's characteristics, its pre-existing productive system (assessed quantitatively and qualitatively), human capital and technological knowledge determine the extent to which location in the area by a multinational company affects the local economy. A recent body of literature stresses that a multinational's input/output relations with local firms are crucially important for local development – which recalls the growth-pole theory and its emphasis on the importance of intersectoral relations for local economic development. This more recent school of thought mathematically models the effects of input/output relations on economic growth as increasing returns in an aggregate production function that are entirely absent from Perroux and Boudeville's theory.[20]

The development of this school of thought was boosted in the 1980s by numerous technological innovations which altered the standard functional division of labour. The reprogrammable systems made possible by CAM/CAD applications, and the computerization of numerous administrative and managerial procedures, gave rise to a new organization of industry characterized by closer functional integration (production, design, research, marketing and strategy), deverticalization, and reorganization of the production cycle. This inevitably had spatial impacts, which were at first centripetal but then centrifugal, pushing higher-level functions towards weak regions.[21]

Finally, the literature on the role of multinationals in local development has more recently focused on aspects of technology transfer (or technological spillovers) from multinational firms to local economies.[22] These spillovers are more frequent in advanced areas with high levels of innovation. They also occur most frequently in industrial areas similar to the sector in which the multinational operates and with already-existing specific knowledge that the additional knowledge generated by the multinational enriches.[23] Moreover, the innovativeness already possessed by a local system is important if the latter is to exploit the technological externalities produced by a large multinational. It is accordingly useful to examine two features: the endogenous technological potential of an area, and the mechanisms by which innovation spreads through space.

THE SPATIAL DIFFUSION OF INNOVATION

Hägerstrand's model: geographical distance

We have not yet examined the role of innovation in local development. The interregional theories and models of local growth presented in Part 2 of this book conceived innovation, in typically neoclassical manner, as 'manna from heaven' available to all economic actors at no cost, and as such with no influence on the growth capacity of systems: technological progress, these theories and models believed, came about at the same pace and simultaneously in all sectors, among all economic actors, and in all territorial contexts.

However, if the assumption of perfect information is abandoned for the more modern notion adopted in the 1980s of information asymmetry, the simplistic framework assumed thus far no longer holds. Innovation comes about in entirely different ways in different areas and is thus a key factor in explanation of the differing capacities of regions to grow.

It accounts for the process of output growth, which cannot be directly attributed to an increase in the production factors, in equilibrium and with constant returns to scale.[24] Innovation is therefore of key importance for an explanation of why local systems grow; and any thoroughgoing theory of regional development must be able to specify the sources of innovation and the factors that give a local system innovative capacity.

An early approach to analysis of these matters thought of innovation as an exogenous factor in development: innovation, this approach maintained, propagates through specific territorial channels to generate positive impacts on a local area from outside. Analysis should therefore examine the territorial routes whereby innovation reaches a particular area: routes formalized in models of the spatial diffusion of innovation.

The best-known, and probably earliest, of these models was developed by the Swedish geographer Torsten Hägerstrand.[25] His pioneering work on innovation diffusion, on which numerous subsequent studies were based, maintained that the temporal development of an innovation displays an S-shaped pattern represented by a logistic function, and that temporal phases of the cycle must be combined with spatial ones to depict a spatial-temporal diffusion of innovation moving through the following three phases:

1   the first 'adoption' stage, when the urban hierarchy canalizes the course of diffusion: the innovation centre is often the primary city or some other metropolitan centre; the centres next in rank then follow (Figure 7.2a);
2   the second 'diffusion' stage, when the hierarchical effect and the 'neighbourhood effect' (the latter illustrated by Figure 7.2b) act simultaneously, with different weights according to the moment in time. Initially, the hierarchical effect still predominates; however, as time passes, the friction of space puts outlying large centres out of the immediate range of the diffusion's influence, and the neighbourhood effect predominates;[26]
3   the third 'saturation' stage, when the spatial diffusion of the innovation becomes random. Saturation may be reached around the innovation centre while the rate of diffusion is still low in distant areas. The overall deceleration in the diffusion pattern may conceal a catching-up process in which the innovation is still spreading through distant areas although adoption at the centre has halted.

In Hägerstrand's model, an innovation is diffused by an epidemic process: the pure likelihood of contact between people who have already adopted an innovation and its potential adopters explains innovation diffusion in this model, which implicitly assumes that every potential adopter has the same opportunity to adopt, and that spatial variations in adoption are due solely to information flows that spread territorially at different times. The model assumes that information about innovation automatically entails its adoption; and when Hägerstrand seeks to include the uneven distribution of receptiveness among an innovation's potential adopters, he once again resorts to a measure of information intensity.[27]

It should be borne in mind that the use of a logistic function is only acceptable if it can be assumed that potential adopters are all equally likely to adopt a particular innovation. The element that makes this assumption unacceptable is space: it is very difficult, in fact,

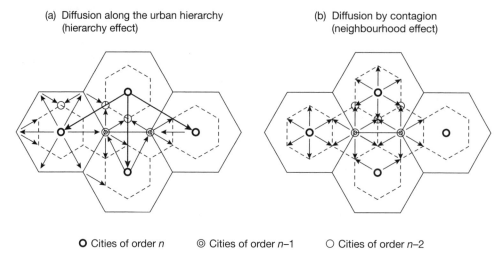

Figure 7.2 *Hägerstrand's channels of innovation diffusion*

to hypothesize that potential adopters located in two territorial areas different in structure and productive performance will have the same receptiveness to innovative processes. Hence space does not perform a significant role in Hägerstrand's model except in its form as pure geographical distance between actual and potential adopters.

The contribution of Griliches and Mansfield: economic distance

The economists Zvi Griliches and Edwin Mansfield have examined the spatial characteristics that condition the innovation adoption process. They introduce into Hägerstrand's model the idea that the spatial diffusion of innovation is influenced less by geographic distance among adopters than by economic distance: the amount of productive activity in an area, and its levels of income, consumption and investment, can straightforwardly explain the greater receptiveness of an adoption area.[28]

Griliches and Mansfield formulate a two-stage methodology for the empirical analysis of innovation diffusion. The first stage involves estimation of a logistic function taking the following form:

$$D = K/(1 + e^{-(a+bt)}) \qquad\qquad (7.1)$$

where D is the density of adoption, or the cumulated number of adopters, a the moment in time when the first adoption occurs (origin of the logistic curve), b the speed of adoption (the slope of the logistic curve), and K the asymptote towards which the curve tends (the ceiling of the logistic curve), i.e. the maximum number of potential adopters that the innovation can reach (Figure 7.3). The analytical properties of the logistic function enable simple estimation of its parameters.[29]

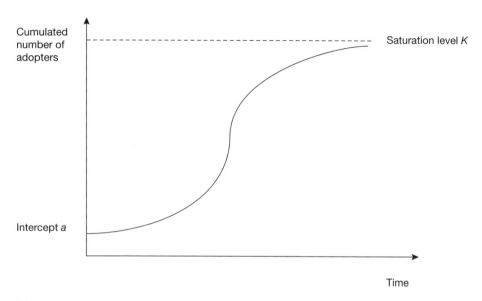

Figure 7.3 *The logistic function*

Once the parameters of the logistic function are known, the next stage is estimation, by means of interregional cross-section regressions, of the incidence of the local economy's main characteristics on the historical moment of the innovation's adoption, on the speed of its penetration, and on its level of saturation. This furnishes a clear 'snapshot' of the various spatial patterns of the innovation's adoption.[30]

Griliches applied this methodology to explain the wide cross-sectional differences in the rates of use of hybrid seed corn in the United States. He found that the lag in the development of adaptable hybrids for particular areas and the lag in the entry of seed producers into these areas (differences in origins) were explained by varying profitability of entry, 'profitability' being a function of market density, and innovation and marketing costs. Differences in the long-run equilibrium use of hybrid corn (ceilings) and in the rates of approach to that equilibrium (slopes) were explained, at least in part, by differences in the profitability of the shift from open pollinated to hybrid varieties in different parts of the country.[31]

When the same methodology was applied to interpret the diffusion of fixed telephony services in the twenty Italian regions, it provided clear evidence that adoption of the innovation (origins) differed markedly among regions because of socio-economic factors: the industrial performance of regions and the educational level of the local population amply explained both the level of saturation and the speed of adoption of the service (i.e. the ceilings and the slopes). The urban structure of a region was instead important in determining the historical moment when the innovation was adopted (expressed by the value of the *a* parameter) – thus highlighting the role of cities in the birth of innovations.[32]

In the case of process innovation adoptions (industrial automation, robotization, etc.), one may logically expect the adoption rate to be lower in weak areas. At macro level, an important obstacle against adoption in weak regions is the lower cost of labour, which reduces the relative profitability of new labour-saving technologies. From a microeconomic point of view, there are factors of cultural and organizational backwardness which generate high adjustment costs in the switch from an old to a new technology. These costs are such that the latter is much less profitable in weak than in advanced regions.

From a dynamic perspective, there are two further critical elements in explaining the late adoption of innovations in weak regions. The first is the irreversibility of non-adoption choices, which may condemn an area to a permanent state of technological backwardness. Irreversibility springs from complex, irreversible processes of cumulative learning and investment in knowledge which accompany transition to a new technological trajectory. These processes influence the costs of, and revenues from, adoption of the new technology, and they alter its relative profitability. In the first period, when the innovation is adoptable, it may well be the case that the costs of adopting a new technology exceed the revenues, justifying, from a static point of view, the non-adoption decision (Figure 7.4). But the time trend of the costs and revenues of adoption shows that there is a temporal interval within which adoption of the new technology is profitable. However, beyond a certain point (time 2 in Figure 7.4), the non-adoption decision becomes irreversible because the costs of adoption are greater than the revenues, and the trend increases in time. As a result, the weak region is condemned to competing against the advanced regions with a more limited and obsolete technological endowment.[33]

The second critical element concerns the need for anticipatory and far-sighted public policies: in fact, if incentives for new technologies are allocated in the first phases of adoption, they may be less than those that are subsequently necessary when the technologies are being developed. As Figure 7.5 shows, if a new technology starts to be developed at time 0, its development may involve a limited extra cost with respect to the old technology. But if the new technology is adopted at time 1, the public costs required to support the late adoption are higher. Consequently, anticipatory and far-sighted policies supporting the introduction of new technologies are all the more necessary and desirable, but generally more difficult to put in place in backward regions.

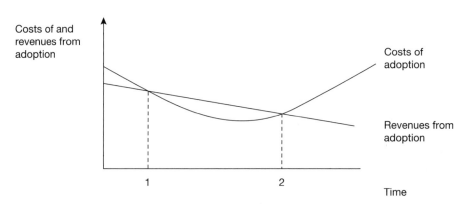

Figure 7.4 Time trend of the costs of and revenues from adoption

Source: Camagni and Capello, 1998

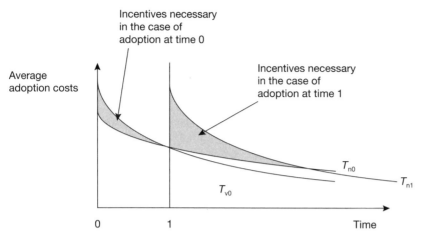

Figure 7.5 *Temporal evolution of the incentives necessary for the adoption of a new technology*

Source: Camagni, 1996

The limitations of the logistic-epidemic model

Although the logistic model is well known in the literature on the spatial diffusion of innovation, it has not been immune to criticisms centred on its evident interpretative short-comings.[34] First, the logic of the model does not envisage the technological evolution of an innovation – i.e. a post-innovation improvement. Even less does it contemplate para-digmatic shifts to other technological trajectories brought about by radical innovations. Yet changes in technological knowledge may induce product innovations, with the conse-quence that they change or even halt the development predicted by the logistic pattern on the old product. At the same time, a process of new product development is generated, represented by a new logistic function, which may co-exist with the old technology for some time, giving rise to a technological pluralism inconceivable on the logic of the logistic model.[35]

A second shortcoming of the logistic approach is that it sees technological development as resulting from the behaviour of potential adopters and from demand for technology, while taking for granted the existence of a completely flexible supply able to satisfy that demand. However, it is now recognized that innovation is the result of a virtuous 'demand/supply' circle in which both components interact to influence the time scale of the innovative process and the ways in which it comes about.

Finally, the logistic model defines the number of potential adopters *ex ante*, exogenously; an aspect which has a considerable negative bearing on the model's interpretative capacity.

173

The product life-cycle and the life-cycle of regions

The notion that the spatial diffusion of innovation is a continuing process in time represents the central component of the logistic model used by the regional life-cycle theory proposed by Norton and Rees and based on Hirsch and Vernon's well-known product life-cycle theory.[36] Norton and Rees's life-cycle theory interprets regional differences in technological capacity as stemming from physiological processes due to technological ageing. Technological development has three stages associated – through analysis of demand, production and innovative processes – with three specific locations of innovation (Figure 7.6a), as follows:

1 *Take-off of a new product.* When incremental innovations in the characteristics of a product are frequent, and production processes have not yet been standardized, the strategic factors necessary for the innovation are research and innovation capabilities, the quality of labour, and ready access to specific information. The natural location is an urban and metropolitan area where demand is more inelastic (rigid) to prices and there is a greater receptiveness to innovation.

2 *Product maturity.* Here incremental process innovations predominate, and the strategic factors for innovation are managerial ability and the availability of capital. Production processes require large-scale plants because they are now highly capital-intensive. The more peripheral areas of advanced countries, where land costs less, are the best locations for manufacture of the innovative product.

3 *Standardized production of the innovative good.* The strategic factor is now the cost of labour, and the optimal location is a developing country.

The result of the above process is the progressive diffusion of the product innovation from more central metropolitan areas to the periphery. This comes about through a mechanism whereby the innovation 'filters down' from stronger areas to weaker ones.

A strength of this theory – one which distinguishes it from the logistic-epidemic model – is its ability to conceive of an *interregional technological pluralism*. This results from a 'snapshot' taken in a particular time-frame of the interregional movement of technologies – a movement driven by the simple process of the physiological ageing of technologies. It may happen, in fact, that while central areas stagnate, the periphery experiences notable innovation characterized by 'creative imitation'.[37]

However, this reasoning has a number of flaws. The first is that, whilst the life-cycle theory was well suited to interpreting the spatial diffusion of innovation in the 1950s and 1960s, when technological change in products took the form of long waves comprising the traditional stages of take-off, maturity and decline, the same cannot be said of the 1980s, when the new technological paradigm associated with high-tech industry imposed an extremely rapid pace on product evolution. The life-cycles of products were therefore drastically reduced; and the patterns of spatial adoption changed as a consequence (Figure 7.6b).[38] The pressure exerted by the shorter life-cycles of products was not in fact accompanied by a more rapid spatial diffusion of innovation from the centre to the periphery. Moreover, the nature of the new technological paradigm in the 1980s was such that it

174

(a) the traditional curve

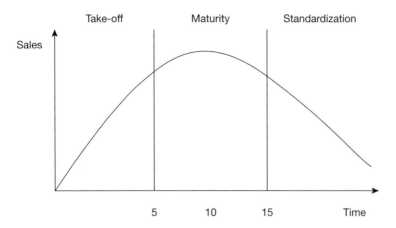

(b) the curve for the high-tech sector

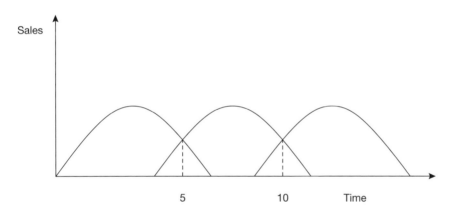

Figure 7.6 *The product life-cycle*

revitalized 'traditional' production, inducing it to relocate from the periphery to the centre. The new electronic technologies introduced in traditional sectors such as textiles, cars, clothing, and precision instruments, enabled them to renovate production by improving products and processes; and this gave central regions, rather than peripheral ones, ample opportunities for economic recovery.

The second weakness of the life-cycle model is that it entails, with no apparent exceptions, a view of interregional technological development as a simple and linear process of technology transfer between territorial areas. By so doing, it rules out the possibility that there might be some subjective element in the diffusion process, such as the interest, ability and receptive capacity of one area compared to another.[39] It thus makes the same mistake as committed by Hägerstrand when he assumed that information necessarily entails adoption.

It will be evident from the foregoing discussion that the spatial diffusion of innovation is a highly complex process in which demand components (characteristics of the potential adopters) interact with supply components (characteristics of the prevailing technological paradigm) and, not least, with elements specific to the context in which the innovation diffuses (structural characteristics of the area). All this is very difficult to incorporate into models for which the diffusion mechanism is an epidemic process. Excluded by definition is the existence of areas able to absorb innovation in a different manner. Yet this is to overlook one of the key elements in explanation of the spatial diffusion of innovation. Nonetheless, the efforts made by the various models to include this element in their analyses are to be commended: either in the form of 'economic distance', as in Griliches and Mansfield, or (and this will be examined in detail later[40]) local endogenous factors – most notably the greater presence of the knowledge and learning that support the adoption process and account for an area's greater capacity to adopt and exploit innovation.

INFRASTRUCTURES AND REGIONAL DEVELOPMENT

Many of the growth theories discussed agree on the importance of infrastructures for regional development. The theories of balanced development, stages of development, the export base, and growth-poles, underline the role of infrastructures in determining a local system's growth and development path. According to these theories, export capacity, the production system's competitiveness, and an area's capacity to attract new activities result, *inter alia*, from a developed infrastructural endowment.

In the light of these theories, more recent analyses have paid closer attention to infrastructures, seeking to identify, among the many possible determinants of an area's growth, the real contribution made thereto by infrastructures. These analyses consider infrastructural endowment to be one of the factors which, together with geographical location and an agglomerative sectoral structure, determine a regional development potential.[41] A better infrastructural endowment attracts new firms into an area, and it is a source of competitiveness for the firms already operating in that area. It heightens the productivity of the production factors, and by increasing accessibility, reduces their purchase costs, thus generating positive externalities on local development.[42] Because the production of infrastructures is indivisible, they are often produced by the public sector: for which reason they are termed 'public capital' or 'social fixed capital'.

The theoretical analysis described has been accompanied by a large number of empirical studies intended to measure the contribution of 'social fixed capital' to factor productivity.[43] The most common method is to estimate an aggregate production function (at the regional or provincial level) in order to verify the existence of scale economies; or (which is easier from an econometric point of view) a multiplying coefficient connected with the infrastructural endowment.[44]

The most important contribution to such analysis has been David Aschauer's study which estimated a production function to show that public capital exerted a strong positive influence on total factor productivity in the United States between 1945 and 1985.[45] Since Aschauer's study, a large number of other empirical surveys have shown (for different geographical areas and different time periods) that greater public capital intensity has positive and significant effects on output elasticities, meaning that a greater provision of public capital increases the magnitude of the impact on regional output. Table 7.1 summarizes the range of alternative estimates of the impact in the recent literature.[46]

The discovery by these empirical analyses of a correlation between infrastructural endowment and economic growth suggests that 'social fixed capital' is a determinant of local competitiveness and factor productivity. The closeness of the correlation largely depends on the type of public capital considered: 'economic' infrastructures (transport facilities, roads, motorways, railways, airports, and electricity-generating stations) – these being directly functional to firms – give rise to greater increases in productivity compared to 'social and civil infrastructures' (hospitals, schools, universities, public housing projects and sewerage systems). Although the latter infrastructures directly affect the quality of life and human capital, they influence production only in the longer run – and with effects not necessarily restricted to the area in which the infrastructures are installed. Moreover, the numerous estimation methods and the diverse territorial disaggregations used by studies on the matter account for the marked variability in the values of income elasticity to social fixed capital (Table 7.1).

Yet the infrastructural policies implemented over the years have had only very limited positive impacts on regional disparities. Besides national policies, 80 per cent of the structural funds allocated by the European Union in the 1970s and 1980s to the development of infrastructures in the Objective 1 regions did not reduce regional disparities: these remained constant in the 1970s, indeed worsened in the 1980s, and only improved in the 1990s.[47]

These results show that it is necessary to proceed with caution if infrastructural investment is to generate economic development.[48] Infrastructural development must necessarily match the needs expressed by the industrial specialization of the area in which the infrastructures are to be installed – as already amply evidenced by the theory of balanced development.[49] Even more misguided is the idea that the creation of infrastructures alone in a weak economic region can engender economic growth, if there is no 'fertile' productive context on which to graft development. Moreover, the building of a transport infrastructure may increase competition in the area because it makes the local market accessible to external firms. Finally, in the presence of an already well-developed infrastructural endowment, further investment in fixed social capital produces – as in the case of any intensively used factor – a very small increase in local production.[50]

In sum, whilst it can be argued that an endowment of fixed social capital is a necessary condition for local development (as also shown by the results of empirical surveys), it is wrong to believe that it is a sufficient one. A series of other, equally necessary, factors must exist – among them entrepreneurship, specialization, and innovative capacity – if an infrastructural policy is to be truly effective.

NEW COMMUNICATION TECHNOLOGIES AND REGIONAL DEVELOPMENT

New opportunities, but also new threats, for the development of local systems arise from the advent of the technological paradigm of the new information and communication technologies (ICTs). The adoption and use of ICTs (or 'computer networks') open up

Table 7.1 *Alternative estimates of the impact of infrastructure on output*

Studies	Output elasticity	Levels of analysis	Infrastructure variable	Output variable
Aschauer (1989)	0.39	National	Public capital	National output
Munnell (1990)	0.33	National	Public capital	National output
Aschauer (1989)	0.24	National	Core public capital	National output
Hulten and Schwab (1995)	0.39	National	Public capital	National output
Moomaw et al. (1995)	0.07–0.26	State	Public capital	Gross state product
Moomaw and Williams (1991)	0.25	State	Highway density	Total factor productivity
Costa et al. (1987)	0.20	State	Public capital	Ouput
Munnell (1990)	0.15	State	Public capital	Gross state product
Aschauer (1990)	0.11	State	Core public capital	Per capita output
Munnell (1990)	0.06	State	Highway capital	Gross state product
Deno (1988)	0.31	Metropolitan	Highway capital	Manufacturing output
Duffy-Deno and Eberts (1991)	0.08	Metropolitan	Public capital	Personal income
Eberts (1986)	0.19–0.26	Metropolitan	Core public capital	Manufacturing value added

Source: Guild, 1998

broad avenues for innovation which encourage local development. Product innovations (e-business, e-commerce), innovations in product distribution (on-line marketing), and process innovations (just-in-time production, functional integration) spring from the presence and exploitation of these technologies, giving the local production system greater competitiveness and efficiency.

The opportunities for development afforded by the new communication technologies depend on the strategic use made of those technologies – a use, that is, which conjugates new technological potentialities, new organizational methods (required by the innovations themselves), and new ways to penetrate markets with more innovative and qualitatively better products (business ideas). Appropriation of the potential profits and higher levels of competitiveness offered by these technologies therefore requires knowledge and innovative and creative skills which are certainly not distributed uniformly in space. Knowledge results from slow processes of learning fuelled by information, and investments in research and training stemming from local experience and expertise embodied in human capital and local relational networks, and in the local labour market. Knowledge is increasingly embedded in the local production system, so that learning processes are highly selective, and they determine capacities for technology use which differ markedly across regions.[51]

This last point has an important implication which relates to what was said earlier about infrastructures in general: the mere adoption of these technologies is a necessary but not sufficient condition for local development. Technologies in the strict sense exert a neutral influence on the growth patterns of local production systems, in fact; they represent a set of opportunities available at a certain cost, a 'quasi-public good'. The discriminating factor – and this is by no means a 'public good' – is the cultural and organizational capacity to exploit their potential with a creative array of technologies, organizational styles and business ideas. These capacities are very likely to be present in central areas, especially in the early phases of adoption and, at least initially, they boost the centripetal forces of development. This point reminds us that the effect of ICTs on regional disparities is still dubious.

In the past fifteen years two currents of thought have interpreted the impact of ICTs on regional disparities.[52] The first maintains that new ICTs are able to resolve the problem of peripherality: greater access to information, knowledge and specific services to production reduce the disadvantages of a peripheral location – the disadvantages emphasized by the 'centrality-peripherality' approach described in Chapter 4. The second, and contrary, current of thought argues that the diffusion of these technologies takes the form of a centripetal process driven by the presence in stronger areas of greater potential demand, and of more knowledge about these technologies and the ability to exploit them. On this view, the centripetal adoption process gives the centre broad opportunities to maintain and widen the gap between it and the weak regions.

Empirical studies demonstrate that in the first phases of adoption, and in all the phases of technological progress which require new strategies of technology adoption, the diffusion of technologies is a centripetal process. A study carried out in the early 1990s on the impact of ICTs on regional development in Northern and Southern Italy showed the existence of an 'ICT adoption/local development' nexus in the North. But this appeared to be entirely absent in the South, owing to a lack of the knowledge necessary for its strategic use. A similar conclusion was reached by an empirical study on the USA: a state-by-state regression analysis showed the variation in returns on telecommunications investments across states. This variation may have been due to the inefficient utilization of telecommunications infrastructure as a factor of production. The same study found that the states obtaining significantly positive benefits were those in which firms used the telecommunications infrastructure more efficiently.[53]

More recent studies have again stressed that if knowledge on how to use these technologies is not sedimented in the local labour market and fuelled by strong relations among local firms, the adoption of new technologies will not generate processes of local development.[54]

CONCLUSIONS

This chapter has surveyed the first theories based on a notion of *diversified space* which enables production activities and factors, demand, and sectoral structure to be conceived as unevenly distributed within a region. According to this approach, the economic and social relations that arise in a geographical area perform an important role in explaining a local system's development: hence the expression *diversified-relational space*.

Of the numerous approaches to diversified-relational space, the chapter has described those which identify elements exogenous to the system as determining long-period competitiveness: the presence of a dominant firm or a multinational, the diffusion of an externally originating innovation, the creation of transport and social infrastructures, and the adoption of new communication technologies. The next chapter will instead examine the theories which, with intriguing and impressive insight, have sought to identify the endogenous factors that determine local competitiveness.

REVIEW QUESTIONS

1   What is meant by a diversified-relational space? How does this definition of space impact on theories of regional development?

2   What is the conception of growth behind the theories based on a diversified-relational space?

3   What is meant by exogenous development?

4   Which are the main novelties of the growth-pole theory? What are the limits of this theory?

5   What role do multinationals play in local development?

6   What is the aim of Hägerstrand's model? What are the limits of this model? What is added to this model by Griliches' and Mansfield's contributions?

7   Is the statement 'infrastructures generate growth' true? Explain why.

8   Is the statement 'ICTs decrease regional disparities' true? Explain why.

SELECTED READING ON EMPIRICAL FINDINGS

About infrastructure and regional development

Biehl, D. (1986) *The contribution of infrastructure to regional development, regional policy division*, Brussels: European Community.

Bröcker, J. and Schneekloth, N. (2006) 'European transport policy and cohesion: an assessment by CGE analysis', *Scienze Regionali – Italian Journal of Regional Science*, vol. 5, no. 2, pp. 47–71.

Fabiani, S. and Pellegrini, G. (1997) 'Education, infrastructure, geography and growth: an empirical analysis of the development of Italian provinces', Banca d'Italia, *Temi di Discussione*, no. 323.

Spiekermann, K. and Wegener, M. (2006) 'Accessibility and spatial development in Europe', *Scienze Regionali – Italian Journal of Regional Science*, vol. 5, no. 2, pp. 15–46.

About ICTs and regional development

Butler, J., Gaspar, J. M. B. and Jeppesen, E. (1986) 'Telecommunications and regional development in Portugal', *Arbejdsrapport*, vol. 16, Aarhus Universitet.

Capello, R. and Nijkamp, P. (1996) 'Telecommunications policy for regional development: theoretical considerations and empirical evidence', *The Annals of Regional Science*, vol. 30, no. 1, pp. 7–30.

Ding, L. and Haynes, K. E. (2004) 'The role of telecommunications infrastructure in regional economic growth of China', paper presented at the Telecommunications Policy Research Conference, Washington, D.C., October, pp. 1–3.

Yilmaz, S. and Dinc, M. (2002) 'Telecommunications and regional development: evidence from the U.S. States', *Economic Development Quarterly*, vol. 16, no. 3, pp. 211–28.

About multinationals and regional development

Cantwell, J. and Piscitello, L. (2002) 'The location of technological activities of MNCs in European regions: the role of spillovers and local competencies', *Journal of International Management*, vol. 8, pp. 69–96.

Li, S. and Ho Park, S. (2006) 'Determinants of locations of foreign direct investment in China', *Management and Organization Review*, vol. 2, no. 1, pp. 95–119.

Nachum, L. and Wymbs, C. (2002) 'Firm-specific attributes and MNE location choices: financial and professional service FDI to New York and London', ESRC Centre for Business Research, University of Cambridge, Working Paper no. 223.

Resmini, L. (2007) 'Regional patterns of industry location in transition countries: does the economic integration with the EU matter?', *Regional Studies*, forthcoming.

Urata, S. and Kawai, H. (2000) 'The determinants of the location of foreign direct investment by Japanese small and medium-sized enterprises', *Small Business Economics*, vol. 15, no. 2, pp. 79–103.

FURTHER READING

Antonelli, C. (1992) (ed.) *The economics of information networks*, Amsterdam: North-Holland.

Biehl, D. (1986) *The contribution of infrastructure to regional development, regional policy division*, Brussels: European Community.

Boudeville, J.-R. (1966) *Problems of regional economic planning*, Edinburgh: Edinburgh University Press.

Capello, R. (1994) *Spatial economic analysis of telecommunications network externalities*, Aldershot: Avebury.

Ding, L. and Haynes, K. E. (2004) 'The role of telecommunications infrastructure in regional economic growth of China', paper presented at the Telecommunications Policy Research Conference, Washington, D.C., October 1–3.

Gillespie, A. and Williams, H. (1988) 'Telecommunications and the reconstruction of regional comparative advantage', *Environment and Planning A*, vol. 20, pp. 1311–21.

Holland, S. (1971) 'Regional underdevelopment in a developed economy: the Italian case', *Regional Studies*, vol. 5, pp. 71–90.

Vickerman, R. (ed.) (1991) *Infrastructure and regional development*, London: Pion.

Chapter 8

Territorial competitiveness and endogenous development

SUMMARY

1 The endogenous sources of competitiveness: agglomeration economies
2 Space and static efficiency
3 The Marshallian industrial district
4 Space and dynamic efficiency
5 Knowledge spillovers: geographical proximity
6 Collective learning and the *milieu innovateur*: relational proximity
7 The 'learning regions': institutional proximity
8 The urban structure and regional development

THE ENDOGENOUS SOURCES OF COMPETITIVENESS: AGGLOMERATION ECONOMIES

Throughout this book thus far, space has performed two distinct roles in models and theories: (a) the role of a physical barrier – or of a spatial friction – against economic activity, taking the form of the physical distance between input and output markets conceptualized by models as a generic transportation cost;[1] (b) that of a 'physical container' of development, a simple geographical area often associated with the administrative region by aggregate macroeconomic theories – but also with smaller local areas (simple geographic agglomerations within a region, as envisaged by the more microeconomic theories examined in the previous chapter). In both cases, space plays no part in determining the development path of a local economy. The same economic logic explains the development of regions, metropolitan areas, or more generally, densely-populated industrial areas. The export-base theory can be applied just as well to a region as to a country, with no change in the logic of its underlying reasoning. The Harrod–Domar model, too, and likewise the neoclassical growth models, fit both regional cases and national ones, which testifies to its aspatiality.

In this chapter, a radical change in the conceptualization of space gives it a very different role in development. No longer a simple geographical container, space is imagined as an

183

economic resource, as an independent production factor. It is the generator of static and dynamic advantages for firms, and a key determinant of a local production system's competitiveness. According to the theories examined in this chapter, space is a source of increasing returns, and of positive externalities taking the form of agglomeration and localization economies. Higher growth rates are achieved by local production systems where increasing returns act upon local productive efficiency to reduce production and transaction costs, enhance the efficiency of the production factors, and increase innovative capacity. Regional development consequently depends upon the efficiency of a concentrated territorial organization of production, not on the availability of economic resources or their more efficient spatial allocation.

This new conception of space has several implications. Space can only be *diversified* space in which it is easy to distinguish (even internally to a region) the uneven distribution of activities. Development comes about selectively in areas where the concentrated organization of production exerts its positive effects on the parameters of static and dynamic efficiency. At the same time, space is *relational*, in that the economic and social relations which arise in an area perform crucial functions in various respects. They ensure the smoother operation of market mechanisms, more efficient and less costly production processes, the accumulation of knowledge in the local market, and a more rapid pace of innovation – all of which are factors that foster local development.

Second, on adopting this new notion of space it is no longer possible to treat development as exogenous in origin. Development is now by definition *endogenous*. It is fundamentally dependent on a concentrated organization of the territory, embedded in which is a socio-economic and cultural system whose components determine the success of the local economy: entrepreneurial ability, local production factors (labour and capital), relational skills of local actors generating cumulative knowledge-acquisition, together with a decision-making capacity which enables local economic and social actors to guide the development process, support it when undergoing change and innovation, and enrich it with the external information and knowledge required to harness it to the general process of growth, and to the social, technological and cultural transformation of the world economy. The theories presented in this chapter accordingly endeavour to identify the genetic local conditions which determine the competitiveness of a local production system and ensure its persistence over time. They seek out the local factors which enable areas, and the firms located in them, to produce goods demanded internationally with an (absolute) competitive advantage, to maintain that advantage over time by innovating, and to attract new resources from outside.

As we shall see, theories of local endogenous development divide into two broad strands. On the one hand neo-Marshallian inquiry, which views local growth as resulting from externalities acting upon the static efficiency of firms, has been expanding and consolidating for years. On the other, the neo-Schumpeterian literature, which has arisen more recently, interprets development as resulting from the impact of local externalities on the innovative capacity of firms.

The logical leap of interpreting space as an active factor in development forcefully imposed itself upon the history of economic thought in the early 1970s, when unprecedented patterns of local development in Italy surprised theoreticians by resisting explanation based on conventional models. During the early 1970s, the sudden and rapid growth achieved by certain Italian regions – those of the North-East and the Centre in particular[2] – when the country's industrialized areas[3] were showing evident signs of economic crisis, could be explained neither by a neoclassical paradigm of interregional mobility of production factors (which greatly decreased in those years), nor by a paradigm centred on large firm efficiency (à la Perroux), nor by a Keynesian paradigm of development driven by external demand.

Numerous neo-Marshallian theorists around the world pursued very similar lines of theoretical inquiry during the 1970s and 1980s (and there is no shortage of theory on the subject): Walter Stöhr developed the concept of 'bottom-up development', Enrico Ciciotti and Reinhart Wettmann that of 'indigenous potential', Bengt Johannison of 'local context', Bernardo Secchi and Gioacchino Garofoli of 'system areas', and Claude Courlet-Bernard Pecqueur and Bernard Ganne of 'localized industrial system'.[4] But the first systematic theory of endogenous development was produced in Italy by Giacomo Becattini with his seminal study on the 'Marshallian industrial district' published in the mid-1970s.[5] The theory of the industrial district – which originated in the work of the great neoclassical economist Alfred Marshall – was the first to conceptualize external economies (of agglomeration) as sources of territorial competitiveness.[6] It did so with a model in which the economic aspects of development are reinforced by a socio-cultural system which fuels increasing returns and self-reinforcing mechanisms of development.

These neo-Marshallian studies, in which space generates and develops mechanisms of productive efficiency, bred theories which identified the territory as the generator of dynamic external economies – that is, all those advantages which favour not only the productive efficiency of firms but also their *innovative efficiency*. In the neo-Schumpeterian strand of analysis on local development, space reduces the uncertainty associated with every innovative process.

Finally, when space is viewed as generating advantages for firms, and therefore as an active component in the development process, scholars of local development shift their attention to the role of the urban space (the city) as the place where agglomeration economies are generated – be these localization or urbanization economies – and therefore as the place where the economic development of the entire region is rooted and structured. Hence, as the models of Christaller and Lösch show, the existence of an advanced and efficient city, and of an urban system organized into a network of vertical and horizontal relationships reflecting an efficient division of labour, may determine the success and development of a region.

In what follows, no criticism will be made of the qualitative nature of the theories examined, even though this is an aspect to which orthodox economists have often objected. On the contrary, it will be argued that these theories have enriched economic analysis by identifying the intangible elements (knowledge, learning, relationality, social capital) which come together to form local competitiveness. Far from being of scant economic significance, the chapter maintains, these elements should be valued and appreciated for their contribution to knowledge of local development processes.

SPACE AND STATIC EFFICIENCY

The Marshallian industrial district

The 1970s witnessed the miracle of the 'Third Italy'[7]: the north-eastern and central regions of the country which recorded surprisingly high growth rates in a period of general economic crisis provoked by severely adverse macroeconomic conditions (oil shocks, inflation, unemployment, stagnating consumption and investment, devaluation of the national currency, the lira). The miracle was interpreted first as a short-term phenomenon due to industrial conflict in the large companies of the industrialized areas, and then as the territorial effect of production decentralization (and therefore again as a process dependent on the centre). Finally, when empirical analyses demonstrated the autonomy and originality of the Third Italy development model, it was hailed as a new form of capitalist economic development.[8]

Numerous case studies on 'success stories' in non-metropolitan, diffused development prompted analysis of the factors responsible for the economic success of Third Italy areas, the distinctive features of which were close concentrations of small-sized firms and a form of entrepreneurship that seemingly stemmed from the historical structure of local agricultural systems. These studies on success factors were flanked and enriched by surveys on the flexibility of local labour markets – which permitted part-time work in the agro-food industry and rapid and easy labour mobility among firms – and by sociological analyses of a cultural, social and political homogeneity that underpinned a long tradition of cooperation in agricultural and trade.[9]

The seminal theory which derived from the empirical results of these studies, and which subsequently bred a large and ramified body of literature, was that of the *Marshallian industrial district*. This term denotes a local area with a strong concentration of small and medium-sized firms, each specialized in one or a few phases of the production process (or activities subsidiary to it) serving the needs of the area's principal sector.

A spatial concentration of small firms is the first genetic element necessary, though not sufficient, for an area to be an industrial district. A district's economic-productive organization is rooted in a social and cultural system of shared values which penetrates the market and structures its workings.[10] It is this relationship between economy and social structure which drives development: the symbiosis between market and society produces the synergy, cooperation and interaction which give rise to the increasing returns and location advantages of district firms. The genetic conditions that must be in place for a geographical area to be an industrial district are the following:

- spatial proximity, or geographical contiguity among firms;
- social proximity: a system of institutions, codes and rules shared by the entire community regulates the market; this system induces firms to cooperate and, in general, to resort to the local market when activities, phases or services prove too costly for them to produce internally;
- a concentration of small firms, the main features of which are productive flexibility and rapid adjustment to market volatility;

■ marked industrial specialization of the area, in which all phases of the production chain are undertaken: from design of the product, through production of all intermediate goods necessary for the product's manufacture, to its marketing world-wide.

District economies

The combined presence of the above economic-territorial conditions gives rise to the competitive advantages which make firms successful. Put in purely economic terms, these conditions generate increasing returns in the form of agglomeration economies: or more precisely, localization economies, or again 'district economies', which are the advantages (in terms of lower costs or increased productive efficiency) accruing to firms from proximity to other firms operating in the same sector.[11] They enable small firms to overcome the obstacles due to their small size, without their having to forgo the advantages which that same small size gives them.[12]

District economies derive from the factors now described (and set out in Table 8.1).

1 *Lower production costs.* The existence in districts of numerous, highly specialized local suppliers reduces the costs of transporting intermediate goods. A local labour market with high levels of elasticity – in the sense of rapid and smooth adjustment of the labour force to quantitative changes in demand – also reduces production costs. At the same time, easy recourse to the labour market, made possible by shared social rules and social sanctions on opportunistic behaviour, enables firms to draw on external labour and, above all, to outsource more complex and costly production phases. These are further factors which reduce production costs.

2 *Reduced transaction costs* (i.e. the costs of economic transactions). The geographical proximity that characterizes a district market facilitates the matching of labour supply and demand through a close-knit local information network. But even more important is social proximity: the system of shared rules of behaviour, the code of conduct internalized through socialization, and the sense of belonging to a community partly inherited from the farm-management system characterizing the history of industrial districts.[13] Social proximity generates governance mechanisms which discourage opportunism or dishonesty in transactions; it thus substantially reduces costs and recourse to the market. The sense of belonging to a specific community and the social identity which pervade local society underpin trust relations which foster inter-firm cooperation in the form of informal, non-bureaucratized and flexible contracts: to use Becattini's apt metaphor, 'the Marshallian industrial district is a localized thickening of inter-industrial relations'.[14] Finally, the strict specialization of firms gives them the technical expertise they need to assess the quality of the large number of suppliers in the area efficiently. Consequently, recourse to the market is again less costly than it is in a differentiated production system.

3 *Increased efficiency of the production factors.* External economies do not have positive effects on costs alone. Production resources remaining equal, the system of shared social values, the spatial concentration of specialized firms, and their small size, act

Table 8.1 A district's genetic conditions and advantages: a taxonomy

Genetic conditions (sources) / Advantages (effects)	Spatial proximity	Social and cultural proximity	Concentration of small firms	Industrial specialization
Reduction of production costs	Lower transportation costs for intermediate goods	System of local agents Recourse to external labour (home work) Outsourcing of production phases	Production flexibility	Availability of skilled labour Inter-firm division of labour
Reduction of transaction costs	Labour demand/supply match Broad local market upstream and downstream	Networks of inter-personal relations System of shared rules and institutions Common code of behaviour Sense of belonging Explicit capacity for inter-actor cooperation Informal contracts	Flexible, non-bureaucratized relationships among firms	Adequate technical knowledge for choice of suppliers
Increase in the efficiency of the production factors	Existence of a critical mass for specialized and infrastructural services Broad market for specialized inputs	Widespread industrial culture Mobility of tacit information Widespread entrepreneurial expertise	Flexibility in the quantity and quality of inputs to the production process	Information services for specialization sectors
Increase in innovative capacity (dynamic efficiency)	Localized accumulation of knowledge	Socialization to the risk associated with innovative activity Accumulation of shared knowledge	Competition-driven stimulus to innovation	Accumulation of specific knowledge

upon the production capacity of firms to increase the efficiency of the production factors. Upstream and downstream from the production process, the presence of a critical mass of firms generates a series of services which enable better use to be made of local production, and which also have synergic effects on the market image of the local economy. Social proximity engenders what Marshall called 'industrial atmosphere', by which he meant an industrial culture consisting in the indivisible 'intangible assets' of the production system as a whole: an entrepreneurial mentality, a spirit of cooperation, local technical knowledge about the production cycle, and the socialization of knowledge make firms – other conditions remaining equal – more productive. Specialization of firms in different stages of the filière, the vertical and horizontal division of labour, and close purchase/sale relations among firms give rise to a greater overall efficiency manifested in increased earnings and profits (and the area's greater attractiveness for the location or creation of new firms).

4   *Increased dynamic efficiency*, in the sense of the innovative capacity possessed by firms operating in the district. Industrial district theory has adopted Marshall's view of a specialized area – 'where so great are the advantages which people following the same skilled trade get from near neighbourhood to one another. The mysteries of the trade become no mysteries; but are as it were in the air, and children learn many of them unconsciously'[15] – to underline the decisive importance of locally accumulated knowledge for the innovative capacity of firms. This aspect has been subsequently reprised and amplified by the theories examined below.[16]

The high level of collective efficiency achieved by firms in industrial districts is therefore explained mainly by district economies. Accordingly, these theories see the territory, with its networks of inter-firm and social relations, as the source of economic growth – as a factor, that is, which actively contributes to determining the development path and productive capacity.

Beyond district economies

Although district economies are the most evident economic advantages springing from the co-presence in an area of small firms operating within the same sector, they are generated and reinforced by factors present in the economic and social context.

A first factor is the inextricable interweaving of economic, geographical and social elements. It has often been stressed, regarding the concept of 'industrial district', that a simple clustering of small firms in a particular area does not in itself constitute an industrial district. Social proximity – defined as a shared code of behaviour and a set of common values penalizing opportunistic behaviour – is a typical feature of a district. Social proximity penetrates the market, structures it around clearly-defined rules, and gives it efficiency. The strength of this organizational model is the close relationship between the economy and the social structure. In this regard, analysts have formulated the notion of a 'community market' – this being the level of transactions governance which lies between the market and the community – because the information which transactions require resides both in the prices system and in an implicit code of behaviour that economic agents internalize through socialization.[17]

A second factor enhancing the efficiency of district firms is the integration between cooperation and competition; indeed, striking an appropriate balance between these two processes determines the survival of the district organizational model itself.[18] Notwithstanding the impression that might be gained from industrial district theory's constant emphasis on cooperation, the firms operating in a district engage in aggressive competition with each other, being obliged to do so by the ready substitutability of the goods which they produce. Competition is the driving force behind district firms obliged to maintain their goods at high quality levels and to innovate their production techniques (even if only by imitation). Simultaneously, forms of explicit cooperation characterize a market regulated by social norms and sanctions which punish opportunistic behaviour: in 'repeated games' (i.e. transactions which take place several times sequentially between the same economic actors) 'reputation' is an intangible asset that ensures a firm's survival in the market.[19]

Finally, the presence of a governance structure (local agents and institutions), which buttresses the transactions regulation system, ensures the efficient operation of the 'community market' by explicitly supporting forms of competition and cooperation. In order that competition does not degenerate into aggression damaging to firms, the district's industry associations impose price controls in the form of agreed and indicative tariffs, modifiable according to the manufacturing process. The risk of information asymmetry is thus abated, and transaction costs are reduced. The local governance system likewise prevents cooperation from degenerating into financial agreements or protectionist cartels which cancel out the positive effects of competition.[20]

Thirty years since its first conceptualization, the Marshallian notion of the industrial district is still largely unsurpassed as a tool for the study of local systems. Although its appeal may have been diminished by a plethora of redundant and repetitive empirical studies, the Italian industrial-district model has recently been used by development economists to interpret the small-firm systems now arising in the developing countries.[21] However, as often happens when conclusions drawn from specific empirical cases are applied to other contexts, analyses conducted in Latin America suggest that there is a substantial difference between the Italian industrial district and the clusters of small firms now emerging in Brazil, Mexico and Argentina – especially because of the lower degree of cooperation in those countries.[22]

Identifying the determinants of the success or crisis of industrial districts – the 'catastrophic' patterns in their evolution – is still the most interesting and fruitful aspect of research in this field, since the dynamics of industrial districts still lacks sound conceptual interpretation.

Some critical remarks

Industrial district theory has had the outstanding merit of being the first theory to give space an active role in economic development, thereby enriching the concept of agglomeration economies with social, psychological and cultural dimensions.

A second merit of the theory is that it highlights the endogenous factors in development: entrepreneurship, production flexibility, district economies, and the presence of a social and cultural context and an institutional structure able to catalyse 'indigenous potential'. The theory of bottom-up development indirectly entails the immobility of certain factors, such as skilled labour, specific knowledge and expertise, but also of intangible elements like a socio-cultural system which supports transaction and market mechanisms. This explains the selectivity of territorial development, and the difficulty of generating development processes artificially.

Industrial district theory has had the further virtues of producing a conceptual model able to explain what was 'inexplicable' at the time of the theory's formulation, and of opening analysis of regional development to consideration of genuinely territorial elements.

However, having acknowledged these various virtues of district theory, mention should also be made of weaknesses in its logical-conceptual structure. First, as often happens at the moment of a 'catastrophic' break with already-existing theories, the approach has an evident tendency to emphasize the novel and to undervalue the findings of previous theories. It places pronounced emphasis on endogenous aspects and tends entirely to ignore the exogenous and objective elements that accompany a development path, in particular the macroeconomic and macro-territorial conditions which act upon the economies of individual areas. The influence exerted by these elements on the birth, development and crisis of district areas is undeniable. In the early 1970s, for example, the manufacturing and exporting difficulties of the large industrial areas in Italy led to general medium-period exchange rate weakness, and to a decrease in the cost of labour (expressed in international currency), which worked mainly to the advantage of the NEC regions because of their specialization in labour-intensive 'tradeable' manufactures with greater elasticity to price.[23] The same situation arose in 1992, when the general weakness of the Italian economy, together with instability in the European financial markets, induced the Italian economic policy authorities to heavily devalue the lira outside the 'monetary snake' bands, taking Italy out of the European monetary system.

It is therefore necessary to analyse not only the internal elements of dynamism and entre-preneurial ability present in individual regions but also the interdependence among regional economic systems and the feedbacks that occur over time.[24] A useful way to consider these connections is to apply the concept of a region's 'relative locational advantage'. This is measured by means of two indicators – productivity defined in the broad sense as the overall efficiency of the local social-productive system, and the cost of labour, also defined in the broad sense as the cost of 'labour force reproduction' – which are used to determine all the socio-environmental factors that affect the real purchasing power of wages in each region. The relative locational advantages of the three Italian macro-regions highlight very clearly the favourable conditions enjoyed by the NEC regions during the 1970s, and the contemporaneous loss of competitiveness by the North-West (Figure 8.1a).[25]

Finally, comparison between productivity and cost of labour evidences the economic revival of the 'central' regions in the 1980s and, more interestingly, the crisis of relative competitiveness that hit some regions, especially those of central Italy: a crisis which was neither foreseen nor explained by industrial district theory (Figure 8.1b).

This last point introduces a second shortcoming of district theory: its static theoretical framework and its tendency towards ex-post descriptivism of spatial phenomena. The theory is able to quantify the relative advantage of the Third Italy entirely satisfactorily. But it is

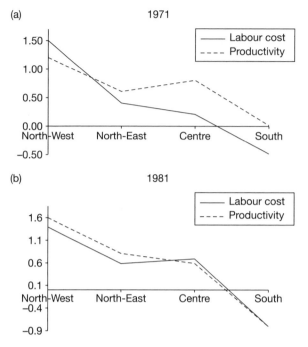

Figure 8.1 *Regional locational advantages in Italy – 1971 and 1981*
Source: Camagni and Capello, 1990

less successful in identifying the determinants of the growth and dynamics of the Third Italy areas, their ability to respond to increasing worldwide competition, rapid technological change, negative feedbacks in the form of manpower shortages, increased costs of labour and production factors, and the physical and infrastructural congestion generated by economic success. These elements may cancel out some of the locational advantages on which the success of these areas was initially based.

A further weakness (one particularly apparent in subsequent schools of thought) is the theory's excessive emphasis on specialization and flexibility. Characteristic of the small firm and of a 'post-Fordist' model of production organization, flexibility is today also a distinctive feature of large firms if they utilize modern flexible production technologies (CAD/ CAM) and the new forms of production organization (just-in-time).[26] Likewise, external economies, which lend themselves well to interpretation of the increasing returns achieved by district firms, also arise and develop in metropolitan areas where large firms are located. Once again, therefore, consideration of subjective, endogenous and local factors alone fails to account for the competitiveness of more recently industrialized areas, and even less for their ability to maintain this competitiveness over time.

Finally, the importance, richness and strength of industrial district theory are evident. But equally obvious is the extreme difficulty of measuring the economic advantages that it theorizes. This difficulty may in part explain the large number of qualitative studies produced with the purpose of determining the presence of genetic elements and success factors in

individual districts. The problem with this approach is that it may lapse into mere anec-
dotal description, thus clogging the literature without adding a great deal to the conceptual
framework already developed. Consequently those recent studies are to be welcomed which
have sought to make quantitative measurement – using statistical tools and cross-section
econometric analyses – of a firm's external economies, using either municipal-level data
(for inter-district analyses) or data disaggregated at the level of the individual district firm
(for intra-district analyses). These studies have the indubitable merit of removing the anec-
dotal content from empirical analysis and of furnishing quantitative measures of phenomena
difficult to gauge.[27]

We may therefore conclude that the theoretical/conceptual contribution of industrial
district theory has been very fruitful. Nevertheless, today, thirty years after its first formulation, the theory is still better suited to describing spatial phenomena than to interpreting
their dynamics.

SPACE AND DYNAMIC EFFICIENCY

Innovation and local development

Thus far, we have examined the role of space as a generator of locational advantages: lower
production and transaction costs, and a more efficient use of resources, which enable firms
to achieve higher levels of productivity and profit. However, the effects of space on
economic activity do not consist solely in improvements to the static efficiency of production processes (that is, an increase in firms' revenues or a decrease in their costs); they
are also manifest in the innovative and creative capacity of firms. In this case, space is a
source of *dynamic efficiency*. Areas with high concentrations of economic activity enjoy easy
information exchange, frequent face-to-face encounters, the presence of research and development activities and advanced services, an availability of skilled labour, cooperativeness
facilitated by shared rules and codes of behaviour, and local social capital, which facilitate
and encourage innovation by the firms located within those areas.[28]

These features are easily explained in the case of urban areas, which have always been
the main sites of innovative activity, the 'incubators' of new knowledge: cities are the
principal centres of research, given their large pools of expertise, and the availability of
advanced services (finance and insurance) ready to carry the risk of any innovative activity.
Yet it is indisputably also the case that certain non-metropolitan areas of small size display
an innovative capacity which persistently outstrips that of other geographical areas, and they
achieve levels of innovation sometimes greatly disproportional to their manufacturing
weight. They thus testify to the presence of some form of increasing returns on the concentration of innovative activity. Cases in point are Silicon Valley in California, 'Route 128'
in the Boston area, Baden-Württemberg in the South of Germany, Jutland in Denmark,
Småland in Sweden, Sophia-Antipolis close to Nice, to cite only some examples.

Understanding these phenomena became of particular interest in the 1980s. In those
years, under the impetus of profound technological changes, innovation came to be considered the driving force of economic development, and knowledge the key factor in local

193

economic success. The uneven spatial distribution of innovative activity was taken to be the primary cause of regional imbalances. In periods when there are evident signs of the hyper-mobility of labour and capital, the most immobile of factors are knowledge and the intangible elements connected with culture, skill, and innovative capacity: it is on these elements that the competitiveness of local systems depends.

From what has just been said, it is clear why the identification of the endogenous, local conditions determining an area's innovative capacity became the most important aim of regional development theories developed in the 1980s. These theories differed sharply from the studies on the spatial diffusion of innovation discussed in the previous chapter: their primary aim was no longer to interpret territorial patterns of innovation and exogenous factors, but to identify the local endogenous determinants of innovations. Their emphasis on elements endogenous to the innovative process fully justifies their inclusion in this chapter.

For these various theories, the endogenous determinants of innovation are increasing returns in the form of dynamic location advantages deriving from:

- *spatial, geographical proximity* among firms, which facilitates the exchange of tacit knowledge: this characterizes reflection by economic geographers concerned to explain the concentration of innovative activities;
- *relational proximity* among firms, defined as interaction and cooperativeness among local agents, the source of collective learning processes and socialization to the risk of innovation (i.e. territorialized relations among subjects operating in geographical and social proximity): this was the approach taken by territorial economists in explaining the dynamic of local systems in terms of local innovative capacity;[29]
- *institutional proximity* taking the form of rules, codes and norms of behaviour which (a) facilitate cooperation among actors and therefore the socialization of knowledge and (b) assist economic actors (individual people, firms and local institutions) to develop organizational forms which support interactive learning processes: this aspect was emphasized by more systemic approaches seeking to understand the evolution of complex systems like the innovative system.

Knowledge spillovers: geographical proximity

That innovative activity has a natural tendency to concentrate in space has been confirmed by numerous empirical studies. Using both input indicators (e.g. spending on research and development) and output indicators (e.g. number of patents) of innovative activity, these studies show that innovation is concentrated in central and metropolitan areas. Moreover, in all the industrialized countries, analyses of the location of high-tech firms reveal marked polarization effects due to the pronounced preference of these firms for central locations with strong sectoral specialization.[30]

Explanation of the phenomenon is straightforward: concentrated location facilitates exploitation of technological and scientific knowledge developed by research centres and universities; it gives easier access to the tacit uncodified knowledge required for imitation and reverse engineering; and it ensures the ready availability of skilled labour and advanced services.

Moreover, the complex and systemic nature of innovative processes explains their cumulative character: clusters of incremental innovations follow an initially radical innovation which marks out a 'technological trajectory' along which knowledge grows and develops within well-defined technological boundaries. At local level, demand for and the supply of innovative factors interact and mutually reinforce each other. Advanced firms enrich the surrounding environment by diffusing their technological and organizational expertise, while the surrounding environment simultaneously sustains their activity. The outcome is a cumulative polarization of research and innovation activities which reinforces the natural tendency for innovation to concentrate in space.

The role of agglomeration economies, both urban and sectoral, in explaining the concentration of innovative activity was demonstrated long ago by Marshall. But interest in dynamic agglomeration economies (the agglomerative advantages that foster innovation by firms) has grown considerably in recent years, as recognition has gained ground of the importance of innovation for the competitiveness of local systems.

The *theory of technological spillovers* developed in the 1990s linked the spatial concentration of innovative activities with the increasing returns that concentrated location generates on those innovative activities themselves. Cross-fertilizations, dynamic interactions between customers and suppliers, synergies between research centres and local production units occur within circumscribed geographical areas such as highly-specialized metropolitan areas. They do so as the result of the rapid exchange of information and transmission of tacit knowledge made possible by face-to-face encounters. In a concentrated location, the beneficial effects of a firm's research and development activities are not confined within the boundaries of firms; they 'spill over' into the surrounding environment, to the advantage of innovative activity by other firms.

A large number of empirical analyses, mainly econometric, have successfully measured the technological spillovers and the knowledge advantages enjoyed by spatially concentrated firms. Now briefly outlined are two of the methods employed to measure these effects:[31]

1   estimation of an aggregate knowledge production function at regional level, in order to verify the existence of technological spillovers; or in simpler econometric terms, to verify the existence of differing effects exerted by research and development (R&D) activities, conducted within and without a region, on its patenting activity.[32] The results confirm the existence of spillovers from innovative activity, in that the significance of the parameter associated with local R&D is greater than that of the parameter for external R&D;[33]

2   estimation of a disaggregated knowledge production function for individual local sectors which separately includes not only expenditure on local and external R&D, but also expenditure on R&D by the same sector and by different ones. The purpose is to determine the differing impacts on innovative activity of diversified and specialized knowledge. Once again, the results show that expenditure on local R&D is, for the majority of sectors, more significant than expenditure on external R&D, and that diversified rather than specialized knowledge is important for local innovative capacity.

195

However, the theory can be criticized on various grounds. First, it should be borne in mind that research and development expenditure and number of patents are highly selective indicators of innovative capacity. Both capture only product innovations: that is, breakthroughs often associated with the innovative activity of large firms. They entirely neglect the process innovation, the creative imitation, and the reverse engineering which characterize the innovative processes of small firms.

Even more dubious is the concept of space assumed by the theory. This space is purely geographical, a physical distance among actors, a pure physical container of spillover effects which come about – according to the epidemiological logic adopted – simply as a result of physical contact among actors. Important consequences ensue. First, this view is unable to explain the processes by which knowledge spreads at local level, given that it only envisages the probability of contact among potential innovators as the source of spatial diffusion. Second, it concerns itself only with the diffusion of innovation, not with the processes of knowledge creation. It thus imposes the same limitations as did Hägerstrand's pioneering model in regard to the spatial diffusion of innovation: the diffusion of knowledge means adoption, and adoption means more innovation and better performance.[34] This ignores the most crucial aspect of the innovation process: how people (or the context) actually learn. This is the aspect of overriding interest not only for scholars but also, and especially, for policy-makers, should they wish to explore the possibilities of normative action to promote local development.

Collective learning and the *milieu innovateur*: relational proximity

In the 1980s, an international group of scholars set out to analyse the phenomenon of the spatial concentration of small firms. Their conclusion was that social interactions, interpersonal synergies, and collective action among actors – in short, what they called 'relational proximity' – are the factors which account for the greater innovative capacity of spatially-concentrated small firms, and of the areas in which they are located.[35] This current of thought thus brought space as the generator of dynamic efficiency into the central focus of analysis on territorial development.

For this theory, economic and social relations among local actors condition the innovative capacity and economic success of specific local areas termed '*milieux innovateurs*'.[36] Synergies among actors are enhanced by spatial proximity and economic and cultural homogeneity, and thus produce dynamic advantages for small firms because they underpin processes of collective learning and socialization of knowledge.

Economic and social relations take two different forms in a *milieu*: first, a set of mainly informal, 'untraded' relationships – among customers and suppliers, among private and public actors – and a set of tacit knowledge transfers which take place through job-mobility chains and inter-firm imitation processes. These informal relationships have been widely studied by the French 'proximity school', and they have recently been labelled 'untraded interdependencies'.[37] Second, more formalized, mainly trans-territorial co-operation agreements – among firms, among collective agents, among public institutions – in the field of technological development, vocational and on-the-job training, infrastructures and services provision.

196

Relationships of the former type constitute the 'glue' which creates a milieu effect; they are complemented by the latter, more formalized, kinds of relationship, which can be interpreted as 'network relations' proper. Both sets of relationships can be viewed as tools or 'operators' that assist the (small) firm in its competitive endeavour, enhancing its creativeness and reducing the dynamic uncertainty intrinsic to innovation processes.

The partners in trans-territorial networks are selected single economic units – enterprises, banks, research centres, training institutions, or local authorities – for which location is only one coordinate among the many that serve to identify the unit. At first glance, therefore, these networks merely link different economic actors together and have no necessary relation with space. But when the location of a unit takes on significant meaning, inasmuch as it reveals a set of relations which generate territorial development and identity (e.g. Apple at Cupertino, Silicon Valley), and when these network relations start to multiply, they do indeed become territorial. When carefully observed, the identity of the local *milieu* often prevails over the identity of the individual partner, which highlights the importance of the territorial aspect: the strategic importance of links with a company in Silicon Valley resides more in the opening of a 'technological window' in Silicon Valley than in gaining access to that specific company's know-how.[38]

'Relational capital' is defined as the set of norms and values which govern interactions among people, the institutions where they are incorporated, the relationship networks set up among various social actors and the overall cohesion of society. It has the same role in *milieu* theory as spatial proximity has in the knowledge spillover theory, in that it generates dynamic advantages taking the following forms (see Table 8.2):[39] collective learning and socialization processes; reduction in the risk and uncertainty associated with the innovation process; and the *ex ante* coordination of routine and strategic decisions made possible by reduced transaction costs.

These functions are performed in a large firm by its R&D department, and they are facilitated by internal diversification and complexity. A small firm finds the same functions in a highly specialized territory. Learning in a *milieu* takes place in a spontaneous and socialized manner within the local labour market through forms of stable and enduring collaboration between customers and suppliers based on loyalty and trust. These relations produce a codified and tacit transfer of knowledge between customers and suppliers which triggers processes of incremental innovation and specific technological trajectories. Relations in the local labour market likewise perform an important role in the local production system because high turnover of skilled labour within the area and scant external mobility cross-fertilize knowledge among firms and upgrade workers' skills. Finally, firm spin-offs – independent firms created by workers previously employed by a local firm – also participate in the knowledge socialization process.

The accumulation of knowledge in large firms is ensured by the presence of R&D departments; and it is permanent because large firms are long-lived and develop their own internal capabilities and cultures. By contrast, small firms have very short life-cycles, with the consequence that they are unable to develop a solid stock of firm-specific knowledge. This difficulty is remedied by the *milieu* and by the relations within it, which guarantee continuity of knowledge through labour market stability, high people mobility within the area, and stable relations between customers and suppliers.

197

Table 8.2 *Functions of the local milieu*

Conditions	Geographical proximity	Relational proximity
Functions		
Reduction of uncertainty	Information collection/ selection	Information transcoding
	Vertical integration within 'filières'	Selection of decision routines
	Local signalling (collective marketing)	Risk sharing among partners
Reduction of coordination costs	Information collection	Reduction of control costs through trust and loyalty
	Reduction of transaction costs (*à la* Williamson)	Social sanctions on opportunistic behaviour
	Ex ante co-ordination of day-to-day decisions (*à la* Marshall)	*Ex ante* coordination in strategic decision-making
Durable substrate for collective learning	Labour turnover within the milieu	Cooperation on industrial projects
	Imitation of innovation practices	Tacit transfer of knowledge
		Public/private partnerships in complex development schemes

Source: Camagni and Capello, 2002

In *milieu innovateur* theory, therefore, collective learning is the territorial counterpart of the learning that takes place within firms. In large firms, knowledge and information are transferred via internal functional interaction among the R&D, production, marketing and strategic planning departments.[40] In *milieux*, and in local small firms systems, this function is performed by the high level of people mobility, by intense innovative interactions between customers and suppliers, and by firm spin-offs (Table 8.3).

Milieu theory flanks these channels of learning available to firms with a third and complementary one: learning through 'network cooperation' (Table 8.3). Through strategic alliances and/or non-equity cooperation agreements, firms acquire some of the strategic assets that they require externally, thus avoiding the costs of developing them internally. This knowledge-acquisition process stands midway between internal learning and collective learning, in that the firm comes into contact with the outside but still maintains a set of selected and targeted relationships. This form of learning assumes an important role in *milieu innovateur* theory because it permits local knowledge – which is produced by socialized and collective processes liable to isolation and lock-in – to enrich and innovate itself. Only through the cooperation with external firms that ensures an influx of new knowledge can a *milieu* avoid death by entropic uniformity. It is with this conceptual tool that the

Table 8.3 Preconditions and channels for learning processes in innovative milieux

Preconditions	Continuity	Dynamic synergies	
Contexts (channels)			
Firms	R&D functions	Functional interaction	INTERNAL LEARNING
		Tacit transfer of knowledge	
Territory	Low mobility of the labour force outside the milieu	High mobility of the labour force within the milieu	COLLECTIVE LEARNING
	Stable linkages with suppliers and customers	Cooperation for innovation with suppliers and customers	
		Local spin-offs	
Networking	Stability as a consequence of the complexity of strategic alliances	Transfer of knowledge via cooperation	LEARNING THROUGH NETWORKING

Source: Camagni and Capello, 2002

theoreticians of the *milieu innovateur* interpret the growth of small firms areas, among them the Marshallian industrial district.

However, collective learning is not the only dynamic advantage generated for local firms by the *milieu*, with its assets of relational capital. A further factor facilitating firms' innovative capacity is reduction of the uncertainty that accompanies innovative processes. In large firms, the functions of information-gathering, the codification of knowledge, and the selection of decision-making routines – all of which are geared to reducing static and dynamic uncertainty – are performed by the R&D department, or by the planning unit. In the case of a *milieu innovateur*, they are undertaken in socialized and collective manner by the *milieu* itself, in which information rapidly circulates because of geographical and collective proximity.[41]

Finally, the reduction of the costs of *ex ante* coordination among decision-making units, and the facilitation of 'collective action' (undertaken to furnish collective goods or simply to integrate private investment decisions), is a further element enhancing the innovative process in a *milieu*. Such coordination generally suffers from the limited and costly nature of the availabile information, and from the possible existence of opportunistic behaviour. The presence of the *milieu* reduces these costs because it enables information to circulate more easily; it facilitates the taking of coordinated decisions through proximity and social homogeneity/cohesion; while it discourages opportunistic behaviour by fostering trust and threatening social sanctions. This last social/psychological element is crucial: it derives from the sharing of common values and of similar codes of behaviour, and it acts positively by developing trust and loyalty. Conversely, it develops rapid processes of isolation and punishment for opportunistic behaviour.[42]

The influence exerted by Marshallian district theory on this approach is evident: the *milieu* theory reiterates the importance of geographical proximity, but even more so of social and cultural proximity, in guaranteeing forms of stable and enduring cooperation in small firm areas. For industrial district theory, these forms of cooperation give rise to a 'community market', the form of production organization which ensures the static efficiency of firms. For *milieu* theory, cooperation generates processes of knowledge socialization, and it reduces the risk associated with innovation, and collective learning – that is, factors of dynamic efficiency.

In recent years, econometric empirical analyses have corroborated the theory. In the case of three *milieux* in Italy, a production function was estimated using data collected at individual firm level in which efficiency parameters of the production factors were connected to:

- for labour: effects of collective learning, these being identified in the intensity of local spin-offs, and appreciation of the stability and quality of the local labour market;
- for intangible capital: effects of 'industrial atmosphere' and collective learning, these being identified in the importance to the individual firm of specialised knowledge internal to the local area, and the lesser importance of acquiring knowledge from outside.

The results showed that labour productivity is subject to increasing returns (given the small average size of firms) which are substantially reinforced by the presence of collective learning processes. Conversely, (intangible) capital productivity is subject to decreasing returns, but is greatly augmented by an increase in the appreciation and use of local specialized knowledge (Figure 8.2).[43]

In terms of economic theory, the *milieu innovateur* approach has recently been indirectly validated by stylized analytical models *à la* Romer and Lucas.[44] The rigidly neoclassical and aggregate form of these endogenous growth models distorts neither the hypotheses nor the intrinsic logic of the *milieu* theory – which testifies to the latter's ability to depict the endogenous economic laws underpinning the dynamic of local economic systems.

Finally, it should be pointed out that the *milieu innovateur* theory remedies the limitation intrinsic to the theory of knowledge spillovers: it explains the channels through which knowledge disseminates, not in terms of pure probability of contact, but rather in those of well-evidenced economic-territorial phenomena – supplier/customer relations, high local labour turnover, and spin-offs. The theory accordingly returns territorial factors to centre-stage in analysis of an area's endogenous innovative capacity, and it reinstates space to the active role in the economic dynamic which the theory of the Marshallian industrial district attributed to it within a framework of pure static efficiency.

The 'learning regions': institutional proximity

The theory of the *milieu innovateur* has been paralleled by the international development of wide-ranging analysis of the endogenous factors at the basis of local innovative capacity. This approach has shifted its attention to institutional aspects, and specifically to the set of

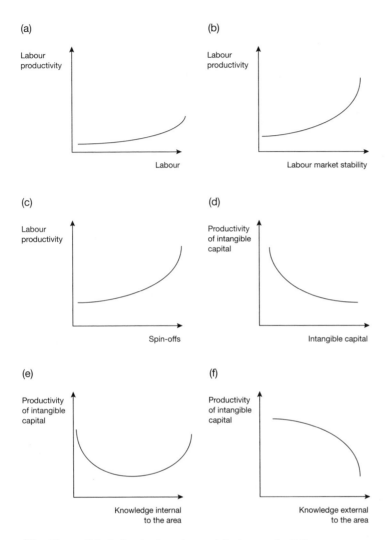

Figure 8.2 *Collective learning and factor productivity*
Source: Capello, 1999b

social, economic and cultural rules embedded in a territorial setting. It originated with the Danish school of Aalborg, and in the works of its founder, the economist Bengt-Åke Lundvall, and it has subsequently been widely adopted, mainly in the UK and the USA.[45]

The main components of this approach can be summarized as follows. The principal resource of modern economies is knowledge. Consequently, the principal processes on which an economy's competitiveness depends are learning and the acquisition of knowledge. Moreover, the complexity and systemic nature of innovation, and the brevity of the product life-cycle characteristic of technological change in recent years, entail that learning is an interactive process. Put otherwise, learning springs from cooperation and interaction between firms and the local scientific system, between different functions within the firm (between production and research and development, between marketing and R&D), between producers and customers, and between firms and the social and institutional structure. The feedbacks, interdependencies and complementarities among the various functions internal to the firm, and between the firm and external actors, required by the innovative process evince the need for cooperative and interactive forms of organizational learning. Finally, innovation is increasingly the result of an informal learning process, based on direct experience or that of others, which comes about through activities focused on finding solutions to specific technological, productive or market problems.

The consequence of these various features is that the innovative process is strongly localized: it results from the variety of traditions, norms, habits, social conventions, and cultural practices that constitute what has been called 'institutional thickness'.[46] Innovation therefore cannot be understood properly unless it is examined within the socio-cultural and institutional context in which it takes place. In areas where there is 'institutional proximity' – meaning the set of norms, codes and rules of behaviour which help economic actors (people, individual firms, public and private institutions) to adopt forms of organization that facilitate interact learning – the innovative process comes about more rapidly and gives competitiveness to the economic system.[47]

A 'learning region' is in this sense:

■ a region in which norms of social and institutional behaviour support interactive learning: the horizontal organization of corporate functions, cooperation and agreements among firms, and cooperation between firms and research centres, facilitate the exchange of knowledge and support the learning process;

■ a region with an 'organized market' in which implicit and generally shared rules of behaviour guarantee the tacit exchange of information and the creation of knowledge. These come about through an interactive and creative learning process centred on the implementation of new products, and new technological solutions. Likewise, a 'destructive' learning process (a 'creative disruption') teaches the system to abandon obsolete and inefficient technological trajectories, and guides it through the profound transformation brought about by the technological – all the more so organizational – changes imposed by a new technological trajectory.[48]

In short, a 'learning region' is a socio-economic system able gradually to develop forms of interactive learning. It is on this 'learning ability' that a region's competitiveness depends. It is accordingly a concept that identifies the condition necessary for an economic system's competitiveness as a process (learning) more than a state (the stock of knowledge).[49]

Despite its necessary abstraction, which makes its empirical application impossible, the concept of the 'learning region' has gained general consensus, not just in a particular scientific community (that of Britain and North America) but also at institutional level, given the European Union's need to devise new policy instruments with which to support regional cohesion. However, the results obtained when the concept of 'learning region' is translated into regional economic policies are rather perplexing: the interventions proposed concern the creation of educational and training services, incentives for learning, the sharing of successful experiences in creating organizational forms to support interaction, and financial aid to firms undergoing corporate restructuring: all of which are interventions in support of weak regions which are well known and already applied in the past.

An apparently major weakness in the theory also needs to be stressed. Although it envisages a system of homogeneous socio-economic and institutional conditions in the region, and interaction and cooperation among actors, it is nevertheless markedly a-spatial. Nothing in the theory explains how and why these relations must necessarily be local; nor does it explain what territorial conditions must be in place for the 'organized market' to arise; or what territorial factors fuel the process of interactive learning.

These shortcomings are all the more evident when one considers that the concept of the 'learning region' is derived from that of the 'learning economy', and that the concept of 'learning economy' is in its turn used to denote a '*national* system of innovation' where the set of institutional rules and norms allow, strengthen and emphasize forms of interactive learning. The fact that the concept can be shifted among different territorial levels of analysis demonstrates its a-spatial nature. One should therefore be wary of the current debate on whether the concept of 'national innovation system' can be applied to regions to produce a 'regional innovation system'.[50] The necessarily a-spatial nature of the concept of 'innovation system' may thwart any attempt to territorialize it, because any such attempt is intrinsically incapable of evincing the endogenous elements which underpin processes of territorial innovation.

THE URBAN STRUCTURE AND REGIONAL DEVELOPMENT

Special emphasis has recently been given to the idea (also mooted by authors in the past) that an efficient, modern and advanced urban structure able to grow in balanced manner, and pursuing goals of equity, competitiveness and sustainability, determines a region's economic success.[51]

On this view, regional development springs substantially from the balanced growth of individual cities – these being sources of increasing returns for the people who live and work in them – and of the city system in which each individual city is embedded.[52] Each individual city must therefore find a growth path which reinforces the elements from which its static and dynamic efficiency derive. Such growth, moreover, is enhanced when the individual city is embedded in a system of cities in its turn able to develop in a harmonious and balanced manner, with an even mix of well-connected and integrated urban centres.

In economic terms, these assertions are borne out by numerous theoretical findings. Maintaining the distinction between analysis of the efficiency of the individual city and that of the city system, the theoretical underpinnings of these statements emerge very clearly, from both the static and dynamic points of view (Table 8.4).

First, a city is a spatial cluster of productive and residential activities. The concentration of activities, the density of the contacts that develop within them, and easy access to advanced information and knowledge are evident advantages springing from an urban location. They are opposed to localization (or district) economies because they stem from the presence of a mix of sectors.[53] A broad and diversified labour market, the availability of

203

Table 8.4 Sources of static and dynamic urban economies

Spatial dimension	Cities	City systems
Temporal dimension		
Static	The City as a Cluster	The City System as an Efficient Production System
	Presence of pronounced sectoral mix	Balanced urban structure
	Density of proximity contacts	Efficient networks of interconnection
	Reduction of transaction costs	Specialization economies
		Network externalities from complementary activities
Dynamic	The City as a Milieu	The City System as an Efficient System of Innovative Cooperation
	Reducer of uncertainty: – information transcoder – *ex ante* coordinator of collective action – substrate for collective learning	Generator of dynamic network externalities

typically central and urban services (advanced, financial, insurance, managerial, etc.), a supply of managerial and executive skills, communication and information structures, characterize an urban location, and they affect the factor productivity of the firms situated therein.

But the importance of the city as the engine of development also resides in its ability to generate dynamic economies and become the preferred location for new high-tech companies, and, in general, for innovative functions. Besides the well-known role attributed in the 1950s and 1960s to cities as 'incubators' of the new, or as the 'nurseries' of small firms, and supported by empirical data,[54] a new interpretative factor has recently been adduced in explanation of the dynamic efficiency of cities. Like the *milieu*, the city performs the crucial function of reducing dynamic uncertainty and creating processes of collective learning to the advantage of local actors. The urban environment comprises the cooperation, synergy, and relational proximity which in *milieu* theory determine the dynamic efficiency of firms. Shared values, common codes of behaviour, a sense of belonging, and mutual trust can be characteristics of urban systems; when this is the case, urban systems share the same features with the *milieu*. These also account for the ability of the urban system to reduce uncertainty and generate processes of the socialization of knowledge and collective learning.[55]

However, it is not solely in the efficiency of the individual city that one grasps the effect of the urban system on regional economic development. As shown by the first theorists of general spatial equilibrium and the structure of city systems, Christaller and Lösch, a well-balanced urban system with an even mix of large, medium and small cities and towns, endowed with efficient transport networks, is the ideal territorial system in terms of efficiency and well-being. A city system of this kind, in fact, makes it possible to exploit the geographical, historical and cultural specificities of each individual city, to provide a broad and diversified range of possible locations for firms and households, and to avoid the hyper-concentration of production and residential activities in a few large-sized cities, where the advantages of scale economies are easily eroded by the high social and environmental costs associated with large urban size.

Again in regard to city systems, an important theoretical contribution to understanding of their dynamic efficiency has been made by the theory of city networks discussed earlier.[56] A network organization of urban centres, hierarchically ordered or of similar size, gives rise to evident advantages associated *inter alia* with the innovative cooperation necessary for the undertaking of innovative projects (infrastructures, or service provision, or even large-scale urban planning).

The sources of an urban system's static and dynamic efficiency are evident in the theories just discussed. But it should be pointed out that the theory which associates regional development with the dynamism of the urban structure rightly gives great importance to social aspects (cohesion) and environmental ones (sustainability) as well. These too are sources of static and dynamic advantages, and they are decisive factors in the balanced growth of an urban system in that they act upon the location choices of firms, and upon the ability of a city to retain businesses already operating in it, and to attract new ones. In the age of globalization, success in the fierce competition among the large European cities for direct foreign investments hinges on their economic efficiency and environmental and social quality.

CONCLUSIONS

The chapter has surveyed the theories which, since the mid-1970s, have endeavoured to have economic analysis incorporate a concept of space which performs an active role in defining the patterns of a local area's economic development. With these theories, the concept of 'space' gives way to that of 'territory' as a factor generating economic advantages for the activities located in it. For these theories, economic development depends on a concentrated spatial organization of production activities, rather than on a greater endowment of economic resources, or on their more efficient spatial allocation.

These theories are widely studied still today, and they have been enriched with numerous conceptual and empirical studies. They represent the maximum of cross-fertilization between location theory and local development theory, where locational features explain and are explained by economic development processes inextricably bound up with each other. All this comes about within a microeconomic and micro-behavioural framework, and therefore without the rigorous mathematical formulation of macroeconomic growth models which, until the end of the 1980s, were only possible on the assumption of perfect competition and constant returns. In the next chapters we shall see that theories have been developed in recent years which include spatial aspects and the increasing returns that derive from them in macroeconomic growth models but are only able to do so because they adopt a different conception of space as 'diversified-stylized'.

REVIEW QUESTIONS

1 What is meant by endogenous development?

2 What role is played by space in local endogenous development theories?

3 Which conception of growth is behind the theory of endogenous development?

4 What stimulated the conceptualization of the endogenous development approach?

5 How would you define an industrial district? How would you define district economies? What advantages exist in industrial districts which go beyond district economies? What are the strengths and weaknesses of this theory?

6 What is conceptualized by the knowledge spillover approach? What are the limits of this approach?

7 How would you define a '*milieu innovateur*'? What are the genetic elements for the existence of a *milieu*? Does the theory of the *milieu innovateur* overcome some of the limits of the knowledge spillover approach and how?

8 What is conceptualized in the learning regions theory? How would you define a learning region? Which are the main strengths and weaknesses of the theory?

9 What is the role of space in the knowledge spillover approach, in the *milieu innovateur* theory and in the learning region approach?

10 Which theoretical elements support the idea that regional development depends on an efficient urban system within the region?

SELECTED READING ON EMPIRICAL FINDINGS

About industrial districts

Alam, G. (1994) 'Industrial districts and technological change: a study of the garment industry in Delhi', in *Technological dynamisms in industrial districts: an alternative approach to industrialisation in developing countries?*, New York/Geneva: UNCTAD, pp. 257–66.

Dawson, J. (1988) 'Flexibility together: surviving and growing in a garment cluster, Ahmedabad, India', *The Journal of Entrepreneurship*, vol. V, no. 2, pp. 153–77.

Dei Ottati, G. (1996) 'Economic changes in the district of Prato in the 1980s: towards a more conscious and organised industrial district', *European Planning Studies*, vol. IV, no. 1, pp. 35–52.

Nadvi, K. and Schmidz, H. (1994) 'Industrial clusters in less developed countries: review of experiences and research agenda', Discussion Paper no. 339, IDS, University of Sussex.

Rabellotti, R. (1997) *External economies and cooperation in industrial districts. A comparison of Italy and Mexico*, London: Macmillan.

Rabellotti, R. and Schmidz, H. (1997) 'The internal heterogeneity of industrial districts in Italy, Brazil and Mexico', *Regional Studies*, vol. 33, no. 2, pp. 97–108.

Saxenian, A. L. (1994) *Regional advantage: culture and competition in Silicon Valley and Route 128*, Cambridge, Mass.: Harvard University Press.

Scott, A. J. (1992) 'The role of large producers in industrial districts: a case study of high technology systems houses in Southern California', *Regional Studies*, vol. 26, no. 3, pp. 265–75.

About innovation and regional development

Aydalot, Ph. and Keeble, D. (eds) (1988) *High technology industry and innovative environment*, London: Routledge.

Breschi, S. (2000) 'The geography of innovation: a cross-sector analysis', *Regional Studies*, vol. 34, no. 2, pp. 213–29.

Camagni, R. and Capello, R. (1998) 'Innovation and performance in SMEs in Italy: the relevance of spatial aspects', *Competition and Change*, vol. 3, pp. 69–106.

Ciciotti, E. and Wettmann, R. (1981) 'The mobilisation of indigenous potential', Commission of the European Community, *Internal Documentation on Regional Policy*, no. 10.

Cooke, Ph. and Morgan, K. (1994) 'The creative milieu: a regional perspective on innovation', in Dodgson, M. and Rothwell, R. (eds), *The handbook of industrial innovation*, Cheltenham: Edward Elgar, pp. 25–32.

Decoster, E. and Tabariés, M. (1986) 'L'Innovation dans un pôle scientifique et technologique: le cas de la cité Scientifique Ile-de-France', in Aydalot, Ph. (ed.), *Milieux Innovateurs en Europe*, Paris: GREMI, pp. 79–100.

Frenkel, A. (2001) 'Why high-technology firms choose to locate in or near metropolitan areas', *Urban Studies*, vol. 38, no. 7, pp. 1083–1101.

Goddard, J. and Thwaites, A. (1986) 'New technology and regional development policy', in Nijkamp, P. (ed.), *Technological change, employment and spatial dynamics*, Berlin: Springer Verlag, pp. 91–114.

Maggioni, M. (2002) *Clustering dynamics and the location of high-tech firms*, Berlin: Physica-Verlag.

Malecki, E. and Varaiya, P. (1986) 'Innovation and changes in regional structure', in Nijkamp, P. (ed.), *Handbook of regional and urban economics*, Amsterdam: North-Holland, pp. 629–45.

Oakey, R., Nash, P. and Thwaites, A. (1980) 'The regional distribution of innovative manufacturing establishments in Britain', *Regional Studies*, no. 13, pp. 141–51.

Paci, R. and Usai, S. (2000) 'Technological enclaves and industrial districts: an analysis of the regional distribution of innovative activity in Europe', *Regional Studies*, vol. 34, no. 2, pp. 97–114.

Schatzl, E. L. and Revilla Diez, J. (eds) (2002) *Technological change and regional development in Europe*, Berlin: Springer Verlag.

Sternberg, R. (1996) 'Reasons for the genesis of high-tech regions – theoretical explanation and empirical evidence', *Geoforum*, vol. 27, no. 2, pp. 205–23.

About milieux innovateurs

Amin, A. and Thwaites, A. (1986) 'Change in the local economy: the case of the Northern Region (UK)', in Aydalot, Ph. (ed.), *Milieux innovateurs en Europe*, Paris: GREMI, pp. 129–62.

Camagni, R. and Rabellotti, R. (1997) 'Footwear production systems in Italy: a dynamic comparative analysis', in Ratti, R., Bramanti, A. and Gordon, R. (eds), *The dynamics of innovative regions*, Aldershot: Ashgate, pp. 139–64.

Capello, R. (1999) 'SMEs clustering and factor productivity: a milieu production function model', *European Planning Studies*, vol. 7, no. 6, pp. 719–35.

Capello, R. (2001) 'Urban innovation and collective learning: theory and evidence from five metropolitan cities in Europe', in Fischer, M. M. and Froehlich, J. (eds), *Knowledge, complexity and innovation systems*, Berlin, Heidelberg, New York: Springer Verlag, pp. 181–208.

Gordon, R. (1993) 'Structural change, strategic alliances and the spatial reorganisation of Silicon Valley's semiconductor industry', in Maillat, D., Quévit, M. and Senn, L. (eds), *Reseaux d'innovation et milieux locaux*, Neuchâtel, EDES: GREMI, pp. 51–72.

Lambooy, J. (1986) 'Regional development trajectories and small enterprises. The case study of the Amsterdam Region', in Aydalot, Ph. (ed.), *Milieux innovateurs en Europe*, Paris: GREMI, pp. 57–78.

Tabariés, M. (1992) 'Nouvelles PME et cité scientifique en formation: Ile-de-France Sud', in Maillat, D. and Perrin, J.-C. (eds), *Entreprises Innovatrices et Développement Territorial*, Neuchâtel, EDES: GREMI, pp. 23–40.

About knowledge spillovers and regional development

Acs, Z., Audretsch, D. and Feldman, M. (1994) 'R&D spillovers and recipient firm size', *Review of Economics and Statistics*, vol. 76, pp. 336–40.

Audretsch, D. and Feldman, M. (1996) 'R&D spillovers and the geography of innovation and production', *American Economic Review*, vol. 86, pp. 630–40.

De Groot, H., Nijkamp, P. and Acs, Z. (2001) 'Knowledge spillovers, innovation and regional development', *Papers in Regional Science*, vol. 80, no. 3, special issue.

Maier, G. and Sedlacek, S. (eds) (2005) *Spillovers and innovations – space, environment and the economy*, Vienna: Springer Verlag.

Ruslan, L. and Plasmans, J. (2003) 'Measuring knowledge spillovers in the new economy firms in Belgium using patent citations', *Global Business and Economics Review*, vol. 5, no. 1, pp. 75–99.

About regional innovation systems

Bacaria, J., Borràs Alomar, S. and Fernàndez-Riba, A. (2004) 'The changing institution structure and performance of the catalon innovation system', in Cooke, P., Heidenreich, M. and Braczyk, H.-J. (eds), *Regional innovation systems*, London: Routledge, pp. 63–90.

Boekhold, P. and de Jager, D. (2004) 'South-east Brabant: a regional innovation system in transition', in Cooke, P., Heidenreich, M. and Braczyk, H.-J. (eds), *Regional innovation systems*, London: Routledge, pp. 44–62.

Cooke, P. (2004) 'The regional innovation system in Wales: evolution or eclipse?', in Cooke, P., Heidenreich, M. and Braczyk, H.-J. (eds), *Regional innovation systems*, London: Routledge, pp. 214–33.

Maskell, P. (2004) 'Learning the village economy in Denmark: the role of institutions and policy in sustaining competitiveness', in Cooke, P., Heidenreich, M. and Braczyk, H.-J. (eds), *Regional innovation systems*, London: Routledge, pp. 154–85.

FURTHER READING

Becattini, G. (1990) 'The Marshallian Industrial District as a socio-economic notion', in Pyke, F., Becattini, G. and Sengenberger, W. (eds), *Industrial districts and interfirm cooperation in Italy*, Geneva: International Institute of Labour Studies, pp. 37–51.

Becattini, G. (ed.) (2004) *Industrial districts: a new approach to industrial change*, Cheltenham: Edward Elgar.

Camagni, R. (1991) 'Local *milieu*, uncertainty and innovation networks: towards a new dynamic theory of economic space', in Camagni, R. (ed.), *Innovation networks: spatial perspectives*, London: Belhaven-Pinter, pp. 121–44.

Capello, R. (1999) 'Spatial transfer of knowledge in high-technology milieux: learning vs. collective learning processes', *Regional Studies*, vol. 33, no. 4, pp. 353–65.

Dei Ottati, G. (2003) 'The governance of transactions in the industrial district: the "community market"', in Becattini, G., Bellandi, M., Dei Ottati, G. and Sforzi, F. (eds), *From industrial districts to local development*, Cheltenham: Edward Elgar, chapter 4.

Keeble, D. and Wilkinson, F. (2000) *High-technology clusters, networking and collective learning in Europe*, Aldershot: Ashgate.

Lundvall, B.-A. (ed.) (1992) *National systems of innovation. Towards a theory of innovation and interactive learning*, London: Pinter.

209

Part 4

Theories of regional growth: diversified-stylized space

Chapter 9

Territorial competitiveness and cumulative demand/ supply growth

SUMMARY

1   Increasing returns, competitiveness and cumulative growth
2   Equilibrium in conditions of non-linearity
3   Increasing returns external to the firm: the circular and cumulative causation model
4   Increasing returns internal to the firm: the new economic geography

INCREASING RETURNS, COMPETITIVENESS AND CUMULATIVE GROWTH

The previous chapter stressed the active role that space may play in economic development as the source of advantages for the firms located within it: static and dynamic agglomeration economies in the form of localization or urbanization economies significantly influence the productivity and innovative capacity of firms and, in aggregate terms, also of the area in which those firms are situated. Increasing returns arise from concentrated production, and they determine the efficiency of the economic system.

The previous chapter also stressed the qualitative nature of the theories of endogenous development that were examined. This qualitativeness was in some cases due to an explicit methodological choice; in others to the difficulty of including increasing returns in an analytical model. In mathematical terms, the hypothesis of scale economies entails that the relations among the variables which determine development cannot be based on linear equations: instead, higher-level equations are necessary, which inevitably require a descriptive mathematical language more complex than that of linear systems.[1] In economic terms, the existence of increasing returns (at the individual firm level) requires abandonment of the perfect competition hypothesis, and the contrary assumption of imperfect competition, a notion which was never formalized prior to the 1970s.[2]

In the 1980s, major progress was achieved in the fields of both non-linear mathematical models and of economic modelling in conditions of imperfect competition. This opened the way for new theories on local economic growth. Thanks to the advent (a) of mathematical approaches to study of the qualitative behaviour of non-linear dynamic systems (bifurcation, catastrophe, and chaos theory) and (b) in economics, of Avinash Dixit and Joseph Stiglitz's formalized model of imperfect competition, increasing returns became the decisive factor in development, not only for qualitative theories but for analytical theories and models as well.[3]

This part of the book describes the theories of local growth which for the most part use advanced mathematical tools and draw on recent economic analytical models. They are of particular importance for local development theory because they take analysis beyond Edwin von Böventer's already-mentioned distinction between 'pure and exact' regional theory without agglomeration economies, on the one hand, and 'applied regional theory', which is inexact but takes agglomeration factors into account, on the other.[4]

The first innovative feature of these more formalized theories is that they enable elegant growth models of a strictly economic nature to include agglomeration economies, in the form of increasing returns, as determinants of local development. They then demonstrate that these phenomena can be treated using the traditional tools of economic theory (optimizing choices for firms and individuals). They have thus induced orthodox economists to (re-)discover the spatial dimension of economic phenomena, and it is to this aspect that they owe a large part of their continuing success.

The second innovative feature of these approaches is their ability to escape the mechanicism of the formalized models which preceded them and to introduce elements of uncertainty into both growth trajectories and the final equilibrium towards which the development path tends. Real phenomena accompanying development trajectories – synergy and positive cumulativeness (agglomeration economies) as well as negative feedbacks (congestion or saturation in growth processes) – are incorporated into the logic of the models through the non-linearity of growth relations. This makes possible multiple equilibria associated with diverse initial conditions, with diverse values of the variables and parameters of the structural relations of development, and with convergent or divergent, explosive or implosive, stable or unstable, growth paths.

These models generate a growth path which recalls that of the theories surveyed in the previous chapter: once again, this is a path of *cumulative, endogenous and largely selective growth*. The models now described envisage a diversified space, in fact. That is to say, they assume the existence of sharp polarities where development takes place and cumulates due to increasing returns in the form of learning processes, scale economies (at the area or firm level), and localization and urbanization economies which engender a virtuous circle of cumulative development. Moreover, because increasing returns are included in the structural relations that characterize the dynamic behaviour of the local system (or of the individual firms located in it), they are produced by the workings of the local economic system themselves, and they mark out an endogenous growth path.

These theories are all the more similar to those of the previous chapter in that they pursue the same goal of identifying the elements which determine long-period competitiveness, and the conditions under which an area can acquire and maintain a role in the international division of labour. The increasing returns hypothesis, in fact, entails the assumption that when the market expands, either production increases with resources remaining equal, or cost decreases with production remaining equal. In other words, it entails the assumption that associated with increases in production are ever greater savings of resources, and therefore increasingly greater rises in productivity, with positive and growing effects on local competitiveness. These effects are expressed differently by each theory: in terms of a greater capacity to capture larger shares of world demand by the theory of cumulative circular development; of greater capacity to attract external capital in search of good financial and productive opportunities by the most recent models of the 'new economic geography'; and of greater capacity to (re-)create over time the conditions for constant economic growth of productive resources by the theory of endogenous growth.

However, also to be emphasized are the marked differences and discontinuities between these theories and the endogenous development theories discussed previously. The first of these differences/discontinuities concerns the formalized, macroeconomic and aggregate nature of the theories that this chapter examines, which stand in sharp contrast to the micro-territorial and micro-behavioural approach taken by the models in the previous chapter. Owing to their aggregate macroeconomic nature, the theories now presented aim to explain the growth rate of aggregate income interpreted as a synthetic indicator for the various aspects of development. Unlike those seen in the previous chapter, these theories do not seek to provide a qualitative interpretation of all the tangible and intangible elements, economic or otherwise, which characterize the dynamic of local economic systems. Once again, therefore, the dynamic path of a local economy is interpreted by *growth theories*. But there are two major differences between these and the growth theories of the 1950s and 1960s: (a) returns are no longer constant but increasing, and (b) the conception of growth assumed is a dynamic and long-term one: theories seek to define the elements with which the competitiveness conditions of a local system can be maintained and recreated, rather than to highlight the mechanisms that increase long-term employment and production, or individual well-being and per capita income, as in previous theories.

A second difference with respect to the theories discussed in the previous chapter resides in the treatment of space, which now becomes *diversified* and *stylized*. These approaches envisage the existence of polarities in space where development takes place, diversifying the level and rate of income growth even among areas of the same region. However, although diversified, space is now stylized into points devoid of any territorial dimension. Localized technological externalities do not exist in this space; nor does a set of tangible and intangible factors which may act upon firms' productivity and innovative capacity because of proximity and reduced transaction costs; nor a system of economic and social relations constituting the relational or social capital of a certain geographical space. Yet all these are elements able to differentiate spatial elements on the basis of strictly territorial aspects. These approaches thus reprise the simple, somewhat banal view of space as the simple container of development, and they therefore necessarily abandon the more inter-esting and intriguing interpretation of space as an additional resource and as an independent factor in development.

These considerations introduce the third discontinuity with respect to the theories discussed in the previous chapter: increasing returns no longer take the form of specific advantages involuntarily generated by individual firms. According to the theories now exam-ined, increasing returns are economies of scale or of learning stylized in systems of equations which explain the structure and dynamics of a local system through non-linear relations which give rise to multiplicative effects in the aggregate growth rate.

215

Whilst these are the main features of the most recent theories of regional growth, this chapter also deals with models which assume the existence of increasing returns (at the firm or area level) to interpret development as resulting from a *cumulative process of demand/supply growth*. Left for treatment in the next chapter are theories which conceive growth as resulting from increasing returns on production resources, in a production function of neoclassical derivation; for these theories, growth depends exclusively on *supply elements*.

According to the logic of the models presented in this chapter, therefore, the competitiveness (exogenously assumed) of strong areas generates greater production (supply); more investments (induced by an 'acceleration' mechanism for some theories, and by the creation of greater profits in the local market for others); and higher employment, which fuels immigration. This process drives the development of a broad local market (demand) which in its turn attracts new investments and creates new employment (supply), in a circle of cumulative growth. In parallel with this circuit of increasing local production, increases come about in the level (or rate) of productivity because of technical progress embodied in capital goods, to firm- and system-level learning processes, and scale economies deriving from larger production volumes.

The modern theories now presented are rooted in a model, formulated at the end of the 1950s and then formalized in the 1970s by Nicholas Kaldor, which already conceived the existence of increasing returns as being intrinsic to the structural relations that characterize a local economy's aggregate growth. In this model, economies of scale are assumed to be external to firms, taking the form of learning economies – or learning-by-doing economies *à la* Arrow. The rich and dynamic advanced economies, with their high growth rates, also display (in these models) greater rates of productivity growth which generate a cumulative circle of growth. Reasoning on the basis of increasing returns at territorial level, the model is able to formalize these returns on the assumption of perfect competition.[5]

Myrdal's and Kaldor's idea of giving increasing returns a key role in local development was taken up by a school of thought which developed in the 1990s under the guidance of the well-known economist Paul Krugman. Exploiting the formalization of the imperfect competition model, Krugman and his followers produced elegant economic growth models which incorporated the location choices of firms. These were made to depend on three economic factors – transportation costs, increasing returns, and migratory flows – which determine, according to the values that they assume, the existence of agglomerative phenomena (what Krugman calls 'geographic concentration') or diffusion processes. When the concentration of productive activities prevails in an area, the conditions for cumulative local growth are generated.

Before the theories are introduced, it may help the reader to understand the new logics of 'equilibrium' if an outline is provided of the most recent mathematical instruments used to interpret economic growth.[6]

EQUILIBRIUM IN CONDITIONS OF NON-LINEARITY

The novel aspects of the approach

There are two reasons for the great success of non-linear dynamic models since the 1980s in socio-economic sciences. The first has just been mentioned: that these models make it possible to represent in stylized form real phenomena which manifestly affect the formation, dynamic and structure of economic systems. In the case of local systems in particular, they enable the inclusion in growth models of scale and agglomeration economies (diseconomies), synergies and idiosyncrasies among the various components of a complex system, oscillatory movements in variables like price, income, and technological innovation: all of which are elements likely to affect the development path of a local economic system.

The second reason for the success of these models is that it is today possible to overcome the difficulties that often accompany solution of these models by using *numerical simulations*, on the one hand, and mathematical analyses of the qualitative behaviour of non-linear dynamic systems on the other. Recent mathematical approaches allow study to be made of the nature of solutions, rather than of their exact value. Mathematical analyses of this kind are the 'bifurcation and catastrophe theories' which emphasize the existence of multiple equilibria in which the transition from one equilibrium to another may take place through a 'break' or 'catastrophic change' in the time pattern of the variables.[7]

The distinctive feature of these theories is their ability to describe qualitative changes in the state of a system resulting from variation in variables expressing the system's dynamic (also known as 'state variables'), which describe the state of a system at each moment t, and the values of which change rapidly in time; and parameters (or 'control variables') which instead change relatively slowly.

The catastrophe and bifurcation theories have several innovative features. First, they allow for the existence of *multiple system equilibria*, in contrast to the unique dynamic equilibrium (whether stable or unstable) that characterized previous theories. The prevalence of one equilibrium over another, as well as the choice among possible equilibria, depends on the values of the parameters conditioning the temporal dynamic of the unknown variable and on the initial conditions which, as we shall see, significantly influence the system's development trajectories.

It is therefore possible to stylize time patterns of development in which small variations in the parameter values may trigger *sudden catastrophic changes* so that, according to the alternative that prevails, entirely different growth paths ensue. These models are thus able to simulate an endogenous series of complex phenomena which in the past could only be replicated by means of exogenous shocks introduced *ad hoc*.

The customary distinction between stable and unstable dynamic equilibria – which represent 'dynamic stability'[8] – has been supplemented with a further meaning of 'stability' which concerns the conditions in which the very nature of solutions may change (for example, instead of a single solution, periodic or chaotic ones are propounded). In this case, analysis centres on the 'structural stability' of systems.[9] Indeed, the most recent approaches to non-linear dynamic systems have studied this 'structural stability' of systems, the quality and nature of solutions, and the form that the system may assume. Unlike linear dynamic models, they have not concerned themselves with analysis of the existence and stability of the system's equilibrium (its 'dynamic stability'). This helps explain why we shall often find that the models do not yield unequivocal results, but instead offer a range of possible solutions according to the initial conditions and the values assumed by the parameters.

There is a further and equally important feature of these models: when time trajectories undergo an abrupt change, they are rarely able to return to their initial state. They appear

217

to be largely *irreversible* if the direction of time is reversed, because the system spontaneously reorganizes itself around the new state; no development trajectory can be replicated by chance, and no development trajectory can move in reverse direction.

An example of catastrophic growth: the export-base model in conditions of non-linearity

The exposition thus far can be made clearer if we take a model already discussed – the dynamic export-base model set out in Chapter 5 – and rework it with the aim of determining the existence and the stability of dynamic equilibrium.

Reprising the structural relations between population (P) and employment (total, in the base sector, and in services, respectively L_T, L_b, L_s) which characterized Hoyt's model:

$$P = aL_T \tag{9.1}$$

$$L_T = L_b + L_s \tag{9.2}$$

$$L_s = bP \tag{9.3}$$

$$L_b = \overline{L_b} \tag{9.4}$$

we introduce a time lag in (9.3)

$$L_s(t) = \beta P(t - 1) \tag{9.5}$$

and non-linearity in the structural relations (9.1) and (9.3):

$$P = \alpha(L) \qquad \text{with } \alpha' > 0 \tag{9.6}$$

$$L_s = \beta(P) \qquad \text{with } \beta' > 0 \tag{9.7}$$

Relation (9.6) states that there exists a certain threshold of employment above which a marginal increase produces a very large increase in the population (presumably because of the positive effects of agglomeration economies). Relation (9.7) states that there exists a critical mass of the population beyond which a population increase has an extremely marked effect on the services sector.[10] On these hypotheses, (9.1) becomes:

$$P(t) = \alpha \left\{ L_b + \beta[P(t - 1)] \right\} \tag{9.8}$$

and the region's growth can be depicted as in Figure 9.1. It is easy to identify the differences with respect to Figure 5.1, which shows the linear growth of income (though the same figure would apply for a model expressing the physical growth of the region, to which the dynamic hypotheses describing the trend in Figure 5.1 are applied). In the model incorporating non-linearity (Figure 9.1a):

(a) Stable and unstable multiple equilibria

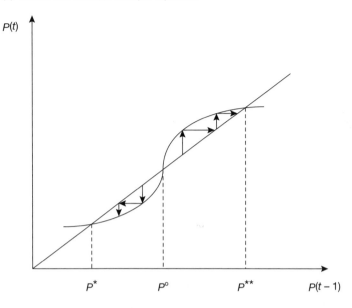

(b) 'Catastrophic' change in the region's size

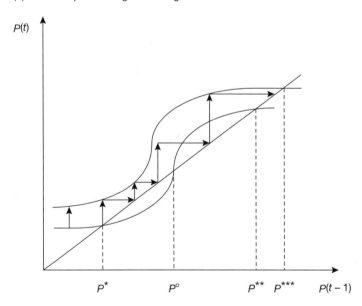

Figure 9.1 The export-base model on the hypothesis of non-linearity
Source: Miyao, 1984

(a) Stationary stable equilibrium

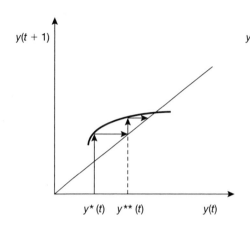

(b) Stationary unstable equilibrium

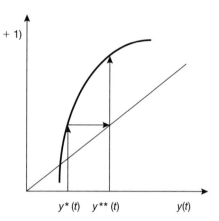

(c) Convergent oscillatory equilibrium

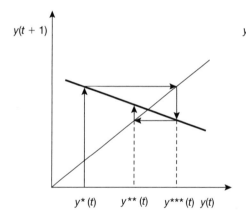

(d) Divergent oscilatory equilibrium

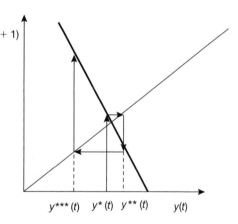

Figure 9.2 *Diagram of the phases in the finite differences equations (time as the discrete variable)*

- there exist *multiple possible equilibria*: P^*, P° and P^{**};
- there exist equilibria *of different kinds*: P^* and P^{**} are stable equilibria; P° is an unstable equilibrium;[11]
- the equilibrium which comes to prevail depends on the initial conditions of the system: if the initial population of the region is less than P°, it will tend to a stable dynamic equilibrium equal to P^*; if instead the initial population is greater than P°, the system will tend to shift to size P^{**}.

Moreover, on assuming exogenous increases in base sector employment (which here performs the role of the control variable or 'parameter' mentioned earlier), the curve expressed by (9.5) shifts upwards. If the increases in base employment are small, the shift does not generate major changes in the region's size. However, there exists a value of employment increase, which may even be very small, at which a break-point, a catastrophic jump, occurs, with a shift to a very much larger size (Figure 9.1b): the size of the city may in fact grow abruptly from $P*$ to $P***$. In this case, the system is rarely able to return to $P*$ and is more likely to reorganize itself around a new and larger size.

INCREASING RETURNS EXTERNAL TO THE FIRM: THE CIRCULAR AND CUMULATIVE CAUSATION MODEL

At the end of the 1950s, Myrdal formulated a model which ran counter to the neoclassical belief in the existence of spontaneous processes of re-equilibrium.[12] Myrdal's 'circular and cumulative causation model' was able to explain the persistent interregional disequilibria reported by empirical research in terms of self-fuelling virtuous/vicious circles. According to the logic of Myrdal's model, rich regions grow increasingly richer, and poor regions increasingly poorer, if spontaneous market forces alone are permitted to operate.[13]

The results yielded by Myrdal's model – which, as said, was entirely at odds with the traditional neoclassical view – are explained by the assumptions on which it was constructed. These were, first, the existence of an investment function which depends on the real or expected level of demand (accelerator theory), rather than on the rate of return on capital, as suggested by the neoclassicals; and second, the existence of increasing returns at territorial level; that is, agglomeration economies generated by the territorial concentration of productive activities and by the accumulation of knowledge embodied in capital goods – as opposed to the constant returns of the neoclassical production function. Assuming this hypothesis signified (for the first time in the history of economic thought on development) that a role must be given to *increasing returns* when the trajectories of local economic growth are defined.[14] It also means relinquishing a single production function with equal technological progress across regions, as imposed by the neoclassical logic, and instead accepting the more realistic assumption that richer regions are endowed with superior technologies which partly explain their greater productivity and competitiveness.

Under these hypotheses, two virtuous processes operate in strong regions (Figure 9.3). These regions attract workers because they have high levels of production (which the model assumes to be exogenous) and a consequent strong demand for labour. Unlike in the neoclassical theory, where the production factors are assumed to be homogeneous, this is a selective migratory process which involves more highly-skilled human capital and consequently deprives the weak areas of better-quality labour. The migratory flows to the rich areas expand the local market, stimulate new investments, and attract new capital, in a virtuous circle of development. At the same time, the close concentration of production activities in a particular area generates agglomeration economies which act upon the area's productivity and competitiveness, boosting development. Greater supply generates further labour demand, increased (internal and external) demand for locally produced goods, new investments, new business start-ups, closer concentration, greater advantages deriving

221

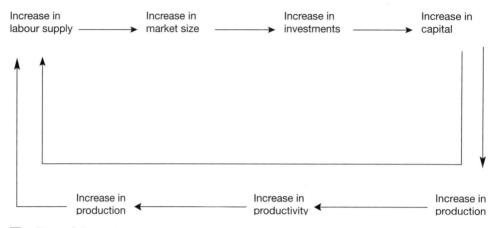

Figure 9.3 *Myrdal's virtuous circle of cumulative development*

from concentrated locations, and further productivity increases, in a virtuous demand/supply circle.

Conversely, the reverse processes of emigration, capital loss, decreasing internal demand, and a decline in productivity due to diminished agglomeration economies characterize the poor areas: according to the logic of the model, these are bound to suffer desertification and poverty.

However, Myrdal's model sets limits on the infinite evolution of the circular cumulative process; limits which consist mainly in territorial and supply-side factors. A constant and concentrated development process generates diffusion effects ('spread effects' in Myrdal's terminology) due to physical congestion, the growing scarcity of the production factors, and their increasing costs. These diffusion processes may arise in the area because of spatial contiguity and then spread along transport and communication axes, or they may 'filter down' through the branches of the urban hierarchy.[15]

The great explanatory potential of Myrdal's model was realized by Nicholas Kaldor, who in the 1970s produced a formalized model of cumulative circular causation.[16]

The dynamic of local income (y) is made to depend on the growth of exports (e).[17] The latter exhibits a dynamic which depends partly on exogenous factors connected with the development of the world economy (b) and partly on endogenous elements connected with the trend of local competitiveness, which depends on domestic price variation (p). In its turn, domestic price variation is explained by variation in the cost of labour per unit of output, also termed 'efficiency wage', and therefore by the difference between the rates of wage growth (w) and of productivity growth (π). Finally, productivity growth is governed by the well-known 'Verdoorn's Law', according to which the rate of productivity growth consists of an exogenous component (d) and a component endogenous to the system expressed by the output growth rate.[18] This last relation states that more than proportional productivity growth rates are associated with higher output growth rates: the existence of scale economies and learning effects explain this relation, and they are comprised in the positive parameter (f) of the mathematical equation:[19]

(a) Cumulative regional development (explosive growth)

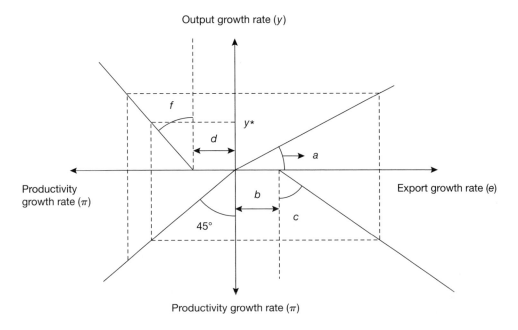

(b) Cumulative regional decline (implosive growth) (for values of a, c, f, different from those in case a)

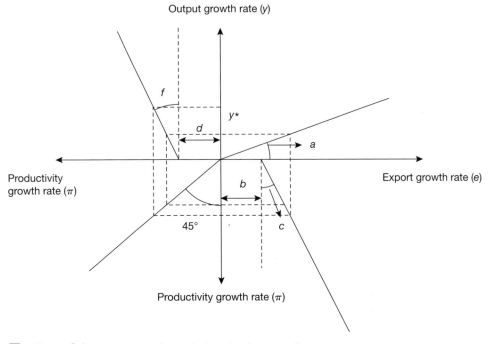

Figure 9.4 *The process of cumulative circular causation*

223

$$y = ae \qquad\qquad a > 0 \qquad\qquad\qquad (9.9)$$

$$e = b - cp = b - c(w - \pi) \qquad b > 0, c > 0, w > 0 \qquad\qquad (9.10)$$

$$\pi = d + fy \qquad\qquad d > 0, f > 0 \qquad\qquad\qquad (9.11)$$

These three relations are depicted by Figure 9.4, where equation (9.9) is shown in the upper-right quadrant, equation (9.11) in the upper-left quadrant, and equation (9.10) in the lower-right quadrant. The lower-left quadrant transposes the variables on the axes. It is easy to see from the figure that, according to the values taken by parameters a, c, and f, the system starts from an initial growth rate y^* and enters either a virtuous and cumulative circle of development (Figure 9.4a) or a vicious one of underdevelopment (Figure 9.4b). The economic conditions that determine a trajectory of growth rather than of decline are the following:

- greater elasticity of demand for exports (parameter a);[20]
- higher increasing returns which associate output growth with productivity growth (parameter f);
- greater elasticity of exports to variation in productivity (and in domestic prices) (parameter c).

Moreover, it is evident that when the economic system suffers from weak structural conditions – expressed by a low initial rate of output growth (y), limited growth of the exogenous component of productivity (d) and of competitiveness (b) – a vicious circle of decline ensues, even with parity of endogenous conditions represented by equal values for the parameters a, c and f (Figure 9.4c).

The same result can be obtained if the dynamic properties of the system are analysed. Solving equations (9.9), (9.10) and (9.11), and introducing a time lag into the last of them, yields:

$$y(t) = a(b - cw + cd) - acfy(t - 1) \qquad\qquad (9.12)$$

(9.12) is represented graphically by Figure 9.5, where it is again evident that equilibrium depends on the parameter values and the initial conditions. If $acf > 1$ (i.e. if the endogenous components of competitiveness are favourable to development), the system is unstable and diverges from the equilibrium development rate, undergoing an explosive or implosive process according to the initial conditions (Figure 9.5a). An initially low growth rate, accompanied by slight exogenous components of productivity and competitiveness, leads to economic decline (Figures 9.4c and 9.5a for initial growth rates less than y^*). Better initial structural conditions, by contrast, engender explosive cumulative development (Figures 9.4a and 9.5a for initial growth rates greater than y^*). These conditions of explosive or implosive development bear out the theoretical expectations of the first proponents of the model, Myrdal and Kaldor.[21]

(c) Cumulative regional decline (implosive growth) (for values of *b* and *d* different from those in case a)

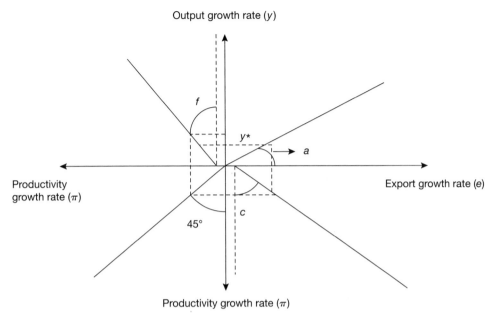

Figure 9.4 *The process of cumulative circular causation (continued)*

By contrast, if $acf < 1$, the system converges on a constant rate y^*. The growth rate is positive if the first term of the right-hand member is positive, i.e. if $w < (b - cd)/c$ – that is, if wages do not grow to such an extent that they compromise the external competitiveness of the local economic system (Figure 9.5b). If wages are instead so high that they thwart the competitiveness of the local system, the latter will nevertheless tend towards a steady-state growth rate, but this growth rate will be negative (y^{**} in Figure 9.5b).

In this case, too, non-linearities can be introduced into the system. One can hypothesize in particular that the productivity growth rate increases with very high growth rates, as follows:

$$\pi = d + \varphi(y) \qquad d > 0,\ \varphi' > 0 \tag{9.13}$$

(9.12) thus becomes:

$$y(t) = a(b - cw + cd) - ac\varphi y(t - 1) \tag{9.14}$$

(9.14), which is expressed by Figure 9.6a, shows that there are always stable rates of growth y^* or decline, but if the local system experiences an increase in the independent component of productivity growth (d), in exports (b), or in wages beyond a certain threshold, the system will abruptly 'jump' to much higher rates of income growth (y^{***} in Figure 9.6b), even eliminating any possibility of negative growth.

225

(a) The case of cumulative divergence ($acf > 1$)

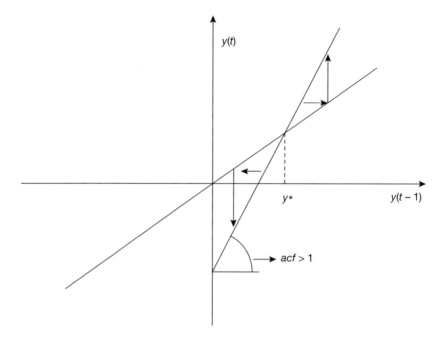

(b) The case of convergence to constant rates of development ($acf < 1$)

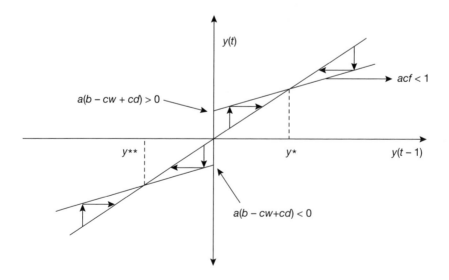

Figure 9.5 *The dynamic equilibrium of the cumulative circular causation model*
Source: Miyao, 1984

226

(a) Two points of stable dynamic equilibrium

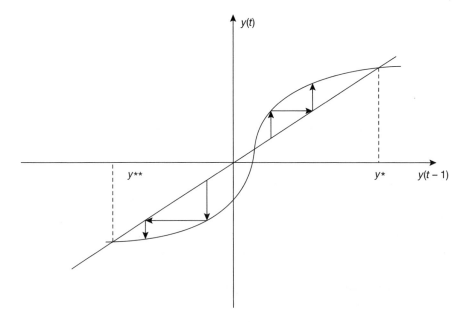

(b) The case of sudden 'catastrophic' growth

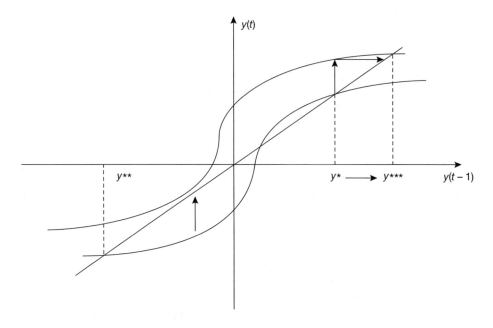

Figure 9.6 *The cumulative circular causation model on the hypothesis of non-linearity in returns*

Source: Miyao, 1984

227

INCREASING RETURNS INTERNAL TO THE FIRM: THE NEW ECONOMIC GEOGRAPHY

The specific nature of the approach

Myrdal and Kaldor's model conceived increasing returns as economies of scale external to the firm: a simple assumption which enables formalization of the growth process in accordance with a market logic of perfect competition.

In the 1990s, thanks to the prolific work of its founder, Paul Krugman, a current of thought known as 'new economic geography' arose in regional studies, provoking considerable criticism by claiming its independence from regional science and from the discipline's 'founding fathers'.[22]

The most distinctive feature of this approach is that it eschews the direct assumption of economies external to the firm. Instead, it highlights local externalities as the consequences of market interactions among firms able individually to exploit internal scale economies, and it does so by making necessary reference to a market structure of imperfect competition.[23]

The aim of 'new economic geography' is to interpret the phenomena of industrial agglomeration – or of 'geographic concentration' to use Krugman's expression – on which local growth processes depend, and to do so by going beyond a simple explanation based on an unequal spatial distribution of resources and production factors.[24] This aim was in fact achieved by the first versions of the model, on the hypothesis of an initially homogeneous distribution of resources, through analysis of the location choices of firms and individuals within a neoclassical framework of the maximization of profits and individual well-being.

Like location theory, these models conceive the organization of productive activities in space as resulting from centrifugal and centripetal forces. In economic terms, the centrifugal forces are represented by the tendency of firms to cover spatially diffused demand and to avoid direct competition with other firms on small local markets. The centripetal forces enable firms to exploit increasing returns for broader outlet markets, and individuals to access markets offering a wider range of goods at more competitive prices and a higher standard of living.

Three fundamental elements affect agglomerative phenomena: increasing returns, transportation costs, and migratory movements. Increasing returns encourage activities to concentrate in space because they guarantee that relocation will be profitable, and also that profitability will increase because of the local market's expansion. The second element, transportation costs, induces firms to locate close to broad outlet markets. The third, migratory movements, influences both an area's labour pool and the size of the local market, both of which affect potential profits and incentivize agglomeration. The agglomeration (dispersion) in space of firms and households generates cumulative conditions of growth (decline) in production: the process is irreversible unless contrary external forces intervene.

Krugman's base model incorporates the cumulative development model *à la* Myrdal and Kaldor as the increasing size of the market. Entry by new firms into a local market attracts new workers and population: these enlarge the local market, increase potential profits, and off-set the downturn in profits suffered by local firms because of greater local competition

(competition effect). The larger size of the local market then stimulates entry by new firms, in a virtuous circle of agglomeration and development.

Operation of the cumulative mechanism is guaranteed by the externalities accruing to the firms located in the area. These externalities are generated by market interactions among firms which individually exploit internal economies of scale. In the presence of imperfect competition, in fact, the decision by a firm to enter a market unintentionally influences demand for a good produced by another firm – the entering firm's potential supplier – which is already operating in the area. This latter firm obtains pecuniary advantages from the expansion of its production because its average production costs diminish. Increasing returns thus turn into externalities which are termed 'pecuniary' in that they come about solely by virtue of trade activity, and take the form of greater potential profits for local firms.[25]

Innumerable models have been developed by 'new economic geographers' over the past decade. They can be distinguished according to the different ways in which inter-firm relations generate externalities: in some cases, these are associated with demand elements; in others with input/output relations among firms; and in others with research and development activities producing knowledge spillovers for local firms.[26] However, the logical framework within which agglomerative phenomena are studied does not change. It is set out in the next section in its original and simplest form.

The centre-periphery model: the 'demand effect' and the 'cost effect'

The base model, which goes by the name of the 'centre-periphery' model, seeks to explain the concentration of industrial activities on the hypothesis of an initially homogeneous distribution of productive resources – that is, in the absence of geographic and economic elements which might easily account for the agglomeration of manufacturing activities.[27]

The model's reasoning is based on the following assumptions:

- there are two regions, with two sectors: agriculture and manufacturing. The good in the manufacturing sector is produced at increasing returns, i.e. in conditions of imperfect competition, while the agricultural good is produced at constant returns, i.e. in conditions of perfect competition;[28]
- each manufacturing firm produces a good of different quality;
- the utility of consumers is influenced by both the quantity and the quality of the manufacturing goods produced;[29]
- transportation costs exist if the manufacturing good is produced in one region and purchased in another. Transportation costs are presumed to take Samuelson's 'iceberg' form: that is, they are calculated on the basis of the fraction of the good which does not reach the destination;[30]
- the labour force of the agricultural sector is immobile, while that of the manufacturing sector is free to migrate from one region to another;
- the labour force of the agricultural sector is homogeneously distributed between the two regions; and so too, at the initial stage of the process, is the labour force of the manufacturing sector.

229

Assuming an initially homogeneous distribution of activities (firms) in the two regions, a firm's decision (introduced exogenously into the model) to move from one region to the other alters the initial equilibrium[31] and triggers the following two effects (Figure 9.7a):

1   *a competition effect*. Made possible by the hypothesis of increasing returns in the manufacturing sector, the new firm's entry into the market on the one hand squeezes the market shares of the other firms, and on the other reduces the prices of the goods produced, with the inevitable consequence that profits fall on the local market and the location becomes less profitable;
2   *a demand (or market-size) effect*. The new firm's presence on the market increases the demand for labour. The wage differential between the two regions consequently widens in favour of the expanding local market, which attracts new workers, and with them new residents. The local market grows further in size, with positive effects on the profits of local firms. The increased profit makes the location more attractive.

These two effects therefore have opposite impacts on the profitability of the new location.[32] It is obvious that agglomeration of manufacturing activities will only come about when the net effect on profits generated by the entry of a new firm into the market is positive – that is, when the demand effect surpasses the competition effect. Whichever effect prevails over the other depends on the values assumed by certain parameters, which either amplify or reduce those effects. As regards the competition effect in particular, its intensity depends on:

■   *the substitution elasticity among the goods produced by the manufacturing firms*: the greater the substitution elasticity among goods, the larger the fall in prices due to increased competition, and hence the larger the fall in the profits of already-existing firms;
■   *transportation costs*: the more transportation costs increase, the more the prices of goods diminish. In this case, competition by firms situated in the other area is low, and any relocation will markedly alter competition.

As for the demand effect, its intensity depends on:

■   *increasing returns*: higher increasing returns ensure wider profit margins for entrant firms, so that a larger number of firms are attracted into the local market. This determines the size of the market and the amount of profit that firms (new entrants and already-existing ones) can realistically expect;
■   *the share of income spent on manufacturing goods*: the more this share of income increases, the greater the demand effect generated by a new firm's entry into the market.

If an area is to grow, the demand effect must exceed the competition effect. This happens if the varieties are difficult to substitute, returns to scale are intense, transportation costs are low, and the share of income spent on agricultural goods is small. Under these conditions, the relocation of a firm produces a net increase in profit for all the firms operating

(a) The 'competition effect' and the 'demand effect'

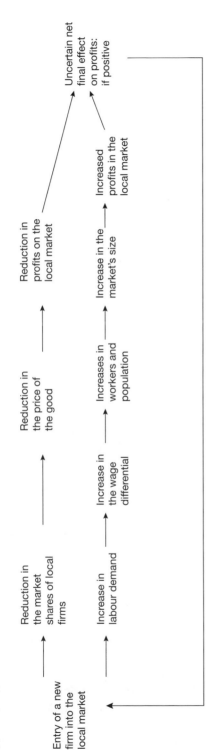

(b) The 'competition effect' and the 'cost effect'

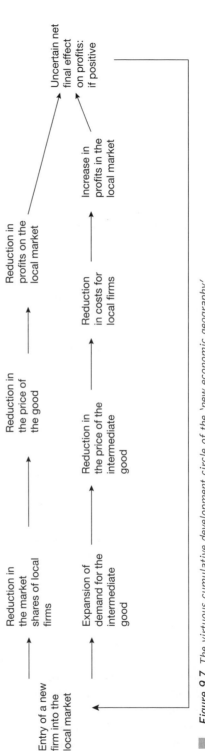

Figure 9.7 The virtuous cumulative development circle of the 'new economic geography'

in the area. Rising profits attract new firms, which further expand the size of the market, in a process of circular causation and cumulative growth.

Since empirical evidence has shown scant labour force mobility in Europe compared with the United States, and this despite wide wage differentials among the European countries and also among regions of the same country, various refinements have been made to the centre-periphery model.[33] One of the best known is comprised in the model developed by Anthony Venables, who reprises the original centre-periphery model. In his version of the model Venables stresses pecuniary externalities deriving from the presence of input–output linkages with other firms ('cost effect') instead of those due to a larger number of workers (and therefore of consumers) in the region ('demand effect').[34] In this manner, Venables is able to derive the mechanism of cumulative circular causation also on the assumption of labour force immobility.

In this version of the centre-periphery model, a new firm's location in a region reduces the costs of its goods, and it generates pecuniary advantages for firms downstream from its production. Furthermore, the presence of the new firm increases the demand of intermediate goods for its manufacturing process; and this demand increases the profits of upstream firms.

Also in this model, two effects ensue from a new firm's entry into the market (Figure 9.7b):

- a *competition effect*, as already described, which causes profits to decrease in the local market because of a reduction in the good's price resulting from greater local competition;
- a *cost effect* which conversely generates an increase in profits through expansion of the market for the intermediate good; this expansion results from a decrease in the intermediate good's price for downstream firms, and an increase in the size of the market for upstream ones – on the assumption that all local firms use the same intermediate good.

Once again, the net effect on profit depends largely on the values of certain parameters. As before, the competition effect is strong if the varieties can easily be substituted for each other, and if transportation costs are high. The cost effect is strong if – on the assumption that the manufacturing good is at once an intermediate good for firms and a final good for consumers – final demand for the good by consumers is less than intermediate demand for it by firms.

It is evident from the foregoing discussion that the final outcome is largely indeterminate in the models of the 'new economic geography'. Concentration in a single region or the equal distribution of manufacturing activities on the market result from different values of the parameters. One way to analyse the dynamic properties of the system is to conduct numerical simulation. Assuming constant values for certain parameters – for example, the share of spending on products from the industrial sector, and the substitution elasticity among industrial goods – it is possible to show the trend in the advantage of location in a particular region: this advantage is represented by the wage differential (in real terms) with variation of a third parameter representing the share of industry present in the region (μ)

at different levels of transportation costs.[35] If transportation costs are very high, there is a unique long-period equilibrium in the location choices of firms which consists in the equidistribution of manufacturing activity between the two areas.

As illustrated by Figure 9.8a, a share of manufacturing activity amounting to less than 0.5 in region 1 gives rise to a wage differential in favour of region 1, with the consequent attraction of manufacturing workers from region 2. The reverse happens when the share of manufacturing workers is greater than 0.5. In the case of low transportation costs, as Figure 9.8b shows, there is a positive relation between wage differentials and the share of manufacturing activity in region 1. No longer is there one possible equilibrium, but three, of which two are stable and long-period. The stable equilibria are represented by the two extreme situations of total concentration in one of the two regions. Low transportation costs allow access to a broad market and make concentration in a region more convenient than territorial dispersion. The equidistribution of activity between the two regions is again an equilibrium, but it is only a short-period one: the transfer of even a single firm from one region to the other will trigger a cumulative process of growth/decline which leads in the long period to one of the two stable extreme equilibria.

Finally, for transportation costs intermediate between the two cases just seen, the results of the model are those shown by Figure 9.8c. They are more complex because they give rise to five possible equilibria. The situation of perfect symmetry between the regions with equidistribution of manufacturing activity is now a stable equilibrium, as in Figure 9.8a, and the same applies to the centre/periphery-type equilibria highlighted in Figure 9.8b. However, there are two further, unstable, equilibria depicted by the white rectangles in Figure 9.8c. This means that if the values of the share of the manufacturing sector in the region are either too high or too low, the system 'collapses' into a polarized equilibrium where manufacturing activity is concentrated solely in one of the two regions – as in the case of low transportation costs.

The base centre-periphery model demonstrates that multiple equilibria – of the concentration or equidistribution of activities – may exist according to the values of the parameters. However, if the tendency is towards concentration, whichever of the regions comes to 'host' the concentration of productive activities will depend on the regions' historical endowment of industrial activities. In this sense, history determines the economy's growth path towards one rather than another stationary equilibrium, just as in Myrdal's model a region's initial economic structure determines – endogenous competitiveness conditions remaining equal – an explosive or implosive process of 'circular causation'.

A CRITICAL ASSESSMENT OF THE MODEL

As already pointed out, the strength of the theory developed by the 'new economic geography' is its capacity to include firm-level increasing returns in models of location choice, and at the same time to express them with the elegant modelling of imperfect competition: these features represent the main innovations introduced by the new economic geography.[36]

The success of the new economic geography approach resides in the formal elegance with which it accounts for spatial phenomena, such as location choices, the concentration of

(a) At high transportation costs

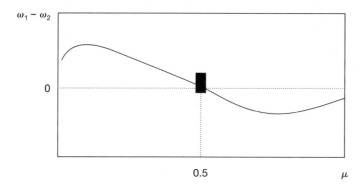

(b) At low transportation costs

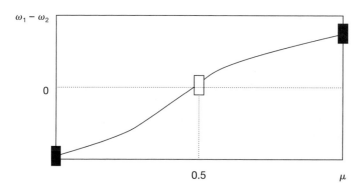

(c) At intermediate transportation costs

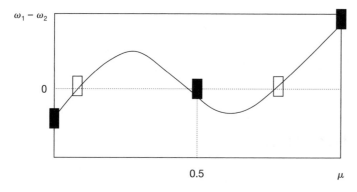

Figure 9.8 *Multiple locational equilibria*
Source: Fujita *et al.*, 1999

activities, and the economic growth deriving from agglomeration economies, within a framework of general economic equilibrium (final equilibrium in the markets of final goods and production factors). The location choices of firms and workers are matched by economic choices for profit maximization by firms and for welfare maximization by individuals, in a strictly neoclassical economic framework.

Furthermore, this neoclassical economic logic comprises positive (or negative) feedback mechanisms which render the process cumulative and have it tend towards concentration (rather than diffusion) and to growth (or decline). The process prior to equilibrium is therefore a path-dependent one in which the well-known elements of cumulativeness, learning, and cross-fertilization of knowledge, and an economic system's feedbacks find appropriate systematization. This family of models conceives choices as being rendered *irreversible* by increasing local advantages or disadvantages which induce firms and workers – on the basis of entirely rational decisions – either to concentrate or diffuse. With these effects of path-dependency and irreversibility, these models closely resemble the modern economic theories of innovation and technological development,[37] and even more closely Myrdal and Kaldor's theory of cumulative circular development: hence, development is a cumulative process, and intrinsic to its workings are self-reinforcing mechanisms which push inexorably towards one or other extreme, concentration or dispersion, explosive development or decline, with no evident possible reverse trajectories.

The success and enthusiasm aroused by the 'new economic geography' in its early years of formulation tended to obscure the interpretative shortcomings of the approach. The first of these shortcomings is that the theory identifies the sources of increasing returns in elements which are economic but not necessarily territorial. Increasing returns, in fact, arise within the firm and then become external economies taking the form of pecuniary externalities, cost advantages, and profits generated by market relations, which do not necessarily require a territorial logic for their explanation.[38] The proximity advantages – physical but above all social and relational – of such importance for regional economists do not perform a central role in the generation of agglomeration economies. An implicit consequence is the necessary sacrifice of a finding now well established by local development theory: that the territory is an independent factor, an additional economic resource, and an active determinant of the development process. Not surprisingly, therefore, as happens with all a-spatial theories, the logic of these models does not change when they are applied to countries or to regions or to urban areas.[39] Although it is space characterized by physical poles at which growth cumulates, the new economic geography approach banally conceives space as punctiform, as the mere container of development, with scant economic-geographic influence upon it.

A second shortcoming is the fact that a firm's location or its decision to relocate (according to whether the model hypothesizes an initially uneven or homogeneous distribution of activities), enters the model exogenously and determines its final result of concentration in one or the other region according to the values assumed by certain fundamental parameters. In a more recent version of his model, Krugman has investigated the role of history in determining the final equilibrium and introduced the possibility that in reality the development path follows the profit expectations of economic actors. But he lapses into the same type of paradox: these profit expectations are not determined by the model but are assumed to be

235

exogenous.[40] Under some very specific conditions, their existence may indeed induce firms and workers to choose locations contrary to the historical development path, and they may give rise to equilibria completely opposed to those determined by history. Yet the model provides no definitions of the elements that determine the profit expectations of firms and workers in economic systems, and no explanations as to how those expectations are fulfilled. One may accordingly state that the models of the 'new economic geography' suffer from the same weakness as Perroux's and Boudeville's 'development poles' model and as the export-base model, where the source of an area's growth, an *industrie motrice* for the former and export capacity for the latter, is left entirely unexplained.

Moreover, because of the underlying theoretical structure, it is impossible to introduce limits to growth and concentration into the model, so that it generates an accumulation of activities without this ever encountering physical obstacles (congestion) or economic ones (shortages of land and productive resources). Yet it would be more realistic to set limits on what is otherwise infinite growth by incorporating net disadvantages of concentration into the model. The onset of these disadvantages (even if only foreseen) would generate profit expectations in regions with lower locational advantages, thus explaining why spatial concentration may go into reverse.

To conclude, the new economic geography makes a commendable effort to include space in strictly economic models. Also to be commended is the implicit merging in its theoretical structure of the various conceptions of space put forward over the years: the merging, that is, of the physical-metric space represented by transportation costs with the diversified space which assumes the hypothesis of the existence of certain territorial polarities where growth cumulates. However, the new economic geography is still unable to combine the economic laws and mechanisms that explain growth with territorial factors springing from the intrinsic relationality present at local level. An approach that did so would represent the maximum of cross-fertilization among location theory, development theory and macro-economic growth theory and would give rise to a framework able to blend specifically local territorial features into a single macroeconomic model. Today, the frontier of knowledge in regional economics consists precisely in defining the territorial micro-foundations of macroeconomic growth models.

CONCLUSIONS

The chapter has examined the first large group of the most recent theories on growth, whose distinctive feature is the resumption of macroeconomic models based on the increasing returns hypothesis. These new theories are rooted in Myrdal and Kaldor's model of cumulative circular causation, which they employ to interpret growth as a cumulative, endogenous and selective process. The models described hypothesize the existence of specific polarities in which development comes about as a result of increasing returns in the form of learning processes, economies of scale (at area or firm level), localization economies, and urbanization economies which set off a virtuous circle of cumulative development.

The models illustrated in this chapter are non-linear dynamic systems. As in all the most recent approaches to such systems, they analyse the 'structural stability' of systems, the nature and quality of solutions, and the form that the system may assume. For this reason, these models do not yield unequivocal results; rather, they offer a range of possible solutions, which vary according to the initial conditions and to the values assumed by the parameters.

These models envisage growth as a cumulative demand/supply process. But those examined in the next chapter include increasing returns to productive resources in a production function of neoclassical derivation. As we shall see, these theories regard growth as depending exclusively on supply-side elements.

REVIEW QUESTIONS

1 What is meant by diversified-stylized space?

2 What have been the obstacles to the analytical formulation of increasing returns up to the middle of the 1980s and which elements have recently been allowed to overcome these obstacles?

3 What is meant by an equilibrium in non-linearity conditions? What are the peculiarities of such an equilibrium?

4 What are the main aims of the circular and cumulative causation model? What is explained by the Verdoorn law? How are the increasing returns embedded in this theory?

5 Does the circular and cumulative causation model contain a concept of regional divergence? Explain your reasoning.

6 Which are the main new elements contained in the 'new economic geography' theory?

7 What is meant by 'competition effect' and 'cost effect'?

8 Is the 'new economic geography' explaining concentration or diffusion of activities in space?

9 Which are the weaknesses and strengths of the 'new economic geography'?

10 Which aspects contained in the 'new economic geography' were already contained in the circular and cumulative causation model?

SELECTED READING ON EMPIRICAL FINDINGS

About the new economic geography

Davis, D. R. and Weinstein, D. E. (1999) 'Economic geography and regional production structure: an empirical investigation', *European Economic Review*, vol. 43, no. 2, pp. 379–407.

Giarratani, F., Gruver, G. and Jackson, R. (2005) 'Empirical evidence concerning the economic geography of market entry in the U.S. steet industry: plant location and the advent of slab casting by U.S. steel minimills', Center for Industries Study Research, University of Pittsburgh.

Hanson, G. H. (1998) 'Market potential, increasing returns, and geographic concentration', Working Paper no. 6429, National Bureau of Economic Research.

Midelfart-Knarvik, K. and Steen, F. (1999) 'Self-reinforcing agglomerations? An empirical industry study', *Scandinavian Journal of Economics*, vol. 101, pp. 515–32.

Mucchieli, J. L. and Mayer, T. (2004) *Multinational firms' location and the new economic geography*, Cheltenham: Edward Elgar.

Naudé, W. A., Krugell, W. F. and Gries, T. (2005) 'The new economic geography: empirical evidence from South Africa', paper presented at the Regional Studies Association's international conference on 'Regional growth agendas', University of Aalborg, Denmark, 28–31 May.

Overman, H. G. and Puga, D. (2002) 'Unemployment clusters across European regions and countries', *Economic Policy*, vol. 34, pp. 115–47.

Redding, S. and Venables, A. (2000) 'Economic geography and international inequality', Discussion Paper no. 2568, Centre for Economic Policy Research.

FURTHER READING

Barentsen, W. and Nijkamp, P. (1989) 'Modelling non-linear processes in time and space', in Andersson, Å., Batten, D., Johansson, B. and Nijkamp, P. (eds), *Advances in spatial theory and dynamics*, Amsterdam: North-Holland, pp. 175–92.

Dixit, A. and Stiglitz, J. (1977) 'Monopolistic competition and optimum product diversity', *American Economic Review*, vol. 67, no. 3, pp. 297–308.

Feenstra, R. E. (2003) *Advanced international trade: theory and evidence*, Princeton, N.J.: Princeton University Press.

Fujita, M., Krugman, P. and Venables, A. J. (1999) *The spatial economy: cities, regions and international trade*, Cambridge, Mass.: MIT Press.

Krugman, P. (1991) *Geography and trade*, Cambridge, Mass.: MIT Press.

Krugman, P. and Venables, A. J. (1996) 'Integration, specialisation and adjustment', *European Economic Review*, vol. 40, pp. 959–67.

Myrdal, G. (1957) *Economic theory of under-developed regions*, London: Duckworth.

Verdoorn, P. J. (1949) 'Factors that determine the growth of labour productivity', in Ironmonger, D., Perkins, J. O. N. and Van Hoa, T. (eds) (1988) *National income and economic progress: essays in honour of Colin Clark*, Basingstoke: Macmillan, pp. 199–207.

Chapter 10

Territorial competitiveness and endogenous growth

SUMMARY

1   Endogenous growth and increasing returns

2   The endogenous sources of growth: the knowledge stock and learning

3   The knowledge stock: Romer's model

4   Learning and human capital: the Lucas model

5   The neoclassical interregional model with increasing returns

ENDOGENOUS GROWTH AND INCREASING RETURNS

This chapter examines the last group of growth models, which represent – together with those of the 'new economic geography' – the most recent of such models. They closely resemble the ones presented in the previous chapter in that they have a high level of formalization and a strictly dynamic structure. As the chapter proceeds, we shall again be dealing with models that investigate the endogenous determinants of an aggregate growth rate, as opposed to the individual microeconomic and micro-territorial elements of competitive or locational advantage typical of development theories. Once again these will be models with a high degree of mathematical formalization, which conceive increasing returns as economies of scale or learning, and which stylize them in equations explaining the growth rate of per capita output.

These are therefore theories and models which conceive space as diversified-stylized; a space in which growth results from increasing returns but does not have a real and proper territorial dimension. More specifically, increasing returns are included in a neoclassical production function, where they off-set the effect of the marginal productivity of the individual factors, which the traditional neoclassical approach assumes to be decreasing.

The strictly neoclassical logic of these models accounts for the interpretation that they give to growth. As in the neoclassical models discussed in Chapter 6, growth is once again associated with an increase in labour productivity, with a rise in per capita income, and therefore with an increase in individual well-being.

239

The origin of these new neoclassical growth models is Robert Solow's well-known model developed in the 1960s. On the assumption that the only reproducible factor (capital) is characterized by decreasing marginal returns, Solow demonstrated that the economy is bound to register nil per capita output growth in the long period unless the existence of technical progress is exogenously hypothesized. By so doing, however, Solow identified the engine of economic growth as an exogenous factor linked to the progress of knowledge.

However, the assumption that increases in factor productivity stem from endogenous factors – such as innovation, scale economies, and learning processes – requires the removal of perfect competition and constant returns from the theoretical framework, and the inclusion in their stead of increasing returns or imperfect markets. This shift requires complex modelling based on the only recently-developed theoretical and analytical tools outlined in the previous chapter.

Chronologically, the first of these models introduced advantages external to firms and therefore continued to assume perfect competition. Subsequent ones included aggregate increasing returns, or constant marginal productivity of a single accumulable factor, in their production functions, but still envisaged a perfectly competitive market structure. Finally, the most recent models introduce technological innovation endogenous to firms in conditions of monopoly or monopolistic competition.[1] On each of these assumptions, the possibility arises of prolonged and balanced growth at a constant and positive rate. For these models, such growth is possible because the economy is able over time to accumulate a resource which yields non-decreasing returns and is a perpetual source of development.

The aim of the models now described – called 'models or theories of endogenous growth' – is therefore to identify the conditions *endogenous* to the productive system which ensure long-term positive growth. The latter is made to depend solely on increasing returns to productive resources (individual or in aggregate), and therefore on supply-side elements. It is this feature that differentiates these models from those analysed in the previous chapter, for which increasing returns gave rise to virtuous circles of demand/supply development.

The next section will examine two initial models which identified the sources of growth in local knowledge embodied in physical capital, and learning – elements already emphasized by some of the development models examined in Chapter 8. An interesting application of increasing returns is then presented. This adopts a more strictly territorial production function in which the physical size of the region (or the city) is the factor which generates increasing returns. The final section shows how the results of the neoclassical interregional growth model discussed in Chapter 6 change if non-linearity is introduced into economic processes.

THE ENDOGENOUS SOURCES OF GROWTH: THE KNOWLEDGE STOCK AND LEARNING

The limitations of the traditional model

We saw in Chapter 6 that the neoclassical model of regional growth is based on technical progress on the one hand, and on growth of the production factors on the other. These are synthesized by the model into a regional economy production function of generally Cobb–Douglas type:

$$Y = AK^{\alpha}L^{1-\alpha} \qquad 0 < a < 1 \tag{10.1}$$

where Y is income, A technical progress, K capital, L labour, and α and $1 - \alpha$ are the contributions of capital and labour respectively (and consequently their distributive shares).

In logarithms, the variation income Y over time is written as:[2]

$$y = a + \alpha k + (1 - \alpha)l \tag{10.2}$$

where the lower-case symbols y, a, k and l denote the growth rates of income, technical progress, capital and labour respectively. Equation (10.2) states that the possibility of growth in local output depends on the growth of technical progress, of capital and labour. Equation (10.2) can also be written as:

$$y - l = a + \alpha(k - l) \tag{10.3}$$

The steady state (i.e. long-term dynamic equilibrium) in which the rate of output growth is constant is guaranteed if and only if the rate of capital growth is equal to that of labour. This situation is equivalent to nil long-term growth of per capita income, unless one assumes an increase in technical progress as represented by parameter a. This parameter, which is also called 'the Solow residual', represents the part of an economy's growth not due to growth of the production factors, and which is therefore not 'explained' by the model.[3]

As pointed out in Chapter 6, the model of interregional growth suggests that regions grow at the same rate in the long run. This is because the distribution of the production factors is equal among regions, and so too is technical progress, given the assumption that all regions have the same production function.

This result is perplexing, for several reasons. First, the sole long-term determinant of growth, namely technical progress, is exogenous to the model; nothing explains the real capacity of a system to grow. Second, as seen earlier when the diffusion of innovation was discussed, the capacity to utilize external and available technical progress differs greatly among regions, and the assumption that parameter a is equal for all regions can only be accepted if it is hedged about with caveats. Besides these theoretical problems, the lack of systematicity in the empirical results on convergence among the growth rates of countries and regions casts further doubt on the validity of the theoretical model.[4]

All the models now described seek to determine an endogenous mechanism which explains the growth rate of per capita output.[5] They identify this mechanism in non-decreasing returns, and in externalities which may have various origins:[6]

- investment cumulated in physical capital and the consequent increase in 'technological capacities' over time (learning-by-doing);
- the aggregate impact of investment by individual firms, which generates a positive externality (and increasing returns to scale) at aggregate level;

241

- the constancy of the marginal return on capital if this includes all the accumulable factors, among them 'human capital';
- the investment in human capital, scientific and technical knowledge which improves the physical productivity of labour;
- investment in R&D to foster the technological innovation that improves the physical productivity of all the factors, i.e. the creation of intermediate and final goods with high value added.

Among the numerous models that have been propounded, those developed by Paul Romer and Robert Lucas are discussed here, for which the sources of growth are factors – the knowledge stock and learning – already identified by the theory of local development, and in particular by the theory of the *milieu innovateur*.[7] Moreover, as regards formalization, these models employ two methods to endogenize growth: Romer's model – by introducing a source of externalities which converts decreasing returns into constant or increasing ones; or Lucas's model – by introducing a production factor into the production function for which a law of motion is hypothesized such that the share of the factor used is re-generated in the same quantity (whatever that quantity may be).

The knowledge stock: Romer's model

One of the first models of endogenous growth was formulated by Paul Romer. Its central assumption concerning the source of growth was that the externalities generated by technical knowledge, and then embodied in the investments accumulated in fixed capital until a certain time t, have the nature of public goods. They are in fact available to all firms whether or not these have participated in creation of that knowledge.[8] Romer incorporates knowledge into his model as 'public capital', which is a further accumulable resource besides private fixed capital. Its existence gives rise to economies of scale in aggregate factor productivity even though the returns on the individual production factors are decreasing.

Romer's model assumes the existence of N identical firms (i) with the same production function, as follows:

$$Y_{it} = K_{it}^{\alpha} L_{it}^{1-\alpha} K_t^{\beta} \quad \text{where } 0 < \alpha < 1; \ 0 < \beta < 1 \tag{10.4}$$

As well as the usual production factors – capital (K_i) and labour (L_i) – the production function comprises a third factor (K) which represents the state of technical knowledge at time t, doing so with typical logic *à la* Arrow whereby knowledge is embodied in accumulated experience; or in other words, embodied in the stock of accumulated investments in capital until time t. The difference between the two types of capital is that the former (with the index) is the traditional physical capital wholly exploited by only the firm which possesses it; the latter is the capital represented by the stock of technical knowledge acquired through action by all firms; and it is a public good because it is available to all firms.

In this model, therefore, firms benefit not only from their investments but also from the knowledge acquired by other firms. Capital and labour combine with the usual decreasing returns to the factors K_i and L_i. The third factor, without the index, is also characterized by decreasing returns, but its presence – which takes the form of an externality – enables firms to off-set the decreasing returns on individual factors so that aggregate factor productivity increases (the sum of the exponents is greater than 1).[9]

Using logarithms, deriving with respect to time, and denoting the growth rates of the variables with lower-case letters, we obtain:

$$y_{it} = \beta k_t + \alpha k_{ti} + (1 - \alpha)l_{it} \tag{10.5}$$

which can be rewritten as:

$$y_{it} - l_{it} = \beta k_t + \alpha(k_{ti} - l_{it}) \tag{10.6}$$

Equation (10.6) shows that the growth rate of per capita output – i.e. the growth rate of average labour productivity (left-hand member of the equation) – increases the higher the capital/labour ratio $(k - l)$ and the greater the amount of knowledge that the firm obtains from outside as an externality (k). The steady state – i.e. the condition in which the rate of growth of per capita capital is nil $(k - l = 0)$ – is here averted by the presence of a public good embedded in the knowledge externalities firms that exploit.

Omitting the index i to simplify the notation, (10.6) can be rewritten as:

$$y_t - l_t = (\alpha + \beta)k_t - \alpha l_t \tag{10.7}$$

On the hypotheses that $0 < \alpha < 1$ and $0 < \beta < 1$, but $\alpha + \beta > 1$, as in the above model, the growth of per capita income will be positive and cumulative, and the economy will have a perpetual source of growth of productivity, and consequently of individual well-being.

Learning and human capital: the Lucas model

The model developed by Robert Lucas envisages two types of capital: physical and human. Combined in a production function of usually Cobb–Douglas type, these give rise to a certain level of output:[10]

$$Y_t = AK_t^\alpha (u_t H_t L_t)^{1-\alpha} H_t^\phi \tag{10.8}$$

where A is a proportionality factor constant in time (and which can therefore be eliminated by choosing an appropriate unit of measurement: it is *not* an indicator of technical progress as previously), K is physical capital, L the number of workers, u the fraction of their time that individuals devote to work, and H is the average amount of knowledge possessed by workers (i.e. it is an indicator of the quality of human capital).

Lucas hypothesizes that workers accumulate knowledge by taking time off work in order to acquire skills ('learning by schooling'), under the following law:[11]

$$h_t = H_t \varphi (1 - u_t) \tag{10.9}$$

where h denotes the rate of growth of human capital over time, H the stock of human capital (or the average amount of knowledge possessed by workers), $(1 - u)$ the time devoted to education, which is indicated as a percentage of the total amount of time available to individuals, and where φ is learning ability, which is assumed to be positive and linear with respect to the level of knowledge attained.[12]

In steady state, u must be a value such that workers are able to produce the tangible goods that directly generate utility and well-being but also have sufficient opportunities to accumulate knowledge and to increase the labour productivity which indirectly influences utility. In this model, human capital is simultaneously the result of a productive process and the source of increased labour productivity, and therefore of greater per capita income.

On the hypothesis that u is constant over time, on switching to logarithms, the rate of output growth can be straightforwardly obtained from (10.8) and (10.9):

$$y_t = \alpha k_t + (1 - \alpha) l_t + (1 - \alpha + \phi) h_t \tag{10.10}$$

where y, k, l and h are respectively the rates of growth of output, physical capital, labour, and human capital at time t.

Recalling that human capital grows according to the law represented by (10.9)[13] and rewriting (10.10) in terms of the rate of growth of per capita output, we obtain:

$$y_t - l_t = \alpha (k_t - l_t) + (1 - \alpha + \phi) \varphi (1 - u_t) \tag{10.11}$$

In steady state, where the growth rate of capital equals that of labour, $\alpha(k_t - l_t)$ is equal to zero. In this situation, there are two endogenous elements generating growth in per capita output: the externalities of a skilled labour market, expressed by the parameter ϕ, which enables the economic system to achieve increasing returns; and learning ability φ, which determines the law of human capital accumulation.

Interestingly, contrary to Romer's model, even if there are no external effects in knowledge ($\phi = 0$), the economy's growth is endogenous, and it depends on learning ability. According to the logic of the model, in fact, the growth rate converges on a steady state and is equal to a constant rate $\varphi (1 - u)$.

A CRITICAL ASSESSMENT

One of the main merits of these models is their ability to endogenize the elements responsible for growth by considering increasing returns in the form of local externalities or laws of direct resource accumulation, without these having first to be converted into output.[14] These models thus elegantly deal with the problem encountered by Solow: when estimating the growth of per capita output in the US economy, he found that the largest part of it could be explained by technical progress, and therefore by precisely the element which his model did not explicitly consider.

244

A further interesting aspect of the Romer and Lucas models is their conception of growth, which in many respects resembles that of the more traditionally territorial development theories set out in Chapter 8, and the *milieu innovateur* theory especially. The similarities between Romer's model and the *milieu innovateur* theory concern:

- *the element that determines growth*, which consists in the positive externalities resulting from a process of collective learning. In Romer's model, growth derives from the increasing marginal returns that knowledge generates in production. This process converts decreasing marginal returns to the production factors into increasing returns and thus enables the economic system to grow. In the *milieu innovateur* theory, the engine of local development is the presence of advantages external to firms which generate dynamic efficiency. Among these advantages are the 'collective' learning mechanisms which enable the spatially concentrated system of small firms to become more innovative.
- *the specific features of knowledge*. Both theories conceive knowledge as a public good. In Romer's model, knowledge is a public good because it is available to all firms; in the *milieu innovateur* theory, learning is likewise a public good because all the firms belonging to the milieu can access it, doing so, for example, through high mobility of the local labour force;
- *external effects of knowledge on the growth process* as a consequence of its nature as a public good. In Romer, knowledge generates positive externalities for all firms and enables them to off-set the effects of decreasing marginal returns to the production factors. This idea is exactly the same as the *milieu innovateur* theory's conception of collective learning as coming about through socialization, rather than through an explicitly cooperative process, in a dynamic local labour market with high internal turnover;
- *hypotheses on returns to the production factors – in particular returns to knowledge*. Romer maintains that knowledge, like the other production factors, yields decreasing marginal returns. The *milieu innovateur* theory also assumes decreasing returns to local knowledge, which the local system must overcome lest it be set on a development path at decreasing returns until its inability to shift to more advanced technological trajectories causes it to atrophy.

There are also similarities between Lucas's model and the *milieu innovateur* theory, as follows:

- *learning as the key to growth*. In Lucas, human capital accumulation is the source of economic growth because it stimulates labour productivity and generates productive capacity. The *milieu innovateur* theory likewise stresses learning by human capital as the source of innovative capacity, and therefore of local development: for this theory, the accumulation of knowledge is facilitated by spatial, cultural and institutional proximity among firms;
- *the external acquisition of human capital with positive effects on growth*. In both theories, the acquisition of knowledge from outside has positive effects on growth. In Lucas's

model, the positive effect of human capital accumulated externally to the firm ($\phi = 0$) is amplified by a typical externality mechanism. In the *milieu innovateur* theory, knowledge accumulated externally to the *milieu* drives the long-term development of the area and prevents the system from falling irremediably victim to the decreasing returns on local knowledge.

However, it should be stressed that endogenous growth models have a serious weakness: their *a-spatiality*, which makes them very different from the *milieu innovateur* theory. Like all endogenous growth models, those of Romer and Lucas suffer from the lack of any active role performed by territorial variables. Indeed, the same models apply at different territorial levels, whether national or regional (the criticism holds for the new economic geography as well). Romer's and Lucas's models consequently differ radically from the *milieu innovateur* theory, which assumes that territorial features – spatial cultural and institutional proximity, the area's sectoral specialization, the structure and dynamic of the local labour market – are the determinants of knowledge socialization, and of local development. The Romer and Lucas models instead more closely resemble those of the new economic geography, or even the early models of regional growth, which were typically a-spatial.

Attempts to remedy this detachment from the territorial context have been made by the numerous empirical analyses that go by the name of β-conditional estimation methods. These seek to identify socio-economic variables – such as human capital, schooling, the infrastructure level of the country or region – which explain why advanced regions achieve higher growth rates than do backward regions, also taking account of differences at territorial level.[15] From the theoretical point of view, this means moving beyond Solow's traditional model to consider the more recent models of endogenous development; but above all it requires the introduction into specific models of the idea that growth results from the structural and socio-economic features of the local economy.

THE NEOCLASSICAL INTERREGIONAL MODEL WITH INCREASING RETURNS

An interesting application of increasing returns in a strictly territorial production function is the neoclassical interregional model at increasing returns proposed by Takahiro Miyao. This model takes the physical size of the region (or city) to be the factor that generates increasing returns:

$$Y = L^{\beta}K^{\alpha}L^{1-\alpha} \tag{10.12}$$

where $0 < \alpha < 1$ and $0 < (1 - \alpha + \beta) < 1$, in which Solow's generic technical progress is replaced by the size of the region (indicated by the number of workers L), and with agglomeration economies or diseconomies depending on whether β is positive or negative.

As in the original neoclassical model, the time paths of the variables K and L depend on the accumulation rate, and on differences with respect to the other regions in factor remuneration.[16] In symbols, this means that the growth rate of capital k is given by:

$$k = \frac{sY}{K} + \mu\,(i_r - i_m) \tag{10.13}$$

where sY represents the total savings available for the financing of investment (ΔK), i_r the rate of capital remuneration in the region, and i_m in the rest of the world. In its turn, the rate of labour growth l is given by:

$$l = n + \lambda(w_r - w_m) \tag{10.14}$$

where n is the natural growth rate of the population, $w_r - w_m$ the difference in wage remuneration between the region and the rest of the world, and μ and λ respectively the sensitivity of capital and labour to change in wage differentials.

Assuming as known the parameters (μ, λ, w_m, i_m, s, n) of equations (10.2n) and (10.3n), which represent the steady-state equilibrium curves (that is, the constant growth trajectories of the production factors), it is possible to examine the properties of the possible solutions by drawing these curves as in Figure 10.1.[17] In the presence of agglomeration economies, i.e. for β greater than zero, the steady-state equilibrium is unstable. As Figure 10.1a shows, when the K/L ratio is less than the steady-state ratio (and therefore lies below the main diagonal), labour increases at a greater rate than capital, so that the K/L ratio is increasingly distanced from the level that ensures dynamic equilibrium. If the K/L ratio is instead greater than the steady-state ratio, capital grows at a higher rate than labour, and the consequence is once again that the local economy cannot achieve constant growth. In other words, the area's economic growth explodes or implodes according to the initial factor endowment: a situation very different from the tendency to convergence expressed by the base model of the 1960s. Conversely, in the presence of agglomeration diseconomies, the region's economic growth converges on a steady-state equilibrium with constant values of K and L (z in Figure 10.1b).[18]

It is also possible to hypothesize the case in which agglomeration economies exist up to a size threshold L_0 beyond which these economies turn into diseconomies. In this case the production function is:

$$Y = \left(\frac{L}{L_o}\right)^{\beta} K^{\alpha} L^{1-\alpha} \tag{10.15}$$

where $\beta > 0$ for $L < L_0$ and $\beta < 0$ for $L > L_0$. For values of K/L at which the $k = 0$ curve lies above the $l = 0$ curve,[19] the region's economy converges on a steady-state equilibrium with K and L constant (E in Figure 10.2a).

Finally, it is interesting to analyse what happens in the case of 'slow' exogenous shocks on the values of the parameters. In the case of a decrease in the parameters representing the forces (rate of saving or the rate of natural population growth) of the region's economy, or if those representing the economic forces (interest or wage rates) in the 'outside world' increase, the $k = 0$ and $l = 0$ curves shift (to the position shown in bold) until they reach a point at which the steady-state equilibrium suddenly disappears, and the local economy declines in a catastrophic process until disintegration (Figure 10.2b).

247

(a) Presence of agglomeration economies (unstable equilibrium $\beta > 0$)

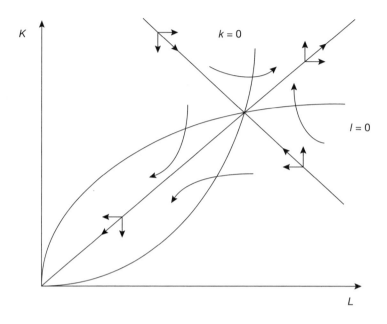

(b) Presence of agglomeration diseconomies (stable equilibrium $\beta < 0$)

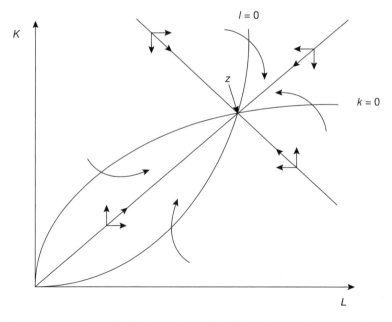

Figure 10.1 A neoclassical growth model with agglomeration economies and diseconomies
Source: Miyao, 1984

(a) Dynamic equilibrium with agglomeration economies ($L < L_0$) and diseconomies ($L > L_0$) (dynamic stability)

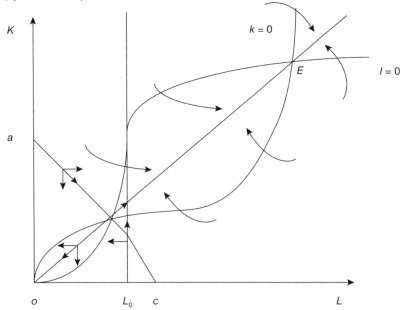

(b) Catastrophic disappearance of equilibrium due to a shift of the $k = 0$ and $l = 0$ curves (structural instability)

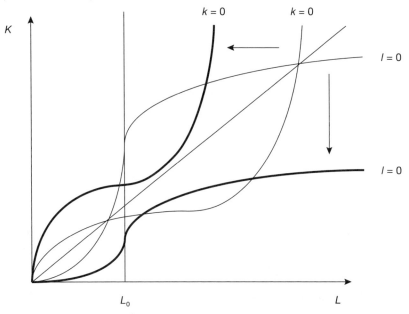

Figure 10.2 A neoclassical growth model with agglomeration economies and diseconomies: *dynamic stability and structural instability*

Source: Miyao, 1984

It is therefore evident that, by introducing agglomeration economies (diseconomies), the neoclassical model successfully simulates a series of behaviours and tendencies, both continuous and 'catastrophic', very different from the mechanistic and univocal ones predicted by the simplified model of the 1960s.

CONCLUSIONS

The chapter has surveyed the last group of modern growth models. In these, cumulativeness is stylized in increasing returns to productive resources (individual and in aggregate) and growth consequently comes to depend solely on supply-side elements.

Like those of the previous chapter, these models are mathematically formalized as nonlinear dynamic systems which enable increasing returns – in the form of scale economies or learning – to be inserted into equations which explain the growth rate of per capita output. In these models, increasing returns are included in a neoclassical production function, where they off-set the effect of the marginal productivity of factors traditionally assumed to be decreasing.

As in the case of previous models, the ones examined in this chapter only achieve their objective by conceiving a diversified-stylized space in which growth is generated by increasing returns; a space, however, bereft of a genuinely territorial dimension. This is the main shortcoming of the most recent models of regional economics, and finding a remedy for it is the challenge that regional economists must address in the next decade.

REVIEW QUESTIONS

1   What is the aim of endogenous growth models?

2   What is the conception of growth behind the endogenous growth models?

3   Which are the ways to make a growth model endogenous?

4   What are the similarities and differences between the theory of the *milieu innovateur* and Romer and Lucas's models?

5   What is demonstrated by the interregional neoclassical growth model with increasing returns?

SELECTED READING ON EMPIRICAL FINDINGS

About human capital and regional development

Bryson, P. J. (2005) 'Regional development and human capital infrastructure in China: lessons from European Union regional policy experience', Proceedings of International Conference on Regional Disparities, Economic Integration and Development, pp. 1–26, Wuhan University, Wuhan, China, December.

Garlick, S. (2005) 'Regional growth, enterprising human capital and community engagement', working paper, Institute for Sustainability, Health and Regional Engagement (ISHaRE), Queensland, Australia: University of the Sunshine Coast, available on line.

Mackay, R. R. (1993) 'Local labour markets, regional development and human capital', *Regional Studies*, vol. 27, no. 8, pp. 783–95.

Mankin, N., Romer, D. and Weil, D. (1992) 'A contribution to the empirics of economic growth', *Quarterly Journal of Economics*, vol. 107, May, pp. 739–74.

FURTHER READING

Aghion, P. and Howitt, P. (1997) *Endogenous growth theory*, Cambridge, Mass.: MIT Press.

Baldwin, R. E., Braconier, H. and Forslid, R. (1999) 'Multinationals, endogenous growth and technological spillovers: theory and evidence', paper presented at the seminar of the Research Institute of Industrial Economics (IUI) on *Multinational production, international mergers and welfare effects in a small open economy*, held in Stockholm, June.

Magrini, S. (2004) 'Regional (di)convergence', in Henderson, V. and Thisse, F. J. (eds), *Handbook of regional and urban economics*, vol. 4, Amsterdam: North-Holland, pp. 2741–96.

Nijkamp, P., Stough, R. and Verhoef, E. (eds) (1998) 'Endogenous growth in a regional context', special issue, *Annals of Regional Science*, vol. 32, no. 1.

Romer, P. (1986) 'Increasing returns and long-run growth', *Journal of Political Economy*, vol. 94, no. 5, pp. 1002–37.

Sala-i-Martin, X. (1996) 'Regional cohesion: evidence and theories of regional growth and convergence', *European Economic Review*, vol. 40, pp. 1325–52.

Chapter 11

Towards a synthesis

SUMMARY

1   The critical elements in local development today
2   The challenge for the future

THE CRITICAL ELEMENTS IN LOCAL DEVELOPMENT TODAY

It seems appropriate to conclude this book on the economic theory of space, and in particular on the economics of local growth/development, by emphasizing a number of implications that have emerged from the analysis.

In recent years, regional growth theories have evolved considerably in their interpretation of the concept itself of growth. Demand-oriented theories on short-term processes of employment creation, in conditions of given but largely under-utilized productive resources, have given way to supply-oriented approaches, developed first in regard to the achievement of individual well-being, and then to the determination of the real productive capacities of local systems.

Without wishing to deny the interpretative capacity and interest of the former theories, it is today evident that the problem of growth should be associated with the endogenous local elements that generate local competitiveness. Competitiveness is the keystone of development, and upon it depends the survival itself of a local economy in the current circumstances of fierce worldwide competition.

It is also necessary to develop theories able to explain an absolute, not relative, competitiveness; a competitiveness which springs from real productive and innovative capacities, and by virtue of which regions or territories can acquire a specific role in the international division of labour, and maintain it over time.

It is by now well established that regions do not compete according to the principle of 'comparative advantage' – the principle that assigns to each area a role within the international division of labour regardless of its productive efficiency. The macroeconomic mechanisms (exchange rates, wage and price flexibility) that protect countries against competition do not operate at regional level, and thus theoretically impose a principle of absolute advantage. On this view, local development is substantially a problem of identifying the elements on which to construct and maintain this 'absolute' or 'competitive' advantage.

History teaches, first, that these elements should be sought within the area itself, and that they arise from the area's specific nature. This supports the idea of 'generative regional growth', or an endogenous development based on the efficient and creative use of local resources. Second, a region's capacity for autonomous development is driven above all by the increasing returns and agglomeration economies generated at local level. The territory should be viewed as an active element in the development process, the generator of advantages for firms and for local actors. It thus becomes the source of agglomeration economies – and consequently of locational advantages – when internal synergies and the local production system reduce static and dynamic uncertainty, production and transaction costs; and today more than ever, when they foster processes of collective learning, technological innovation, and new organizational and managerial methods.

History also teaches that regional and local development is a complex process. It results from the balanced presence of tangible and intangible elements originating in the economic and social spheres, from which derives the importance of theoretical approaches to development which take these elements into account. The endowment of production factors, infrastructures and human capital should be linked with the presence of social capital, a propensity for cooperation among actors, and the ability of people, firms and local institutions to learn. Of equal importance in this 'balanced development' are the endowment of production factors, the ability of suppliers and customers to establish synergies and co-operation, the infrastructural endowment, the tacit diffusion of information, the availability of real or financial capital, as well as processes of collective learning in workforce training, the evolution of managerial styles, and the use of new technologies.

The success of a territorial system therefore does not depend solely on the quantity and quality of the material resources with which it is endowed. It also, and crucially, depends on the richness of economic and social relations, and on local 'social' or 'relational' capital. Because capital is hyper-mobile, the competitiveness of regions depends on intangible resources and their development. Intangible elements connected with culture and innovative capacity accumulate through slow processes of individual and collective learning fuelled by information, interaction, and investments in research and training. They are therefore intrinsically localized and cumulative, embodied in human capital and local relational networks, in the labour market, and in the local context – and they are consequently highly selective in spatial terms.

All these factors have major repercussions on regional disparities. It is likely that the territorial embeddedness of intangible resources boosts the centripetal and cumulative forces of development (economies of scale and scope, increasing returns of various kinds) and the centrifugal forces of territorial exclusion and decline. The divergence between strong and weak areas, between areas with greater or lesser endowments of intangible resources such as knowledge and the ability to learn, is therefore more likely than their convergence – at least in the short-to-medium term. This tendency will strengthen because the traditional elements giving absolute advantage to weak areas, such as low labour costs, tend to disappear in the medium-to-long period owing to social factors (migration), institutional factors (the imposition of national-level collective bargaining), and cultural ones (social expectations within a monetary union).

Necessary as a consequence is a modern conception of local development which concerns itself with the creative and innovative use of local tangible and intangible resources, and with the creation of the knowledge and models of cooperation and decision-making on which the innovativeness of firms is based.

THE CHALLENGE FOR THE FUTURE

The theories described in this handbook have highlighted the increasingly complex and intriguing ways in which models of economic growth treat space. The simple (and in certain respects banal) interpretation of space as uniform-abstract and straightforwardly relatable to administrative units – a space conceived as internally homogeneous and uniform, and which can therefore be synthesized into a vector of aggregate socio-economic-demographic features – has in recent years been replaced by a notion of diversified-relational space which restores to theories of regional development some of the founding principles of location theory: agglomeration economies and spatial interaction.

It is this more complex interpretation of space that has enabled regional economics to take decisive steps forward in analysis of local dynamics by conceiving space as the source of increasing returns and positive externalities. The development process also depends on the efficiency of the territorial organization of production, rather than solely on the quantity of economic resources available. Not only are the tangible elements of development (for example, the quantity of existing productive resources) important, so too are the intangible ones mentioned above: the learning processes, local relational networks, and governance mechanisms that have increasing weight in defining an area's development path.

Finally, most recent years have seen an endeavour to escape from the impasse which caught regional economics between, on the one hand, growth theories of pure macroeconomic origin formalized into elegant models, and on the other, theories which abandon the rigour of formal treatment to consider new qualitative and territorial elements synthesizable – with due caution – into the concept of agglomeration economies. The most recent theories on local growth are able to incorporate increasing returns into the economic and formal logic of macroeconomics, and they are viewed (sometimes all too enthusiastically) as a new way to conceive space; as a means to merge previous conceptions together. Space is conceived as diversified; while territorial development is conceived as selective, cumulative, and at increasing returns, and it is interpreted on the basis of a macroeconomic growth model.

It has been emphasized that this merger is in fact only an initially positive result. More detailed analysis shows that space is indeed conceived as diversified, but it receives no territorial explanation apart from one taking the form of the agglomeration/non-agglomeration dichotomy. The territorial features (and the above-mentioned intangible elements) that play an important role in diversified-relational space theories by explaining and interpreting the level of competitiveness achieved entirely disappear in the macroeconomic models.

Still needed, therefore, is a convincing 'model' which comprises the micro-territorial, micro-behavioural and intangible elements of the development process. Required for this purpose is definition of patterns, indicators, and analytical solutions to be incorporated into formalized models necessarily more abstract and synthetic in terms of their explanatory variables. A move in this direction is the quantitative sociology that embraces the paradigm of methodological individualism and seeks to 'measure' the social capital of local communities. It is obviously necessary to bring out territorial specificities within a macroeconomic model. Or in other words, it is necessary to demonstrate the territorial micro-foundations of macroeconomic growth models. This is the challenge facing regional economists in the years to come.

REVIEW QUESTIONS

1 How would you define local development today?

2 Which are the main elements for local development today?

3 Which are the theoretical aspects which require further attention today?

FURTHER READING

Camagni, R. (2002) 'On the concept of territorial competitiveness: sound or misleading?', *Urban Studies*, vol. 39, no. 13, pp. 2395–411.

Capello, R. and Nijkamp, P. (2004) 'The theoretical and methodological toolbox of urban economics: from and towards where?', in Capello, R. and Nijkamp, P. (eds), *Urban dynamics and growth: advances in urban economics*, Amsterdam: Elsevier, pp. 1–30.

Postscript

Peter Nijkamp

Regional economics has left its stage of infancy and has increasingly and convincingly demonstrated its intrinsic maturity as a vital discipline. Over the years it has consistently and successfully emphasized the scientific and policy relevance of spatial dimensions in economic research. In this way a significant enrichment of traditional a-spatial economic thinking has been achieved, as space is the vehicle *par excellence* for the emergence of agglomeration phenomena, distance frictions and externalities. The blend of vigorous economic analysis and geographical thinking has not only made a bridge between two traditionally disjoint disciplines, but has also created innovative scientific synergies of both a theoretical and applied nature. The scope of regional economics is not confined to industrial nations or regions, but also covers the developing world where issues such as regional deprivation or mass urbanization play a prominent role. The spatial dimension appears to offer a fruitful analytical anchor point for an integrated perspective on regional issues in a broad sense, such as regional development in the context of resource availability, industrial growth in the context of favourable labour market conditions, or the rise of metropolises in the context of global network developments. Regional economics has been able to offer powerful analytical and theoretical concepts for a better understanding of the spatial-economic complexity of our world. It is, therefore, no surprise that it has attracted thousands of scholars all over the world who share a scientific concern on the regional question. The vitality of the discipline can be further illustrated by referring to numerous journals and books published in the field of regional economics.

The present book written by Roberta Capello is another landmark in the history of regional science and regional economics. It offers both a stock-taking of achievements made thus far in the past decade as well as integrating contributions and fascinating perspectives on new departures in the field. This book may be seen as an important pedagogical instrument through which a new generation can be introduced to a field of research that is rapidly evolving and that has also attracted the interest of policy-makers. Roberta Capello has done a superb job in bringing together a wealth of material and filtering the abundant contributions to the field on the basis of standard economic principles.

In reflecting on likely future developments in the field of regional economics, a few dominant themes seem to prevail. In the first place, there is the growing awareness in the field that regional or urban development has to be seen in the framework of complex spatial dynamics that are taking place in a multi-faceted evolutionary environment. Second, we have observed that the structural position of regions or cities is not so strongly determined any more by its physical-geographical position, but increasingly by its position in global (or at least international) network constellations with a multiplicity of actors, and/or institutional ramifications. Finally, given the trend towards spatial interdependencies and communications, regions and cities are not individual economic players any more, but exhibit a great variety of spatial externalities of various nature which deserve close analytical-economic investigation.

The treatment of these substantive issues will require a major research effort, not only theoretically and methodologically, but also empirically and oriented towards policy. There will be a clear need for exchange of research findings, in which comparative analysis – preferably based on new approaches in meta-analysis – may play an important role. Against the background of a globalizing world, and hence against the background of globalizing science, there will be a clear need for more research collaboration world-wide, an endeavour in which network-instigated scientific research and meta-analysis experiments will have a dominant position.

The book written by Roberta Capello offers the intellectual ingredients to come to grips with future scientific challenges in the field of regional economics. It will no doubt exert a great influence on the intellectual mindset of new generations of regional economists.

Department of Spatial Economics
Free University, Amsterdam
February 2006

Notes

INTRODUCTION

1 See Isard, 1956.

2 See the well-known model of Dixit and Stiglitz, 1977.

3 Geographical (physical) features are removed from models and theories by assuming the existence of a homogeneous plain with equal fertility of land (Von Thünen, 1826) or uniform infrastructural endowment (Alonso, 1964a; Christaller, 1933; Hoover, 1948; Lösch, 1954; Palander, 1935).

4 See Camagni, 1999a. This definition has the merit of combining the two concepts of growth and development in a programme of research typical of the current phase of development of regional economics.

5 Ohlin defines a 'region' as a territory characterized by perfect mobility of production factors. See Ohlin, 1933.

6 See Perroux, 1955, p. 308.

7 See Camagni, 2002.

8 Von Böventer, 1975, p. 3.

9 The notion of 'backwardness' employed by regional economics should not be confused with the underdevelopment analysed by development economics. Although there are points of contact between the two disciplines – indeed, some of the early models of regional economics were decisively influenced by those of economic development theory – there are also important differences. The underdevelopment treated by regional economics is contextualized within a broader economic system (the country as a whole) with an already advanced level of industrialization on which backwardness can count: the 'Objective 1' regions of the European Union, termed such because they have levels of per capita income below the average of European regions, are parts of economically advanced countries with infrastructures, technologies, labour forces, and industrial systems typical of the industrialized world. The concern of development economics is instead with the underdevelopment of entire countries, and therefore also with the 'preconditions' for development: industrialization, population support, the creation of basic infrastructures and services for people and firms. Moreover, because regional economics deals with subnational territorial areas, it must disregard certain macroeconomic policy instruments, like the exchange rate or the interest rate, which belong among the public policy instruments available for country-level development.

10 See Meyer, 1963; Isard, 1956.

1 AGGLOMERATION AND LOCATION

1 Location theory – the branch of regional economics which explains the economic mechanisms responsible for location choice – concerns itself not only with the location of economic activities, in particular industrial production, but also with the location of residential activities, and with the economic processes that configure large territorial systems such as cities. This chapter, however, will examine only the mechanisms that condition the location choice of productive activities, leaving treatment of the other topics to subsequent chapters.

2 Isard, 1956.

3 Hoover, 1933, 1936, 1948; Isard, 1949, 1956.

4 Economies of scale arise when, on increasing the inputs to the production process, output grows more than proportionally.

5 Optimal city size is achieved when an urban agglomeration is able to maximize the advantages of agglomeration while also minimizing its costs, thereby obtaining a maximum net advantage (Alonso, 1971; Richardson, 1972). However, the constant physical growth of cities (whether small, medium or large) suggests that the benefits and costs of agglomeration stem from factors other than size: for instance the city's functional specialization and its spatial organization of production (Camagni *et al.*, 1986). The urban environmental diseconomies often exacerbated by the large size of cities now figure on the agendas of policy-makers. Local and national governments, and indeed the European Union, are currently considering the economic and territorial policies best able to render urban economic growth compatible with the natural and social environment. The intention is to achieve urban sustainability, for this is one of the factors on which the competitiveness of cities – and of the regions where cities lie – depends: see Chapter 8. On the concept of urban sustainability see e.g. Banister, 1998; Camagni, 1998; Nijkamp, 1999; Nijkamp and Perrels, 1994.

6 The theory of industrial districts has made much use of the concept of agglomeration economies to explain local development. It has thus prepared the ground for analysis of the role of proximity in local development. Over time, the concept of proximity has assumed a decreasingly physical connotation and an increasingly economic one (see Chapter 8).

7 Only if demand is uniformly distributed in space does the minimization of costs equal the maximization of profits. If, instead, demand is concentrated at some points in space, a location with higher costs than another may coincide with better revenue conditions (sales) and thus increase the firm's profits.

8 Weber's original work was published in 1909. However, it became widely known in 1929, when it was translated for the first time into English. Weber drew on a previous work by Launhardt (1882 and 1885) in developing his theory.

9 Demand (or supply) is said to be inelastic when the price of a good changes but the quantity of the good demanded (or supplied) varies less than proportionally or remains the same.

10 The per unit costs of transportation are assumed to be the same in all directions. In a subsequent version of his model, Weber substituted the concept of real weight with that of ideal weight, which is the actual weight multiplied by the unit cost of transportation in a certain direction. The reasoning does not change, however, and the location solution is found using the same procedure: the only difference is that a further element of realism has been introduced by giving greater importance to the cost per unit of distance than to the weight per distance to cover.

11 Hypothesized here is a situation in which P is the production site, M_1 and M_2 are the raw material sources, and C is the market for the final good, these being located at distances from P which are respectively a, b and c (Figure 1.1a). It is also hypothesized that, in these conditions, the location of P guarantees a minimum total transportation cost. Hence, the forces of attraction ax, by, and cz must stand in the relation $ax + by = cz$, which is the equilibrium condition of the forces of attraction. If $cz > ax + by$, for point P to be the point

of minimum transportation costs, it must shift towards C, while if $cz < ax + by$, it must shift closer to the raw materials market, as described in the main text.

12 Also Palander and Hoover have worked on the concept of isodapane. Palander shows that isodapanes change shape when the hypothesis of non-uniform transportation costs is introduced. See Palander, 1935. Hoover uses the concept of isotime (curve along which the sale price of the good is constant) to define the division of market areas among producers. He shows how different firms, whose production is characterized by different transport and production costs, and therefore by different sale prices and different distances from the production site, divide up the market. See Hoover, 1937a.

13 Weber uses a very similar procedure to find the best location for a firm on the hypothesis that there exists a specific place, coinciding neither with the raw materials market nor with the final goods market, where there is an abundance of low-cost labour. Once the least-cost location has been found, the decision to relocate to the point of lowest labour cost is taken on the basis of a comparison between the saving that the firm obtains in terms of labour cost from the new location and the increased transportation cost that the latter entails. If the advantage is greater than the increased cost, the firm relocates.

14 Weber was nevertheless aware of the importance of distributive aspects and the manner in which they countervail agglomerative forces to disperse activities geographically. He argues, in fact, that deglomerative factors 'all depend on the growth of the value of land, which is caused by the increased demand for land which accompanies all agglomerations', and that they operate through a redistribution of the advantages of agglomeration in favour of rents and wages at the expense of profits. See Weber, 1929.

15 See Smith, 1971.

16 Hoover argues that Weber's model is more easily applicable to the location of firms operating in some sectors rather than others, for example the steel and coal industries. In the case of these sectors, in fact, it is easier to identify raw materials and their incidence in the production of the final good. See Hoover, 1933, 1937b, 1948.

17 Greenhut, 1959a, 1964, 1966.

18 The first studies on the subject date as far back as Launhart, 1882; Fetter, 1924; Hotelling, 1929. Subsequently, Palander analysed market size and spatial competition in order to produce a solution that incorporated the partial findings of previous scholars in a more general explanation. For this reason, Palander is widely considered to be the first theoretician able to conceptualize market areas. See Palander, 1935. The economist Lösch was the first to formulate a general spatial equilibrium on the basis of definition of market areas. See Lösch, 1954.

19 As said in note 9, by rigidity of demand is meant a situation in which, if the price of the good varies, consumers alter the quantity of the good that they want to purchase less than proportionally (or they do not change it at all).

20 For analysis of all the location equilibria in the various cases of price discrimination, see Beckmann, 1968. For critical discussion of the effects of price discrimination on the location equilibrium, see Smith, 1971, chapter 8. On the consequences of different price elasticities of demand on price discrimination and on the location equilibrium, see Hotelling, 1929.

21 Chamberlin, 1936; Lancaster, 1975.

22 This hypothesis amounts to saying that above a certain threshold of production, the law of decreasing marginal returns to the production factors applies. As more and more units of production factors are introduced, their contribution in terms of additional output grows less than proportionally. When this is the case, above a certain threshold there arise decreasing marginal returns and increasing marginal and (average) production costs.

23 For detailed analysis of the effects of changes in factor prices, production techniques, and the combination of production factors, on the position and slope of the overall average cost curve, see Smith, 1966.

24 The supply curve is defined by the firm's operating conditions (costs profile and economies of scale), which the model assumes as given.

25 See Cappellin, 1980; Camagni, 1992a, chapter 1. In analytical terms, with x_i denoting individual demand, we have:

$$p = p^* + \tau d \qquad\qquad \text{(1.1n) Price-distance: Figure 1.5a}$$

$$p = a - bx_i \qquad\qquad \text{(1.2n) Individual demand curve: Figure 1.5b}$$

Therefore:

$$P^* + \tau d = a - bx_i$$

$$x_i = \frac{a - p^*}{b} - \frac{\tau d}{b} \qquad\qquad \text{(1.3n) Individual spatial demand curve: Figure 1.5d}$$

26 For the analytical solution of the quantity demanded in a linear and circular market, see Camagni, 1992a, chapter 1; Segal, 1977, chapter 2.

27 An increase in the production price p^* produces a parallel upward shift of the curve in panel a, and a parallel downward shift of the firm's spatial demand curve in panel d. An increase in τ instead causes the individual spatial demand curve to slope more steeply (Figure 1.5d) and reduces the market area. Interestingly, these results correspond to those obtained by the market areas model.

28 Microeconomics defines 'market equilibrium' as a situation in which, given certain demand conditions, the firm can produce a quantity of goods that enables it to maximize profits. The equilibrium achieved may be short- or long-period. In the former case, the equilibrium is altered by conditions in the market (e.g. the existence of surplus profits) that attract new firms, with which the firm finds itself having to share the market. In the latter case, the equilibrium persists over time until conditions external to the market (technological innovations, variations in the prices of raw materials and the production factors) change the initial rules of the game (costs structure, relative prices of the factors).

29 Because profit is defined as total revenues minus total costs ($\pi = R - C$), profit maximization requires equality between marginal cost (C') and marginal revenue (R'). In fact, $\pi' = 0$ entails that $R' - C' = 0$, i.e. $R' = C'$. In this situation, the firm maximizes the so-called 'normal' profit, i.e. the entrepreneur's normal remuneration. However, there exist cases in which the producer obtains a surplus profit, in addition to its normal profit deriving from market conditions, whereby the good can be sold at prices higher than the average cost. This situation is one of short-term equilibrium, however, because the availability of surplus profits induces new firms to enter the market. In the long period, as the surplus profits are absorbed, the incentive for firms to enter the market disappears, and a stable equilibrium is reached.

30 Before Hotelling, only Fetter had envisaged the possibility that two firms might compete to control the broadest market area possible. Thereafter, other economists conducted interesting analyses on the workings of a market with imperfect competition or a monopolistic market. See Chamberlin, 1936; Fetter, 1924; Hotelling, 1929; Robinson, 1934.

31 We shall see later that discarding this hypothesis changes the final result of the model.

32 Hotelling addressed the problem of location choice also in analytical terms (see Hotelling, 1929). Let τ be the unit cost of transportation, p_a and p_b the sale prices of firm A and B respectively, and x_a and x_b the quantities of the good manufactured by the two firms. Moreover, let c, f, g and h be, respectively, the distances between the origin and A, between A and L, between L and B, and between B and the end of the linear market, as in Figure 1.9a. The lengths of the segments f and g depend on the difference between the two producers'

prices: f increases if $p_a - p_b$ increases; conversely g decreases when $p_a - p_b$ increases.

The location point L in Figure 1.9 represents the division of the market between the two producers in so far as the following relation holds:

$$p_a + \tau c = p_b + \tau g \qquad (1.4n)$$

In L, consumers are indifferent between purchasing from A or B because their sale prices are the same. The market, whose total size is l, is divided into four segments (Figure 1.9a):

$$l = c + f + g + h \qquad (1.5n)$$

Rewriting (1.5n) for f and (1.4n) for g, and substituting the latter in (1.5n), yields:

$$f = \frac{1}{2}\left(l - c - h + \frac{p_b - p_a}{\tau}\right) \qquad (1.6n)$$

and likewise:

$$g = \frac{1}{2}\left(l - c - h + \frac{p_a - p_b}{\tau}\right) \qquad (1.7n)$$

With these lengths of the segments f and g (or, in economic terms, with these market sizes served by the two firms) their profits become:

$$\pi_a = p_a x_a = p_a(c + f) = \frac{1}{2}(l + c - h)p_a - \frac{p_a^2}{2\tau} + \frac{p_a p_b}{2\tau} \qquad (1.8n)$$

$$\pi_b = p_b x_b = p_b(g + h) = \frac{1}{2}(l - c + h)p_b - \frac{p_b^2}{2\tau} + \frac{p_a p_b}{2\tau} \qquad (1.9n)$$

Each firm decides to sell the good at the price which enables it to maximize profit. In analytical terms, the price is decided by differentiating the profit functions from the price and setting them equal to zero:

$$\frac{\partial \pi_a}{\partial p_a} = \frac{1}{2}(l + c - h) - \frac{p_a}{\tau} + \frac{p_b}{2\tau} = 0 \qquad (1.10n)$$

$$\frac{\partial \pi_b}{\partial p_b} = \frac{1}{2}(l - c + h) - \frac{p_b}{\tau} + \frac{p_a}{2\tau} = 0 \qquad (1.11n)$$

from which one obtains:

$$p_a = \tau\left(l + \frac{c - h}{3}\right) \qquad (1.12n)$$

$$p_b = \tau\left(l - \frac{c - h}{3}\right) \qquad (1.13n)$$

and

$$x_a = c + f = \frac{1}{2}(l + \frac{c-h}{3}) \qquad (1.14n)$$

$$x_b = g + h = \frac{1}{2}(l - \frac{c-h}{3}) \qquad (1.15n)$$

The maximum profits become:

$$\pi_a = p_a x_a = \frac{\tau}{2}(l + \frac{c-h}{3})^2 \qquad (1.16n)$$

$$\pi_b = p_b x_b = \frac{\tau}{2}(l - \frac{c-h}{3})^2 \qquad (1.17n)$$

It is evident from equations (1.16n) and (1.17n) that firm A, given the location of B, increases its profit by relocating to A' (Figure 1.9): in fact, c increases and h decreases, so that B's profit diminishes and A's profit increases. Firm A will therefore seek to maximize segment c. In its turn, B wants to relocate closer to A, for example to B' (Figure 1.9), so that it can increase segment h to the detriment of segment c. By so doing, it increases its profit by appropriating from A. Once point L has been reached, neither of the two firms has any further interest in relocating.

33 See Chamberlin, 1936; Lösch, 1954.
34 See Isard, 1970.
35 See Greenhut, 1959a and 1964.
36 Cf. Camagni, 1992a, chapter 1. Recent studies have highlighted the role of logistic costs, in addition to transportation costs, in the location choices of industrial activities. On this see McCann, 1998. For a recent critical review on industrial location theory, see McCann and Sheppard, 2003.

2 ACCESSIBILITY AND LOCATION

1 See Isard, 1956; Beckmann, 1969; Wingo, 1961. An unpublished version of Beckmann's study dates back to 1957, which was prior to Alonso's work. See Alonso, 1964b.
2 See Beckmann, 1969; Montesano, 1972; Solow, 1972; Mirrlees, 1972; Mills, 1972; Anas and Dendrinos, 1976; Richardson, 1977; Fujita, 1989.
3 For firms see Alonso, 1960, 1964b; for households see Alonso, 1964b; Muth, 1961, 1969.
4 See Von Thünen, 1826.
5 Interestingly, the problem that induced Von Thünen to develop his theoretical model was a highly practical one: how to organize agricultural production on his own estates.
6 This result is important, because it has been obtained by all the models developed since Von Thünen's. It states that rent is nothing other than a saving in transportation costs made possible by more central locations. From this follows the 'indifference to alternative locations' condition, which is reached by an individual or a firm when a move in space costs nothing, i.e. when the saving in transport costs obtained by moving one kilometre closer to the centre equals the cost of the land that must be purchased to do so. See Samuelson, 1983.
7 See Ricardo, 1971 [1817].
8 As repeatedly pointed out, by eliminating everything except the distance between land and the town from concrete geographic space, Von Thünen defined a new type of space: namely economic space. See Huriot, 1988.

9 See Alonso, 1960, 1964b; Muth, 1961, 1968, 1969.

10 See Ricardo, 1971.

11 See Camagni, 1992a, chapter 9.

12 Microeconomics defines the utility function as the relation between a person's well-being (expressed in terms of the level of satisfaction – i.e. utility – that possession of a good generates for him/her) and the quantity of goods that s/he possesses.

13 The curve slopes downwards and is convex, thus indicating that the law of the diminishing marginal utility of goods applies. This law states that if a person possesses a large quantity of a particular good, the utility accruing to him/her from acquiring additional units of that good is so small that s/he is willing to exchange units of goods for even very small quantities of another good without this altering his/her satisfaction (utility). Conversely, if the person possesses limited quantities of a good, his/her utility will be increased by possession of additional units to such an extent that a very large quantity of the other good must be offered before s/he is willing to exchange units of the first good. Only thus will his/her utility remain constant.

14 House size remaining equal, if the individual obtains greater quantities of other goods, his/her satisfaction (expressed in terms of utility) will increase.

15 Equation (2.8) is obtained by using the Lagrangian ($\mathcal{L}$):

$$\mathcal{L} = u(q, z) = \lambda(r_d q + p_z z + \tau d) - Y) \tag{2.1n}$$

Setting the partial derivatives with respect to q and z equal to zero, we obtain:

$$\frac{\partial \mathcal{L}}{dz} = u'_z - \lambda p_z \qquad u'_z = \lambda p_z \tag{2.2n}$$

$$\frac{\delta \mathcal{L}}{dq} = u'_q - \lambda r_d \qquad u'_q = \lambda r_d \tag{2.3n}$$

Dividing (2.2n) by (2.3n) and bearing in mind that by definition $u'_z dz = -u'_q d_q$ we obtain (2.8).

16 This situation reflects the traditional consumer optimal choice equilibrium of microeconomic consumption theory. Here the situation is complicated by the fact that the price of one of the two goods (the size of the house) is influenced by the quantity of the other good, distance, chosen by the household.

17 In analytical terms, this problem can also be solved by taking (2.5) as the constraint and maximizing, for that level of utility, the rent offered by households:

$$max \; r(d) = \frac{Y - p_z z - \tau d}{q(d)} \tag{2.4n}$$

$$s.t. \; u^* = u(q, z, d) \tag{2.5n}$$

The system can be solved with the Lagrangian in function of distance and u^*. This system is the dual of the one outlined at note 15. The results do not change, and in particular (2.9) still holds. See Alonso, 1964b, chapter 2.

18 See Fujita, 1989, chapter 2, p. 23.

19 This condition is obtained by setting the third partial derivative of the Lagrangian (2.1.n) equal to zero with respect to distance:

$$\frac{\partial \mathcal{L}}{\partial d} = -\lambda(\frac{\partial r(d)}{\partial d} q + \tau) = 0 \qquad (2.6n)$$

Solving (2.6n) for $\partial r(d)/\partial d$, we obtain:

$$\frac{\partial r(d)}{\partial d} = -\frac{\tau}{q} \qquad (2.7n)$$

which is equation (2.9).

20 When an individual obtains a higher income, the time taken to commute rather than work (called the opportunity cost of transportation) is of greater value.

21 Because of the enormous number of studies published in this field, it is impossible to provide an exhaustive list of references. To be mentioned in particular, however, are Fujita, 1985, 1989; Kanemoto, 1987; Miyao and Kanemoto, 1987; Miyao, 1981, 1984, 1987a. For surveys see Derycke, 1996; Huriot, 1994; Wheaton, 1979.

22 Hypotheses on the model's exogenous variables vary according to the approach. Solow and Mills take the population wanting to settle as given and thereby obtain, *inter alia*, individual utility. See Solow, 1972; Mills, 1972. Fujita instead hypotheses a situation in which utility is known, instead of the population. See Fujita, 1989, chapter 2.

23 The first part of this model, which identifies the indifference to alternative locations conditions for an individual firm (to be then extended to n firms), has an entirely similar logical structure to that of the partial equilibrium location model for firms described above. Here the size of the house is substituted by the firm's intensity of land use.

24 A production function is the relation between the quantity of a firm's output and the quantity of production factors used by the firm in its productive process. The functional form expressed by (2.10) was first proposed by Cobb and Douglas. See Cobb and Douglas, 1928.

25 The expression 'returns to scale' refers to the relation between variations in output and equiproportional variations in all the inputs. If the inputs are increased and the output increases proportionally, the firm produces at constant returns to scale; if the output increases more than proportionally, the firm achieves increasing returns to scale (economies of scale); if the output increases less than proportionally, the firm has decreasing returns to scale (diseconomies of scale).

26 This problems translates into a system which minimizes costs (C) at each distance (d) from the centre, under the constraint of achieving a certain total revenue ($\bar{V}$):

$$\min C_d = r(d) T_d + p_k K_d \qquad (2.8n)$$

$$s.t.: \bar{V} = (p_y - \tau d) Y_d = (p_y - \tau d) a T_d^\alpha K_d^{1-\alpha} \qquad (2.9n)$$

where p_y represents the price of the good y, τ the unit transport costs, and d the distance from the centre. The solution of the system is obtained by means of the Lagrangian:

$$\mathcal{L} = r(d) T_d + p_k K_d - \lambda(p_y - \tau d) \bar{Y}_d - \bar{V} \qquad (2.10n)$$

Setting the partial derivatives equal to zero, we obtain:

$$\frac{\partial \mathcal{L}}{\partial T_d} = r(d) - \lambda(p_y - \tau d) \frac{\partial Y_d}{\partial T_d} = 0 \qquad (2.11n)$$

265

$$\frac{\partial \mathcal{L}}{\partial K_d} = p_k - \lambda(p_y - \tau d)\frac{\partial Y_d}{\partial K_d} = 0 \tag{2.12n}$$

from which we get:

$$r(d) = \lambda(p_y - \tau d)\frac{\partial Y_d}{\partial T_d} = \lambda(p_y - \tau d)\,MaP_{T_d} \tag{2.13n}$$

$$P_K = \lambda(p_y - \tau d)\frac{\partial Y_d}{\partial K_d} = \lambda(p_y - \tau d)\,MaP_{K_d} \tag{2.14n}$$

where MaP represents the marginal productivity of land and capital respectively; i.e. the variation in production when one additional unit of a factor is included in the input. Dividing (2.13n) by (2.14n), we obtain:

$$\frac{r(d)}{p_K} = \frac{\partial K_d}{\partial T_d} = \frac{MaP_T}{MaP_K} \tag{2.15n}$$

The firm will obtain maximum profit (or minimum cost, given a certain revenue) when the ratio between the marginal productivity of the two goods (MaP_{T_d}/MaP_{K_d}) equals the ratio between the prices. In other words, the firm gains by substituting one factor with the other until the productivity of the latter compared to that of the former is higher than its relative price.

27 (2.11) is obtained by deriving the Lagrangian expressed in (2.10n) with respect to d and setting the first derivative equal to zero. This yields:

$$\frac{\partial \mathcal{L}}{\partial d} = \frac{\partial r(d)}{\partial d}T_d + \lambda Y_d \tau = 0 \tag{2.16n}$$

whence:

$$\frac{\partial r(d)}{\partial d} = -\tau\frac{Y_d}{T_d}(\lambda) \quad \text{or} \quad \frac{\partial r(d)}{\partial d}\frac{T_d}{Y_d} = -\tau(\lambda) \tag{2.17n}$$

which is (2.11).

28 A distinctive feature of 'new urban economics' models is their introduction of a production function which allows for substitutability between production factors. The bid-rent curve is thus convex and slopes downward as the distance from the centre increases. This pattern shows that closer to the centre of the city (Von Thünen's market place), the location equilibrium is also defined by the elasticity of substitution between the two factors (goods in the residential activity equilibrium). The term 'elasticity of substitution' between factors (goods) denotes the percentage by which the quantity of one of the two factors (goods) must be increased in order to offset the reduction by one unit of the other factor (good) so that the producer's (consumer's) total production (utility) remains the same.

29 The boundary rent curve was first proposed by Fujita in his outstanding book of 1989.

30 In mathematical terms, this means that in order to obtain a general equilibrium, two further conditions besides those already stated must be imposed. The first concerns land use: the demand for urban land use must exhaust the supply of land:

$$T_d = 2\pi ds \tag{2.18n}$$

where s is the percentage of urban land used for production, and $2\pi d$ represents the area of the circle.

The second condition is that the market for the good must be in equilibrium, thereby ensuring stability in the number of firms operating in the market:

$$\int_{d=0}^{d_{max}} Y_d \, \partial d = D(p) \qquad \text{with} \qquad D'(p) < 0 \tag{2.19n}$$

where $D(p)$ is demand for the good, which is a function of its price p. Conditions (2.18n) and (2.19n) are both fulfilled along the boundary rent curve: hence, the firms in the market occupy a quantity of land equal to the available supply of urban land; at the same time the number of firms exactly covers demand for the good in the market.

Assuming as known the rent on the edge of the city, which is equal to agricultural rent:

$$r(d_{max}) = r_a \tag{2.20n}$$

it is possible to solve the system of equations (2.10n–2.11n; 2.13n–2.14n and 2.18n–2.20n) and obtain the equilibrium values: from equation (2.10), (2.13n) and (2.18n) the values for land and capital (T and K) and for production (Y) at every distance from the centre in function of the price of the good (p), of the price of capital (p_K) and of the cost of land (r); from equations (2.11n) and (2.14n) the profit rate and rent for every distance (except for one constant, the urban edge rent, which is given as exogenous); finally, from (2.19n) the price of the good for which demand equals supply. (2.20n) defines the extreme boundary of the city, its size, and closes the model with definition of the absolute value of rent.

31 The size of the city whereby total population equals the population given exogenously, equal to $\bar{n}$, is given by:

$$\int_{d=0}^{d_{max}} \frac{2\pi d}{q(d, u)} \, \partial d = \bar{n} \tag{2.21n}$$

If the amount of space required by each household (q) increases – for instance because the utility of location in the city increases – residential density ($1/q$) decreases. See Fujita, 1989, chapter 3, p. 57.

32 Once again surprising is how these models turn out to be only more modern versions of Von Thünen's model.

33 See Camagni, 1992a, chapter 6.

34 Various theories have been propounded regarding the relation between territorial phenomena and the law of gravitation of celestial bodies. It was not until the early 1970s, however, that the first convincing account appeared in the form of Wilson's entropy principle. See Wilson, 1970, 1971. For previous theories see Stouffer, 1940, 1960, and his interposed opportunities approach. See also Niedercorn and Bechdolt, 1969, 1972, who developed the individual utility approach to movements in space.

35 Zipf, 1949. Several theories had been formulated before Zipf, most notably Reilly's 'law of retail gravitation'. See Reilly, 1931. For recent empirical examinations of Zipf's law, see Ioannides and Overman, 2003; Soo, 2005.

36 According to the law of universal gravitation, two celestial bodies attract each other with a force proportional to the product of their masses and inversely proportional to the square of the distance between them:

$$T_{ab} = K(M_a M_b)/d_{ab}^2 \qquad\qquad (2.22n)$$

On inserting a generic parameter γ as the exponent of distance, and substituting population for the mass of the two bodies, we obtain (2.12).

37 Also (2.13) derives from an analogy with gravitational physics which states that every unit mass a in the gravitational field of a mass b has a potential energy E equal to the work that a would yield by falling to b:

$$E_{ab} = K M_b/d_{ab} \qquad\qquad (2.23n)$$

Assuming different force fields, the total potential produced on a by a set of masses is defined as:

$$E_a = K\sum_j M_j/d_{aj} \qquad\qquad (2.24n)$$

which is equation (2.13) when the exponent of distance assumes value 1.

38 See Camagni, 1992a, chapter 3.

3 HIERARCHY AND LOCATION

1 See Chapter 2, 'Recent developments: general equilibrium models'.

2 See Christaller, 1933; Lösch, 1954, although the original work dates to 1940.

3 For surveys of this literature see Mulligan, 1984; Beguin, 1988. The latter also conducts interesting critical analysis of the base models.

4 Unlike the models described in Chapter 2, which hypothesized punctiform demand and spatially distributed supply, the models discussed here envisage punctiform supply and demand uniformly distributed in space. They thus recall those described in Chapter 1 which sought to explain how market areas are divided between firms.

5 Christaller defines the threshold as the minimum range within which a service can be supplied from the central place (Christaller, 1933).

6 See Mills and Lav, 1964. It has been erroneously claimed that Christaller's market areas hark back to Von Thünen's circular areas (see Ullman, 1941): in Christaller's theory the circular areas are market areas (of demand), whereas in Von Thünen's they are areas of production (of supply).

7 An equilateral triangle or a square also guarantees the complete coverage of a space without overlaps, but it does not also guarantee the minimization of transport costs, which a hexagonal market area instead does.

8 The constant k may also be defined as the equivalent number of market areas of a given level that nest with a market area of the next higher level.

9 If a is the distance between two original settlements and R is the number of ranks in the hierarchy (excluding the original agricultural settlements), the various progressions are:

No. of market areas: k^0, k^1, k^2, k^3 ...

No. of central places of a certain order R: 1, $k^0(k-1)$, $k^1(k-1)$, $k^2(k-1)$ ...

Distances among central places of the same order: $a\sqrt{k^{R-0}}$, $a\sqrt{k^{R-1}}$, $a\sqrt{k^{R-2}}$ ...

On applying Christaller's three principles, we obtain in numerical terms:

Order	Market principle		Transportation principle		Administrative principle	
	Central places	Market areas	Central places	Market areas	Central places	Market areas
n	1	1	1	1	1	1
n − 1	2	3	3	4	6	7
n − 2	6	9	12	16	42	49
n − 3	18	27	48	64	294	343
...						

10 The relationship between specialization and urban size had already been analysed by previous studies (see Clark, 1945).

11 See Beguin, 1988.

12 The first attempt at mathematical formalization was made by Beckmann, 1958. The definitive version was produced by Beckmann and McPherson, 1970, who were able to solve the problem of the demographic size of centres of different orders – a problem which Christaller did not address. Described here is the version set out in Segal, 1977, which is derived from Beckmann and McPherson.

13 $s + 1$ is k, the proportionality factor in Christaller's model.

14 See Dacey, 1964.

15 See Segal, 1977.

16 For this reason it has been suggested that Lösch's model is better suited to describing urban systems with a predominant industrial sector in which internal, scale or localization economies prevail to produce more 'specialized' agglomerations. Christaller's system is better suited to analysis of tertiary urban systems: in this case, transportation costs, which are mainly paid by consumers, still decisively determine the size of a service's market. An example is the role played by transportation costs in defining the market area of a baker compared to that of a specialist doctor.

17 See Lösch, 1954, p. 435. Lösch numbers the ranges of cities in an order which is the reverse of the one used here, in that he gives higher values to higher-order centres. However, in order to maintain the notation of Christaller's model, here Lösch's numbering is inverted.

18 See Segal, 1977.

19 Presented here is the mathematical formulation by Paelink and Nijkamp, 1976.

20 The reference is to the models of 'new urban economics' (see Chapter 2, 'Recent developments'), which were developed much later chronologically than those of Christaller and Lösch. As said, there are doubts concerning the ability of the 'new urban economics' models to explain the existence of city systems: in order for firms and households to be indifferent among locations in different cities, these models require equal levels of profit and utility, but these are conditions fulfilled only on the hypothesis that all cities are of the same size.

21 For criticisms see Beckmann, 1958; Berry and Garrison, 1958; Mills and Lav, 1964; Mulligan, 1979; Eaton and Lipsey, 1982; Evans, 1985; Fujita et al., 1999; Valavanis, 1955.

22 The lack of analysis of demand in these models has always been regarded as one of their major weaknesses. Even recently it has prompted attempts to develop – at the cost of considerable analytical complexity – general equilibrium models comprising both demand and supply components. See Fujita et al., 1999.

23 In economics, two goods are said to be 'complementary' when a percentage increase in the price of one of them causes a percentage decrease in the quantity sold of the other. Goods are instead termed 'substitute goods' when a percentage increase in the price of one of them causes a percentage increase in the quantity sold of the other.

24 See Beguin, 1988.

25 Beckmann and McPherson, 1970.

26 Beguin, 1984.

27 Long, 1971.

28 Parr, 1978, 1981, 1985.

29 Camagni, 1994.

30 Camagni, 1994.

31 In microeconomics, 'externalities' are the advantages (or disadvantages) which arise from activities of exchange or production between two actors and involuntarily affect a third actor extraneous to the transaction, which gains an advantage (or suffers a disadvantage) without monetary compensation. For detailed treatment of the concept of externality see Meade, 1954; Scitovski, 1954; Mishan, 1971. In the present case, cooperation among cities generates advantages for which the cities do not pay the exact monetary equivalent. For example, they achieve a critical mass of demand for jointly produced services, and they enjoy the relative economies of scale in supplying and managing the service. For a critical survey of the concept of network externalities see Capello, 1994, chapter 2.

32 For empirical analyses of the network organization of urban systems see Boix, 2004; Camagni, 1994; Cappellin and Grillenzoni, 1983; Dematteis, 1994; Emanuel, 1988; Emanuel and Dematteis, 1990; Gottman, 1991; Pumain and Saint-Julien, 1996; Subirats, 2002; Taylor, 2001. For a synthesis of theoretical and empirical aspects on city networks, see Camagni and Capello, 2004.

33 See Capello, 2000.

4 PRODUCTIVE STRUCTURE AND DEVELOPMENT

1 In macroeconomics, the income multiplier effect is generated by the following process: an increase in one of the components of aggregate demand – for example demand for goods produced in the area (local consumption) – gives rise to a general increase in income. However, an increase in income in its turn generates an increase in consumption, and therefore in aggregate demand. The latter once again produces an increase in income, which once again generates increased consumption. The 'Keynesian multiplier' yields a value, by definition greater than unity, which measures the variation in output resulting from a unit change in some component of aggregate demand (consumption, investments, public spending, exports).

2 Note that per capita income as an indicator of disparity has the major shortcoming from the statistical point of view of associating better conditions of relative well-being with emigration from an area. In fact, increased per capita income is obtained either through real growth in regional income (the numerator in the income/population ratio) or through real growth in regional population level (the denominator in the ratio). While the two effects are statistically recorded in the same way by the indicator, from the economic point of view they represent two very different cases: the former that of real economic growth; the latter that of possible social hardship and crisis.

3 The marginal productivity of a production factor, labour for example, measures the extent to which output varies with a change in one unit of labour. If the neoclassical law of decreasing marginal productivity holds, marginal productivity diminishes as the workforce of a firm (or an area) increases. Inevitably, therefore, surplus labour has nil marginal productivity. If new workers were included in the production process, they would be unable to produce additional units of output; for this reason, they remain unemployed.

4 On this see also Graziani, 1983.

5 In Chapter 9.

6 See Introduction, 'Local development and diversified-relational space', for a more detailed interpretation of the notion of 'territory' by economists.

7 See Fisher, 1933; Hoover, 1948; Hoover and Fisher, 1949. More recently see Poratt, 1977; Rostow, 1960.

8 At the time, the hypothesis that factor productivity grew from one stage to the next was empirically confirmed by Fisher's and Clark's studies on the linkage between growth in per capita income and employment in agriculture, industry and services. See Fisher, 1933; Clark, 1940.

9 See Young, 1928.

10 For the definition of 'externalities' see Chapter 3, note 31.

11 See Rosenstein-Rodan, 1943, 1959.

12 See Nurkse, 1952.

13 Nurkse writes: 'a balanced increase in production generates external economies by enlarging the size of the market for each firm or industry' (Nurkse, 1952, p. 574); the same idea is put forward by Rosenstein-Rodan, 1943, 1959.

14 See Hirschman, 1957; Hirschman and Sirkin, 1958.

15 See the export-base theory discussed in Chapter 5.

16 The reference is the export-base theory discussed in Chapter 5.

17 See Williamson, 1965.

18 See Richardson, 1969.

19 See Vernon, 1957.

20 See Perloff, 1957; Perloff *et al.*, 1960.

21 On this see Chapter 8.

22 The three geographical areas have been identified as NUTS2 areas in the Eurostat classification.

23 See Richardson, 1978.

24 The model was developed by geographers at Cambridge in the 1970s. See Keeble *et al.*, 1982, 1988.

25 See Giersch, 1949; Isard, 1954; Isard and Peck, 1954; Friedmann, 1966.

5 DEMAND

1 This circular process is driven by the Keynesian multiplier as defined at note 1, Chapter 4.

2 In the case of a region, exports (imports) comprise sales to (purchases from) subjects in other regions, and even the country itself.

3 Henceforth, 'balance of payments' will be used to denote the current account and the capital account balances. The financial account balance, which, as explained, equalizes the balance of payments, will be excluded.

4 The national accounts are published by the national statistical offices. Most of them furnish statistics on value added, consumption, investments, and incomes which can be used to calculate savings and therefore the gross disposable income and its appropriation account and the capital formation account. The availability of publications on regional accounts varies among countries. Single items of the accounts are made available by Eurostat at different geographical levels (NUTS0, NUTS1 and NUTS2).

5 In macroeconomics, the gross disposable income account (Table 5.2a) is the balance between aggregate demand and supply expressed by the following relation:

$$Y + R = C + I + G + X - M + T \qquad (5.1n)$$

where Y denotes output, R public transfers, C consumption, I investments, G public spending, $X - M$ the trade balance, and T the tax yield.

6 This relation is written in macroeconomics as:

$$Y + R = C + S + T \qquad (5.2n)$$

7 Equalizing equations (5.1n) and (5.2n) we obtain:

$$I + G + X - M = S + T \qquad (5.3n)$$

and therefore:

$$I + (G - T) = S + (M - X) \qquad (5.4n)$$

If the public budget is in equilibrium $(G - T = 0)$, investments can be financed with either internal savings or external savings (business loans and capital investments) $(S + (M - X) = I)$. This becomes clear if we assume that an economic system is initially in macroeconomic equilibrium $(S + (M - X) = I)$ and that a direct investment takes place from outside. This investment is recorded in the capital account as a receipt, while its monetary counterpart is recorded as a monetary inflow: thus the account is balanced. At national level, the increase in investment obtained is entered in the capital formation account as an inflow. Given the assumption of initial macroeconomic equilibrium, the saving is sufficient to cover only the internal investment: the investment from outside therefore engenders an increase in the imports (machinery, raw materials, etc.) necessary for the investment and equal to its value. The current account balance thus perfectly counterbalances the balance of the capital formation account.

8 This circumstance highlights that a fiscal policy intended to assist backward regions by means of greater public transfers only affects the income level. It gives no stimulus to the region's productive capacity, nor does it ameliorate unemployment and stagnation.

9 Stabler argues: 'The size of the area in question also has a major bearing on the importance of what phenomena are most important in generating growth'. See Stabler, 1970, p. 53 (1st edn 1968). See also Aydalot, 1985.

10 See Weimer and Hoyt, 1939; Hoyt, 1954.

11 See North, 1955, Tiebout, 1956; Andrews, 1953, 1954. Andrews is also the author of numerous articles on the subject published in issues of *Land Economics* between 1953 and 1956. North developed his export-base model in critical reaction to the theory of the stages of development (see Chapter 4). The latter was ill-suited to interpreting the growth of certain states (regions) of America, and especially those on the West coast. In these regions, the earliest phases of development had not been characterized by a subsistence economy, but by the industrial production of large quantities of goods, the bulk of which were sold on external markets.

12 $1/(1 - (c - m))$ is the analytical expression of the Keynesian multiplier; its economic meaning is defined at note 1 of Chapter 4.

13 In this case, aggregate demand is defined as:

$$Y - T + R = C + I + G + X - M \qquad (5.5n)$$

and the multiplier becomes, if an income tax rate equal to t is hypothesized (i.e. setting $Y_d = Y - tY + R$):

$$\frac{1}{1 - (1 - c)(1 - t)} \qquad (5.6n)$$

applicable to changes in any of the components of aggregate demand.

14 In this case, the aggregate demand of a generic region r is defined by the equation:

$$Y_r = C_r + I_r + G_r + X_r - M_r \qquad (5.7n)$$

Exports are the sum of imports by all the other regions, and income is disposable income, once taxes have been subtracted, as follows:

$$X_r = \sum_j M_{rj} = \sum_j m_{rj} Y_j^d \qquad (5.8n)$$
$$Y_{d_r} = Y_r - tY_r$$
$$T_r = t_r Y_r$$

where j denotes the generic other regions, m_{rj} the propensity to import from outside the region, t the tax rate, tY the tax revenue, and Y_d the disposable income. Defined m_{ra} as the propensity to import from abroad, the multiplier becomes:

$$\frac{1}{1 - (c_r - m_{ra} - \sum_j m_{rj})(1 - t_r)} \qquad (5.9n)$$

15 See Tiebout, 1960; Richardson, 1978, p. 87 for the dynamic formulation of the model. See Tiebout, 1956; Weiss and Goodwin, 1968 for criticisms against this model.
16 The income differential is given by:

$$\Delta Y = \frac{1}{1 - a_1} \Delta Y_b \qquad (5.10n)$$

Bearing in mind that income is defined by equation (5.10), the percentage variation in income thus obtained is:

$$\frac{\Delta Y}{Y} = \frac{\Delta Y_b}{1 - a_1} \bigg/ Y = \frac{\Delta Y_b}{1 - a_1} \bigg/ \frac{a_0 + Y_b}{1 - a_1} = \frac{\Delta Y_b}{1 - a_1} \frac{1}{\dfrac{a_0 + Y_b}{1 - a_1}} \qquad (5.11n)$$

17 See Miyao, 1984.
18 If external demand for locally-produced goods is hypothesized as increasing exponentially over time at a constant rate $g > 0$:

$$X(t) = X(0)(1 + g)^t \qquad (5.12n)$$

the solution of the differences equation (5.15) is given by:

$$Y(t) = \frac{X(0)(1 + g)^{t+1}}{1 + g - (c - m)} + K(c - m)^t \qquad (5.13n)$$

where K is a constant defined by the initial income condition:

$$K = Y(0) - \frac{X(0)(1 + g)}{1 + g - (c - m)} \qquad (5.14n)$$

If $c - m < 1$, the $\lim_{t \to \infty} K(c - m)^t = 0$. It follows that the regional income converges on a development path at a constant equilibrium rate g, as illustrated by Figure 5.1. The appendix to this chapter contains the mathematical solution of the differences equation (5.15).

273

19 See Chapter 9.

20 This weakness can be remedied by using an input–output table in which the sectoral and geographical disaggregation of commercial interrelations (internal and external to the region) shows the actual multiplier mechanism operating at local level.

21 See Chenery et al., 1953; Chenery, 1962. Sirkin (1959) stressed that multiplier effects change not only according to the sector of specialization but also according to the level of specialization. More specialized areas necessarily require greater openness to interregional trade, especially if there exists highly diversified internal demand which stimulates greater commercial exchanges. It is therefore highly unlikely that the multiplier effect will be the same in regions with different structural features.

22 Greenhut pointed out as early as 1959 that 'the region's export base is not a datum. That is to say, the base changes with time, as currently produced private and social goods help bring forth new goods that change the base'. See Greenhut, 1959b, p. 71; Greenhut, 1966.

23 Use of the location quotient to define the base sector was first proposed by Hildebrand and Mace in 1950. See Hildebrand and Mace, 1950.

24 See Pratt, 1968.

25 See Ullman and Dacey, 1960.

26 Knowing the size (in units of employment or in value) of the base sector and the total sector, from equation (5.7) it is possible to obtain the value of the multiplier: in fact, $Y/X = 1/(1 - c + m)$. Of course, this is an average value when instead a marginal value is required ($\Delta Y/\Delta X$). The two values are only equal, in fact, if there are no autonomous expenditure items apart from exports.

27 See Archibald, 1967. A similar approach has been applied by McGuire, 1983, who calculated the multiplier for two localities in Scotland. For an application to England, see Steele, 1969. For a critical review, see Wilson, 1968.

28 In our case, we assume that:

$$C_l = a + bY_d \tag{5.15n}$$

i.e. that a proportion (b) of local spending C_l depends on income, while a proportion (a) does not. The regression method allows estimation of the values of the parameter, and in particular b, which is the marginal propensity to spend disposable income locally.

29 See Allen, 1969. The logic of this method can be understood by recalling that if regions were closed systems, the only variable reducing the value of the multiplier would be the propensity to save the increase in income. However, the inverse of the propensity is nothing but the Keynesian multiplier. This method has been recently used to estimate the multiplier for Italian regions: see Faggian and Biagi, 2003.

30 In order to sum the flows of diverse kinds of goods, they must obviously be expressed in value terms, not in quantities.

31 The same method of analysis is used at national, regional or urban level. In the case of a regional or urban input–output matrix, what is meant by 'imports' and 'exports' are flows into or out of the region (or city), not just flows to or from abroad. For a critical description of the theory see Tiebout, 1957.

32 For example, the technical coefficients between the car industry and the rubber industry express the value of the rubber necessary to produce the value of a car.

33 Expressing equation (5.21) in matrix form, where R and D are the two sectoral vectors of the value of production and the value of final demand, A is the matrix of the technical coefficients and I the identity matrix, produces:

$$R = AR + D \tag{5.16n}$$

$$(I - A)R = D \qquad\qquad (5.17n)$$

$$R = (I - A)^{-1} D \qquad\qquad (5.18n)$$

With $B = (I - A)^{-1}$ defined as the Leontief inverse matrix, we have:

$$R = BD \qquad\qquad (5.19n)$$

which is nothing other than (5.22).

34 If the area happens to be an island, use can be made of harbour and airport statistics documenting the value of goods entering and leaving the island. These statistics are excellent means with which to separate local and interregional effects. They have been used in Italy to assess the impact of a building project for the Costa Smeralda on the growth of the Sardinian economy. See Camagni, 1982. For detailed discussion of input/output analysis see Hewings, 1977; Hewings *et al.*, 2001; Martellato, 1982.

35 See Harrod, 1939 and Domar, 1957. For a critical examination of Harrod's theory see Hawtrey, 1939.

36 See Richardson, 1969.

37 Equation (5.25) is constructed by setting $I = sY$, i.e. $I = S$, which is the macroeconomic equilibrium condition. In fact, the $I = S$ equality is an accounting identity which always holds after the fact. On the hypothesis of an economy closed to foreign trade and in the absence of a public sector, output is either wholly consumed or wholly invested ($Y = C + I$). Income, on the other hand, is allocated between consumption and investments ($Y = C + S$). If $C + S = C + I$ – a condition which holds only if $I = S$ – the output offered is equal to the output sold, and the value of output is equal to the income earned, which in its turn is either spent or saved.

38 The $Y = C + S$ equality states that income is either spent or saved. If actual saving is less than planned investment, this means that effective consumption is greater than planned investment, and therefore that effective demand (defined by the level of consumption) is greater than expected demand.

39 The constraint for the system as a whole is that interregional trade must be balanced, i.e. that:

$$\sum_i \sum_j M_{ij} = \sum_i \sum_j X_{ij} \qquad \text{for each } i \neq j \qquad (5.20n)$$

40 This condition is analysed, and explained in accounting terms, in 'Interregional relations' (above).

41 The importance of imports for the growth and competitiveness of countries has recently been re-examined by the eminent economist Paul Krugman. The real purpose of international trade, Krugman argues, is to obtain imports, not to export. Exporting is only a way to finance imports, which are less costly than the direct production of what one needs. See Krugman, 1996, p. 19.

42 In Thirlwall's words: 'export demand is a vital element in regional demand, which is necessary to compensate for a region's appetite for imports, in the absence of other compensating expenditure'. See Thirlwall, 1980, p. 422. See also Thirlwall, 1983; McCombie, 1992; McGregor and Swales, 1985.

43 Thirlwall argues, in fact, that 'regional problems are balance of payments problems': see Thirlwall, 1980.

44 In microeconomics, the elasticity of the quantity demanded (supplied) to income measures in percentage terms the extent to which the quantity demanded (supplied) varies with a one per cent change in income.

6 FACTOR ENDOWMENT

1 Two important theoretical notions should be borne in mind if this reasoning is to be properly understood. First, in a neoclassical world, factor productivity is governed by the law of decreasing marginal returns: a larger quantity of factors entails lower factor productivity. Second, according to the neoclassical theory, the production factors can only be remunerated at their marginal productivity: the firm pays the additional factor exactly for the value of the good which the additional factor is able to produce, thus maximizing its profit. On this view, a region with a large endowment of a particular factor can only expect low productivity by, and therefore low remuneration of, that factor.

2 See Chapter 10.

3 The reference is to Borts, 1960; Borts and Stein, 1964, 1968 (original edition 1962).

4 See Camagni, 1999a; Krauss and Johnson, 1974.

5 See Cobb and Douglas, 1928.

6 Rewriting equation (6.1) in logarithms gives:

$$\ln Y = \ln A + \alpha \ln K + (1 - \alpha)\ln L \tag{6.1n}$$

The derivative over time of a variable is calculated as:

$$\frac{d \ln Y}{dt} = \frac{1}{Y} \frac{\partial Y(t)}{\partial t} \tag{6.2n}$$

Setting $\dfrac{\partial Y(t)}{\partial t} = \dot{Y}$, equation (6.2n) can be rewritten as follows:

$$\frac{d \ln Y}{dt} = \frac{\dot{Y}}{Y} = y \tag{6.3n}$$

Deriving all the variables of equation (6.1n) over time, we obtain equation (6.2).

7 See Smith, 1975; Miyao, 1987a. These curves are obtained by setting equations (6.4) and (6.5) equal to zero. As regards equation (6.1), if we substitute equation (6.1) in (6.4), we obtain:

$$k = sL^{\beta}\left(\frac{K}{L}\right)^{\alpha-1} + \mu(i_r - i_m) = 0 \tag{6.4n}$$

i_r is by definition equal to the marginal productivity of capital, i.e. it is equal to:

$$i_r = \alpha L^{\beta}K^{\alpha-1}L^{1-\alpha} \tag{6.5n}$$

which when substituted in equation (6.4n) yields:

$$sL^{\beta}\left(\frac{K}{L}\right)^{\alpha-1} + \mu(\alpha L^{\beta}K^{\alpha-1}L^{1-\alpha} - i_m) = 0 \tag{6.6n}$$

which can be rewritten as:

$$sL^{\beta}K^{\alpha-1}L^{1-\alpha} + \mu\alpha L^{1-\alpha+\beta}K^{\alpha-1} - \mu i_m = 0 \tag{6.7n}$$

In its turn, equation (6.7n) can be written as:

$$\left(\frac{s + \mu L}{i_m \mu}\right)^{\frac{1}{1-\alpha}} = KL^{\frac{\alpha - 1 + \beta}{1-\alpha}} \tag{6.8n}$$

Solution of equation (6.8n) for K produces:

$$K = \left(\frac{s + \mu L}{i_m \mu}\right)^{\frac{1}{1-\alpha}} L^{\frac{1-\alpha+\beta}{1-\alpha}} \tag{6.9n}$$

Likewise, as regards equation (6.5) we have:

$$l = n + \lambda(w_r - w_m) = 0 \tag{6.10n}$$

Setting w_r equal to marginal productivity, we obtain:

$$n + \lambda((1 - \alpha)L^\beta K^\alpha L^{-\alpha} - w_m) = 0 \tag{6.11n}$$

which with simple steps leads to:

$$K = \left(\frac{w_m \lambda - n}{\lambda(1-\alpha)}\right)^{\frac{1}{\alpha}} L^{\frac{\alpha-\beta}{\alpha}} \tag{6.12n}$$

8 The trend of equation (6.3) depends on the time trend of the growth rate of per capita capital $(k - l)$, which for convenience may be called $H(k - l) = d(k - l)/dt$. From equations (6.4) and (6.5) we obtain:

$$H(k - l) = sA(k - l)^{\alpha-1} + \mu(\alpha A(k - l)^{\alpha-1} - i_m) - n - \lambda((1 - \alpha)A(k - l)^\alpha - w_m) \tag{6.13n}$$

when $\lim_{(k-l)\to\infty} H(k - l) = \mu i_m - n + \lambda w_m$ and $\lim_{(k-l)\to 0} H(k - l) = \infty$ and $H'(k - l) < 0$. These relations explain the trend of the per-capita growth rate curve in Figure 6.3 and imply, for the differential equation (6.9n), the existence, uniqueness and stability of equilibrium growth. See Miyao, 1987b.

9 One implication of the one-sector model (see p. 135) is that low-wage regions should exhibit higher rates of growth of both capital and the capital/output ratio, and consequently of per capita income. Moreover, low-wage regions should also record a higher rate of wages growth because of the increase in the capital/output ratio. However, statistical tests conducted by the authors of the theoretical model showed that this was not the case. On examining the American regions, Borts and Stein found that in the periods 1919–29 and 1948–53 capital flowed to high-wage regions – regions, moreover, with higher rates of wages growth. Only in one period, between 1929 and 1949, did the empirical reality seem to support the theoretical hypotheses: a result which, as Borts and Stein themselves acknowledged, was too weak to give empirical validity to their model. See Borts, 1960; Borts and Stein, 1964, 1968 (original edition, 1962). Numerous neoclassical authors, convinced that the original model was fundamentally sound, blamed its contradiction by the empirical evidence on erroneous methodology: Smith argued that the problem was due to the excessive sectoral disaggregation of the data used by Borts and Stein, while Coelho et al. pointed to the erroneous use of nominal wages as a proxy for individual well-being, given substantial differences in the costs of living among regions. See Smith, 1974; Coehlo and Ghali, 1971; Coehlo and Shepherd, 1979.

10 In Borts and Stein's words: 'The forces we have outlined produce a *permanent divergence of regional growth rates*. The only way in which growth rates might converge is through the role played by other autonomous forces operating within the framework of such a set of economic relations.' Borts and Stein, 1968, p. 184 (emphasis added); original edition 1962.

11 The value of marginal product is the price of the good produced multiplied by the marginal productivity of the factors used to produce that good. It represents the revenue obtained by the firm from the use of the extra unit of the production factor. The value of marginal product has to be equal to the cost of the production factor in order for a firm to maximize its profit. In the case of labour, therefore:

$$VPMa_l = P_x{}^*PMa_l = w \tag{6.14n}$$

where VPM_{al} is the value of marginal product (i.e. the marginal revenue), P_x the price of good x, PM_{ai} the marginal productivity of the labour factor, and w the wage. Likewise, for capital:

$$VPMa_k = P_x{}^*PMa_k = i \tag{6.15n}$$

where i represents the remuneration of capital. When marginal revenue equals marginal costs, i.e. when equations (6.14n) and (6.15n) hold, the firm achieves profit maximization.

12 With this assumption, the model resembles the export-base model: external demand — which is not explained but assumed exogenously — is the source of growth.

13 The migration of labour from the agricultural to the manufacturing sector induced by indus-trialization is a good example of this source of local growth. There is a version of the model which assumes the existence of a single region with two sectors: one with low, the other with high factor productivity. Under standard neoclassical assumptions, the migration of workers to the higher-wage sector is followed by higher income levels produced by the reallocation of resources which guarantee conditions of optimal intra-regional allocation of resources. See Borts and Stein, 1964, chapter 7; McCombie, 1988.

14 Recall the item 'Compensation of employees and property income owned by non-residents in the region' in the current account of the balance of payments (see Table 5.1). These incomes do not enter the formation of disposable income: in Table 5.2, in fact, the remuneration of employees and property incomes entering the formation of gross disposable income are net incomes, i.e. the only ones earned by residents outside the region; see Chapter 5.

15 Borts writes: 'Migration does not appear sufficient to produce convergence. It clearly produces less divergence than would occur were migration to halt': Borts, 1960, p. 346.

16 See Chapter 10.

17 A case in point is North-Eastern and Central Italy in the 1970s, where growth was driven by traditional labour-intensive light manufacturing industries characterized by a high level of productivity and a low labour cost, compared to the North-Western (Lombardy, Piedmont and Liguria) and Southern regions of the country. See Camagni and Capello, 1990, and Chapter 8 in this book.

18 See Camagni, 1999a; Holland, 1977.

19 See Okun and Richardson, 1961.

20 See Lutz, 1962. For discussion of the Italian dual economy see Ackley and Spaventa, 1962; Spaventa, 1959; Graziani, 1983. For a critical examination of Lutz's theory see Holland, 1971.

21 Interesting in this regard is Ohlin's observation that the theory of international trade is a particular case of the theory of interregional trade with the exclusion of production factor mobility. See Ohlin 1933.

22 See Ricardo, 1971, original edition, 1817. Historians of economic thought are still unsure as to who originally developed the notion of comparative advantage, which is present in the works of both Torrens (1815) and Ricardo (1817). However, there is no disputing that both authors made a crucial contribution to the development of the theory of comparative advantages.

23 The advantage in terms of labour-hours is calculated as follows: by obtaining from the trade one-third of good B, when it could itself produce one-quarter, the region obtains an extra 1/12 of a unit of good B (1/3 − 1/4 = 1/12) from the trade. Given that each unit of B is produced in 4 hours, 1/12 of B is produced in 1/3 of an hour, which represents the advantage in terms of labour-hours saved obtained from the trade.

24 'For Ricardo, the main benefit deriving from imports is that wage goods can be obtained at lower prices': Onida, 1984, p. 65.

25 Armstrong and Taylor's observation (2000, p. 123) is emblematic: 'that trade is based on comparative advantage and not absolute advantage is universally accepted'.

26 See Camagni, 2002.

27 See Heckscher, 1919.

28 See Leontief 1953, 1956.

29 See Moroney and Walker, 1966.

30 See Camagni, 1999a.

31 See Keesing, 1966.

32 See Posner, 1961; Vernon, 1966; Nelson and Norman, 1977.

33 In a recent work, Roberto Camagni responds to the provocative thesis of the noted international economist Paul Krugman that territories, unlike firms, can only compete on the basis of comparative advantage: see Camagni, 2002, on Krugman, 1996, 1998a. For broader treatment of the arguments presented in the main text see Camagni, 2002.

34 Ricardo's model was developed from a normative perspective: it concludes that it is economically convenient for regions (or countries) to trade, but nothing in the model is able to determine whether or not trade actually takes place. Moreover, the Ricardo model, which demonstrates the existence of comparative advantages in the economies of two nations, is based on a barter economy in which 'units of goods' are exchanged. But the model lacks a theory of wages, prices and money necessary to understand real trade decisions. 'The monetary conditions of trade are an advantage in absolute costs': Onida, 1984, p. 81.

35 'Specie' denotes commodity-money or international means of payment, whose net flow reflects the deficits-surpluses in the trade balances of countries. See Onida, 1984, p. 85.

36 See Chapter 5, 'Interregional relations'.

37 On the effects of the creation of the European Common Market see Thirlwall, 1974; Balassa, 1975; Scitovski, 1958. On those of the creation of the Single Market see Cecchini, 1988; Quévit, 1992; Camagni, 1992b.

38 On 1 May 2004, with the entry into the European Union of eight countries in Eastern Europe and two from the Mediterranean area (Malta and Cyprus), the European Union changed from a Europe of 15 to a Europe of 25.

39 See Bachtler and Downes, 1999; Petrakos, 2000; Resmini, 2007; Traistaru et al., 2003.

40 See Camagni and Pompili, 1990; Capello, 2002a.

41 See Linder, 1961; Lancaster, 1980. For comments on the models see Barker, 1977.

7 TERRITORIAL COMPETITIVENESS AND EXOGENOUS DEVELOPMENT

1 The reference is, for example, to formalization of equilibrium in non-linearity conditions and equilibrium under monopolistic competition. The latter was proposed towards the end of the 1970s by Dixit and Stiglitz, and it provides the basis for some of the models presented in Part 4.

2 See Von Böventer, 1975, p. 3. When Von Böventer refers to '"pure and exact" regional theory without agglomeration economies', he means the theories presented in Part 2 of this book; when he refers to '"applied regional theory" which is inexact but takes agglomeration factors into account', he means theories expounded in more qualitative form, which will be the ones developed in this part of the book.

3 'Transaction costs' are the costs which arise from the exchange of information and documents relative to commercial transactions, for which reason they are also called 'costs of market use'. See Williamson, 1975.

4 This is the case of the weak region achieving greater growth than the rich region in Borts and Stein's one-sector model. It needs to be stressed that the view of development adopted by other neoclassical models, such as the Heckscher–Ohlin model, is one of generative development, not of competitive development. On the distinction between competitive and generative development see Richardson, 1973, 1978.

5 Perroux, 1955, p. 308, my translation. The same ideas are set out in embryonic form in Perroux, 1950.

6 Higgins proposes the following definition: a firm A can be called a 'dominant firm' if its investment decisions influence the investment decisions of a group of firms (B) connected with it, and therefore if the following holds:

$$I_B = f(I_A) \qquad \text{with } \Delta I_B / \Delta I_A > 0 \tag{7.1n}$$

where I is the level of investments. See Higgins, 1977.

7 See Paelink, 1965; Boudeville, 1964 (English trans. 1966).

8 Hansen, 1967.

9 Paelink, 1965.

10 See also Chapter 8.

11 Note that, chronologically, the growth-pole theory preceded shift-share analysis: the technique already discussed and which sought to describe the productive structure and sectoral dynamic of an area in order to explain its development.

12 See Chapter 3.

13 For a critical survey of the normative application of growth-pole theory see Parr, 1999a and 1999b.

14 Hirschman, 1958.

15 An example is provided by the steelworks constructed in Taranto (Southern Italy) during the 1960s, the direct consequence of which was the closure of small crafts firms, which were forced to leave the urban area by the increases in living costs, land rents and wages caused by the external intervention.

16 On this see Holland, 1977; Massey and Meegan, 1978; Lipietz, 1980; Carney et al., 1980; Damette, 1980.

17 Lipietz, 1980.

18 On this see Holland, 1977; Damette, 1980; Carney, 1980. In particular, Damette introduced the idea of the hyper-mobility of capital.

19 For this interpretation see e.g. Young et al., 1988; Nauwelaers et al., 1988. In the 1990s the extraordinary economic growth achieved by Ireland thanks to its ability to attract FDIs (the so-called 'Irish miracle') amply demonstrated that the relationship between FDIs and a country's growth is not always negative, and that it is more complex than the 'radical' school envisaged.

20 See Rodriguez-Clare, 1996; Borensztein et al., 1998; Markusen and Venables, 1999, and Chapter 9 in this book.

21 See Camagni, 1988.

22 On multinationals and technological spillovers see Blomström and Kokko, 1988; Cantwell, 1989; Cantwell and Iammarino, 1998; Cantwell and Piscitello, 2002.

23 On this see Holland, 1977; Massey and Meegan, 1978; Lipietz, 1980; Carney et al., 1980; Damette, 1980.

24 In a celebrated study, Solow showed that more than 40 per cent of US growth between 1900 and 1949 was due to a factor (Solow's famous 'residue') which could not be explained in terms of factor growth: see Solow, 1957. In subsequent years, empirical surveys carried out at national, regional and local level showed that more than one-third of output growth in the second half of the twentieth century was due to the growth of factor productivity achieved through technological progress. It is debatable whether the assumption of constant returns made by these studies is necessary. Nevertheless, it proves useful in several respects: in the presence of increasing returns to scale, output increases more than input, and it is conceptually and empirically difficult to determine the specific contribution of technological change to economic growth. Instead, on the hypothesis of constant returns, the entire increase in input not obtained from increases in the production factors is due to technological progress. For discussion of the role of the spatial diffusion of innovation in the regional development process see, among others, McCombie, 1982.

25 Hägerstrand, 1967. For the preliminary reflections which gave rise to the model see Hägerstrand, 1952 and 1966.

26 'This accounts for the fact that though most innovations are adopted at a higher rate than the economy's mean rate in cities and large towns (obvious exceptions are innovations in the agricultural sector, such as new agricultural machines), certain rural districts surrounding the innovation centre may also apply the innovation at a rate above the mean'. Richardson, 1973, p. 313.

27 In Hägerstrand's words: 'a person becomes more and more inclined to accept an innovation the more often he comes into contact with other persons who have already accepted it'. Hägerstrand, 1967, p. 264.

28 Griliches, 1957; Mansfield, 1961, 1968.

29 The linearity of the function obtained with a transformation into logarithms allows estimation of its parameters with ordinary least squares regression – an easily applicable econometric technique. In Griliches' words 'the logistic was chosen because it is simpler to fit and in our context easier to interpret'. Griliches, 1957, p. 503.

30 In this case, too, the determinants of the values assumed by the three parameters are easily identified by means of multiple linear regression models based on ordinary least squares.

31 See Griliches, 1957, p. 501.

32 See Capello, 1988. The same analysis has been conducted on the adoption of industrial automation technologies. See Camagni, 1985.

33 The pattern of adoption costs is explained as follows: adoption costs are at first decreasing because of the creation of local knowledge in the new technology and because of the reduction of sunk costs on the old technology, made possible by increasing depreciation of the old technology. They then increase because of the constant accumulation of knowledge in the old technology. In their turn, the revenues (net of the opportunity-cost of still using the old technology) decrease over time because of learning processes centred on the old technology. Figure 7.4 shows that if the new technological trajectory is not chosen immediately, it may never be introduced; in fact, the more the adoption is postponed, the greater the risk of lock-in to the knowledge developed for the old technology, and the more costly the transition from the old to the new technology. See Camagni and Capello, 1998. The pattern of adoption costs and revenues is also affected by the structure of the market in which the innovation is produced. See Capello et al., 1999, chapters 5–6.

34 See Brown, 1981; Davies, 1979; Stoneman, 1986. For a critical analysis of epidemic models see Haggett et al., 1977, chapter 7.

35 The logistic model used to analyse the telephone service would find it very difficult today to describe its real diffusion *ex post*. The model was developed in the mid-1980s and did not foresee the advent of the cell-phone, which has radically changed the trend in adoption of the fixed telephone service.

36 See Norton and Rees, 1979; Hirsch, 1967; Vernon, 1966.

37 See Davelaar and Nijkamp, 1990.

38 In the words of Abernathy and Utterback, the curve of the product life-cycle 'lost its tail'. See Abernathy and Utterback, 1978.

39 As Davelaar puts it, 'the "swarming" processes are "creative" processes and not simple "carbon copy" processes of imitation': see. Davelaar, 1991, p. 29. On this statement, see also Davelaar and Nijkamp, 1990.

40 See Chapter 8.

41 The 'regional development potential' model was first formulated by Biehl, who maintained that 'an essential requirement for a theory which claims to establish the contribution of infrastructures to regional economic development is that it must not restrict itself to the infrastructures themselves but also considers other possible determinants of regional economic development; and this is precisely the case of the regional development potential approach'. See Biehl, 1986.

42 For analysis of infrastructures as the source of endogenous growth see Barro, 1990.

43 Infrastructural endowment is estimated using two methods. The most frequent one measures public capital in monetary terms as a proportion of the total stock of capital. The method less frequently used – mainly because of the difficulty of obtaining suitable data – calculates it on the basis of 'physical' indicators of infrastructural endowment.

44 Besides infrastructural endowment, often included in the production function are further factors deemed decisive in the overall competitiveness of the local system considered. For example, Biehl emphasizes location, sectoral composition and the agglomerative structure; Ferri and Mattesini highlight the role of human capital; Fabiani and Pellegrini stress the importance of geographical factors, the environment, and the sectoral structure. See Biehl, 1986; Fabiani and Pellegrini, 1997; Ferri and Mattesini, 1997. See Elhance and Lakshmanan, 1988, for the solution of some methodological problems in estimates of a quasi-production function.

45 See Aschauer, 1989, 1990.

46 On the theoretical and empirical aspects of the subject, see, among others, Aschauer, 1989, 1990; Costa *et al.*, 1987; Deno, 1988; Duffy-Deno and Eberts, 1991; Eberts, 1986; Guild, 1998; Hansen, 1965a, 1965b; Hulten and Schwab, 1995; Moomaw and Williams, 1991; Moomaw *et al.*, 1995; Munnell, 1990; Rietveld, 1989.

47 See European Commission, 2004.

48 On this see Bruinsma *et al.*, 1990; Vickerman, 1991.

49 See Rosenstein-Rodan, 1943, and Chapter 4 of this book.

50 Hansen, a pioneer of these studies, showed that development in Belgium varied by region according to the classes of investment. Lagging regions benefited more from increased social overhead capital (e.g. social services including health and education), while intermediate regions benefited more from increased spending on economic overhead capital (e.g. roads and power supplies). Congested regions were less affected by changes in both types of social capital. See Hansen, 1965a, 1965b. Paci and Saddi have obtained different levels of income elasticities to infrastructures for the North and the South of Italy: 0.14 for Northern Italy and 0.20 for Southern Italy. See Paci and Saddi, 2002.

51 See Amin and Wilkinson, 1999; Asheim, 1996; Camagni, 1991; Keeble and Wilkinson, 2000; Lundvall and Johnson, 1994. For a definition of collective learning see Chapter 8.

52 On the debate concerning convergence or divergence in development rates following the advent of ICTs see Goddard and Pye, 1977; Gillespie and Williams, 1988; Gillespie *et al.*, 1989; Capello, 1994; Hepworth and Waterson, 1988.

53 See Yilmaz and Dinc, 2002. For empirical analyses on the effects of telecommunications on regional development in China see Ding and Haynes, 2004; for Portugal, see Butler *et al.*, 1986.
54 See Capello, 1994; Capello and Spairani, 2004.

8 TERRITORIAL COMPETITIVENESS AND ENDOGENOUS DEVELOPMENT

1 The allusion is to all the location theory models examined in Part 1 of the book.
2 Hence the name 'NEC areas'.
3 The 'industrial triangle' comprising Lombardy, Liguria and Piedmont, i.e. the regions of north-western Italy.
4 See Ciciotti and Wettmann, 1981; Johannisson and Spilling, 1983; Stöhr and Tödtling, 1977; Stöhr, 1990; Secchi, 1974; Garofoli, 1981; Courlet and Pecqueur, 1992; Ganne, 1992. See Vásquez-Barquero, 2002, for a well-structured survey of theories of endogenous development.
5 Becattini set out his main ideas in a study published in 1975 (see Becattini, 1975) and then developed them in a subsequent study of 1979 (see Becattini, 1979; English trans. 1989). There followed a series of works in which Becattini expanded and deepened the concept of the 'Marshallian industrial district'. Recent volumes containing seminal works on the issue are Becattini, 2004.
6 See Marshall, 1920. For detailed analysis of the links between Marshall's work and the theory of industrial districts see Bellandi, 1989.
7 The 'Third Italy' is the geographical macro-area comprising the regions of the North-East and the Centre (the NEC areas). The term was coined in order to underline the inadequacy of the North/South 'dualistic' model hitherto applied to Italian economic development, and to mark the birth of a new (third) macro area of such development. See Bagnasco, 1977.
8 See Benedetti and Camagni, 1983.
9 Unfortunately, none of the pioneering studies on the subject have been translated into English and are therefore only available in Italian. See Bagnasco, 1977 and 1983 on entrepreneurship; for detailed analyses of the workings of local labour markets see Brusco, 1982, 1990; Paci, 1973; for analysis of social and political cohesion see Bagnasco, 1985; Bagnasco and Trigilia, 1984; Trigilia, 1985.
10 Becattini's original definition of an industrial district was as follows: 'a socio-territorial entity characterised by the active presence of both a community of people and a population of firms in one naturally and historically bounded area': Becattini, 1990, p. 38. This definition highlights the genetic features of an industrial district: the geographical and social proximities of economic actors.
11 In his *Principles of Economics* Marshall stresses the importance of '[. . .] those very important external economies which can often be secured by the concentration of many small businesses of a similar character in particular localities: or, as is commonly said, by the localization of industry'. See Marshall, 1920, 8th edn, p. 221.
12 Because of its limited size, in fact, a small firm cannot exploit 'economies of scale', namely the advantages deriving to a firm from production of a large and increasing volume of output in the same place. In an industrial district, this disadvantage is off-set by localization economies, which Marshall calls 'external economies' because they depend on conditions external to the firm (the sector's volume of business) rather than internal to it (the volume of output by the firm). In *Principles of Economics*, Marshall argues that the advantages of large scale may in general be achieved either by grouping a large number of firms into a single district or by constructing a few large-scale factories. See Marshall, 1920.
13 The historical structure of the agricultural systems of industrial districts has been researched by Bagnasco, who wrote in 1977: 'The family of peasant origin (although it is today different

in nature) is the pivot of the production system, and we can also understand why industrialization arises as a result of the local presence of this original type of family'. See Bagnasco, 1977, p. 153, my translation. To be noted is that Becattini initially used the expression 'urbanized countryside' to denote diffused industrialization, his purpose being to emphasize the agricultural origins of areas of recent industrialization. See Becattini, 1979; Engl. vers. Becattini, 1989.

14 Becattini, 1987, p. 47, my translation.

15 Marshall, 1920, 8th edn, p. 225.

16 See 'Collective learning and the *milieu innovateur*'.

17 The idea of a 'community market' was first developed by Dei Ottati. See Dei Ottati, 2003 (original version, Dei Ottati, 1987). Also proposed has been the notion of 'market socialization': see Bagnasco, 1985. The importance of social aspects in industrial district theory is such that some authors have claimed that 'despite the many insights of genuinely economic character, the picture is still predominantly sociological': Benedetti and Camagni, 1983, p. 22, my translation.

18 On the symbiosis between competition and cooperation see Becattini, 1990; Bianchi, 1994; Dei Ottati, 1995, 2003. On the concept of cooperation, or 'collective efficiency', see Rabellotti, 1997; Schmitz, 1995, 1998.

19 In this regard Becattini writes: 'The dynamic and self-reproducing nature of the district consists of a continuous comparison between the cost of performing any given operation inside the firm and the cost of having it done outside [. . .]. It should be noted that it is not a matter of a generic comparison between doing and buying, but a specific comparison between doing and having done [. . .]. It should also be noted that this is almost always "doing together"': Becattini, 1990, p. 48. For detailed analysis of reputation as capital see Dei Ottati, 1995.

20 See Dei Ottati, 1995.

21 I would point out – and not just as a matter of pride – that while regional economists drew their initial theories (for example the theory of stages of development) from analysis conducted by development economists, today the reverse is happening: the tools developed by regional economics are being used by economists of development. This demonstrates the significant evolution and autonomization undergone by thought on regional economic development in the past fifty years.

22 See Rabellotti, 1997; Schmitz and Musyck, 1994.

23 See Benedetti and Camagni, 1983; Cappellin, 1983.

24 The reference is to the fact that, in order to understand the performance of the north-eastern Italian regions in the 1970s or 1980s, analysis must be made of the performances in those years of the north-eastern and southern regions as well.

25 The economic reasoning is as follows. When goods prices (P_n) are assumed equal at national level, and fixed with a mark-up $(1 + \lambda)$ differentiated regionally (r) on the cost of labour per unit of output (w_r / π_r), they become:

$$P_n = (1 + \lambda)_r (w_r / \pi_r) \qquad (8.1n)$$

where w denotes wages and π productivity. On rearranging elements in (8.1n), a regional locational advantage, indicated by a positive gross profit rate (λ), is obtained in regions where:

$$\pi_r > (w_r / P_n) \qquad (8.2n)$$

and, in relative terms, above-average profit is obtained in regions where:

$$\pi_r / w_r > \pi_n / w_n \qquad (8.3n)$$

For economic treatment see Benedetti and Camagni, 1983; for application to the Italian case see Camagni and Capello, 1990.

26 See Piore and Sabel, 1984.

27 For a quantitative study of industrial districts using municipal-level data see Pietrobelli, 1998. For a methodology based on firm-level data see Rabellotti, 1997; Signorini, 2000.

28 For a critical survey of neo-Schumpeterian theories see Mouleart and Sekia, 2003.

29 The concept of proximity gave rise to a school of thought in France which analysed the relatively greater importance for local development of organizational and cultural proximity compared with geographical proximity. The French school's notion of 'organizational and cultural proximity' and the one proposed here of 'relational proximity' have many features in common. On the French school of the 'economics of proximity' see Bellet *et al.*, 1993; Rallet and Torre, 1998.

30 Wide-ranging empirical studies on innovative activity have been carried out in the UK by the CURDS (Centre for Urban and Regional Development Studies) of the University of Newcastle (see Goddard and Thwaites, 1986; Oakey *et al.*, 1980) and by the SPRU (Science Policy Research Unit) of the University of Sussex (see Clark, 1971); in the USA by Malecki (see Malecki and Varaiya, 1986); and more recently also in Italy (see Breschi, 2000; Paci and Usai, 2000). Studies on the concentrated location of high-tech firms have been conducted by Keeble on the UK, Sternberg on Germany, Ciciotti on Italy, Decoster and Tabariés on France, Malecki on the USA, Frenkel on Israel, and Maggioni on a group of OECD countries. See Keeble, 1990; Sternberg, 1996; Ciciotti, 1982; Decoster and Tabariés, 1986; Frenkel, 2001; Maggioni, 2002. For detailed studies on the role of innovation in regional development see e.g. Cappellin and Nijkamp, 1990; Ewers and Allesch, 1990; de Groot *et al.*, 2004. For a recent theoretical and empirical analysis of spatial spillovers see Maier and Sedlacek, 2005.

31 Among the numerous empirical studies on knowledge spillovers, to be mentioned in particular are the seminal work by Jaffe, 1989, which was followed by other studies: Acs *et al.*, 1994, who examined the differing abilities of small and large firms to exploit knowledge spillovers; Audretsch and Feldman, 1996 and Feldman and Audretsch, 1999, who distinguished between scientifically diversified and specialized spillovers; and Anselin *et al.*, 2000, who defined the distance beyond which spillover effects disappear. For a recent critical review of the role of knowledge spillovers in regional development see de Groot *et al.*, 2001.

32 Given expenditure on research and development as the input to innovative activity (*R&D*) and the number of patents (*B*) as the output, the knowledge production function shows the quantity of innovative input required to obtain a certain amount of innovative output:

$$B = f(R\&D) \tag{8.4n}$$

Recent econometric tests have shown the existence of a certain simultaneity between *R&D* and patents. This evidences that applications for patents tend to be made very early on in the innovative process and are consequently less indicative of a capacity to produce innovative output.

33 More refined methods, such as the inclusion of 'lagged' variables taking different values according to the geographical distance between the areas analysed, have recently been used. The results of the analysis do not change: they confirm the existence of technological spillovers through the greater significance of university expenditure on R&D for the innovative capacity of areas geographically closer to where the university is located, finding that 50 miles is the distance beyond which spillover effects disappear.

34 See Chapter 4, 'The spatial diffusion of innovation'.

35 The reference is to studies conducted by GREMI, Groupe de Recherche Européen sur les Milieux Innovateurs, headquartered in Paris, whose members were scholars from all the European countries. The group's research results were set out in a series of publications,

most notably Aydalot, 1986; Aydalot and Keeble, 1988; Camagni, 1991; Maillat *et al.*, 1993; Ratti *et al.*, 1997; RERU, 1999.

36 It should be stressed that 'the concept of "innovative milieu" is necessarily abstract; the milieu must be considered an economic and territorial archetype more than an empirical reality. Its conceptualisation in economic terms enables us to generalise some recent empirical findings showing the importance of relational assets in the success of some specific areas, and to find an economic rationale for the manner in which they support innovative processes. The characteristics of the innovative milieu are never fully realised in real territorial systems, however. The relationship between the presence of these characteristics and the innovative outcome has been verified in some empirical cases, and it is above all theoretically justified. But it can never be considered a precondition, either necessary or sufficient, for innovation; it is only an element which increases the probability of an innovative outcome.' Camagni and Capello, 2002, p. 17.

37 See Bellet *et al.*, 1993; Storper, 1995.

38 See Camagni and Capello, 2002, p. 18.

39 The concept of relational capital is similar to that of social capital developed by Putnam (see Putnam, 1993). It has been argued that the main difference between the two concepts is that social capital exists wherever a local society exists, while relational capital consists in the (rare) ability of actors to inter-relate their different skills, interact with each other, trust each other, and cooperate even at a distance with other complementary organizations. See Camagni, 2001.

40 Since the concept of collective learning was first formulated by the GREMI group (see Camagni, 1991), it has been used by numerous other authors. See Capello, 1999a; Keeble and Wilkinson, 1999, 2000; Lawson and Lorenz, 1999. On the concept of cognitive dimension of agglomeration economies, see Cappellin, 2003.

41 See Camagni, 1991.

42 This recalls the theory of the Marshallian industrial district and the role performed by social and cultural homogeneity in producing forms of transaction regulation which deter opportunistic behaviour. See Camagni and Rabellotti, 1997; Arrighetti *et al.*, 2001.

43 For details on the methodology used see Capello, 1999b. After this pioneering study, subsequent analyses have also examined the effect of collective learning and the local atmosphere on the innovative activity of firms.

44 Romer's and Lucas's theories are set out in Chapter 10. For 'stylization' of the *milieu innovateur* theory within a neoclassical endogenous growth framework see Capello, 2002b.

45 For the main studies produced by the Danish school see Lundvall, 1992; Lundvall and Johnson, 1994; Asheim, 1996; Maskell and Malmberg, 1999; Edquist, 1997; Malmberg and Maskell, 2002. For studies produced in Britain and North America see Cooke and Morgan, 1994; Morgan, 1997; Boekema *et al.*, 1997; Cooke, 2002. The importance of institutional factors for local growth is now so widely recognized that creating institutional performance indicators for inclusion in macroeconometric growth models is considered to be essential. See Stimson *et al.*, 2005.

46 See Amin and Thrift, 1994. The term 'institution' should of course be understood in the sense given to it by North's and Williamson's institutional economics, namely as a set of societal norms and 'rules of the game' (North, 1990, p. 3). See on this also WIlliamson, 2002.

47 'Institutions are here defined as the sets of habits, routines, norms and laws that regulate the relations between people and thus shape human interaction and learning': Lundvall and Johnson, 1994, p. 33.

48 This definition of 'learning region' has obvious links with the theories already described in this chapter. The concept of 'organized market' recalls that of 'community market' developed – much more convincingly and in richer form – by industrial district theory: social rules and norms regulate the market, making it more efficient and dynamic. The difference between

the 'community' market and the 'organized' market resides in their outcomes: the former generates the factors which determine the coexistence and positive interaction between forms of cooperation and competition; the latter generates a dynamic process of interactive learning. Moreover, the theory of learning regions resembles that of the *milieu innovateur* when it emphasizes the importance of the 'destructive' learning which enables a region to abandon an obsolete technological trajectory. The *milieu innovateur* theory, too, stresses the importance for the local system's dynamic of avoiding 'lock-in' to knowledge that may become, like rules and norms of behaviour, 'barriers to exit' if the *milieu* must rapidly shift to a new technological trajectory. See Bianchi and Miller, 1993.

49 Lundvall and Johnson point out that 'learning economy refers not only to the importance of the scientific and technology system – universities, research organisations, in-house R&D departments and so on – but also to the learning implications of the economic structure, the organisational forms and the institutional set-up': Lundvall and Johnson, 1994, p. 26.

50 On the debate concerning whether the concept of 'national innovation system' can be used to derive a 'regional' version in the form of a 'regional innovation system' see Howells, 1999; Fritsch, 2001; Acs *et al.*, 2000.

51 When commenting on Lösch and Christaller's theories, Beguin observes that 'un bon réseau urbain hiérarchisé peut contribuer à favoriser un développement régional équilibré' (a good hierarchical urban network can contribute to favouring a balanced regional development): Beguin, 1988, p. 242.

52 The official document on the 'European Spatial Development Plan' (ESDP) presented to the European Council of Ministers at Noordwijk in 1997, subsequently supplemented at the meeting of ministers held in Glasgow in June 1998, and definitively approved at Potsdam in June 1999, stresses the importance of an efficient urban system for regional development: 'The development of Europe's cities and the relations between them constitutes the most significant factor affecting the spatial balance of the territory of Europe': ESDP, 1998, p. 47. Again, 'regions as a whole can become competitive only if their towns and cities are motors of economic growth': ibid., p. 51.

53 As early as 1961, Chinitz stressed that cities with more competitive and diversified structures furnishing externalities for small firms have greater growth potential than cities with oligopolized and specialized structures in which the 'internalizing' of service functions by large firms impoverishes the urban environment. See Chinitz, 1961.

54 The pioneering studies by Vernon and Hoover and Vernon in the USA on the concentration of small and medium-sized firms in the heart of cities provided clear evidence of the 'incubator role' performed by cities. See Vernon, 1960; Hoover and Vernon, 1962.

55 On the concept of urban *milieu* see Camagni, 1999b. For empirical evidence on the existence of '*milieu* effects' in five European metropolises, Amsterdam, Milan, Paris, London and Stuttgart, see Capello, 2001.

56 See Chapter 3.

9 TERRITORIAL COMPETITIVENESS AND CUMULATIVE DEMAND/ SUPPLY GROWTH

1 Linear equations (or systems) are equations (or systems) in which the variables are raised to the power one, and in which there are no products of different variables. Higher-level equations (systems) are equations (systems) which comprise terms as the product of two variables (yx) or of variables with superscripts (y^2, y^3, etc.).

2 The increasing returns hypothesis entails that firms have surplus productive capacity to exploit when the market expands. In other words, as the market expands, firms are able to increase their output, moving along the decreasing cost curve and obtaining increasing returns. Perfect competition instead hypothesizes that firms produce in conditions of minimum average cost.

3 Dixit and Stiglitz produced the first formalized model of imperfect competition *à la* Chamberlin. All the models which introduce increasing returns into growth paths presented in this chapter are based on Dixit and Stiglitz's original formulation. See Dixit and Stiglitz, 1977. For surveys of the literature on non-linear dynamic models applied to the dynamic of territorial systems see, among others, Barentsen and Nijkamp, 1989; Nijkamp and Reggiani, 1988, 1992, 1993; Lung, 1987; Reggiani, 2000; Wilson, 1981.

4 See Von Böventer, 1975, p. 3.

5 Some seminal ideas in Myrdal's theory had already been propounded by Young. See Young, 1928.

6 Given that it has been decided here to address these new theories from within a strictly economic framework, the treatment that follows will often use graphical tools, without excessively encumbering itself with mathematics. References will be provided to the specific literature for mathematical aspects.

7 Catastrophe theory originated in a work published in 1972 by the French mathematician, René Thom. It consists in a mathematical account of morphogenesis, or the formation of a system's structure. Like bifurcation theory, it analyses non-linear dynamic systems characterized by multiple equilibria in which the passage from one equilibrium to another may be triggered by a sudden and slight variation in the parameters determining the system's dynamic. See Thom, 1972.

8 A 'stable dynamic equilibrium' exists when, although the system may have been distanced by an external force from a certain value of the unknown variable, for instance $y*$, it is able to return to that value. In this case, $y*$ is also called the 'attractor' of the time path, or of y's trajectory. In the contrary case, it is called the 'repulsor' and the equilibrium is termed an 'unstable dynamic equilibrium'.

9 In the case of non-linear models, the difference between a locally stable equilibrium point and a globally stable equilibrium point is emphasized. A point $y*$ is said to be of locally stable equilibrium if it is possible to define at will a small neighbourhood of $y*$ such that, for initial conditions within the interval, the function $y(t)$ tends to $y*$ for $t \rightarrow \infty$. A point $y*$ is instead called globally stable if the function $y(t)$ tends to $y*$ for $t \rightarrow \infty$ for every initial condition of y. See Barentsen and Nijkamp, 1989.

10 See Miyao, 1987b.

11 The stability of the equilibrium can be straightforwardly verified by using a 'phase diagram': that is, by setting the value of the variable (the population in the case of Figure 9.1) respectively at time t and $t - 1$ on the two axes. If the function is positively sloped, as it is in the present case, there is a stable dynamic equilibrium if the slope is below 1 (see also Figure 9.2.a), and an unstable dynamic equilibrium if the slope is above 1 (Figure 9.2.b). The former case is that of growth at decreasing rates in the variable over time (slope below 1); the latter case is that of growth at increasing rates (slope above 1). If the function is negatively sloped it depicts an equilibrium reached in oscillatory and convergent manner if the slope is below 1 (Figure 9.2.c), and in oscillatory and divergent manner if the slope is above 1 (Figure 9.2.d).

12 We saw in Chapter 6 that convergence is an inevitable result of the one-sector neoclassical model if the growth rates of regions are assumed to be initially different. This result troubled the authors of the model because it was not confirmed by empirical evidence. Using the mathematical tools of the time, Burns and Stein managed to prove divergence with the two-sector model, on the hypothesis of initially equal growth rates among regions. There matters stood until the 1980s, when the neoclassicals were able – by introducing non-linearity into the original model – to prove divergence for certain parameter values even on the assumption of different initial rates of growth. See Chapter 10.

13 See Myrdal, 1957.

14 Young had previously suggested the importance of increasing returns for the development of an economic system. See Young, 1928. In the same period of Myrdal, Perroux stressed, within a microeconomic framework, the importance of agglomeration economies for local development.

15 See Myrdal, 1957, chapter 3.

16 See Kaldor, 1970. A study on a convergent or divergent development of Kaldor's model is contained in Dixon and Thirlwall, 1975.

17 The influence of the export-base theory is evident here.

18 In an article published in 1949, Verdoorn demonstrated empirically, using a typically Smithian approach, the existence of a relationship between the size of the market and productivity gains, and a positive relationship between the rates of output growth and productivity growth. See Verdoorn, 1949. Empirical verification of Verdoorn's Law is still a matter of much controversy. The first empirical tests conducted by Kaldor were criticized for assuming an endogenous relationship between the dependent variable (productivity) and the independent variable (employment), the reason being that the latter is by definition at the denominator of the productivity index. See Rowthorn, 1975. Kaldor rebutted these criticisms with empirical proof that the relationship between the output growth rate (in its turn correlated with the employment growth rate) and the productivity growth rate does not hold in some sectors, in particular agriculture and trade. The debate is still animated today. See Kaldor, 1975; Thirlwall, 1983. For empirical tests of Verdoorn's Law see Leon-Ledesma, 1998, for Spain; McCombie and De Ridder, 1984, for the United States; Rid and Lau, 1998, for the UK; Soro, 2003, for Italy.

19 The presence of a constant d, which explains the exogenous growth of productivity independently of output, can resolve the dispute among regional economists on whether it is the output growth rate that determines the productivity growth rate, as Verdoorn's Law postulates, or conversely whether it is the productivity growth rate that determines the output growth rate. An empirical test of Verdoorn's Law for the Italian regions has shown that the independent component of productivity not explained by the output growth rate accounts for the largest share of the overall growth of productivity. See Soro, 2003.

20 The presence of relatively more export-oriented sectors and of less import-dependent sectors facilitates the onset of virtuous development circles – as was seen earlier (in strictly Keynesian terms) in the case of Thirlwall's Law. With respect to the latter, however, in Myrdal and Kaldor's model development depends on other elements, such as the competitiveness of the local system expressed in the growth rates of wages and domestic prices, and increasing returns: these are entirely absent from Thirlwall's Law.

21 Although these considerations had already been put forward by Richardson, it was Miyao who introduced non-linearity into the structural relations conceived by Kaldor. See Richardson, 1978, p. 148; Miyao, 1984.

22 In 1991 Krugman wrote: 'I could have entitled this book "Location and Trade". I was afraid, however, that this would convey too narrow an idea of what I was trying to say. Although the intellectual tradition of location theory is both wide and deep, what is thought is usually a very narrow set of geometric tricks involving triangles and hexagons (. . .). "Location" seemed too restrictive a term for this field. Location theory, however, is part of a much broader field, that of economic geography' (Krugman, 1991a, pp. x–xi). For criticism of Krugman's claimed independence from regional economics see Martin, 1999. See Gans and Shepherd, 1994, for a well-known critique of Krugman's studies: 'it's obvious, it's wrong and anyway they said it years ago'.

23 The theoretical underpinning of these models is Dixit and Stiglitz's model of monopolistic competition. See Dixit and Stiglitz, 1977.

24 Krugman's interest in analysing the location of productive activities stems from a simple observation: the dense concentration of manufacturing activity in the so-called 'manufacturing

belt' of the north-eastern United States, which, according to an estimate by Perloff and colleagues, in 1957 already accounted for 64 per cent of manufacturing employment in the country. See Krugman, 1991a; Perloff *et al.*, 1960.

25 Krugman regards pecuniary externalities as the great merit of his model. Defined as the externalities (or advantages) that arise from trade, pecuniary externalities can be easily quantified by variations in profit; for this reason they are more readily identifiable than technological externalities, which are generated by proximity among firms and are difficult to quantify and model. See Krugman, 1991b. I would suggest, however, that precisely because pecuniary externalities are tied to market relations, they may arise independently of geographical, social and cultural proximity among firms, impoverishing the role of territorial factors in the determination of local advantages. See Chapter 8 in this book. See Krugman, 1991a, p. 15; Fujita and Thisse, 1996, 2002.

26 See e.g. Faini, 1984; Venables, 1996; Baldwin, 1998; Baldwin *et al.*, 1999; Martin and Ottaviano, 1999; Ottaviano and Puga, 1998; Ottaviano and Thisse, 2001; Krugman and Venables, 1996.

27 The term 'centre-periphery' denotes the geographic dichotomy between an area in growth (the centre) and one in decline (the periphery) generated by the model under certain conditions.

28 Increasing returns to scale are formalized by hypothesizing that the good is produced at a fixed cost:

$$L_M = \alpha + \beta x_M \qquad (9.1n)$$

where L_M is the quantity of workers necessary to produce the variety M of a generic manufacturing good, α the fixed share of workers, x_M the quantity of the manufacturing good M produced, and β the share of workers proportional to the quantity produced. The consequence of this hypothesis is that each firm produces one and only one variety in equilibrium.

29 Consumer interest in the variety of the good – that is, the notion that consumers obtain greater utility, the quantity consumed remaining equal, the larger the number of varieties of the differentiated good available – is formalized by means of the following utility function:

$$U = x_M^{\pi} x_A^{(1-\pi)} \qquad (9.2n)$$

This states that an individual's well-being depends on possession of both the agricultural good (x_A) and the composite industrial good (x_M). π represents the share of spending on products from the manufacturing sector, and its complement to one $(1 - \pi)$ is the share of spending on the agricultural good. The quantity consumed of the composite industrial good x_M is a function of the consumption of individual industrial goods:

$$x_M = \left(\sum_{M=1}^{m} x_i^q \right)^{1/q} \qquad (9.3n)$$

m represents the varieties available, of which there exist a large number, although not all of them are produced, and q the intensity of the 'preference for variety'. When the value of q is close to 1, the manufactured goods are almost perfect substitutes for each other. Conversely, if q tends to 0, the desire of individuals to consume a wide variety of goods is very high, with the consequence that the value of x_M is high as well. Setting $\sigma = 1/(1 - q)$, this is substitution elasticity between two different varieties of manufactures, and equation (9.3n) becomes:

$$x_M = \left(\sum_{M=1}^{m} x_i^{\frac{\sigma-1}{\sigma}} \right)^{\frac{\sigma}{\sigma-1}} \tag{9.4n}$$

30 'Iceberg' transport costs were formally introduced by Samuelson in 1954. But Von Thünen had hypothesized costs of this kind as early as 1826 when he stated that the transportation cost of grain could be identified in the quantity of the grain consumed by the horses used to transport it. See Samuelson, 1954; Von Thünen, 1826. Formalization of this hypothesis is straightforward: if for each unit of a good transported from one region to another, only a fraction $\tau < 1$ arrives at the destination, then in order to transport one unit of the good from one region to another, a quantity $1 + \frac{1}{4}$ must be shipped. $\frac{1}{4}$ denotes the transportation costs incurred by the firm in order to transport the good from one region to another; τ represents the fourth parameter influencing the growth processes of the two regions.
31 Interestingly, if the model does not hypothesize increasing returns, the agglomeration process immediately meets an obstacle: the non-existence of extra profits, which renders the relocation unprofitable, so that the process is blocked at the outset.
32 The formalized version of the model defines the individual demand curve through maximization of the individual's utility (equation 9.2n), given the budget constraint and assuming that all individuals have the same utility functions. Straightforwardly obtained from the individual demand curves is the market curve of a typical variety produced in the region:

$$p = x_M^{-1/\sigma} P(n, \tau)^{1-(1/\sigma)}(A + L)^{1/\sigma} \tag{9.5n}$$

where p represents the price of the variety produced (assumed equal for all varieties), x_M the quantity of the generic variety M required by the market, P the price index, σ substitution elasticity between two different varieties of manufactures, τ the transportation costs, n the number of firms present in the market, and $(A + L)$ the number of residents and therefore the size of the local market. p is therefore a function of the elasticity of demand among the varieties produced, the number of firms in the area, the transportation costs, and the demand for labour, which depends on the fixed cost at which the firm produces the variety of the good.

Given the market demand curve of the variety of the good, the firm fixes the quantity and sale price of the variety of the good on the basis of its marginal costs, the purpose being to maximize its profit. The arrival of a new firm in the area alters the equilibrium reached by each firm. Market demand for each firm on the one hand diminishes because of the fall in prices due to greater competition, but on the other hand increases because of the expansion of the market. Which of the two effects will prevail depends on the values of the other parameters, which represent the elasticity of demand among the varieties produced, the demand for labour (which determines the number of firms in the area), the transportation costs, and the substitution elasticity among the goods produced by the manufacturing firms.
33 See Blanchard and Katz, 1992, for an empirical analysis of the United States; and Decressin and Fatàs, 1995, for an analysis of Europe.
34 See Venables, 1996.
35 See Fujita et al., 1999.
36 As said, apart from attempts (some very successful) to model location choices in imperfect competition, for example by Hotelling and Lösch, the tendency in regional economics has been to use more easily formalized models with perfect competition, and to assume increasing returns external to the firm (localization or urbanization economies). In one of his articles, Krugman himself has summarized the innovative elements of the 'new economic geography' as these: increasing returns in an imperfect competition model à la Dixit and

Stiglitz, transportation costs *à la* Samuelson, multiple equilibria, and numerical simulation for empirical analysis. See Krugman, 1998b.

37 See Dosi, 1982; Dosi *et al.*, 1988; David, 1985; Arthur, 1989, 1990.

38 In a subsequent refinement of their model, Krugman and Venables furnish an explanation for the tendency of local economies to specialize (an aspect hitherto not included in the formalization); on their approach, specialization results from the circular causality mechanism operating in input/output relationships among local firms. The difference with respect to Venables' model presented above is that the advantages generated by a new firm in the market are selective: they accrue solely to the firms of the sector in which the new entrant operates, while the greater competition on the final goods and labour markets impoverishes all the firms in the area. The region is thus induced to specialize in the sector that enjoys agglomeration advantages. See Krugman and Venables, 1996; Venables, 1996.

39 It is important to note that the 'new economic geography' has become an important topic in the most recent handbooks on the economics of international trade. See Feenstra, 2003.

40 See Krugman, 1991c.

10 TERRITORIAL COMPETITIVENESS AND ENDOGENOUS GROWTH

1 Numerous endogenous growth models have been propounded: among the best known of them are Romer, 1986, 1987, 1990; Lucas, 1988; Barro, 1990; Rebelo, 1991; Grossman and Helpman, 1991; Aghion and Howitt, 1992.

2 For the mathematical steps see note 6, Chapter 6.

3 When estimating equation (10.3) for the economy of the United States, Solow found that more than 40 per cent of US growth between 1900 and 1949 was due to a factor (the 'residual' as he termed it) different from factor growth. This he called 'technical progress'.

4 Romer has written that it was the statistically non-significant and non-robust (or at any rate equivocal) results of regression analyses on the initial income and growth levels of countries that stimulated his interest in formulating a new model of growth. Romer, 1994, p. 4.

5 These models in fact pursue an even more complex goal, which stems from their profoundly neoclassical nature. They embrace the idea of rational and optimizing behaviour by economic actors who choose a temporal consumption path that enables them to optimize an intertemporal utility function while respecting a dynamic constraint of capital stock growth per unit of product constant in time. They are therefore models which explain aggregate macroeconomic growth on the basis of microeconomic behaviour. To this end they draw on Ramsey's model of intertemporal consumption as subsequently applied to growth models by Cass and Koopmans. See Ramsey, 1928; Cass, 1965; Koopmans, 1965.

6 See Aghion and Howitt, 1997 and Solow, 2000, among others, for comprehensive surveys of the theoretical and empirical issues raised by modern growth theory. On investment cumulated in physical capital and the consequent increase over time in 'technological capacities' see Romer, 1986; on the impact at aggregate level of investment by individual firms which generates a positive externality (and increasing returns to scale) at aggregate level, see Romer, 1989; on the constancy of the marginal return on capital if this includes all the accumulable factors, among them 'human capital', see Rebelo, 1991, or private and public goods, see Barro, 1990; on investment in human capital, scientific and technical knowledge which improves the physical productivity of labour, see Lucas, 1988; finally, on investment in R&D to foster the technological innovation that enhances the physical productivity of all the factors, i.e. the creation of intermediate and final goods with higher value added, see Romer, 1990; Aghion and Howitt, 1992; Grossman and Helpman, 1991.

7 For the theory of the *milieu innovateur* see Chapter 8.

8 See Romer, 1986. The model's logic closely resembles that of the theory of knowledge spillovers, which here undergoes economic modelling. See Chapter 8.

9 In other models this role is performed by public capital (e.g. infrastructures) or by other public goods: see Barro, 1990; Rebelo, 1991. However, the mechanism of growth endogenization remains the same: the public goods enter the aggregate production function as externalities and convert the decreasing returns to the individual production factors into constant or increasing returns at aggregate level.

10 See Lucas, 1988, pp. 17–27. Lucas drew on Uzawa, 1964.

11 In a second model, Lucas hypothesizes that knowledge is accumulated through experience: 'learning by doing'. See Lucas, 1988, pp. 27–31.

12 Although this latter hypothesis is essential for determining the endogenous growth mechanism, it has major implications: it entails, in fact, that a country's initial conditions do not influence the growth of its economy. This is obviously a highly unrealistic hypothesis.

13 (10.9) can be easily rewritten as:

$$\frac{h_t}{H_t} = \varphi\,(1 - u_t)$$

(10.1n)

where the left-hand member is the rate of growth of human capital over time.

14 For a regional approach to the theory of endogenous growth see Nijkamp et al., 1998 (special issue of Annals of Regional Science), Nijkamp and Poot, 1998; Button and Pentecost, 1999.

15 The first time series and cross-section analyses of convergence or divergence among regions used a methodology known as 'σ-convergence' which measured the standard deviation in the distribution of income among regions or countries: if the standard deviation decreases, this indicates convergence (called 'strong' convergence) among the growth rates of regions and countries. A subsequent widely-used methodology, which has examined 'β-convergence' or 'weak' or 'absolute' convergence, does not measure the standard deviation in the distribution of income among regions but rather the slope of a linear regression line connecting the rates of income growth in the high-income regions in the initial period: a negative slope indicates a higher growth rate in countries or regions with lower levels of income, and vice versa. In other words, this result confirms the hypotheses of Solow's model, which predicts convergence among the growth rates of countries because the decreasing productivity of the factors entails that, in advanced countries with higher levels of per capita capital, the productivity of capital is less than it is in the backward countries. The latter therefore inevitably record higher levels of accumulation and development. See Solow, 1957. For empirical studies on convergence and divergence see, among many others, Baumol, 1986; Chatterji, 1994; Mankin et al., 1992; Romer, 1994; Barro and Sala-i-Martin, 1995; and among regions, Sala-i-Martin, 1996; Cuadrado-Roura and Parellada, 2002; Rodrìguez-Pose and Fratesi, 2004; Magrini, 1997; Pompili, 1992; Terrasi, 2002. For a critical survey of methods used to measure regional disparities see Magrini, 2004; for a survey of empirical results see Abreu et al., 2005.

16 See Chapter 6.

17 The steady-state equilibrium curves (i.e. the constant growth trajectories of the production factors) are obtained by imposing nil variation in the growth rates. They are expressed by the following equations, the first obtained by setting $k = 0$ and the second by setting $l = 0$:

$$K = \left(\frac{s + \mu\,L}{i_m\,\mu}\right)^{\frac{1}{1-\alpha}} L^{\frac{1-\alpha+\beta}{1-\alpha}}$$

(10.2n)

$$K = \left(\frac{w_m\,\lambda - n}{\lambda\,(1 - \alpha)}\right)^{\frac{1}{\alpha}} L^{\frac{\alpha-\beta}{\alpha}}$$

(10.3n)

For the mathematical solution see note 7, Chapter 6.

18 See Rabenau, 1979; Miyao, 1984.

19 This happens for high initial values of K/L, external to the *aoc* area in Figure 10.2a, and on the condition that:

$$\left(\frac{s + \mu L}{i_m \mu}\right) > \left(\frac{w_m \lambda - n}{\lambda (1 - \alpha)}\right) \qquad (10.4n)$$

See Rabenau, 1979; Miyao, 1984.

Bibliographical references

Abernathy, W. and Utterback, J. (1978) 'Patterns of industrial innovation', *Technology Review*, June, pp. 121–33.

Abreu, M., de Groot, H. L. F. and Florax, R. (2005) 'A meta-analysis of β-convergence: the legendary 2%', *Journal of Economic Surveys*, vol. 19, no. 3, pp. 389–420.

Ackley, G. and Spaventa, L. (1962) 'Emigrazione e industrializzazione nel Mezzogiorno', *Moneta e Credito*, vol. 15, no. 58, pp. 144–59.

Acs, Z., Audretsch, D. and Feldman, M. (1994) 'R&D spillovers and recipient firm size', *Review of Economics and Statistics*, vol. 76, pp. 336–40.

Acs, Z., de la Mothe, J. and Paquet, G. (2000) 'Regional innovation: in search of an enabling strategy', in Acs, Z. (ed.), *Regional innovation, knowledge and global change*, London: Pinter, pp. 37–52.

Aghion, P. and Howitt, P. (1992) 'A model of growth through creative destruction', *Econometrica*, vol. 60, no. 2, pp. 323–51.

Aghion, P. and Howitt, P. (1997) *Endogenous growth theory*, Cambridge, Mass.: MIT Press.

Allen, K. J. (1969) 'The regional multiplier: some problems in estimation', in Cullingworth, J. B. and Orr, S. C. (eds), *Regional and urban studies: a social science approach*, London: Allen & Unwin, pp. 80–96.

Alonso, W. (1960) 'A theory of the urban land market', *Papers and Proceedings of the Regional Science Association*, no. 6, pp. 149–57.

Alonso, W. (1964a) 'Location theory', in Friedmann, J. and Alonso, W. (eds), *Regional development and planning: a reader*, Cambridge, Mass.: MIT Press, pp. 78–106.

Alonso, W. (1964b) *Location and land use: towards a general theory of land rent*, Cambridge, Mass.: Harvard University Press.

Alonso, W. (1971) 'The economics of urban size', *Papers and Proceedings of the Regional Science Association*, pp. 67–83.

Amin, A. and Thrift, N. (eds) (1994) *Globalisation, institutions, and regional development in Europe*, Oxford: Oxford University Press.

Amin, A. and Wilkinson, F. (eds) (1999) 'Learning, proximity and industrial performance: an introduction', *Cambridge Journal of Economics*, vol. 23, no. 2, pp. 121–5.

295

Anas, A. and Dendrinos, D. (1976) 'The New Urban Economics: a brief survey', in Papageourgiou, Y. Y. (ed.), *Mathematical land use theory*, Lexington, Mass.: Lexington Books, pp. 23–51.

Andrews, R. (1953) 'Mechanics of the urban economic base', *Land Economics*, vol. 29, no. 2, pp. 161–7.

Andrews, R. (1954) 'Measuring the urban economic base', *Land Economics*, November, pp. 52–60.

Anselin, L., Varga, A. and Acs, Z. (2000) 'Geographic and sectoral characteristics of academic knowledge externalities', *Papers in Regional Science*, vol. 79, no. 4, pp. 435–43.

Archibald, G. (1967) 'Regional multiplier effects in the United Kingdom', *Oxford Economic Papers*, vol. 19, pp. 22–45.

Armstrong, H. and Taylor, J. (2000) *Regional economics and policy*, Oxford: Blackwell.

Arrighetti, A., Serravalli, G. and Wolleb, G. (2001) *Social capital, institutions and collective action between firms*, Paper presented at the EURESCO Conference 'Social Capital: Interdisciplinary Perspectives', Exeter, 15–20 September.

Arthur, W. B. (1989) 'Competing technologies, increasing returns and lock-in by historical events', *The Economic Journal*, vol. 99, pp. 116–33.

Arthur, W. B. (1990) 'Silicon Valley's location clusters: when do increasing returns imply monopoly?', *Mathematical Social Sciences*, vol. 19, pp. 235–51.

Aschauer, D. A. (1989) 'Is public expenditure productive?', *Journal of Monetary Economics*, vol. 23, pp. 177–200.

Aschauer, D. A. (1990) 'Why is infrastructure important?', in Munnell, A. H. (ed.), *Is there a shortfall in public capital investment?* Proceedings of a Conference Sponsored by the Federal Bank of Boston, Federal Reserve Bank of Boston, Boston.

Asheim, B. (1996) 'Industrial districts as "Learning Regions": a condition for prosperity?', *European Planning Studies*, vol. 4, no. 4, pp. 379–400.

Audretsch, D. and Feldman, M. (1996) 'R&D spillovers and the geography of innovation and production', *American Economic Review*, vol. 86, pp. 630–40.

Aydalot, Ph. (1985) *Economie Régionale et Urbaine*, Paris: Economica.

Aydalot, Ph. (ed.) (1986) *Milieux Innovateurs en Europe*, Paris: GREMI.

Aydalot, Ph. and Keeble, D. (eds) (1988) *High technology industry and innovative environment*, London: Routledge.

Bachtler, J. and Downes, R. (1999) 'Regional policy in the transition countries: a comparative assessment', *European Planning Studies*, vol. 7, no. 6, pp. 793–808.

Bagnasco, A. (1977) *Tre Italie. La problematica territoriale dello sviluppo italiano*, Bologna: Il Mulino.

Bagnasco, A. (1983) 'Il contesto sociale', in Fuà, G. and Zacchia, C. (eds), *Industrializzazione senza fratture*, Bologna: Il Mulino, pp. 149–65.

Bagnasco, A. (1985) 'La costruzione sociale del mercato: strategie d'impresa e esperimenti di scala in Italia', *Stato e Mercato*, no. 13, pp. 9–45.

Bagnasco, A. and Trigilia, C. (1984) *Società e politica nelle aree di piccola impresa: il caso di Bassano*, Venice: Arsenale.

Balassa, B. (1975) 'Trade creation and diversion in the European Common Market: an appraisal of the evidence', in Balassa, B. (ed.), *European economic integration*, Amsterdam: North-Holland, pp. 79–118.

296

Baldwin, R. E. (1998) 'Agglomeration and endogenous capital', Discussion Paper CEPR, London.

Baldwin, R. E., Braconier, H. and Forslid, R. (1999) 'Multinationals, endogenous growth and technological spillovers: theory and evidence', paper presented at the seminar of the Research Institute of Industrial Economics (IUI) on *Multinational production, international mergers and welfare effects in a small open economy*, held in Stockholm, June.

Banister, D. (1998) 'Barriers to implementation of urban sustainability', *International Journal of Environment and Pollution*, vol. 10, no. 1, pp. 65–83.

Barentsen, W. and Nijkamp, P. (1989) 'Modelling non-linear processes in time and space', in Andersson, Å., Batten, D., Johansson, B. and Nijkamp, P. (eds), *Advances in spatial theory and dynamics*, Amsterdam: North-Holland, pp. 175–92.

Barker, T. (1977) 'International trade and economic growth: an alternative to the neoclassical approach', *Cambridge Journal of Economics*, no. 1, pp. 153–72.

Barro, R. J. (1990) 'Government spending in a simple model of endogenous growth', *Journal of Political Economy*, vol. 98, no. 5, pp. S103–S125.

Barro, R. J. and Sala-i-Martin, X. (1995) *Economic growth*, New York: McGraw-Hill.

Batten, D. (1995) 'Network cities: creative urban agglomerations for the 21st century', *Urban Studies*, vol. 32, no. 2, pp. 313–28.

Baumol, W. J. (1986) 'Productivity growth, convergence and welfare: what the long run data show', *American Economic Review*, vol. 76, pp. 1072–85.

Becattini, G. (ed.) (1975) *Lo sviluppo economico della Toscana con particolare riguardo all'industrializzazione leggera*, Florence: Guaraldi.

Becattini, G. (1979) 'Dal settore industriale al distretto industriale. Alcune considerazioni sull'unità di indagine dell'economia industriale', *Rivista di Economia e Politica Industriale*, no. 1, pp. 35–48; English edn (1989) 'Sectors and/or districts: some remarks on the conceptual foundations of industrial economics', in Goodman, E. and Bamford, J. (eds), *Small firms and industrial districts in Italy*, London: Routledge, pp. 123–35.

Becattini, G. (ed.) (1987) *Mercato e forze locali: il distretto industriale*, Bologna: Il Mulino.

Becattini, G. (1990) 'The Marshallian Industrial District as a socio-economic notion', in Pyke, F., Becattini, G. and Sengenberger, W. (eds), *Industrial districts and interfirm cooperation in Italy*, Geneva: International Institute of Labour Studies, pp. 37–51.

Becattini, G. (ed.) (2004) *Industrial districts: a new approach to industrial change*, Cheltenham: Edward Elgar.

Beckmann, M. J. (1958) 'City hierarchies and the distribution of city sizes', *Economic Development and Cultural Change*, vol. 6, pp. 243–8.

Beckmann, M. J. (1968) *Location theory*, New York: Random House.

Beckmann, M. J. (1969) 'On the distribution of urban rent and residential density', *Journal of Economic Theory*, no. 1, pp. 60–8.

Beckmann, M. J. and McPherson, J. (1970) 'City size distribution in a central place hierarchy: an alternative approach', *Journal of Regional Science*, vol. 10, pp. 25–33.

Beguin, H. (1984) 'The shape of city-size distribution in a central place system', *Environment and Planning A*, vol. 16, pp. 749–58.

Beguin, H. (1988) 'La Région et les lieux centraux', in Ponsard, C. (ed.), *Analyse Economique Spatiale*, Paris: Presse Universitaire de France, pp. 231–75.

Bellandi, M. (1989) 'The industrial district in Marshall', in Goodman, E. and Bamford, J. (eds), *Small firms and industrial districts in Italy*, London: Routledge, pp. 136–52; orig. edn (1982) 'Il distretto industriale in Alfred Marshall', *L'Industria*, no. 3, July–September, pp. 355–75.

Bellet, M., Colletis, G. and Lung, Y. (1993) 'Introduction au numero special sur l'économie de proximitè', *Revue d'Economie Régionale et Urbaine*, no. 3, pp. 357–64.

Benedetti, E. and Camagni, R. (1983) 'Riflessioni sulla periferia', *Economia e Politica Industrialé*, no. 39, pp. 19–37.

Berry, B. and Garrison, W. (1958) 'Recent development of central place theory', *Papers and Proceeding of the Regional Science Association*, no. 4, pp. 107–20.

Bianchi, G. (1994) 'Requiem per la Terza Italia? Sistemi territoriali di piccola impresa e transizione post-industriale', in Garofoli, G. and Mazzoni, R. (eds), *Sistemi produttivi locali: struttura e trasformazione*, Milan: FrancoAngeli, pp. 59–90.

Bianchi, P. and Miller, L. (1993) 'Collective action, strategic behaviour and endogenous growth', Working Papers 160, Economic Department, University of Bologna.

Biehl, D. (1986) *The contribution of infrastructure to regional development*, Regional Policy Division, Brussels: European Community.

Blanchard, O. J. and Katz, L. F. (1992) 'Regional evolutions', *Brookings Papers on Economic Activity*, vol. 1, pp. 1–75.

Blomstrom, M. and Kokko, A. (1988) 'Multinational corporations and spillovers', *Journal of Economic Surveys*, vol. 12, no. 3, pp. 247–77.

Boekema, F., Morgan, K., Bakkers, S. and Rutten, R. (1997) 'Introduction to learning regions: a new issue for analysis?', in Boekema, F., Morgan, K., Bakkers, S. and Rutten, R. (eds), *Knowledge, innovation and economic growth*, Cheltenham: Edward Elgar, pp. 3–16.

Boix, R. (2004) 'Redes de ciudades y externalidades', *Investigaciones Regionales*, no. 4, pp. 5–27.

Borensztein, E., De Gregorio, J. and Lee, J. W. (1998) 'How does foreign direct investment affect economic growth?', *Journal of International Economics*, vol. 45, no. 1, pp. 115–35.

Borts, G. H. (1960) 'The equalisation of returns and regional economic growth', *The American Economic Review*, pp. 319–47; reprinted in McKee, D., Dean, R. and Leahy, W. (eds) (1970) *Regional economics: theory and practice*, New York: The Free Press, pp. 147–76.

Borts, G. H. and Stein, J. L. (1964) *Economic growth in a free market*, New York: Columbia University Press.

Borts, G. H. and Stein, J. L. (1968) 'Regional growth and maturity in the United States: a study of regional structural change', in Needleman, L. (ed.), *Regional analysis*, Harmondsworth: Penguin, pp. 159–97, orig. edn (1962) in *Schweizerische Zeitschrift für Volkswirtschaft und Statistik*, vol. 98, pp. 290–321.

Boudeville, J.-R. (1964) *Les Espaces économiques*, Paris: Presses Unversitaires de France, English edn (1966) *Problems of regional economic planning*, Edinburgh: Edinburgh University Press.

Breschi, S. (2000) 'The geography of innovation: a cross-sector analysis', *Regional Studies*, vol. 34, no. 2, pp. 213–29.

Brown, L. (1981) *Innovation diffusion: a new perspective*, London: Methuen.

Bruinsma, F., Nijkamp, P. and Rietveld, P. (1990) 'Regional economic transformation and social overhead investments', *Series Research Memoranda*, no. 55, Free University of Amsterdam.

298

Brusco, S. (1982) 'The Emilian Model: productive decentralisation and social integration', *Cambridge Journal of Economics*, no. 6, pp. 167–84.

Brusco, S. (1990) 'The idea of the industrial district: its genesis', in Pyke, F., Becattini, G. and Sengenberger, W. (eds), *Industrial districts and interfirm cooperation in Italy*, Geneva: International Institute of Labour Studies, pp. 10–19.

Butler, J., Gaspar, J. M. B. and Jeppesen, E. (1986) 'Telecommunications and regional development in Portugal', *Arbejdsrapport*, vol. 16, Aarhus Universitet.

Button, K. and Pentecost, E. (1999) *Regional economic performance within the European Union*, Cheltenham: Edward Elgar.

Camagni, R. (1982) 'L'Impatto sull'economia Sarda della spesa e dell'investimento turistico in Costa Smeralda', *Quaderni Sardi di Economia*, no. 4, pp. 371–413.

Camagni R. (1985) 'Spatial diffusion of pervasive process innovation', *Papers of the Regional Science Association*, vol. 58, pp. 83–95.

Camagni, R. (1988) 'Functional integration and locational shifts in the new technology industry', in Aydalot, Ph. and Keeble, D. (eds), *High technology industry and innovative environment*, London: Routledge, pp. 48–64.

Camagni, R. (1991) 'Local *milieu*, uncertainty and innovation networks: towards a new dynamic theory of economic space', in Camagni, R. (ed.), *Innovation networks: spatial perspectives*, London: Belhaven-Pinter, pp. 121–44.

Camagni, R. (1992a) *Economia urbana: principi e modelli teorici*, Rome: La Nuova Italia, French edn. (1996) *Economie Urbaine*, Paris: Economica.

Camagni, R. (1992b) 'Development scenarios and policy guidelines for the lagging regions in the 1990s', *Regional Studies*, no. 4, pp. 361–74.

Camagni, R. (1994) 'From city hierarchy to city networks: reflections about an emerging paradigm', in Lakshmanan, T. R. and Nijkamp, P. (eds), *Structure and change in the space economy: Festschrift in honor of Martin Beckmann*, Berlin: Springer Verlag, pp. 66–87.

Camagni, R. (1996) 'Lo sviluppo urbano sostenibile: le ragioni e i fondamenti di un programma di ricerca', in Camagni, R. (a cura di), *Economia e pianificazione della città sostenibile*, Il Mulino, Bologna, pp. 13–52, eng. edn. (1998) 'Sustainable urban development: definition and reasons for a research programme', *International Journal of Environment and Pollution*, vol. 10, pp. 6–26.

Camagni, R. (1999a) *La teoria dello sviluppo regionale*, Padua: Cusl Nuova Vita.

Camagni, R. (1999b) 'The city as a milieu: applying the GREMI approach to urban evolution', *Revue d'Economie Régionale et Urbaine*, no. 3, pp. 591–606.

Camagni, R. (2001) 'Policies for spatial development', in OECD (ed.), *Territorial Outlook*, Paris, pp. 147–69.

Camagni, R. (2002) 'On the concept of territorial competitiveness: sound or misleading?', *Urban Studies*, vol. 39, no. 13, pp. 2395–411.

Camagni, R. and Capello, R. (1990) 'Towards a definition of the manoeuvring space of local development initiatives: Italian success stories of local development – theoretical conditions and practical experiences', in Stöhr, W. (ed.), *Global challenge and local responses*, London: Mansell, pp. 328–53.

Camagni, R. and Capello, R. (1998) 'Indivisibilità e irreversibilità nei processi di adozione delle tecnologie rinnovabili in ambiente urbano', in Boscacci, F. and Senn, L. (eds), *I luoghi della trasformazione e dell'innovazione*, Turin: SEAT, pp. 223–46.

299

Camagni, R. and Capello, R. (2002) 'Milieux innovateurs and collective learning: from concepts to measurement', in Acs, Z., De Groot, H. and Nijkamp, P. (eds), *The emergence of the knowledge economy: a regional perspective*, Berlin: Springer Verlag, pp. 15–45.

Camagni, R. and Capello, R. (2004) 'The city network paradigm: theory and empirical evidence', in Capello, R. and Nijkamp, P. (eds), *Urban dynamics and growth: advances in urban economics*, Amsterdam: Elsevier, pp. 495–529.

Camagni, R. and Pompili, T. (1990) 'Competence, power and waves of urban development in the Italian city system', in Nijkamp, P. (ed.), *Sustainability of urban systems: a cross-national evolutionary analysis of urban innovation*, Aldershot: Avebury, pp. 37–86.

Camagni, R. and Rabellotti, R. (1997) 'Footwear production systems in Italy: a dynamic comparative analysis', in Ratti, R., Bramanti, A. and Gordon, R. (eds), *The dynamics of innovative regions*, Aldershot: Ashgate, pp. 139–64.

Camagni, R., Diappi, L. and Leonardi, G. (1986) 'Urban growth and decline in a hierarchical system: a supply-oriented dynamic approach', *Regional Science and Urban Economics*, vol. 16, pp. 145–60.

Cantwell, J. (1989) *Technological innovation and multinational corporations*, Oxford: Blackwell.

Cantwell, J. and Iammarino, S. (1998) 'MNCs, technological innovation and regional systems in the EU: some evidence in the Italian case', *International Journal of the Economics of Business*, vol. 5, no. 3, pp. 383–408.

Cantwell, J. and Piscitello, L. (2002) 'The location of technological activities of MNCs in European regions: the role of spillovers and local competencies', *Journal of International Management*, vol. 8, pp. 69–96.

Capello, R. (1988) 'La diffusione spaziale dell'innovazione: il caso del servizio telefonico', *Economia e Politica Industriale*, no. 58, pp. 141–75.

Capello, R. (1994) *Spatial economic analysis of telecommunications network externalities*, Aldershot: Avebury.

Capello, R. (1999a) 'Spatial transfer of knowledge in high-technology milieux: learning vs. collective learning processes', *Regional Studies*, vol. 33, no. 4, pp. 353–65.

Capello, R. (1999b) 'A measurement of collective learning effects in Italian high-tech milieux', *Revue d'Economie Régionale et Urbaine*, no. 3, pp. 449–68.

Capello, R. (2000) 'The city-network paradigm: measuring urban network externalities', *Urban Studies*, vol. 37, no. 11, October, pp. 1925–45.

Capello, R. (2001) 'Urban innovation and collective learning: theory and evidence from five metropolitan cities in Europe', in Fischer, M. M. and Froehlich, J. (eds), *Knowledge, complexity and innovation systems*, Berlin, Heidelberg, New York: Springer Verlag, pp. 181–208.

Capello, R. (2002a) 'Urban rent and urban dynamics: the determinants of urban development in Italy', *The Annals of Regional Science*, vol. 36, no. 4, pp. 593–611.

Capello, R. (2002b) 'Apprendimento collettivo e teorie della crescita endogena: una prospettiva territoriale', in Camagni, R. and Capello, R. (eds), *Apprendimento collettivo e competitività territoriale*, Milan: FrancoAngeli Editore, pp. 57–84.

Capello, R. and Spairani, A. (2004) 'The role of collective learning in ICT adoption and use', in De Groot, H., Nijkamp, P. and Stough, R. (eds), *Entrepreneurship and regional economic development: a spatial perspective*, Cheltenham: Edward Elgar, pp. 198–224.

Capello, R., Nijkamp, P. and Pepping, G. (1999) *Sustainable cities and energy policies*, Berlin: Springer Verlag.

300

Cappellin, R. (1980) 'Teorie e modelli dello sviluppo spaziale delle attività di servizio', *Giornale degli Economisti e Annali di Economia*, nos. 3–4, pp. 205–31.

Cappellin, R. (1983) 'Osservazioni sulla distribuzione inter e intraregionale delle attività produttive', in Fuà, G. and Zacchia, C. (eds), *Industrializzazione senza fratture*, Bologna: Il Mulino, pp. 241–71.

Cappellin, R. (2003) 'Territorial knowledge management: towards a metrics of the cognitive dimension of agglomeration economies', *International Journal of Technology Management*, vol. 26, nos. 2–4, pp. 303–25.

Cappellin, R. and Grillenzoni, C. (1983) 'Diffusion and specialisation in the location of service activities in Italy', *Sistemi Urbani*, no. 2, pp. 249–82.

Cappellin, R. and Nijkamp, P. (eds) (1990) *The spatial context of technological development*, Aldershot: Avebury.

Carney, J. (1980) 'Regions in crisis: accumulation, regional problems and crisis formation', in Carney, J., Hudson, R. and Lewis, J. (eds), *Regions in crisis*, London: Croom Helm, pp. 28–59.

Carney, J., Hudson, R. and Lewis, J. (eds) (1980) *Regions in crisis*, London: Croom Helm.

Cass, D. (1965) 'Optimal growth in an aggregative model of capital accumulation', *Review of Economic Studies*, vol. 32, pp. 233–40.

Cecchini, P. (1988) *The European challenge: 1992*, Aldershot: Wildwood House.

Chamberlin, E. H. (1936) *The theory of monopolistic competition*, Cambridge, Mass.: Harvard University Press.

Chatterji, M. (1994) 'Convergence clubs and endogenous growth', *Oxford Review of Economic Policy*, vol. 8, no. 4, pp. 57–69.

Chenery, H. (1962) 'Development policies for Southern Italy', *Quarterly Journal of Economics*, vol. 76, pp. 515–47.

Chenery, H., Clark, P. and Pinna, C. (1953) *The structure and growth of the Italian economy*, U.S. Mutual Security Agency, Special Mission to Italy for Economic Co-operation.

Chinitz, B. (1961) 'Contrast in agglomeration: New York and Pittsburgh', *American Economic Review*, Papers, vol. 51, pp. 279–89.

Christaller, W. (1933) *Die zentralen Orte in Süddeutschland*, Darmstadt: Wissenschaftlische Buchgesellschaft, English edn (1966) *The central places in Southern Germany*, Englewood Cliffs, N.J.: Prentice-Hall.

Ciciotti, E. (1982) 'Differenze regionali nella capacità innovativa', *Politica ed Economia*, no. 3, pp. 42–8.

Ciciotti, E. and Wettmann, R. (1981) 'The mobilisation of indigenous potential', Commission of the European Community, *Internal Documentation on Regional Policy*, no. 10.

Clark, C. (1940) *The conditions of economic progress*, London: Macmillan.

Clark, C. (1945) 'The economic functions of a city in relation to its size', *Econometrica*, vol. 13, no. 2, pp. 97–113.

Clark, N. G. (1971) 'Science, technology and regional economic development', *Research Policy*, no. 1, pp. 296–319.

Cobb, C. W. and Douglas, P. H. (1928) 'A theory of production', *American Economic Review*, vol. 18, no. 1, March, pp. 139–65.

Coehlo, P. and Ghali, M. A. (1971) 'The end of the North–South wage differential', *The American Economic Review*, vol. 61, no. 5, pp. 932–7.

301

Coehlo, P. and Shepherd, J. (1979) 'The impact of regional differences in prices and wages on economic growth: the United States in 1890', *Journal of Economic History*, vol. 39, no. 1, pp. 69–85.

Cooke, Ph. (2002) *Knowledge economies: clusters, learning and cooperative advantage*, London: Routledge.

Cooke, Ph. and Morgan, K. (1994) 'The creative milieu: a regional perspective on innovation', in Dodgson, M. and Rothwell, R. (eds), *The handbook of industrial innovation*, Cheltenham: Edward Elgar, pp. 25–32.

Costa, J., Da Silva, Ellson R. W. and Martin, R. C. (1987) 'Public capital, regional output and development: some empirical evidence', *Journal of Regional Science*, vol. 27, no. 3, pp. 419–35.

Courlet, C. and Pecqueur, B. (1992) 'Les systèmes industriels localisés en France: un nouvel model de développement', in Benko, G. and Lipietz, A. (eds), *Les Régions qui gagnent. Districts et réseaux: les nouveaux paradigmes de la géograqhie économique*, Paris: Presses Universitaires de France, pp. 81–102.

Cuadrado-Roura, J. R. and Parellada, M. (eds) (2002) *Regional convergence in the European Union*, Berlin: Springer Verlag.

Dacey, M. F. (1964) 'A note on some number properties of a hexagonal hierarchical plane lattice', *Journal of Regional Science*, vol. 5, pp. 63–7.

Damette, F. (1980) 'The regional framework of monopoly exploitation: new problems and trends', in Carney, J., Hudson, R. and Lewis, J. (eds), *Regions in crisis*, London: Croom Helm, pp. 76–92.

Davelaar, E. J. (1991) *Regional economic analysis of innovation and incubation*, Aldershot: Avebury.

Davelaar, E. J. and Nijkamp, P. (1990) 'Industrial innovation and spatial systems: the impact of producer services', in Ewers, H. and Allesch, J. (eds), *Innovation and regional development*, Berlin: de Gruyter, pp. 83–122.

David, P. (1985) 'Clio and the economics of qwerty', *AEA Papers and Proceedings*, vol. 75, no. 2, pp. 332–7.

Davies, D. (1979) *The diffusion of process innovations*, Cambridge: Cambridge University Press.

De Groot, H., Nijkamp, P. and Acs, Z. (2001) 'Knowledge spillovers, innovation and regional development', *Papers in Regional Science*, vol. 80, no. 3, special issue.

De Groot, H., Nijkamp, P. and Stough, R. (eds) (2004) *Entrepreneurship and regional economic development: a spatial perspective*, Cheltenham: Edward Elgar.

Decoster, E. and Tabariés, M. (1986) 'L'innovation dans un pôle scientifique et technologique: le cas de la cité scientifique Ile-de-France', in Aydalot, Ph. (ed.), *Milieux innovateurs en Europe*, Paris: GREMI, pp. 79–100.

Decressin, J. and Fatàs, A. (1995) 'Regional labour market dynamics in Europe', *European Economic Review*, vol. 39, pp. 1627–55.

Dei Ottati, G. (1995) *Tra mercato e comunità: aspetti concettuali e ricerche empiriche sul distretto industriale*, Milano: FrancoAngeli.

Dei Ottati, G. (2003) 'The governance of transactions in the industrial district: the "community market"', in Becattini, G., Bellandi, M., Dei Ottati, G. and Sforzi, F. (eds), *From industrial districts to local development*, Cheltenham: Edward Elgar, chapter 4, orig. edn (1987) 'Il mercato comunitario', in Becattini, G. (ed.), *Mercato e forze locali: il distretto industriale*, Bologna: Il Mulino, pp. 117–41.

Dematteis, G. (1994) 'Global networks, local cities', *Flux*, no. 15, pp.13–17.

Deno, K. T. (1988) 'The effects of public capital on U.S. manufacturing activity: 1970 to 1978', *Southern Economic Journal*, vol. 55, pp. 400–11.

Derycke, P.-H. (1996) 'Equilibre spatial urbain', in Derycke, P.-H., Huriot, J.-M. and Pumain, D. (eds), *Penser la ville*, Paris: Anthropos, pp. 53–90.

Ding, L. and Haynes, K. E. (2004) 'The role of telecommunications infrastructure in regional economic growth of China', paper presented at the Telecommunications Policy Research Conference, Washington, D.C., October 1–3.

Dixit, A. and Stiglitz, J. (1977) 'Monopolistic competition and optimum product diversity', *American Economic Review*, vol. 67, no. 3, pp. 297–308.

Dixon, R. and Thirlwall, A. P. (1975) 'A model of regional growth rate differences on Kaldorian lines', *Oxford Economic Papers*, vol. 27, no. 2, pp. 201–14.

Domar, E. D. (1957) *Essays in the theory of economic growth*, London: Oxford University Press.

Dosi, G. (1982) 'Technological paradigms and technological trajectories: a suggested interpretation of the determinants and directions of technical change', *Research Policy*, vol. 11, pp. 147–62.

Dosi, G., Freeman, C., Nelson, R., Silverberg, G. and Soete, L. (eds) (1988) *Technical change and economic theory*, London: Pinter.

Duffy-Deno, K. T. and Eberts, R. W. (1991) 'Public infrastructure and regional economic development: a simultaneous equation approach', *Journal of Urban Economics*, vol. 30, no. 3, pp. 329–43.

Eaton, C. and Lipsey, R. (1982) 'An economic theory of central places', *The Economic Journal*, vol. 92, no. 365, pp. 56–72.

Eberts, R. W. (1986) *Estimating the contribution of urban public capital stock to regional growth*, working paper no. 8610, Federal Reserve Bank of Cleveland, Cleveland.

Edquist, C. (ed.) (1997) *Systems of innovation*, London: Pinter.

Elhance, A. and Lakshmanan, T. R. (1988) 'Infrastructure-production system dynamics in national and regional systems', *Regional Science and Urban Economics*, vol. 18, pp. 511–31.

Emanuel, C. (1988) 'Recenti trasformazioni nell'organizzazione urbana e regionale: il caso Padano', Papers and Proceeding of the IX Italian Regional Science Conference, Turin.

Emanuel, C. and Dematteis, G. (1990) 'Reti urbane minori e deconcentrazione metropolitana nella Padania centro-occidentale', in Martellato, D. and Sforzi, F. (eds), *Studi sui sistemi urbani*, Milan: FrancoAngeli, pp. 233–61.

ESDP – *European Spatial Development Perspective* (1998) Final Version, Glasgow, 8 June.

European Commission (2004) *A new partnership for cohesion*, Third Report on Economic and Social Cohesion, Office for Offical Publications of the European Communities, Luxembourg.

Evans, A. (1985) *Urban economics: an introduction*, Oxford: Basil Blackwell.

Ewers, H.-J. and Allesch, J. (eds) (1990) *Innovation and regional development*, Berlin: De Gruyter.

Fabiani, S. and Pellegrini, G. (1997) 'Education, infrastructure, geography and growth: an empirical analysis of the development of Italian provinces', Banca d'Italia, *Temi di Discussione*, no. 323.

Faggian, A. and Biagi, B. (2003) 'Measuring regional multipliers: a comparison between different methodologies in the case of the Italian regions', *Scienze Regionali*, no. 1, pp. 33–58.

Faini, R. (1984) 'Increasing returns, non traded inputs and regional development', *Economic Journal*, vol. 94, pp. 308–23.

Feenstra, R. E. (2003) *Advanced international trade: theory and evidence*, Princeton, N.J.: Princeton University Press.

Feldman, M. and Audretsch, D. (1999) 'Innovation in cities: science-based diversity, specialization and localized competition', *European Economic Review*, vol. 43, pp. 409–29.

Ferri, G. and Mattesini, F. (1997) 'Finance, human capital and infrastructure: an empirical investigation of post-war Italian growth', Banca d'Italia, *Temi di Discussione*, no. 321.

Fetter, F. (1924) 'The economic law of market areas', *Quarterly Journal of Economics*, vol. 38, pp. 520–29.

Fisher, A. (1933) 'Capital and the growth of knowledge', *The Economic Journal*, vol. 43, no. 171, pp. 379–89.

Frenkel, A. (2001) 'Why high-technology firms choose to locate in or near metropolitan areas', *Urban Studies*, vol. 38, no. 7, pp. 1083–1101.

Friedmann, J. (1966) *Regional development policy: a case study of Venezuela*, Cambridge, Mass.: MIT Press.

Fritsch, M. (2001) 'Co-operation in regional innovation systems', *Regional Studies*, vol. 35, no. 4, pp. 297–307.

Fujita, M. (1985) 'Existence and uniqueness of equilibrium and optimal land use', *Regional Science and Urban Economics*, vol. 15, pp. 295–324.

Fujita, M. (1989) *Urban economic theory: land use and city size*, Cambridge: Cambridge University Press.

Fujita, M. and Thisse, J.-F. (1996) 'Economics of agglomeration', *Journal of the Japanese and International Economies*, vol. 10, pp. 339–78.

Fujita, M. and Thisse, J.-F. (2002) *Economics of agglomeration: cities, industrial location and regional growth*, Cambridge: Cambridge University Press.

Fujita, M., Krugman, P. and Mori, T. (1999) 'On the evolution of hierarchical urban systems', *European Economic Review*, vol. 43, pp. 209–51.

Fujita, M., Krugman, P. and Venables, A. J. (1999) *The spatial economy: cities, regions and international trade*, Cambridge, Mass.: MIT Press.

Ganne, B. (1992) 'Place et évolution des systèmes industriels locaux en France: économie politique d'une transformation', in Benko, G. and Lipietz, A. (eds), *Les régions qui gagnent. districts et réseaux: les nouveaux paradigmes de la géographie économique*, Paris: Presses Universitaires de France, pp. 315–45.

Gans, J. and Shepherd, G. (1994) 'How are the mighty fallen: rejected classic articles by leading economists', *Journal of Economic Perspectives*, vol. 8, pp. 165–79.

Garofoli, G. (1981) 'Lo sviluppo delle aree periferiche nell'economia italiana degli anni settanta', *L'Industria*, vol. 5, no. 3, pp. 391–404.

Giersch, H. (1949) 'Economic union between nations and the location of industries', *Review of Economic Studies*, vol. 17, pp. 87–97.

Gillespie, A. and Williams, H. (1988) 'Telecommunications and the reconstruction of regional comparative advantage', *Environment and Planning A*, vol. 20, pp. 1311–21.

Gillespie, A., Goddard, J., Hepworth, M. and Williams, H. (1989) 'Information and communications technology and regional development: an information economy perspective', *Science, Technology and Industry Review*, no. 5, April, pp. 86–111.

Goddard, J. and Pye, R. (1977) 'Telecommunications and office location', *Regional Studies*, vol. 11, pp. 19–30.

Goddard, J. and Thwaites, A. (1986) 'New technology and regional development policy', in Nijkamp, P. (ed.), *Technological change, employment and spatial dynamics*, Berlin: Springer Verlag, pp. 91–114.

Gottman, J. (1991) 'The dynamics of city networks in an expanding world', *Ekisticks*, no. 350–1, pp. 227–81.

Graziani, A. (1983) 'La teoria economica di Vera Lutz', *Moneta e Credito*, vol. 36, no. 141, pp. 3–29.

Greenhut, M. (1959a) 'Size of markets versus transport costs in industrial location surveys and theory', *Journal of Industrial Economics*, vol. 8, pp. 172–84.

Greenhut, M. (1959b) 'Comments on economic base theory', *Land Economics*, vol. XXV, pp. 71–4.

Greenhut, M. (1964) 'When is the demand factor of location important?', *Land Economics*, vol. 40, pp. 175–84.

Greenhut, M. (1966) 'Needed – a return to the classics in regional economic development theory', *Kyklos*, vol. XIX, pp. 461–78; reprinted in McKee, D., Dean, R. and Leahy, W. (eds) (1970) *Regional economics: theory and practice*, New York: The Free Press, pp. 65–80.

Griliches, Z. (1957) 'Hybrid corn: an exploration in the economics of technological change', *Econometrica*, vol. 25, no. 4, pp. 501–25.

Grossman, G. and Helpman, E. (1991) *Innovation and growth in the global economy*, Cambridge, Mass.: MIT Press.

Guild, R. L. (1998) *Infrastructure investment and regional development: theory and evidence*, Working Paper no. 3, Working Paper Series of the Department of Planning, The University of Auckland, New Zealand.

Hägerstrand, T. (1952) 'The propagation of innovation waves', *Lund Studies in Geography, Human Geography*, no. 4, pp. 3–19.

Hägerstrand, T. (1966) 'Aspects of the spatial structure of social communication and the diffusion of innovation', *Papers of the Regional Science Association*, vol. 16, pp. 27–42.

Hägerstrand, T. (1967) *Innovation diffusion as a spatial process*, Chicago: University of Chicago Press.

Haggett, P. (1965) *Locational analysis in human geography*, London: Edward Arnold.

Haggett, P., Cliff, A. and Frey, A. (1977) *Locational analysis in human geography*, vol. I, 2nd edn, London: Edward Arnold.

Hansen, N. M. (1965a) 'Unbalanced growth and regional development', *Western Economic Journal*, no. 4, pp. 3–14.

Hansen, N. M. (1965b) 'The structure and the determinants of local public investment expenditures', *The Review of Economics and Statistics*, vol. 45, pp. 150–62.

Hansen, N. M. (1967) 'Development pole theory in a regional context', *Kyklos*, vol. 20, pp. 709–25, reprinted in McKee, D., Dean, R. and Leahy, W. (eds) (1970) *Regional economics: theory and practice*, New York: The Free University Press, pp. 229–42.

Harrod, R. F. (1939) 'An essay in dynamic theory', *The Economic Journal*, vol. 49, no. 193, pp. 14–33.

Hawtrey, R. (1939) 'Mr. Harrod's essay in dynamic theory', *The Economic Journal*, vol. 49, no. 195, pp. 468–75.

Heckscher, E. F. (1919) 'The effects of foreign trade on the distribution of income', *Economik Tidskrift*, pp. 497–512; Eng. edn. in Ellis, H. S. and Metzler, L. S. (eds) (1950), *Readings on the theory of international trade*, London: Allen & Unwin, pp. 270–300.

Hepworth, M. and Waterson, M. (1988) 'Information technology and the spatial dynamics of capital', *Information Economics and Policy*, vol. 3, pp. 148–63.

Hewings, G. J. D. (1977) *Regional industrial analysis and development*, London and New York: Methuen.

Hewings, G. J. D., Okuyama, Y. and Sonis, M. (2001) 'Economic interdependence within the Chicago Metropolitan Region: a Miyazawa Analysis', *Journal of Regional Science*, vol. 41, pp. 195–217.

Higgins, B. (1977) 'Development poles: do they exist?', *Economie Appliquée*, vol. 30, no. 2, pp. 241–58.

Hildebrand, G. and Mace, A. (1950) 'The employment multiplier in an expanding industrial market: Los Angeles County, 1940–47', *Review of Economics and Statistics*, vol. 32, no. 3, pp. 241–9.

Hirsch, S. (1967) *Location of industry and international competitiveness*, London: Clarendon Press.

Hirschman, A. O. (1957) 'Investment policies and "dualism" in underdeveloped countries', *The American Economic Review*, vol. 47, no. 5, pp. 550–70.

Hirschman, A. O. (1958) *The strategy of economic development*, New Haven, Conn.: Yale University Press.

Hirschman, A. O. and Sirkin, G. (1958) 'Investment criteria and capital intensity once again', *Quarterly Journal of Economics*, vol. 72, no. 3, pp. 469–71.

Holland, S. (1971) 'Regional underdevelopment in a developed economy: the Italian case', *Regional Studies*, vol. 5, pp. 71–90.

Holland, S. (1977) 'Capital, labour and the regions: aspects of economic, social and political inequality in regional theory and policy', in Folmer, H. and Oosterhaven, J. (eds), *Spatial inequalities and regional development*, The Hague: Martinus Nijhoff Publisher, pp. 185–218.

Hoover, E. M. (1933) 'The location of the shoe industry in the United States', *Quarterly Journal of Economics*, vol. 47, no. 2, pp. 254–76.

Hoover, E. M. (1936) 'The measurement of industrial localisation', *The Review of Economics and Statistics*, vol. 18, no. 4, pp. 162–71.

Hoover, E. M. (1937a) 'Spatial price discrimination', *The Review of Economics and Statistics*, vol. 4, no. 3, pp. 182–91.

Hoover, E. M. (1937b) *Location theory and the shoe and leather industry*, Cambridge, Mass.: Harvard University Press.

Hoover, E. M. (1948) *The location of economic activity*, New York: McGraw-Hill.

Hoover, E. M. and Fisher, A. (1949) 'Research in regional economic growth', *Problems in the Study of Economic Growth*, New York: N.B.E.R. (National Bureau of Economic Research).

Hoover, E. M. and Vernon, R. (1962) *Anatomy of a metropolis*, Cambridge, Mass.: Harvard University Press.

Hotelling, H. (1929) 'Stability in competition', *The Economic Journal*, vol. 39, no. 153, pp. 41–57.

Howells, J. (1999) 'Regional systems of innovation?', in Archibugi, D., Howells, J. and Michie, J. (eds), *Innovation policy in a global economy*, Cambridge: Cambridge University Press, pp. 67–93.

Hoyt, H. (1954) 'Homer Hoyt on the development of economic base concept', *Land Economics*, May, pp. 182–7.

Hulten, C. R. and Schwab, R. M. (1995) 'Infrastructure and the economy', in Pogodzinski, J. M. (ed.), *Readings in public policy*, Cambridge, Mass.: MIT Press, pp. 213–34.

Huriot, J.-M. (1988) *Von Thünen: économie et espace*, Paris: Economica.

Huriot, J.-M. (1994) 'L'Utilisation du sol', in Auray, J.-P., Bailly, A., Derycke, P.-H. and Huriot, J.-M. (eds), *Encyclopédie d'économie spatiale*, Paris: Economica, pp. 297–306.

Ioannides, Y. and Overman, H. (2003) 'Zipf's law for cities: an empirical examination', *Regional Science and Urban Economics*, vol. 33, pp. 127–37.

Isard, W. (1949) 'The general theory of location and space', *Quarterly Journal of Economics*, vol. 63, no. 4, pp. 476–506.

Isard, W. (1954) 'Location theory and trade theory: short run analysis', *Quarterly Journal of Economics*, vol. 68, no. 2, pp. 305–20.

Isard, W. (1956) *Location and space-economy*, Cambridge, Mass.: MIT Press.

Isard, W. (1970) 'Game theory, location theory and industrial agglomeration', in Richardson, H. (ed.), *Regional economics: a reader*, London: Macmillan.

Isard, W. and Peck, M. (1954) 'Location theory and international and interregional trade theory', *Quarterly Journal of Economics*, vol. 68, no. 1, pp. 97–114.

Jaffe, A. B. (1989) 'Real effects of academic research', *American Economic Review*, vol. 79, pp. 957–70.

Johannisson, B. and Spilling, O. (1983) *Strategies for local and regional self-development*, Oslo: NordREFO.

Kaldor, N. (1970) 'The case of regional policies', *Scottish Journal of Political Economy*, no. 3, pp. 337–48.

Kaldor, N. (1975) 'Economic growth and the Verdoorn Law – a comment on Mr. Rowthorn's article', *The Economic Journal*, vol. 85, pp. 891–6.

Kaldor, N. (1985) *Economic without equilibrium*, Cardiff: University College of Cardiff Press.

Kanemoto, Y. (1987) 'Externalities in space', in Miyao, T. and Kanemoto, Y. (eds), *Urban dynamics and urban externalities*, Chur, Switzerland and New York: Harwood Academic Publishers, pp. 43–103.

Keeble, D. (1990) 'Small firms, innovation and regional development in Britain in the 1990s', *Regional Studies*, vol. 31, no. 3, pp. 281–93.

Keeble, D. and Wilkinson, F. (1999) 'Collective learning and knowledge development in the evolution of regional clusters of high-techology SMEs in Europe', *Regional Studies*, vol. 33, pp. 295–303.

Keeble, D. and Wilkinson, F. (eds) (2000) *High-technology clusters, networking and collective learning in Europe*, Aldershot: Ashgate.

Keeble, D., Offord, J. and Walker, S. (1988) *Peripheral regions in a community of twelve member states*, Luxembourg: Office for Official Publications of the European Communities.

Keeble, D., Owens, P. L. and Thompson, C. (1982) 'Regional accessibility and economic potential in the European Community', *Regional Studies*, vol. 16, pp. 419–32.

Keesing, D. (1966) 'Labour skills and comparative advantage', *The Review of Economics and Statistics*, vol. 56, nos. 1–2, pp. 249–58.

Koopmans, T. (1965) 'On the concept of optimal economic growth', *Econometric approach to development planning*, Amsterdam: North-Holland, pp. 225–87.

Krauss, M. B. and Johnson, H. G. (1974) *General equilibrium analysis*, London: Allen & Unwin.

Krugman, P. (1991a) *Geography and trade*, Cambridge, Mass.: MIT Press.

Krugman, P. (1991b) 'Increasing returns and economic geography', *Journal of Political Economy*, vol. 99, no. 3, pp. 484–99.

Krugman, P. (1991c) 'History vs. expectations', *The Quarterly Journal of Economics*, May, pp. 651–67.

Krugman, P. (1996) 'Making sense of the competitiveness debate', *Oxford Review of Economic Policy*, vol. 12, no. 3, pp. 17–25.

Krugman, P. (1998a) *Pop internationalism*, Cambridge, Mass.: MIT Press.

Krugman, P. (1998b) 'What's new about the new economic geography', *Oxford Review of Economic Policy*, vol. 14, no. 2, pp. 7–17.

Krugman, P. and Venables, A. J. (1996) 'Integration, specialisation and adjustment', *European Economic Review*, vol. 40, pp. 959–67.

Lancaster, K. (1975) 'Socially optimal product differentiation', *American Economic Review*, vol. 65, pp. 567–85.

Lancaster, K. (1980) 'Intra-industry trade under perfect monopolistic competition', *Journal of International Economics*, vol. 10, pp. 151–75.

Launhardt, W. (1882) 'Die Bestimmung des Zweckmässigsten Standorts einer Gewerblischen Anlage', *Zeitschrift des Vereins Deutscher Ingenieure*, vol. 26, pp. 106–15.

Launhardt, W. (1885) *Mathematische Begründung der Volkwirtschaftslehre*, Leipzig.

Lawson, C. and Lorenz, E. (1999) 'Collective learning, tacit knowledge and regional innovation capacity', *Regional Studies*, vol. 33, pp. 305–17.

Leon-Ledesma, M. A. (1998) 'Economic growth and Verdoorn's Laws in the Spanish regions, 1962–1991', Discussion Paper no. 1, Department of Economics, University of Kent.

Leontief, W. (1953) 'Domestic production and foreign trade: the American capital position re-examined', *Proceedings of the American Philosophical Society*, vol. 97, pp. 332–49.

Leontief, W. (1956) 'Factor proportions and the structure of American trade: further theoretical and empirical analysis', *The Review of Economics and Statistics*, vol. 38, no. 4, pp. 386–407.

Linder, S. B. (1961) *An essay on trade and transformation*, New York: John Wiley and Sons.

Lipietz, A. (1980) 'The structuration of space, the problem of land, and spatial policy', in Carney, J., Hudson, R. and Lewis, J. (eds), *Regions in crisis*, London: Croom Helm, pp. 60–75.

Long, W. (1971) 'Demand in space: some neglected aspects', *Papers and Proceedings of the Regional Science Association*, vol. 27, pp. 45–62.

Lösch, A. (1954) *The economics of location*, New Haven, Conn.: Yale University Press, orig. edn (1940) *Die Räumlische Ordnung der Wirtschaft*, Jena: Gustav Fischer.

Lucas, R. (1988) 'On the mechanics of economic development', *Journal of Monetary Economics*, vol. 22, pp. 3–42.

Lundvall, B.-A. (1992) 'Introduction', in Lundvall, B.-A. (ed.), *National systems of innovation. Towards a theory of innovation and interactive learning*, London: Pinter, pp. 1–19.

Lundvall, B.-A. and Johnson, B. (1994) 'The learning economy', *Journal of Industry Studies*, vol. 1, no. 2, pp. 23–42.

Lung, P. (1987) 'Complexity and spatial dynamic modelling, from catastrophe theory to self-organising processes: a review of the literature', Institut d'Economie Régionale du Sud-Ouest.

Lutz, V. (1962) *Italy – a study in economic development*, London: Oxford University Press.

Maggioni, M. (2002) *Clustering dynamics and the location of high-tech firms*, Berlin: Physica-Verlag.

Magrini, S. (1997) 'Spatial concentration in research and regional income disparities in a decen-tralised model of endogenous growth', *Research Paper in Environmental and Spatial Analysis*, no. 43, London School of Economics.

Magrini, S. (2004) 'Regional (di)convergence', in Henderson, V. and Thisse, F. J. (eds), *Handbook of regional and urban economics*, vol. 4, Amsterdam: North-Holland, pp. 2741–96.

Maier, G. and Sedlacek, S. (eds) (2005) *Spillovers and innovations – space, environment and the economy*, Vienna: Springer Verlag.

Maillat, D., Quévit, M. and Senn, L. (eds) (1993) *Réseaux d'innovation et milieux innovateurs: un pari pour le développement régional*, Neuchâtel: EDES.

Malecki, E. and Varaiya, P. (1986) 'Innovation and changes in regional structure', in Nijkamp, P. (ed.), *Handbook of regional and urban economics*, Amsterdam: North-Holland, pp. 629–45.

Malmberg, A. and Maskell, P. (2002) 'The elusive concept of localization economies: towards a knowledge-based theory of spatial clustering', *Environment and Planning A*, vol. 34, pp. 429–49.

Mankin, N., Romer, D. and Weil, D. (1992) 'A contribution to the empirics of economic growth', *Quarterly Journal of Economics*, vol. 107, May, pp. 739–74.

Mansfield, E. (1961) 'Technological change and the rate of imitation', *Econometrica*, vol. 29, no. 4, pp. 741–66.

Mansfield, E. (1968) *The economics of technological change*, New York: Norton.

Markusen, J. and Venables, A. (1999) 'Foreign direct investment as a catalyst for industrial development', *European Economic Review*, no. 43, pp. 335–56.

Marshall, A. (1920) *Principles of economics*, 8th edn, London: Macmillan.

Martellato, D. (1982) 'The Tuscany interregional input output model', International Institute for Applied Systems Analysis, IIASA paper series no. 82–30, Vienna.

309

Martin, P. and Ottaviano, G. (1999) 'Growing locations: industry location in a model of endogenous growth', *European Economic Review*, vol. 43, no. 2, pp. 281–302.

Martin, R. (1999) 'The new "geographical turn" in economics: some critical reflections', *Cambridge Journal of Economcs*, vol. 23, pp. 65–91.

Maskell, P. and Malmberg, A. (1999) 'Localised learning and industrial competitiveness', *Cambridge Journal of Economics*, vol. 23, no. 2, pp. 167–85.

Massey, D. and Meegan, R. (1978) 'Industrial restructuring versus the city', *Urban Studies*, vol. 15, pp. 273–88.

McCann, Ph. (1998) *The economics of industrial location: a logistic-cost approach*, Heidelberg: Springer Verlag.

McCann, Ph. and Sheppard, S. (2003) 'The rise, fall and rise again of industrial location theory', *Regional Studies*, vol. 37, nos. 6–7, pp. 649–63.

McCombie, J. S. (1982) 'How important is the spatial diffusion of innovation in explaining regional growth disparities?', *Urban Studies*, vol. 19, pp. 377–82.

McCombie, J. S. (1983) 'Kaldor's Law in retrospect', *Journal of Post Keynesian Economics*, vol. V, pp. 414–29.

McCombie, J. S. (1988) 'A synoptic view of regional growth and unemployment: I – the neoclassical theory', *Urban Studies*, vol. 25, no. 4, pp. 267–81.

McCombie, J. S. (1992) 'Thirwall's Law and balance of payments constrained growth: more on the debate', *Applied Economics*, vol. 24, pp. 493–512.

McCombie, J. S. and De Ridder, J. R. (1984) 'The Verdoorn Law controversy: some new empirical evidence using U.S. state data', *Oxford Economic Papers*, vol. 36, no. 2, pp. 208–83.

McGregor, P. and Swales, J. K. (1985) 'Professor Thirlwall and balance of payments constrained growth', *Applied Economics*, vol. 17, pp. 17–32.

McGuire, A. (1983) 'The regional income and employment impacts of nuclear power stations', *Scottish Journal of Political Economy*, vol. 30, no. 3, pp. 264–74.

Meade, J. E. (1954) 'External economies and diseconomies in a competitive situation', *Economic Journal*, vol. 62, pp. 143–51.

Meyer, J. R. (1963) 'Regional economics: a survey', *American Economic Review*, vol. 53, pp. 19–54.

Mills, E. (1972) *Urban economics*, Glenview: Scott Foresman and Co.

Mills, E. and Lav, M. (1964) 'A model of market areas with free entry', *The Journal of Political Economy*, vol. 72, no. 3, pp. 278–88.

Mirrlees, J. A. (1972) 'The optimum town', *Swedish Journal of Economics*, vol. 74, pp. 114–35.

Mishan, E. J. (1971) 'The postwar literature on externalities: an interpretative essay', *Journal of Economic Literature*, no. 1, pp. 1–28.

Miyao, T. (1981) *Dynamic analysis of the urban economy*, New York: Academic Press.

Miyao, T. (1984) 'Dynamic models of urban growth and decay: a survey and extensions', paper presented at the second world Conferences of Arts and Sciences, Rotterdam, 4–15 June.

Miyao, T. (1987a) 'Dynamic urban models', in Mills, E. (ed.), *Urban economics: handbook of regional and urban economics*, Amsterdam: North-Holland, vol. 2, pp. 877–925.

Miyao, T. (1987b) 'Urban growth and dynamics', in Miyao, T. and Kanemoto, Y. (eds), *Urban dynamics and urban externalities*, Chur, Switzerland and New York: Harwood Academic Publishers, pp. 1–41.

Miyao T and Kanemoto Y. (eds), *Urban dynamics and urban externalities*, London: Harwood Academic Publisher.

Montesano, A. (1972) 'A restatement of Beckmann's model on the distribution of urban rent and residential density', *Journal of Economic Theory*, no. 4, pp. 329–54.

Moomaw, R. L. and Williams, M. (1991) 'Total factor productivity in manufacturing: further evidence from the States', *Journal of Regional Science*, vol. 31, pp. 17–34.

Moomaw, R. L., Mullen, J. K. and Martin, W. (1995) 'The interregional impact of infrastructure capital', *Southern Economic Journal*, vol. 61, no. 3, pp. 830–45.

Morgan, K. (1997) 'The learning region: institutions, innovation and regional renewal', *Regional Studies*, vol. 31, no. 5, pp. 491–503.

Moroney, J. R. and Walker, J. M. (1966) 'A regional test of the Heckscher–Ohlin hypothesis', *Journal of Political Economy*, vol. 74, pp. 573–86.

Mouleart, F. and Sekia, F. (2003) 'Territorial innovation models: a critical survey', *Regional Studies*, vol. 37, no. 3, pp. 289–302.

Mulligan, G. (1979) 'Additional properties of a hierarchical city-size model', *Journal of Regional Science*, no. 1, pp. 1–42.

Mulligan, G. (1984) 'Agglomeration and central place theory: a review of the literature', *International Regional Science Review*, no. 1, pp. 1–42.

Munnell, A. H. (1990) 'How does public infrastructure affect regional economic performance?', in Munnell, A. H. (ed.), *Is there a shortfall in public capital investment?* Proceedings of a Conference Sponsored by the Federal Bank of Boston, Federal Reserve Bank of Boston.

Muth, R. (1961) 'Economic change and rural–urban land conversions', *Econometrica*, vol. 29, no. 1, pp. 1–23.

Muth, R. (1968) 'Urban residential land and the housing market', in Perloff, H. and Wingo, L. (eds), *Issues in urban economics*, London: The Johns Hopkins Press, pp. 285–333.

Muth, R. (1969) *Cities and housing*, Chicago: University of Chicago Press.

Myrdal, G. (1957) *Economic theory of under-developed regions*, London: Duckworth.

Nauwelaers, C., Reid, A. and Desterbecq, H. (1988) *Firmes multinationales et développement régional*, Université Catholique de Louvain, Louvain-la-Neuve: RIDER.

Nelson, R. R. and Norman, V. D. (1977) 'Technological change and factor mix over the product cycle: a model of dynamic comparative advantage', *Journal of Development Economics*, vol. 4, pp. 3–24.

Niedercorn, J. H. and Bechdolt, B. V. (1969) 'An economic derivation of the law of spatial interaction', *Journal of Regional Science*, vol. 9, pp. 273–82.

Niedercorn, J. H. and Bechdolt, B. V. (1972) 'An economic derivation of the law of spatial interaction: further reply and a reformulation', *Journal of Regional Science*, vol. 11, pp. 123–36.

Nijkamp, P. (1999) 'Environment and regional economics', in Van den Bergh, J. C. J. M. (ed.), *Handbook of environmental and resource economics*, Cheltenham: Edward Elgar, pp. 525–38.

Nijkamp, P. and Perrels, A. (1994) *Sustainable cities in Europe*, London: Earthscan.

Nijkamp, P. and Poot, J. (1998) 'Spatial perspectives on new theories of economic growth', *Annals of Regional Science*, vol. 32, no. 1, pp. 7–38.

Nijkamp, P. and Reggiani, A. (1988) 'Entropy, spatial interaction models and discrete choice analysis: static and dynamic analogies', *European Journal of Operational Research*, vol. 36, pp. 186–96.

Nijkamp, P. and Reggiani, A. (1992) *Interaction, evolution and chaos in space*, Berlin: Springer Verlag.

Nijkamp, P. and Reggiani, A. (1993) *Non-linear evolution of spatial economic systems*, Berlin: Springer Verlag.

Nijkamp, P., Stough, R. and Verhoef, E. (eds) (1998) 'Endogenous growth in a regional context', *Annals of Regional Science*, vol. 32, no. 1, special issue.

North, D. (1955) 'Location theory and regional economic growth', *Journal of Political Economy*, vol. 63, pp. 243–58.

North, D. (1990) *Institutions, institutional change and economic performance*, Cambridge: Cambridge University Press.

Norton, D. and Rees, J. (1979) 'The product cycle and the spatial decentralisation of American manufacturing', *Regional Studies*, no. 13, pp. 141–51.

Nurkse, R. (1952) 'Some international aspects of the problem of economic development', *The American Economic Review*, vol. 42, no. 2, pp. 571–83.

Oakey, R., Nash, P. and Thwaites, A. (1980) 'The regional distribution of innovative manufacturing establishments in Britain', *Regional Studies*, no. 13, pp. 141–51.

Ohlin, B. (1933) *Interregional and international trade*, Cambridge, Mass.: Harvard University Press.

Okun, B. and Richardson, R. (eds) (1961) *Studies in economic development*, New York: Holt, Rinehart & Winston.

Onida, F. (1984) *Economia degli scambi internazionali*, Bologna: Il Mulino.

Ottaviano, G. and Puga, D. (1998) 'Agglomeration in the global economy: a survey of the New Economic Geography', *The World Economy*, vol. 21, no. 6, pp. 707–31.

Ottaviano, G. and Thisse, J.-F. (2001) 'On economic geography in economic theory: increasing returns and pecuniary externalities', *Journal of Economic Geography*, no. 1, pp. 153–79.

Paci, M. (1973) *Mercato del lavoro e classi sociali in Italia*, Bologna: Il Mulino.

Paci, R. and Saddi, S. (2002) 'Capitale pubblico e produttività nelle regioni Italiane', *Scienze Regionali*, no. 3, pp. 5–26.

Paci, R. and Usai, S. (2000) 'Technological enclaves and industrial districts: an analysis of the regional distribution of innovative activity in Europe', *Regional Studies*, vol. 34, no. 2, pp. 97–114.

Paelink, J. (1965) 'La théorie du développement régional polarisé', Cahiers de l'ISEA, Série Economie Régionale, no. 3, pp. 5–47.

Paelink, J. and Nijkamp, P. (1976) *Operational theory and method in regional economics*, Westmead, Farnborough: Saxon House.

Palander, T. (1935) *Beiträge zur Standortstheorie*, Uppsala: Almqvist & Wiksells Boktryckeri.

Parr, J. (1978) 'Models of the central place system: a more general approach', *Urban Studies*, vol. 15, pp. 35–49.

Parr, J. (1981) 'Temporal change in a central-place system', *Environment and Planning A*, vol. 13, pp. 97–118.

Parr, J. (1985) 'A note on the size distribution of cities over time', *Journal of Urban Economics*, vol. 18, pp. 199–212.

Parr, J. (1999a) 'Growth pole strategies in regional economic planning: a retrospective view. Part 1. Origins and advocacy', *Urban Studies*, vol. 36, no. 7, pp. 1195–216.

Parr, J. (1999b) 'Growth pole strategies in regional economic planning: a retrospective view. Part 2. Implementation and outcome', *Urban Studies*, vol. 36, no. 8, pp. 1247–68.

Perloff, H. (1957) 'Interrelations of state income and industrial structure', *The Review of Economics and Statistics*, vol. 39, no. 2, pp. 162–71.

Perloff, H., Dunn, E., Lampard, E. and Muth, R. (1960) *Region, resources and economic growth*, Baltimore: Johns Hopkins.

Perroux, F. (1950) 'Economic space: theory and applications', *The Quarterly Journal of Economics*, vol. 64, no. 1, pp. 89–104.

Perroux, F. (1955) 'Note sur la notion de pôle de croissance', *Economie Appliquée*, vol. 7, nos. 1–2, pp. 307–20.

Petrakos, G. (2000) 'The spatial impact of east–west integration in Europe', in Petrakos, G., Maier, G. and Gorzelak, G. (eds), *Integration and transition in Europe*, London: Routledge, pp. 38–68.

Pietrobelli, C. (1998) 'The socio-economic foundations of competitiveness: an econometric analysis of Italian industrial districts', *Industry and Innovation*, vol. 5, no. 2, pp. 139–55.

Piore, M. and Sabel, C. F. (1984) *The second industrial divide: possibilities for prosperities*, New York: Basic Books.

Pompili, T. (1992) 'The role of human capital in urban system structure and development: the case of Italy', *Urban Studies*, vol. 29, pp. 905–34.

Poratt, M. (1977) *The information economy: definition and measurement*, special publication 77–12(1), Office of Telecommunications, US Department of Commerce, Washington D.C.

Posner, M. V. (1961) 'International trade and technical change', *Oxford Economic Papers*, vol. 13, no. 3, pp. 323–59.

Pratt, R. (1968) 'An appraisal of minimum requirement technique', *Economic Geography*, vol. XLIV, pp. 117–24.

Pumain, D. and Saint-Julien, T. (eds) (1996) *Urban networks in Europe*, Paris: John Libbey Eurotext.

Putnam, R. D. (1993) *Making democracy work*, Princeton, N.J.: Princeton University Press.

Quévit, M. (1992) 'The regional impact of the internal market: a comparative analysis of traditional industrial regions and lagging regions', *Regional Studies*, vol. 26, no. 4, pp. 349–60.

Rabellotti, R. (1997) *External economies and cooperation in industrial districts. A comparison of Italy and Mexico*, London: Macmillan.

Rabenau, B. V. (1979) 'Urban growth with agglomeration economies and diseconomies', *Geographia Polonica*, vol. 42, pp. 77–90.

Rallet, A. and Torre, A. (1998) 'On geography and technology: proximity relations in localised innovation networks', in Steiner, M. (ed.), *From agglomeration economies to innovative clusters*, London: Pion, pp. 41–56.

313

Ramsey, F. (1928) 'A mathematical theory of saving', *Economic Journal,* vol. 38, pp. 543–59.

Ratti, R., Bramanti, A. and Gordon, R. (eds) (1997) *The dynamics of innovative regions,* Aldershot: Ashgate.

Rebelo, S. (1991) 'Long-run policy analysis and long-run growth', *Journal of Political Economy,* vol. 99, pp. 500–21.

Reggiani, A. (2000) 'Introduction: new frontiers in modelling spatial and economic systems', in Reggiani, A. (ed.), *Spatial economic science,* Berlin: Springer Verlag, pp. 1–11.

Reilly, W. J. (1931) *The law of retail gravitation,* New York: Knickerbocker Press.

RERU (1999) 'Le paradigme du milieu innovateur dans l'économie contemporaine', *Revue d'Economie Régionale et Urbaine,* no. 3, special issue.

Resmini, L. (2007) 'Regional patterns of industry location in transition countries: does the economic integration with the EU matter?', *Regional Studies,* forthcoming.

Ricardo, D. (1971) *Principles of political taxonomy and taxation,* Harmondsworth: Penguin, orig. edn, 1817.

Richardson, H. W. (1969) *Regional economics,* Trowbridge, Wiltshire: World University, Redwood Press.

Richardson, H. W. (1972) 'Optimality in city size, systems of cities and urban policy: a sceptic's view', *Urban Studies,* vol. 9, no. 1, pp. 29–47.

Richardson, H. W. (1973) *Regional growth theory,* London: Macmillan.

Richardson, H. W. (1977) *The new urban economics: and alternatives,* London: Pion.

Richardson, H. W. (1978) *Regional and urban economics,* Harmondsworth: Penguin.

Rid, H. and Lau, E. (1998) 'Verdoorn's Law and increasing returns to scale in the UK regions, 1968–91: some new estimates based on the cointegration approach', *Oxford Economic Papers,* vol. 50, pp. 201–19.

Rietveld, P. (1989) 'Infrastructure and regional development – A survey of multiregional economic models', *The Annals of Regional Science,* vol. 23, pp. 255–74.

Robinson, J. (1934) *The economics of imperfect competition,* London: Macmillan.

Rodriguez-Clare, A. (1996) 'Multinationals, linkages, and economic development', *The American Economic Review,* vol. 86, no. 4, pp. 852–73.

Rodrìguez-Pose, A. and Fratesi, U. (2004) 'Between development and social policies: the impact of European structural funds in objective 1 regions', *Regional Studies,* vol. 38, no. 1, pp. 97–113.

Romer, P. (1986) 'Increasing returns and long-run growth', *Journal of Political Economy,* vol. 94, no. 5, pp. 1002–37.

Romer, P. (1987) 'Growth based on increasing returns due to specialisation', *American Economic Review, Papers and Proceedings,* vol. 77, pp. 56–67.

Romer, P. (1989) 'Capital accumulation in the theory of long-run growth', in Barro, R. (ed.), *Modern business cycle theory,* Oxford: Basil Blackwell, pp. 51–127.

Romer, P. (1990) 'Endogenous technological change', *Journal of Political Economy,* vol. 98, pp. S71–S102.

Romer, P. (1994) 'The origins of endogenous growth', Journal of Economic Perspective, vol. 8, no. 1, pp. 3–22.

Rosenstein-Rodan, P. N. (1943) 'Problems of industrialisation of Eastern and South-Eastern Europe', *The Economic Journal*, vol. 53, pp. 202–11.

Rosenstein-Rodan, P. N. (1959) 'Due lezioni sui problemi di sviluppo', *L'Industria*, no. 4, pp. 422–42.

Rostow, W. W. (1960) *The stages of economic growth*, Cambridge: Cambridge University Press.

Rowthorn, R. E. (1975) 'What remains of Kaldor's Law?', *The Economic Journal*, vol. 85, pp. 10–19.

Sala-i-Martin, X. (1996) 'Regional cohesion: evidence and theories of regional growth and convergence', *European Economic Review*, vol. 40, pp. 1325–52.

Samuelson, P. (1954) 'The transfer problem and transport costs. Part II: Analysis of the effects of trade impediments', *Economic Journal*, vol. 64, pp. 264–89.

Samuelson, P. (1983) 'Thünen at two hundred', *Journal of Economic Literature*, vol. 21, no. 4, pp. 1468–88.

Sassen, S. (ed.) (2002) *Global networks, linked cities*. New York: Routledge.

Schmitz, H. (1995) 'Collective efficiency: growth path for small-scale industry', *Journal of Development Studies*, vol. 31, no. 4, pp. 529–66.

Schmitz, H. (1998) 'Collective efficiency and returns to scale', *Cambridge Journal of Economics*, vol. 23, no. 4, pp. 465–83.

Schmitz, H. and Musyck, B. (1994) 'Industrial district in Europe: policy lessons for developing countries?', *World Development*, vol. 22, no. 6, pp. 889–910.

Scitovski, T. (1954) 'Two concepts of external economies', *Journal of Political Economy*, vol. 62, pp. 143–51.

Scitovski, T. (1958) *Economic theory and Western Europe integration*, London: Allen & Unwin.

Secchi, B. (1974) *Squilibri regionali e sviluppo economico*, Padua: Marsilio.

Segal, D. (1977) *Urban economics*, Illinois: Richard Irwin.

Signorini, L. F. (2000) *Lo sviluppo locale. Un'indagine della Banca d'Italia sui distretti industriali*, Corigliano Calabro: Meridiana Libri Publisher.

Sirkin, G. (1959) 'The theory of regional economic base', *The Review of Economics and Statistics*, vol. 41, no. 4, pp. 426–9.

Smith, D. M. (1966) 'A theoretical framework for geographical studies of industrial location', *Economic Geography*, vol. 42, pp. 95–113.

Smith, D. M. (1971) *Industrial location: an economic geographical analysis*, London: Wiley & Sons.

Smith, D. M. (1974) 'Regional growth, interstate and intersectoral factor reallocation', *Review of Economics and Statistics*, vol. 61, pp. 353–9.

Smith, D. M. (1975) 'Neoclassical growth models and regional growth in the U.S.', *Journal of Regional Science*, vol. 15, no. 2, pp. 165–81.

Solow, R. (1957) 'Technical change and the aggregate production function', *Review of Economics and Statistics*, vol. 39, no. 3, pp. 312–20.

Solow, R. (1972) 'Congestion, density and the use of land in transportation', *Swedish Journal of Economics*, vol. 74, pp. 161–73.

315

Solow, R. (2000) *Growth theory: an exposition*, 2nd edn, Oxford: Oxford University Press.

Soo, K. T. (2005) 'Zipf's Law for cities: a cross-country investigation', *Regional Science and Urban Economics*, vol. 35, pp. 239–63.

Soro, B. (2003) 'Fattori che regolano lo sviluppo della produttività del lavoro. Fifty years on', in McCombie, J., Pugno, M. and Soro, B. (eds), *Productivity growth and economic performance. Essays on Verdoorn's Law*, Basingstoke: Palgrave–Macmillan, chapter 3, pp. 37–63.

Spaventa, L. (1959) 'Dualism in economic growth', *Banca Nazionale del Lavoro Quarterly Review*, no. 51, pp. 386–434.

Stabler, J. C. (1968) 'Exports and evolution: the process of regional change', *Land Economics*, vol. XLIV, no. 1, pp. 11–23, reprinted in McKee, D., Dean, R. and Leahy, W. (eds) (1970), *Regional economics: theory and practice*, New York: The Free Press, pp. 49–64.

Steele, D. B. (1969) 'Regional multipliers in Great Britain', *Oxford Economic Papers*, vol. 21, no. 2, pp. 268–92.

Sternberg, R. (1996) 'Reasons for the genesis of high-tech regions – theoretical explanation and empirical evidence', *Geoforum*, vol. 27, no. 2, pp. 205–23.

Stimson, R. J., Stough, R. R. and Salazar, M. (2005) 'Leadership and institutional factors in endogenous regional economic development', *Investigationes Regionales*, no. 7, pp. 23–52.

Stöhr, W. (1990) 'On the theory and practice of local development in Europe', in Stöhr, W. (ed.), *Global challenge and local responses*, London: Mansell, pp. 35–54.

Stöhr, W. and Tödtling, F. (1977) 'Spatial equity. Some anti-thesis to current regional development doctrine', *Papers of the Regional Science Association*, vol. 38, pp. 33–53.

Stoneman, P. (1986) 'Technological diffusion: the viewpoint of economic theory', *Ricerche Economiche*, vol. 4, pp. 585–606.

Storper, M. (1995) 'La géographie des conventions: proximité territoriale, interdépendance non-marchandes et développement économique', in Rallet, A. and Torre, A. (eds), *Economie industrielle et économie spatiale*, Paris: Economica, pp. 111–28.

Stouffer, S. A. (1940) 'Intervening opportunities: a theory relating mobility and distance', *American Sociological Review*, no. 5, pp. 845–67.

Stouffer, S. A. (1960) 'Intervening opportunities and competing migrants', *Journal of Regional Science*, vol. 12, pp. 26–35.

Subirats, J. (ed.) (2002) *Redes, territorios y gobierno*, Barcelona: UIMP.

Taylor, P. S. (2001) 'Specification of the world city network', *Geographical Analysis*, vol. 33, no. 2, pp. 181–94.

Terrasi, M. (2002) 'National and spatial factors in EU regional convergence', in Cuadrado-Roura, J. R. and Parellada, M. (eds), *Regional convergence in the European Union*, Berlin: Springer Verlag, pp. 185–209.

Thirlwall, A. P. (1974) 'Regional economic disparities and regional policy in the Common Market', *Urban Studies*, no. 11, pp. 1–12.

Thirlwall, A. P. (1980) 'Regional problems are balance of payments problems', *Regional Studies*, vol. 14, pp. 419–25.

Thirlwall, A. P. (1983) 'A plain man's guide to Kaldor's Law', *Journal of Post Keynesian Economics*, vol. V, pp. 345–58.

Thom, R. (1972) *Stabilité structurelle et morphogenèse: essai d'une théorie générale des modèles*, Paris: Inter Editions.

Tiebout, C. (1956) 'The urban economic base reconsidered', *Land Economics*, February, pp. 95–9.

Tiebout, C. (1957) 'Regional and interregional input–output models: an appraisal', *Southern Economic Journal*, vol. 24, pp. 140–7.

Tiebout, C. (1960) 'The community income multiplier: a case study', in Pfouts, R. (ed.), *The techniques of urban economic analysis*, London: Chandler-Davis.

Torrens, R. (1815) *An essay on the external corn trade*, London: J. Hatchard.

Traistaru, I., Nijkamp, P. and Resmini, L. (eds) (2003) *The emerging economic geography in EU accession countries*, Aldershot: Ashgate.

Trigilia, C. (1985) 'La regolazione localistica: economia e politica nelle aree di piccola impresa', *Stato e Mercato*, no. 14, pp. 181–228.

Ullman, E. (1941) 'A theory of location for cities', *The American Journal of Sociology*, vol. 46, no. 6, pp. 853–64.

Ullman, E. and Dacey, M. (1960) 'The minimum requirements approach to the urban economic base', *Papers and Proceedings of the Regional Science Association*, no. 6, pp. 175–94.

Uzawa, H. (1964) 'Optimal growth in a two sector model of capital accumulation', *Review of Economic Studies*, vol. 31, pp. 1–24.

Valavanis, S. (1955) 'Lösch on location', *American Economic Review*, vol. XLV, pp. 637–44.

Vásquez-Barquero, A. (2002) *Endogenous development*, London: Routledge.

Venables, A. J. (1996) 'Equilibrium location of vertically linked industries', *International Economic Review*, vol. 37, pp. 341–59.

Verdoorn, P. J. (1949) 'Factors that determine the growth of labour productivity', in Ironmonger, D., Perkins, J. O. N. and Van Hoa, T. (eds) (1988) *National income and economic progress: essays in honour of Colin Clark*, Basingstoke: Macmillan, pp. 199–207.

Vernon, R. (1957) 'Production and distribution in the large metropolis', *The Annals of the American Academy of Political and Social Sciences*, pp. 15–29.

Vernon, R. (1960) *Metropolis 1985*, Cambridge, Mass.: Harvard University Press.

Vernon, R. (1966) 'International investment and international trade in the product cycle', *Quarterly Journal of Economics*, vol. 80, no. 2, pp. 190–207.

Vickerman, R. (1991) 'Infrastructure and regional development: introduction', in Vickerman, R. (ed.), *Infrastructure and regional development*, London: Pion, pp. 1–8.

Von Böventer, E. (1975) 'Regional growth theory', *Urban Studies*, vol. 12, pp. 1–29.

Von Thünen, J. H. (1826) *Der isolierte Staat in Beziehung auf Landwirtschaft und Nationalökonomie*, Hamburg: Puthes.

Weber, A. (1929) *Alfred Weber's theory of the location of industries*, Chicago: University of Chicago Press, orig. edn (1909) *Über der Standort der Industrien*, Tübingen: Verlag Mohr.

Weimer, A. and Hoyt, H. (1939) *Principles of urban real estate*, New York: Ronald Press.

Weiss, S. and Goodwin, E. (1968) 'Estimation of differential employment multipliers in a small region', *Land Economics*, vol. 44, pp. 235–44.

Wheaton, W. (1979) 'Monocentric models of urban land use: contributions and criticisms', in Mieszkowski, P. and Straszheim, M. (eds), *Current issues in urban economics*, London: The Johns Hopkins University Press, pp. 105–29.

Williamson, J. G. (1965) 'Regional inequality and the process of national development: a description of the patterns', *Economic Development and Cultural Change*, vol. 13, pp. 3–45.

Williamson, O. (1975) *Markets and hierarchies: analysis and antitrust implications*, New York: The Free Press.

Williamson, O. (2002) 'The lens of contract: private ordering', *American Economic Review, Papers and Proceedings*, vol. 92, no. 2, pp. 438–53.

Wilson, A. (1970) *Entropy in urban and regional modelling*, London: Pion.

Wilson, A. (1971) 'A family of spatial interaction models and associated developments', *Environment and Planning*, no. 3, pp. 1–32.

Wilson, A. (1981) *Catastrophe theory and bifurcation*, London: Croom Helm.

Wilson, T. (1968) 'The Regional Multiplier – a critique', *Oxford Economic Papers,* vol. 20, no. 3, pp. 374–93.

Wingo, L. (1961) *Transportation and urban land*, Washington D.C.: Resources for the Future.

Yilmaz, S. and Dinc, M. (2002) 'Telecommunications and regional development: evidence from the U.S. States', *Economic Development Quarterly*, vol. 16, no. 3, pp. 211–28.

Young, A. (1928) 'Increasing returns and economic progress', *The Economic Journal*, vol. 38, no. 152, pp. 527–42.

Young, S., Hood, N. and Dunlop, S. (1988) 'Global strategies, multinational subsidiary roles and economic impact in Scotland', *Regional Studies*, vol. 22, no. 6, pp. 487–97.

Zipf, G. K. (1949) *Human behaviour and the principle of least effort*, Cambridge, Mass.: Addison Wesley.

Index

319